CHARLES HELM

TUMBLER RIDGE

Enjoying its History, Trails and Wilderness

MCA PUBLISHING
Tumbler Ridge, British Columbia

Copyright © 2001 by Charles Helm

All rights reserved. No part of this book may be reproduced or used in any form by any means – graphic, electronic, or mechanical, including information storage and retrieval systems – without prior permission from the author.

Cover design by Loraine Funk and Charles Helm.
Illustrations by Joan Zimmer.

Published in Canada in 2001 by MCA Publishing
Box 1981, Tumbler Ridge, British Columbia V0C 2W0
(250) 242-5343 email lfunk@pris.bc.ca

Printed in Canada by Quebecor World, Edmonton.

National Library of Canada Cataloguing in Publication Data
Helm, Charles, Date -
   Tumbler Ridge

Includes bibliographical references and index.
ISBN 0-9688558-0-6

1. Tumbler Ridge Region (B.C.)–History. 2. Tumbler Ridge Region (B.C.)–Guidebooks. 3. Trails–British Columbia–Tumbler Ridge Region–Guidebooks. 1. Title.
FC3845.T86H44 2001   971.1'87   C2001-910574-6
F1089.T86H44 2001

> By the same author:
>
> Beyond Rock and Coal
>
> *with Herbert Helm*
> The Helm Family History
>
> *booklets with Peter Sherrington*
> Murray Canyon Overlook Interpretive Trail Guide
> The Stone Corral Interpretive Hiking Trail

Throughout this book a cautious approach is advised. The activities described in it have inherent risks. Some destinations may become inaccessible with the passage of time, access routes may change, and information presented in this book may become obsolete or incorrect. Conditions will vary with weather and seasonal changes. Some destinations have no trails, may have hazardous elements, or may demand wilderness travel. The maps in this book should serve as a guide only, and are not a substitute for topographical maps. There is no guarantee that the events mentioned this book will continue to be organised in future. Although the author and publisher have taken every effort to ensure that the information is as accurate as possible, they accept no responsibility or liability for any errors and omissions, nor for any loss, injury or inconvenience sustained by any person using this book. Readers should seek current information on conditions before setting out. Errors brought to the attention of the publisher will be corrected in subsequent editions.

*Dedicated to my parents
in appreciation of their love
in showing me a way to enjoy the wilderness
...*

and to all those who have believed in the future of Tumbler Ridge

■ CONTENTS

List of Plates vi
List of Figures ix
List of Destinations ix
Introduction xi

1	Overview of the Area 1	
2	Climate 8	
3	Hazards 12	
4	Activities 14	
	Birding 14	
	Botany 16	
	Camping 17	
	Canoeing and Kayaking 17	
	Caving 19	
	Cross–country Skiing 21	
	Dog Sledding 23	
	Exploration 25	
	Fishing 25	
	Harvesting the Wild 26	
	Hiking 27	
	Ice Climbing 29	
	Jet Boating 30	
	Mountain Biking and Cycling 31	
	Road Touring 32	
	Rock Climbing and Peak–bagging 34	
	Running 35	
	Snowmobiling 36	
	Snowshoeing 39	
	Trail Riding 41	
	Waterfall–bagging 41	
	Wildlife Watchimg 42	
5	Geological History 43	
6	Palaeontology – The Fossil Heritage of Tumbler Ridge ... 49	
	Corals, Crinoids and Trace Fossils 51	
	The Triassic Fishes and Reptiles 53	
	Dinosaur Prints and Trackways 55	
	The Cretaceous Plants 61	
7	Prehistory 65	

8	The Explorers	70
	The Search for Railway Passes	72
	The First Local European Explorers	74
	Prescott Fay – The First Scientific Expedition	77
	A Mystery Pass	83
	Vreeland Climbs the Big Peaks from the West	84
	First Descent of the Wapiti	85
	The First Surveyors for Oil and Gas	88
	The Boundary Commission	89
	Holzworth – Another Zoological Expedition	93
	The First Prentiss Gray expedition	94
	Gray's Follow–up Trip	99
	The First Formal Exploration of the Sukunka	103
9	The Settlers	105
	The First Permanent Settlement	105
	The Calliou Family	107
	The First Settlers near Present–day Tumbler Ridge	111
	Ranchers of the Wolverine Valley	113
	The Monkman Pass Epic	117
	The First Tourists, and Almost another Town	123
10	Discovery and Use of the Natural Resources	124
	The Discovery of the Fossil Fishes	124
	Natural Gas	126
	Forestry	127
	Coal	128
11	The Recent Past	135
	Latterday Explorers	135
	The Evolution of Tumbler Ridge	136
12	Maps	137
	Historic Maps	137
	Current Maps	139
13	The Destinations	143
	Around Tumbler Ridge	143
	Highway 29 to Chetwynd	167
	The Wolverine Forest Service Road	175
	The Bullmoose – Windfall Creek Road	197
	The Sukunka Valley	213
	The Heritage Highway to Dawson Creek	221
	The Road to Bearhole Lake	227
	The Hourglass Road	229
	The Boundary Road	231
	The Road to Monkman Park and Kinuseo Falls	239
	Monkman Provincial Park	253
	Beyond Monkman Park	279
	To the Core Lodge and Beyond	285
	The Road to Thunder Mountain	299
	To the Wapiti, Red Deer and Belcourt Valleys	301
	The Murray River	315
	The BC Rail Line	321

14	How Good is it Here?	323
	Local	323
	Regional	326
	Global	331
	Conclusion	332
	Appendices	
	Appendix A – Origin of Place Names	333
	Appendix B – Bird Lists	344
	Appendix C – Plant Lists	348
	Appendix D – Acknowledgements	350
	Appendix E – Chapter Notes	353
	Index	358

■ LIST OF PLATES

Plate 1	Monkman Glacier	6
Plate 2	Bulley Glacier	6
Plate 3	Coral fossil from the Stone Corral	48
Plate 4	Fossilised coral	48
Plate 5	Crinoid fragments from the Stone Corral	50
Plate 6	Detail from The Mural	50
Plate 7	A fish fossil near the shore of Fossil Fish Lake	52
Plate 8	The coelacanth *Whiteia*	52
Plate 9	The ray–finned fish *Albertonia*	54
Plate 10	The ray–finned fish *Bobasatrania*	54
Plate 11	Head of the predatory fish *Saurichthys*	56
Plate 12	A print of *Irenichnetes*	56
Plate 13	The Flatbed Creek dinosaur trackway	58
Plate 14	The footprints on Roman Mountain of *Aquatilavipes*	60
Plate 15	Frond of the fern *Coniopteris*	60
Plate 16	The redwood *Elatides*	62
Plate 17	*Pseudocycas*, a cycad from the Gates Formation	62
Plate 18	Leaf of the seed fern *Sagenopteris*	64
Plate 19	Leaves of the maidenhair tree *Ginkgo pluripartita*	64
Plate 20	Fay's party descended into the Red Deer Valley	76
Plate 21	For 200 miles Fay and his party had to chop their way	76
Plate 22	Cross and Brewster map the way ahead	78
Plate 23	The first photograph ever taken of Kinuseo Falls	78
Plate 24	Prescott Fay and party pose in Hudson's Hope	80
Plate 25	Frederick Vreeland	80
Plate 26	Donald "Curly" Phillips	90
Plate 27	The Boundary Commission, cutting a swath	90
Plate 28	A monument constructed by the Boundary Commission	92
Plate 29	John Holzworth	92
Plate 30	Prentiss Gray	96
Plate 31	Gray took the second photos of Kinuseo Falls	96
Plate 32	Gray's party crosses the Wapiti River	100
Plate 33	Prentiss Gray carried state of the art camera equipment	100

Plate 34	William Sheldon	102
Plate 35	Self portrait by Richard Borden	102
Plate 36	Pete Calliou, veteran guide	108
Plate 37	Bill Taylor, Johnny Napoleon and Pete Calliou	108
Plate 38	Kathleen Peck	110
Plate 39	"Aunt Kate" Edwards	114
Plate 40	John Terry	114
Plate 41	Alex Monkman on horseback	118
Plate 42	Ted Chambers bathing in the Big Spring	118
Plate 43	Leake's 1939 photo of Kinuseo Falls	120
Plate 44	Leake's 1939 photo of Brooks Falls	120
Plate 45	A pioneer sits on the porch of one of the cabins	122
Plate 46	Cliff Duke lights a gas seep, 1950	122
Plate 47	Flatbed Falls	150
Plate 48	Kevin Sharman biking Kevin's Trail	150
Plate 49	The Bald Spot offers a view of Tumbler Ridge	154
Plate 50	Lost Haven Cabin	154
Plate 51	Quality Canyon	160
Plate 52	Upper Quality Falls	160
Plate 53	Kayaking the Wolverine Pools	164
Plate 54	Bergeron Cliffs on the Echo Ridge Trail	164
Plate 55	Gwillim Lake Provincial Park	170
Plate 56	Martin Falls drop into Martin Canyon	172
Plate 57	Perry Falls	176
Plate 58	The Caribou Highway on the trail up Mt. Reesor	176
Plate 59	Mt. Spieker is a family destination for all ages	182
Plate 60	The rocky flat summit of Mt. Spieker	182
Plate 61	Lower Tunnel Falls	188
Plate 62	The Wolverine Waterfall	188
Plate 63	View from the top of the Albright Ridge	192
Plate 64	Ridge–walking, Albright Ridge	192
Plate 65	Hoodoos on the Albright Ridge	193
Plate 66	Sunbathing on the Albright Ridge	194
Plate 67	Jogging on the Albright Ridge	194
Plate 68	Relaxing after a long, hot day's hiking	196
Plate 69	Entrance to Goatbone Grotto, Albright Ridge	196
Plate 70	Ice climbing lesson on Cowmoose Step Falls	200
Plate 71	Backcountry ski trip to Bullmoose Falls	202
Plate 72	Hiking the Reesor Ridge	204
Plate 73	Skiing the Holzworth Meadows	204
Plate 74	Final steps to the top of Mt. Crum	206
Plate 75	Hiking up Pinnacle Peak	206
Plate 76	Hiking up Pinnacle Peak	208
Plate 77	Windfall Lake	208
Plate 78	Tunnel Mountain – Xs mark tunnel exits	212
Plate 79	Looking out of Tunnel Cave onto the Sukunka Valley	212
Plate 80	Prescott Fay took the first photo of Sukunka Falls	216
Plate 81	Hole in the Wall	216
Plate 82	Murray Canyon Overlook Hiking Trail	222
Plate 83	Murray Canyon Overlook	222

Plate 84	Tepee Falls	224
Plate 85	Prentiss Gray took the first photo of Bearhole Lake	224
Plate 86	Skiing Babcock Creek	234
Plate 87	Rappelling lesson above Upper Flatbed Creek	234
Plate 88	Euphemia McNaught captured the beauty of Stony Lake	236
Plate 89	Skiing M20 Creek	236
Plate 90	Barbour Falls	244
Plate 91	Skiing to Nesbitt's Knee Falls	244
Plate 92	Nesbitt's Knee falls in spring flood	246
Plate 93	Summit scrambling, Pyramid Peak	246
Plate 94	The Stone Corral	250
Plate 95	Looking out of Corral Cave	250
Plate 96	Icicles in Corral Cave in spring	254
Plate 97	Cliff scenery, Stone Corral Hiking Trail	254
Plate 98	Kids in Porcupine Cave	258
Plate 99	Exiting Porcupine Cave	258
Plate 100	Kinuseo Falls	262
Plate 101	Al Tattersall leads the winter ascent of Kinuseo Falls	264
Plate 102	The Monkman Lake Trail	266
Plate 103	Monkman Lake	266
Plate 104	Unnamed Cascade	270
Plate 105	Unnamed Cascade	270
Plate 106	Upper Moore Falls	270
Plate 107	Unnamed Cascade	270
Plate 108	Brooks Falls	271
Plate 109	Lower Moore Falls	271
Plate 110	Monkman Falls	271
Plate 111	Glacier view from Paxton Peak	274
Plate 112	Summit view from Paxton Peak	274
Plate 113	The Shark's Fin	282
Plate 114	The unclimbed face of The Shark's Fin	282
Plate 115	The Boulder Gardens	286
Plate 116	Training for the Emperor's Challenge	286
Plate 117	The flat summit of Quintette Mountain	292
Plate 118	Babcock Falls	292
Plate 119	The Back Meadows… some of the finest snowmobiling	304
Plate 120	Belcourt Falls	304
Plate 121	Prentiss Gray in the first photo of Belcourt Lake	308
Plate 122	Wapiti Falls	308
Plate 123	Wapiti Lake	310
Plate 124	Prentiss Gray took the first photo of Onion Lake	310
Plate 125	Camping at Bootski Lake	312
Plate 126	Prentiss Gray took the first photo of Red Deer Falls	312
Plate 127	Snowmobiling the Red Deer area	314
Plate 128	Start of the Murray River canoe trip	314
Plate 129	Murray River canoe trip, Lower Section	316
Plate 130	Bergeron Falls	318

■ LIST OF FIGURES

Fig. 1   River Drainages and Area Boundaries 2
Fig. 2   The Road System 4
Fig. 3   The Tumbler Ridge Town Map 140
Fig. 4   The Area Surrounding Tumbler Ridge 142
Fig. 5   TR Point and Surrounding Trails 144
Fig. 6   Flatbed Falls Regional Park 148
Fig. 7   The Wolverine Trail System 156
Fig. 8   The Quality Falls Trail 162
Fig. 9   Highway 29 to Chetwynd 166
Fig. 10 The Wolverine Forest Service Road 174
Fig. 11 The Mt. Spieker – Mt. Reesor Area 178
Fig. 12 Tunnel Falls and Wolverine Waterfalls 186
Fig. 13 The Albright Ridge 190
Fig. 14 The Bullmoose – Windfall Creek Road 198
Fig. 15 The Windfall Lake Area 210
Fig. 16 The Sukunka Forest Service Road 214
Fig. 17 The Heritage Highway to Dawson Creek 220
Fig. 18 The Murray Canyon Overlook Hiking Trail 223
Fig. 19 The Road to Bearhole Lake 226
Fig. 20 The Hourglass Road 228
Fig. 21 The Boundary Road 232
Fig. 22 The Murray Forest Service Road to Monkman Park 240
Fig. 23 Nesbitt's Knee Falls and Barbour Falls 243
Fig. 24 Monkman Provincial Park 252
Fig. 25 The Stone Corral Hiking Trail 256
Fig. 26 The Kinuseo Falls Area 261
Fig. 27 The Cascades 268
Fig. 28 Beyond Monkman Park 278
Fig. 29 To the Core Lodge and Beyond 284
Fig. 30 The Thunder Mountain Road 298
Fig. 31 The Wapiti and Red Deer Forest Service Roads 302
Fig. 32 The Wapiti Lake Area 306

■ LIST OF DESTINATIONS

Albright Ridge 189
Bald Spot, The 155
Babcock, Mt. 289
Babcock Falls 294
Barbour Falls 245
Bat Lake area 218
Bearhole Lake 229
Becker, Mt. 315

Belcourt Falls/Lake 303
Bergeron Cliffs 165
Bergeron Falls 319
Blackhawk Lake 230
Boot Lake 230
Bootski Lake 311
Boulder Gardens, The 287
Boulder Lake 171

ix

Brooks Falls	272	Moose Lake	168
Bulley Glacier	280	Murray Canyon Overlook	223
Bulley, Mt.	279	Murray River (Lower)	319
Bullmoose Cliffs	197	Murray River (Upper)	317
Bullmoose Falls	199	Nesbitt's Knee Falls	247
Bullmoose Marshes	168	Onion Lake	307
Bullmoose Mountain	199	Paxton Peak	276
Circular Run	153	Perry Falls	177
Crum, Mt.	205	The Pond	165
Cowmoose Step Falls	197	Pinnacle Peak	207
Echo Ridge Trail	165	Pyramid Peak	248
The Five Peak Circuit	297	Quality Canyon	161
Flatbed Creek	152	Quality Falls	162
Flatbed East	235	Quality Lake	227
Flatbed Falls	149	Quality Mouth Trail	161
Flatbed Rock Pools	152	Quintette Mountain	293
Folded Falls	245	Red Deer Falls	313
Ganoid Range	309	Reesor, Mt.	180
Gap Lake	300	Reesor Ridge	201
Gibson Lake	299	Roman Mountain	289
Greg Duke Trail	249	Shark's Fin, The	283
Gwillim Lake	169	Spieker, Mt.	181
Hermann Mountain	242	Stone Corral Trail, The	255
Hole in the Wall	217	Stony Lake	238
Holzworth Meadows	203	Sukunka Falls	215
Hook Lake	219	Sukunka Ridge	219
Horseshoe Falls	167	TR Point	145
Imperial Canyon	281	Tentfire Canyon	248
Jade Falls and Lake	260	Tepee Falls	225
Kevin's Trail	151	Terminator, The	297
Kinuseo Creek	251	Thunder Mountain	299
Kinuseo Falls	261	Tumbler Branch Line	322
Kostuik, Mt.	295	Tumbler Ridge Tower	227
Limestone Lakes	277	Tunnel Falls	183
Linking Trail	147	Tunnel Mountain	211
Lions Campground	146	Upper Quality Falls	162
Lower Babcock Falls	233	Upper Tunnel Falls	187
Lower Tunnel Falls	183	Wapiti Falls	305
Lupin Lake area	275	Wapiti Lake	307
M20 Creek Falls	241	Waptik, Mt.	311
Martin Canyon	173	Warner Pass	313
Meikle Canyon	168	Windfall Lake area	209
Mini–Falls	147	Wolverine Pools	163
Monkman Falls	272	Wolverine Trails	157
Monkman Highway	238	Wolverine Waterfalls	187
Monkman Lake	275	Wong Way, The	242
Moore Falls	269		

INTRODUCTION

For many reasons, I would have been profoundly unhappy if Tumbler Ridge had not survived. On a personal and social level, it would have meant having to move from the community my family and I have grown to enjoy passionately. At a professional level it would have meant starting over somewhere fresh. At a recreational level I would have left numerous projects half finished.

But perhaps most importantly, at a deeper level I would have been disturbed by what would have been an immensely sad reflection on our society and its values. After all, if a community this attractive in an environment this beautiful in a country this fortunate with houses this affordable had *not* survived, it would have been an indictment of what we as a society consider meaningful and desirable.

But there is no reason to be gloomy. Although there are doubtless blips on the road ahead, the future for Tumbler Ridge is much brighter than it was even months ago. Houses have sold at a rate no one could have envisaged, and people are not just buying, but are coming to live here. They bring with them pensions, skills, and innovative ideas. Bullmoose Mine still operates and provides a cushion of a few years for the community to expand its horizons, and the Quintette reclamation team will be busy for a good while. The natural gas exploration and pipelines may offer some jobs to residents, there are promising signs of appropriate forestry development, and electronic communication will allow home businesses to spring up relatively easily in idyllic places like Tumbler Ridge.

This turnaround in fortunes has not come without an incredible amount of dedication, hard work and vision. Few mayors, councillors and administrators can ever expect to have such momentous forces thrust upon them as did ours in 2000. That they were able to weather the crisis and steer a true course is a tribute to them all. A debt of gratitude is owed them by residents new and old, and by the many that will follow and make this community their home or their vacation destination.

And it is in the field of tourism and recreation that the future of Tumbler Ridge is particularly blessed. An ecotourism co-operative in the true sense of the word is poised to capitalize on the potential market. New residents are discovering what a magnificent portion of North America they have settled in and will be bringing their friends and families. The towns of the Peace Country in British Columbia and Alberta have a need for a mountain retreat far from the furious crowds of the over-touristed national parks. The Alaska Highway carries one of the most constant streams of tourist traffic on the continent each summer, one that can be diverted to spend a few days in a wild area that boasts unique features.

Indeed, the challenge is no longer to ensure that Tumbler Ridge survives, but to ensure that it survives in such a way that the very attributes that make it so attractive are not destroyed, and that its clean air and water, excellent facilities, and a wilderness on its doorstep do not disappear. There are enough mistakes of both over-industrialized towns and over-touristed towns to learn from.

In a cynical and materialistic world, I see Tumbler Ridge as a bastion of sanity in which a gentler and infinitely more rewarding life prevails. One of the finest towns in the most beautiful province of a great country …we who have lived here for a while know this intuitively. What is new compared to a year ago is that this secret is out, and those for whom geographical remoteness is not something to be feared have responded.

In the light of these remarkably positive trends, a need arises for accessible information, which is the rationale for this book. Most existing guidebooks on the "Canadian Rockies" stop just north of Jasper. This need is augmented by the fact that the scenery here is not as immediately spectacular as further south – this is a land that visitors and residents really need to get close to in order to appreciate fully. These are not mountains to gawk at from a distance, but they are much more user-friendly and accessible than their higher counterparts.

In *Beyond Rock and Coal* I sought to fill a void, believing that a community needs to understand where it has come from in order to appreciate where it is headed. Because an appreciation of the wilderness around us also depends in part on an understanding of history, some material from *Beyond Rock and Coal* has been incorporated into this book, although in a different format. Another interesting phenomenon which followed its publication was the wealth of new material that interested people brought to my attention. The history contained in these pages includes this new data and seeks to address omissions and valid criticisms.

There is much left to discover here; this is a young land that has not been fully explored. There is something here for all tastes, and this book tries to cater to a broad variety of interests, although it reflects to some extent my personal pastimes and activities, which are non–mechanized and non–consumptive. It is also a big land with lots of room, and one of the defining features of those who use it has been the respect shown to those who enjoy the wilderness in a different way. In so many places there are turf wars between cross–country skiers and snowmobilers, between canoeists and jet boaters. That has never happened here, and the occasional minor incident only serves to highlight how much tolerance and goodwill exists. The Wolverine Nordic and Mountain Society (WNMS) is the local four–season non–mechanised outdoors group (complementing the activities of the Ridge Riders Snowmobile Club and other organizations). I have been privileged to be a member of this group for eight years, and much of the contents of this book is a synthesis of what WNMS has explored and is prepared to share.

As this is a volatile area, details will change as new trails are built, roads are deactivated etc. Some of the destinations mentioned in this book may become inaccessible with time and others will open up. I would appreciate criticism, suggestions for improvements, and new information which could be incorporated into future editions.

If you use this guide to explore the area and become acquainted with its subtle beauty, please tread gently on it and leave it an inspiring place for others to enjoy.

Charles Helm
Tumbler Ridge
2001

1 OVERVIEW OF THE AREA

"The Tumbler Ridge area" as defined in this book has the following boundaries:

– the BC – Alberta border to the east
– the spine of the Hart Ranges of the Rocky Mountains to the west (because the Peace River has its source on the western side of the Rockies, the mountains from Mt. Barton northwards do not form a continental divide
– southwards as far as Belcourt Lake, which excludes the entire Kakwa area; the reason being that Kakwa is most easily accessed either from Alberta via a long road from Grande Prairie, or else via forestry roads from McBride
– to the north, approximately halfway from Tumbler Ridge along the highways to Dawson Creek and Chetwynd, which just includes Gwillim Lake. The Sukunka River valley is something of an anomaly, being closer as the raven flies to Tumbler Ridge but closer as the vehicle travels to Chetwynd. It is included in this book as there is no adequate guidebook for the Chetwynd area that describes it.

Between these arbitrary boundaries is an enormous area of 12 000 square kilometres, within which Tumbler Ridge is the only community. Although certain parts of it have seen development for resource extraction

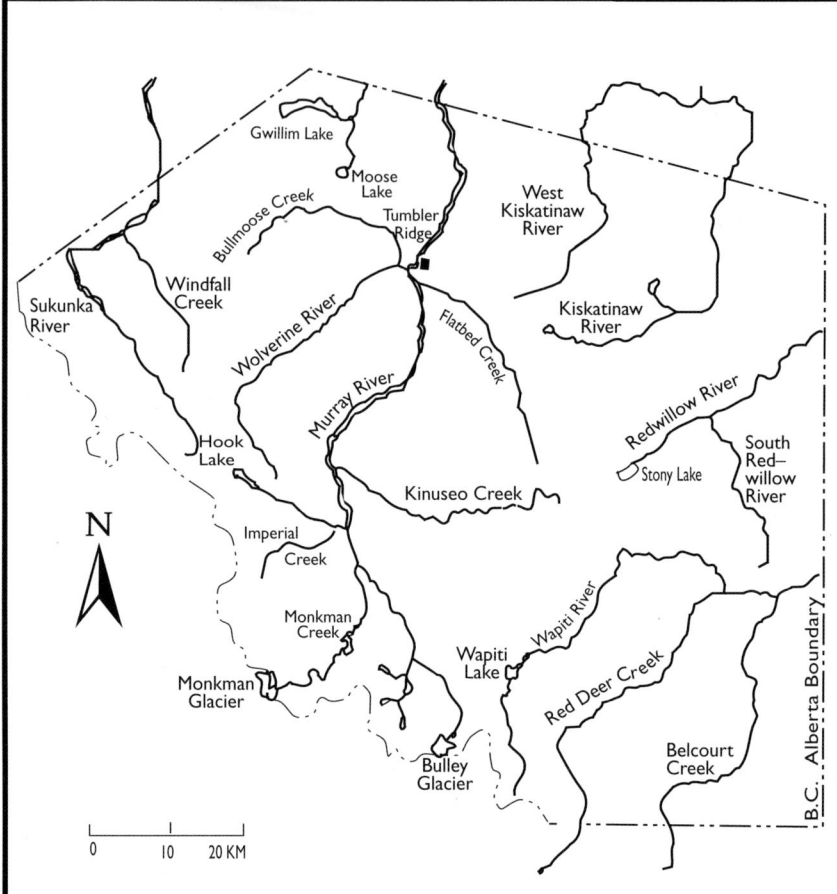

FIG. 1 RIVER DRAINAGES AND AREA BOUNDARIES

Distance from Tumbler Ridge to:

Dawson Creek .... 120 KM.
Fort St. John .... 92 KM.
Prince George .... 400 KM.
Edmonton .... 785 KM.
Calgary .... 1000 KM.
Vancouver .... 1178 KM.

in recent decades, the majority of it remains relatively untouched and there are many areas where humans have not yet set foot.

The road system is easy to grasp. There are three main arteries of travel: the paved highways to Dawson Creek and Chetwynd, and the largely unpaved Boundary Road to the east. All three have offshoots.

Some of these side roads are forestry roads which have radio frequencies posted at the start on which you can announce your presence to oncoming vehicles. These roads are sometimes narrow and logging trucks may use them at scary speeds. If you are unable to communicate on the radio frequency, please drive with extra caution. Although Tumbler Ridge has a small airport, the nearest commercial airport is just outside Dawson Creek.

All rivers flow eventually in to the Peace River and thus drain into the Arctic Ocean. Most of the rivers and their tributaries boast waterfalls.

> The major drainages are:
> – the Sukunka River in the northwest
> – the Murray River through the centre, fed in part by the Monkman (Plate 1) and Bulley (Plate 2) Glaciers. Its tributaries include Bulley Creek, Monkman Creek, Imperial Creek, Hook Creek, Kinuseo Creek, Flatbed Creek, the Wolverine River and the Gwillim River
> – the Kiskatinaw River which drains the Kiskatinaw plateau in the northeast
> – the branches of the Wapiti River system to the east and southeast; from north to south these are the Redwillow River, Wapiti River, Red Deer Creek and Belcourt Creek.

Although the area is not particularly well endowed with lakes, the largest are Bearhole Lake, Gwillim Lake, Hook Lake, Monkman Lake and Wapiti Lake. With the exception of Hook Lake these lie in protected areas.

As the Murray is the main river in the area, it is worth pondering the exact location of its source. The source of a river is best defined by distance, not volume. In other words, at every fork in the river, work out which is the longest branch, follow that, and repeat the process until the source is found. Applying this in the case of the Murray River

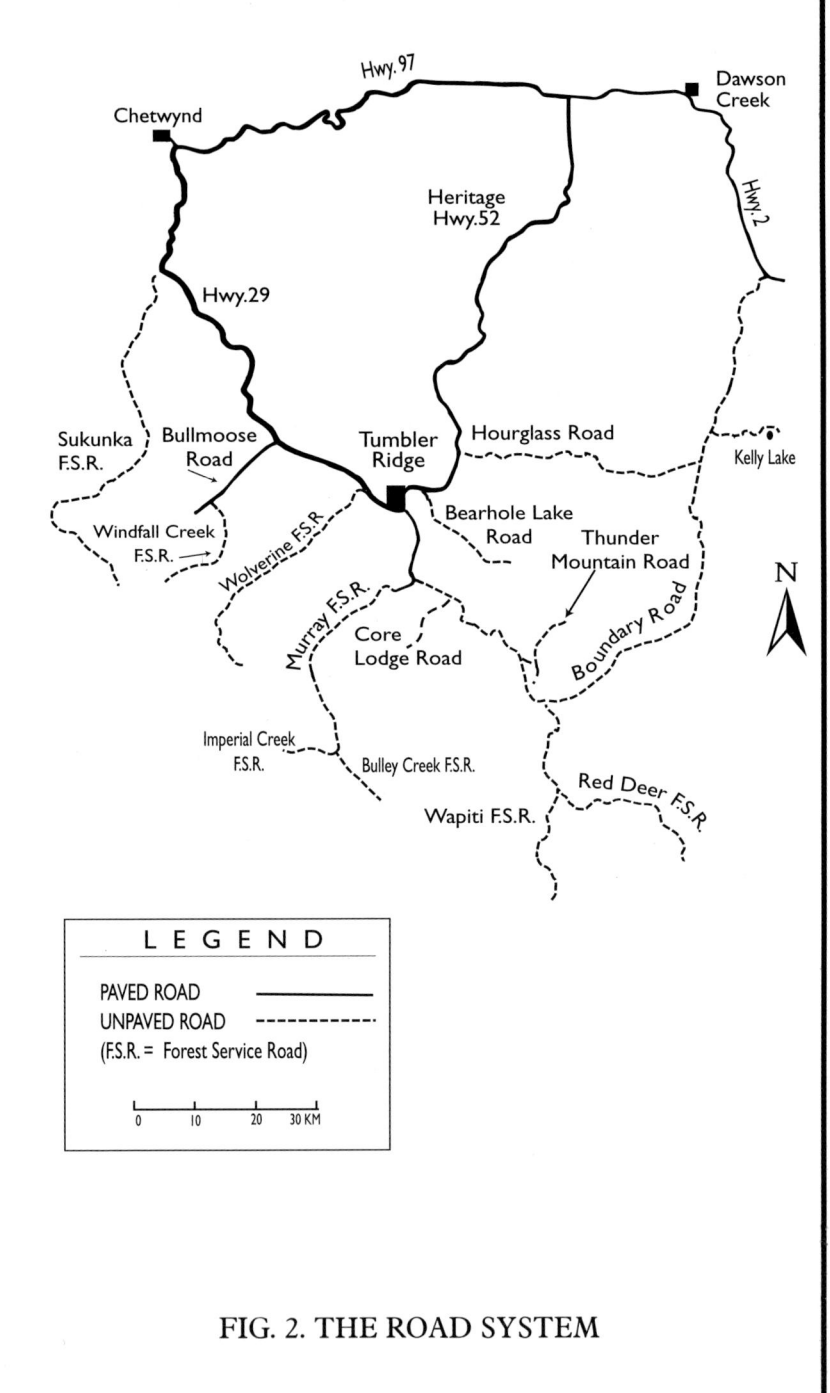

FIG. 2. THE ROAD SYSTEM

yields some surprising results. What is called the upper reaches of the Murray (the river that flows through Upper Blue and Lower Blue Lakes) is actually quite a lot shorter than both Monkman Creek and Bulley Creek. Bulley Creek just pips Monkman Creek, and so the substantial Bulley Glacier is the source of the Murray River.

This seems quite appropriate as the unnamed peak at the head of this glacier is the highest point in the area at 2630 metres (8600 feet) above sea level. The lowest point is 600 metres (1980 feet) above sea level where the Sukunka River leaves the area. The timberline occurs at around 1750 metres (5800 feet) above sea level, considerably lower than in the southern Canadian mountains. This enables easy alpine access. Tumbler Ridge's elevation is 820 metres (2700 feet) above sea level.

A biophysical description of the area becomes quite complicated, if one uses the standard classifications. British Columbia has been divided into a number of ecoregions according to specific parameters. In this area we have the Boreal Plains Ecoregion to the east and the Sub–boreal Interior Ecoregion to the west. The boundary between these two ecoregions bisects the area from north to south, passing just west of town along Flatbed Creek. Ecoregions are further subdivided into ecosections: so here we have the Kiskatinaw Plateau Ecosection of the Boreal Plains Ecoregion, and the Hart Foothills and Hart Ranges Ecosections of the Sub–boreal Interior Ecoregion. This classification is used for wildlife management purposes.

Confused yet? Then try adding this separate Biogeoclimatic Ecosystem Classification System, which often overlaps the Ecoregion Classification System. This one delineates ecological zones by vegetation, soils and climate; B.C. has fourteen Biogeoclimatic zones, of which four occur in the area:

> – the Boreal Black and White Spruce Zone (BWBS) comprises the majority of the lower elevation portions
> – the Engelmann Spruce – Subalpine Fir Zone (ESSF) occupies the higher elevation forested area
> – the Sub-boreal Spruce (SBS) Zone occupies some lowest elevation valley bottoms
> – the Alpine Tundra (AT) Zone occurs above the treeline.

The Murray River is fed by the two largest glaciers in the region.

Plate 1:   Monkman Glacier.   Credit: Paul Jurgens

Plate 2:   Bulley Glacier – the unnamed peak at its head is the highest in the region at 2 630 metres above sea level. Credit: Kevin Sharman

These zones describe the climax vegetation that they can support, therefore species such as aspen and pine are not mentioned.

These classifications are of interest to those involved in resource management and conservation, but have little practical relevance to recreational enjoyment of the area.

The only natural resources that have been exploited thus far are coal, gas and timber. The Peace River Coal Field contains a staggering estimate of 10 billion tons of coal, most of which is in the Tumbler Ridge area. Northeastern British Columbia is the only portion of the province that currently produces natural gas. Approximately 37% of the Dawson Creek Forest District (which includes the Tumbler Ridge area) is classified as "operable for sustainable forest production".

There are other potential resources that could be extracted in future: peat moss, limestone, sand, gravel, coal–bed methane and wind.

The Wolverine Nordic and Mountain Society has opened its own website: www.pris.bc.ca/wnms
This recommended site contains photo galleries of area attractions and activities, including most of the destinations mentioned in this book, as well as information, photos and entry forms for the Emperor's Challenge Mountain Run.

The District of Tumbler Ridge website has links, a guest book, and useful information including accommodations. Check it out at www.district.tumbler-ridge.bc.ca It also contains the regularly updated snow report of the Ridge Riders Snowmobile Club.

For more information on the town itself, look no further than the annual Community Directory. This excellent and comprehensive publication is a goldmine of up to date information.

2 CLIMATE

The town of Tumbler Ridge has a uniquely favourable climate, deriving benefits from the influences of the prairies, the mountains, and the more moderate temperatures to the west. The reasons for this happy state of affairs are briefly discussed in this chapter.

Summers are warm but not hot, relatively dry, and on most days when the mountain ranges are bathed in cloud, the town still basks in sunshine. The long daylight hours provide opportunities for endless outdoor recreation, as well as a fine growing season.

Although Tumbler Ridge's climate is classified as "continental", winters are surprisingly mild for this latitude (55 degrees north) and being east of the mountains. Snowfall is seldom excessive, and temperatures are almost invariably warmer than in the prairie communities of Dawson Creek or Grande Prairie. Year round there is a relative absence of wind – if you want to windsurf or fly a kite, head for the prairies. The exception to the latter rule is to be found on the alpine summits which are usually windy; flying a kite up there provides an exhilarating experience appreciated by only a few. This alpine zone offers potential for harnessing wind energy, perhaps using the existing infrastructure of the Quintette mine. The maximum wind recorded is an impressive 121 km/hr.

Because of the northern latitude, the sun does not rise as high in the sky compared with more southerly locations. This increases the difference between south–facing slopes and north–facing slopes. South–facing slopes get a lot more radiant heat, warm up quicker, are therefore drier, and are sometimes not even forested. The slopes of Mount Bergeron are a good example.

The prevailing winds are from the southwest, but by the time they reach the Rockies they already have deposited much of their precipita-

---

Tumbler Ridge Climate Statistics

Longest day: 21 June   Sunrise 04h25 Sunset 21h50
Shortest day: 21 December   Sunrise 09h29 Sunset 16h38

Tumbler Ridge temp. (Celsius):   January average   -11.1
     July average   14.8

Average of the coldest temperature recorded each January: -32
Average of the warmest temperature recorded each July: 30.9

Rainfall: mm (snowfall has been converted into mm of water): Tumbler Ridge   479
     Bullmoose Mine 721
Wettest month in Tumbler Ridge: July (86 mm)
Driest month in Tumbler Ridge: April (21 mm)
Frost–free days: 90

Sources: Fern Duperreault, Environment Canada, District of Tumbler Ridge.

---

tion. Our mountains often grab the remaining rain and snow, and this results in the comparative dryness of Tumbler Ridge, a typical "rain–shadow" effect. One only has to compare the average snowfall in communities like Mackenzie and Tumbler Ridge to see this, or compare the verdant vegetation on a hike in the mountains such as the Stone Corral Trail with the drier vegetation near town.

Longtime residents know that when the east wind blows, rain or snow is on the way. These are known as "upslope conditions". Air is pushed upwards as it reaches the hills and mountains, and cools as it rises. Moisture condenses and rain falls. Often when this happens, the conditions west of the mountains will be sunny.

Summer thunderstorms are relatively common. These are often preceded by strong winds, often in a direction quite different from the prevailing winds. These sometimes reach high intensity and can cause large blow downs in which whole clumps of trees fall in the same direction. There is a good example of this a few hundred metres behind the Lost Haven ski cabin. Naturally this causes headaches for those who have to come afterwards and reopen hiking trails.

Climate

The usual pattern is of decreasing temperature with increasing elevation, so a hike on the alpine ridges is colder than a walk around town, all other factors being equal. But in winter this is often reversed, with the phenomenon of temperature inversions. This works wonderfully in favor of Tumbler Ridge compared to other communities, because of the higher altitude here (820 metres above sea level). Arctic air flowing down through the prairies is often topped by warmer air. When this happens, conditions at the mines are warmer still, and have sometimes been recorded at a full 15 degrees Celsius higher than in town.

Winter conditions in the mountains are often extreme, and although another general rule is that winter precipitation increases with altitude, the wind blasting effect of the prevailing air movements above the tree line often leads to bare conditions on the summits and ridges. The greatest snow pack is found just below tree line, and this is the elevation at which snowmobilers and backcountry skiers are to be found. Elsewhere, where the mountains are more precipitous, avalanches are a lot commoner. Their infrequency in this area is one of the reasons for its popularity with snowmobilers. However, there is no room for complacency as avalanches do occur here.

To the north and south the Rockies act as more of a barrier to air mass flow, and temperatures vary a lot depending on which side of the mountains you find yourself on. Because the mountains here are lower, this barrier effect is reduced, which again works to the advantage of Tumbler Ridge. Usually winter conditions are colder east of the mountains on the prairies, and warmer to the west. Some of that warmer air manages to sneak through the passes west of Tumbler Ridge, and warm up our neck of the woods. Tumbler Ridge temperatures are not routinely given out yet on the regional weather reports, but residents know that our winter temperatures are usually closer to those of Prince George than Dawson Creek, yet not quite warm enough to melt the snow for skiers – in other words, just right (provided we get enough snow).

That happy equilibrium is sometimes abruptly shattered with the arrival of a chinook. This gusty warm wind from beyond the mountains evokes a wide range of intense emotions in those who brave it. Some are delighted by the warmer temperatures that allow them to resume walking. A chinook is a wholesome break from the grip of winter, these people will tell you. Many folks become grumpy, and statistics show a definite increase in the rates of homicides, suicides etc. before a chinook. The theory is that levels of brain neurotransmitters are altered to cause emotional changes. To skiers and snowmobilers, the chinook is a demon, an ill wind that eats snow or makes for icy conditions. Similar winds occur in Europe, Japan, and many other alpine areas across the globe, resulting in a powerful international anti–chinook solidarity amongst those who love good snow.

So what is a chinook really? It is caused by an intense flow of air from the Pacific, that shoots across the Rockies and causes gigantic standing waves on their eastern slopes where we happen to be. This is what accounts for the fact that some areas seem always to be buffeted more by chinooks than others – these standing waves are fairly constant. The best example in the Tumbler Ridge area is the industrial park about ten kilometres from town on the road to the Quintette mine and Monkman Park. That, of course, is pretty close to the Tumbler Ridge airport, which has caused many to question exactly why the airport was built just there.

Chinooks have an interesting effect on the vegetation. If you work out where these winds are strongest, then go back later in the year and check on the coniferous trees, you will find evidence of this. Dry windy conditions cause these trees to lose moisture. In summer this is combated by a swift flow of sap back to the needles. In winter the trees cannot muster this flow, and the result is damaged needles. In summer these have a sickly reddish–brown appearance.

The combination of climate and latitude makes for poor stargazing. Either one waits seemingly forever in summer for the sky to get dark enough to permit good viewing, or else one freezes rapidly at the end of an outdoor telescope during the long winter night. This is a shame because the clear skies, unpolluted by smog or light, are otherwise ideal. If astronomy is your passion, think about heading south. But in common with most northern Canadian communities, aided by our relative proximity to the magnetic north pole, there is a celestial extravaganza on a big big screen: the Aurora Borealis.

3 HAZARDS

Compared with many other mountain habitats, this is a gentle land. However, there is a great variety of ways in which one can get injured or killed, and one needs to anticipate the unexpected.

The area is a Grizzly Bear and Black Bear stronghold. The rivers are wild and unpredictable enough to cause canoeing accidents. Winter temperatures can be extreme and can kill the unprepared in minutes. Avalanches do occur. The alpine ridges can be dry and hot in summer and heat stroke and dehydration are not impossible. Lightning is a summer reality in the exposed alpine regions.

Because this is a wilderness area, many beautiful parts of it have no trails, and it is quite possible to get lost. Some of the more remote destinations described in this book are mentioned only as exciting areas to explore, without detailed instructions. Therein lies their magic but also potential danger. The term "bushwhacking" crops up a fair amount in the destinations section. A compass and GPS, adequate maps, and the skills to use these tools are essential.

Roads can be icy and dangerous in winter, but the serious motor vehicle accident rate remains thankfully low.

The majority of wilderness accidents are due to ignorance, ill-founded bravado, irresponsibility or poor preparation. Throughout this book a cautious and well-prepared approach is advised. There are many good books that deal in detail with these hazards. A sound knowledge of preventing and treating wilderness emergencies is needed before entering the backcountry.

There is a remote risk of H_2S (hydrogen sulphide) exposure in the portions of the area in which natural gas is extracted. Signs warning that entry is at own risk are posted at the beginning of roads into these areas. H_2S has a typical rotten eggs smell, and is potentially fatal. Unfortunately, one of its characteristics is that it affects one's sense of smell. Therefore, if you smell this odour for a few seconds and then can no longer discern it, one of three things has happened. Either you were imagining it, this was a very small pocket, or else your inability to smell it means you are receiving a toxic exposure and may pass out soon. Do not take a chance! Get out of the area immediately, as quickly as you can. And do not approach gas plants unnecessarily.

Tumbler Ridge is fortunate to have an efficient Search and Rescue team. The risk of having them called out on your behalf will be reduced if you give someone a definite projected return time. And if they do have to come looking for you, their job will be made easier by their knowing your destination and route. Leaving these details with a friend not only increases your chances of rescue, but also decreases the risks for your rescuers.

Throughout this book a cautious approach is advised. The activities described in it have inherent risks. Some destinations may become inaccessible with the passage of time, access routes may change, and information presented in this book may become obsolete or incorrect. Conditions will vary with weather and seasonal changes. Some destinations have no trails, may have hazardous elements, or may demand wilderness travel. The maps in this book should serve as a guide only, and are not a substitute for topographical maps. There is no guarantee that the events mentioned this book will continue to be organised in future. Although the author and publisher have taken every effort to ensure that the information is as accurate as possible, they accept no responsibility or liability for any errors and omissions, nor for any loss, injury or inconvenience sustained by any person using this book. Readers should seek current information on conditions before setting out. Errors brought to the attention of the publisher will be corrected in subsequent editions.

4 ACTIVITIES

■ BIRDS

This is an intriguing and absorbing area for birders, with many unsolved questions, yet not always conducive to easy observation. I am often struck by the relative ease with which many species can be found rapidly in the cleared prairie areas around Dawson Creek, compared with the patience needed in the more forested Tumbler Ridge area.

TROG (Tumbler Ridge Ornithology Group) is devoted to all aspects of bird watching in the area, from systematic atlassing to compiling an area list, assisting visiting birders and arranging outings, to rehabilitating injured birds.

Probably the most interesting ornithological feature of the area is that "this is where East meets West". In other words, many eastern prairie species just reach the western limit of their distribution here, and likewise, many species characteristic of B.C. west of the Rockies spill over into the area and have their easternmost representation here. For example, it is possible to find species pairs such as Black–throated Green Warbler and Townsend's Warbler, or Mourning Warbler and MacGillivray's Warbler, occurring in the same patch of forest.

Some birds such as Clark's Nutcracker and Black Swift also reach their northernmost limit here. The latter is interesting because it is thought to breed in the canyons of the foothills near waterfalls. No birds are thought to reach their southernmost limit here; the closest candidate would be Rock Ptarmigan which is known from the Pine Pass.

Birders from southern B.C. who keep provincial lists find the area of specific interest because of the "northeastern B.C. Specials". Ideally they will combine a trip to Tumbler Ridge with a visit to the Peace Country of Dawson Creek and Fort St. John to add variety.

Another interesting birding feature is the ease of alpine access. This ecosystem is generally poorly birded due to the small numbers of enthusiasts who venture this high. This does not apply in Tumbler Ridge, and the interesting avifauna of the tree line and tundra is approachable and provides for rewarding birding. Quintette Mountain, Babcock Mountain, Mount Hermann and Mount Spieker are the best sites.

Then there is the phenomenon of the Golden Eagle migration. Research into this fascinating phenomenon has been pioneered by Peter Sherrington (see page 184).

There are few places where breeding Trumpeter Swans can so easily be seen. Many of the smaller lakes boast one or two breeding pairs each summer. Gibson Lake offers possibly the best sightings. Blackhawk Lake is another quiet undisturbed lake for swans. Bearhole Lake Provincial Park was recently proclaimed and protects critical Trumpeter Swan habitat and a variety of wetland habitats. It is estimated that there are approximately 25 breeding pairs in the area, easily identifiable by means of an aerial survey.

A complete bird list as of 2001 is provided as Appendix B, along with the eastern specials and western specials. An impressive total of 211 species has been recorded.

Apart from the lakes and the alpine areas mentioned, there are a few specific recommended sites. The TR Point trail has been designated a bird sanctuary and offers a variety of habitats and edge effect in quick succession, with the advantage of being able to scan the forest canopy with ease from the trail. The Sewage Works normally harbour some waterbirds or shorebirds. In May the Quintail Slough alongside the Boundary Road has large numbers of waterfowl and a few pallets have been strategically placed for good viewing. The Murray Canyon Overlook Trail provides good mixed woodland birding and also traverses extensive open country which is good for raptors and many species otherwise uncommon in the area. The Kinuseo Falls area, especially the road just upstream from the falls, and the Stone Corral are also recommended. One of the finest birding sites is along the road past Serpent Lake to its terminus at Kinuseo Creek. This east–west valley funnels a lot of migratory birds, and the relatively open forest and beaver dams around the end of the road offer easy birding.

■ BOTANY

— GETTING TO KNOW THE TREES, PLANTS & FLOWERS

There are only nine large tree species in the area (see Appendix C). What we lack in variety we compensate for in numbers. This allows novices and kids to obtain some sort of mastery of their natural environment fairly quickly, which in turn can lead to branching out into other areas of natural history. Almost all kids enjoy learning to distinguish pine needles from spruce needles from fir needles etc.

The flowering plants are typical for northern climes, but because of the proximity of riverine forest and alpine tundra, with many habitats in between, there is ample opportunity for finding many species in a short period of time without a lot of driving distance.

The TR Point and Linking trails close to town offer excellent wildflower finding opportunities. Early Blue Violet and Calypso Orchid still occur close to town, a tribute to residents who have not wiped these species out as has happened in many other places. Appendix C includes commonly found flowering plants along these trails.

Slightly further afield, the Murray Canyon Overlook trail is a mass of colour on its open second half in season. The Stone Corral Trail shows off the flowers of its more moist environment, and its interpretive booklet describes poisonous plants like Baneberry, Mountain Monkshood and Mountain Death Camas.

However, it is the flowers of the subalpine meadows and the alpine tundra that draw most botanically–minded visitors. Any of the alpine areas described in this book are suitable, but the easiest of access are Mt. Hermann, Quintette Mountain and Mt. Spieker. A sample list of commonly encountered alpine species is provided in Appendix C.

■ CAMPING

Both the Lions Flatbed Campground and the Monkman RV Park are situated close to Tumbler Ridge and cater to visitors. A few years ago a small beach was created near the Lions Flatbed Campground, next to a pleasant pool beneath some cliffs. There is also good access to the trail system.

The most popular regional campgrounds are in Gwillim Lake and Monkman Provincial Parks. The Gwillim campground in particular is very popular and its 49 sites are often full on weekends. The increasing number of recreational opportunities in and around Monkman Park will increase the popularity of its campground, which has 42 sites.

There are at least ten Forest Service campgrounds, which are typically more rustic and offer only a few sites each. These include Windfall Creek, Moose Lake, Bearhole Lake, Boot Lake, Flatbed East, Stony Lake, Redwillow, Thunder Creek, Wapiti West and Wapiti East.

Then there are the unofficial sites that have somehow developed over the years, often situated alongside creeks, with no amenities at all. The use of the Murray River by boaters and canoeists has led to some excellent riverside unofficial sites.

The two official long trails in the region both offer camping facilities with food caches to minimize bear encounters. The Monkman Lake trail has sites at the Murray River crossing and at the lake, and the Wapiti–Onion Trail has sites at both lakes.

The alpine regions offer unlimited camping opportunities for the adventurous. The flat–topped Mount Spieker offers the easiest access for wilderness camping. Further afield, the lakes on the Albright Ridge, Windfall Lake and Bootski Lake all provide idyllic camping opportunities.

■ CANOEING AND KAYAKING

The Tumbler Ridge area offers something for canoeists of all skills. Starting with flat water, many of the local lakes are suitable, and can be combined with fishing and wildlife watching. Examples include Moose Lake, Quality Lake and Boulder Lake. Larger lakes are also attractive but some caution should be used if there is a possibility of strong winds. Examples are Bearhole Lake and Blackhawk Lake, which are both good for birds and other wildlife.

Stony Lake is subject to dangerously strong winds which funnel down the long reach of the lake. However, the downstream (eastern) end of the lake is protected and is good for wildlife and also offers the interesting excursion to the historic old cabins site.

Gwillim Lake's larger size and the prevailing wind direction combine to make canoeing not recommended. This is a boater's lake.

Almost in the flat water category is the excursion up the Upper Flatbed Creek that starts at the Flatbed East Forest Service Site. This involves negotiating some beaver dams and wading through one shallow set of rapids, and offers the opportunity of rappelling down some small cliffs.

Slightly more challenging is the canoe descent of the Murray River from Kinuseo Falls to Tumbler Ridge. This very long day trip can be broken up into four stages by convenient bridges. It is considered suitable for those wishing to learn to extend their abilities beyond flat water, especially the last section from the Quintette bridge down to Tumbler Ridge. It is classified Grade 2.

The Murray River from Tumbler Ridge to the East Pine is a good three–day trip for experienced canoeists, a wild adventure that will thrill those who safely complete it. It is classified Grade 3 and clearly is for experienced and well–equipped parties prepared for any canoeing eventualities.

For kayakers, sections of the Wolverine River and Flatbed Creek provide good whitewater within minutes of town. Note that these are cold rivers – a good wetsuit or a drysuit is advised. The part of the Wolverine that interests kayakers and advanced canoeists is the lowest section (Class 2), from the Bullmoose silos to the Highway 29 bridge. The river passes through a small canyon, with plenty of play spots. There is one drop on river right that must be avoided – scout before you run!

Flatbed Creek "bridge to bridge" ending at the Lions campground offers Class 2 to 3 paddling, depending on the water level. This three to four hour trip has been run in open boats by experts, but is more suitable for kayaks. Features include ledge drops, boulder gardens, a few good side surfing holes, and Flatbed Falls, a 4 m high drop that is runnable at higher levels. The best section from the falls down is about 2 hours. Paddling season on both of these is late April to late June, and later in the year after heavy rainfall in the catchment areas. The Wolverine spring flood occurs a week or two after Flatbed, as the river has more alpine drainage.

■ CAVING

The ingredients for caves are there: a lot of limestone, considerable elevation changes and time. True, the warm temperatures that allow for the creation of the impressive formations of the tropical and temperate parts of the world don't occur here, and as a result speleothem formation (stalactites, stalagmites etc.) is limited. But then again, you don't find our ice caves and underground icefalls in the tropics.

One just needs to consider some of the incredible finds of the past two decades in the mountains to the southwest of our area, characterized by similar rock formations: Fang Cave has yielded almost four kilometres of passageway, and Close to the Edge contains the deepest single pit in North America, a sheer drop of 300 metres.

The search has only just begun here for similar caves. The limited amount of exploration that has been done has given tantalizing hints of interesting finds to come, and has certainly proven that the area does contain caves.

Initial discoveries came after minimal searching in 1996 with the discovery of Goatbone Grotto and Cornice Cave on the Albright Ridge. "Goatbone" proved a misnomer when the ancient bones discovered at the bottom of its pit turned out to be those of a mule deer. The bottom of Cornice Cave was remarkable for a separate chamber named the Attic, adorned with an appealing array of small stalactites. The area holds more potential and there are a number of other caves in this range that have not yet been entered.

1997 saw a focus on the headwaters of the Sukunka River. A helicopter survey arranged by the Ministry of Forests had identified an area high in potential, and had discovered Consolation Cave but not had time to probe it. The entrance was rediscovered and the cave explored to its end, some 70 metres deep. Some of the most impressive formations yet discovered were in this cave's four chambers. Once again, the area is rich in caves for anyone with time, patience, and a passion for the underground world.

In 1998 the Windfall Creek basin was explored, with interesting results. Sausage Cave is probably the first true ice–cave to be found in British Columbia. It leads down a tight ice–filled passage to a chamber forty metres below the surface blessed with an icefall. Below that level the passage is choked with ice. Nearby Caribou Cave is a long gash in the surface of the alpine, with short passages branching off in four directions. Below these caves is Lisa's Cave with an interesting arch at the entrance. Higher up the mountain are two fascinating sites: one is at the bottom of a big sinkhole and hasn't been entered yet because of concerns about the lack of safety of the sidewalls. The second is a vertical pit 60 metres deep, and only awaits the right expertise and equipment.

A few kilometres away lies Tunnel Cave, northwest of Mount Crum. This allows a very different ascent of Tunnel Mountain, by climbing through the long tunnel with its beautiful views of the Sukunka Valley below. Also accessed from the Sukunka Forest Service Road is a large cave with a significant bat population.

In 1999 the Stone Corral and Corral Cave were discovered, with the addition in 2000 of Porcupine Cave and a number of other small cave systems in Monkman Provincial Park. Exploration then ceased as all efforts were put into developing the trail system to these intriguing destinations. These small caves may interest the casual visitor: small stalactites, tubes, fossils, moonmilk, cave popcorn etc. An interpretive pamphlet is available to guide visitors through this karst area. Many caves have been reported from the inaccessible high country of Monkman Park, but have not been formally explored.

In contrast to many of the other caves discovered, Corral Cave and Porcupine Cave are walk–in or crawl–in caves, do not require the use of ropes, and are not as fragile. Most of the other caves are vertical and require technical gear.

As in many areas, there are rumours about enormous caves. One interesting tale is about a huge cave that was discovered during the construction of the Table railway tunnel and was filled with water, 1000 metres below the surface. BC Rail allegedly closed the entrance with concrete to prevent any curious cavers from wandering through this long tunnel. Although there is a hole in the concrete, the most reliable information obtained is that this "cave" is actually very tiny. BC Rail does not permit pedestrian traffic in the tunnel.

Finally, there is the issue of cave diving. The water that percolates down through the limestone often emerges lower down as resurgence springs. The best known regional example is Hole in the Wall. Cave divers can enter such springs. No cave diving has yet occurred in the region. This is a highly specialized field of activity, best left to experts.

It is clear that there is a vast area here waiting to be explored. Aerial photographs are often used and many caves are in remote alpine locations. One area, yet to be visited on foot, has 43 areas identified on aerial photographs that need to be inspected. The majority of these are sinkholes that may lead to cave entrances. Another unexplored area features a series of sunken lakes.

Both for reasons of safety and for protection of the sensitive cave features; no directions are given to any entrances in this book with the exception of the Stone Corral Interpretive Hiking Trail. However, experienced cavers with acceptable credentials, as well as residents with a true interest in minimal impact caving, may contact the Wolverine Nordic and Mountain Society for details or to participate in a field trip.

■ CROSS–COUNTRY SKIING

Tumbler Ridge offers some of the finest and most varied cross–country skiing to be found anywhere. There is only one problem: we live on the eastern slopes of the Rockies and snowfall here is not as plentiful as it is on the western flanks of the mountains. To compound this, a number of chinooks occur every winter. These are the bane of cross–country skiers, who sometimes see their cherished snow and lovingly tended trails vanish over a couple of days.

Activities

There have been occasional years in which the Wolverine Ski Trails have only offered quality skiing for a few weeks per year, but usually a very respectable three to four month season can be enjoyed, and this can be extended if you are prepared to head up into the mountains in spring.

The provision of trackset ski trails of excellent quality is one of the most important functions of the Wolverine Nordic and Mountain Society. Trail construction began in the late 1980s and the trails were expanded in 1996, with the creation of the Lost Haven Ski Cabin, which serves as a warm–up destination and is a focus for a number of events.

For novice and intermediate skiers, a waxing clinic and practical ski clinic is held each year, and there are numerous events, from full moon skis to a New Year's Eve ski to backcountry ski outings. A busy BC Rabbit coaching program guides young skiers. The annual Ridge Ramble ski race, held in February, has become a challenging twenty kilometre event, with shorter recreational distances and a kids' race. This is usually followed the next day by the Kids Triathlon, another event that seeks to foster healthy sporting activities for the youth of the town and the region.

The ski season usually begins with a couple of early snowfalls that provide limited skiing opportunities. Once there is a decent base, the 10 kilometres of the Wolverine trails are groomed and trackset. These trails, which start and finish at the golf course clubhouse, vary from easy to challenging. There is also a wilderness loop of two kilometres from the Lost Haven cabin.

After prolonged cold weather, usually around the New Year, the backcountry creek skiing begins. This is one of the skiing highlights of the region. It is essential to check snow and ice conditions first before venturing out onto the creeks – check with the experienced skiers in town first if in any doubt. Learn to read frozen creeks and how to avoid falling in. Check also as to which creeks have been ski–set – these vary from year to year. This avoids having to break trail.

The Flatbed Creek ski is one of the most popular. Most skiers simply ski up the creek from the Lions campground to the falls and back (7 KMS) but the creek above the falls has its own charm, and a worthwhile slightly longer alternative is to ski 'bridge to bridge' from the upper bridge past the falls down to the campground.

A similar trip lies up Babcock Creek past Lower Babcock Falls to the next two sets of falls. Meikle Creek is another good option, leading through Meikle Canyon and to the Hoodoos. M20 Creek is short but very spectacular, leading through a canyon to a frozen waterfall. For the connoisseur of creek skiing, the trip up Bullmoose Creek to Horseshoe Falls is recommended. Perry Creek offers some unique challenges including negotiating a massive logjam.

Wind at high elevations often creates bare conditions right on the mountain summits, so the area at and just above the tree line is often the best for skiing. There are a number of ways to gain access to these areas, but one year often differs from the next as different roads are plowed open in different years. Again, it is best to check locally. If the pass at the head of Bullmoose Creek is accessible via the Windfall Creek road, this is one of the finest areas, which sometimes needs to be shared with snowmobiles. (One of the distinguishing features of life in Tumbler Ridge has been the excellent relationship between skiers and snowmobilers). Snowmobilers have cut a trail from the lakelet in the pass up through a stretch of forest into the alpine regions, with limitless opportunities for cross–country skiing, and spring ascents of a number of summits (carry a pair of hiking boots in your backpack and change into them when the snow ends and the windswept rocky ridges take over).

Telemark skiing is increasing in popularity and its enthusiasts have pinpointed a number of choice locations for this exhilarating activity. The bowls of Mount Spieker, Mount Reesor and the ridges accessible from the Windfall Creek road offer some of the best sites.

Non-skiers are asked to observe the ethic of never encroaching on any ski trails. Cross–country skis may be rented in town from Budskis.

■ DOG SLEDDING By Mark Bernadet

When most people think of dog–sledding, they think of the Iditarod, in which teams of exceptionally athletic dogs run 1100 miles through the Alaskan wilderness in as little as nine and a half days. But to limit one's thoughts to the Iditarod is to ignore the growing sport of recreational dog mushing. Recreational mushers may have kennels of

2 to 25 dogs, and run sprints of 4-6 miles once or twice a week, racing on the weekends or heading into the mountains for an overnight camp.

Tumbler Ridge has the potential to set up a large kennel and develop fixed trails, but at present it is easiest to load up the dogs, drive a few minutes out of town and run on a different trail each week. Moderate temperatures, a constant snow pack, accessible wilderness in a variety of settings and elevations, and endless trails all provide for enjoyable runs. Some trails are shared with snowmobilers, who inevitably pass with courtesy and caution.

Dog sledding embodies *excitement, magic and joy*. The *excitement* lies in the sprint, in skidding around corners, flying over bumps or careening down hills. There are several 6–10 km runs close to town e.g. past the gun range, adjacent to the highways, the Basset road off Highway 52, Flatbed Creek and along the Murray and Wolverine Rivers when conditions permit. Annually there is a sled dog sprint race in Tumbler Ridge.

Mountain runs into the alpine are hard work, but coming down is best described as a bobsled run. The dogs are running flat out without having to pull the sled and serve only to steer as you weave and bob down the trail. Easiest access is off the Windfall Creek road. Wildlife often creates excitement as the dogs realise why they have canines and take off at a run that can give the musher whiplash.

The *magic* of dog sledding is in the distance run, when the dogs settle into a rhythmic trot, cruise mode, when you are swallowed up by the landscape, crossing a lake guarded by mountains with their heads in the clouds, when you creep above tree line and glide on top of the world. One distance run leaves from the Flatbed Campground and ends at the Quintette spur line. If the line gets taken out of service, this will become an excellent return loop. Bearhole Lake is a good distance run and campsite, 26 kilometres one way with a series of hills. One of the most incredible runs is up Wapiti River to Wapiti Lake. This is a difficult run as there is an open channel of water, which may pin the team against the bank at several points.

The *joy* of dog sledding is in the dogs, spending time with good buddies who are always happy to see you. Each dog has its own personality, strengths and weaknesses, and the team has a pack relationship that is very different from owning a single pet.

Recreational mushing in Tumbler Ridge is a thrilling and expanding activity. Here only one thing can be said for certain: "winter is always too short".

■ EXPLORATION

The early explorers like Fay and Gray identified some of the major features of the region, like Kinuseo Falls, Red Deer Falls, Wapiti Lake, Bearhole Lake, Gwillim Lake and Onion Lake. But in the intervening century not everything else has been found. The recent discoveries of the Stone Corral and the tunnel of Tunnel Mountain are but two exciting examples. We live in the Golden Age of exploration in Tumbler Ridge, with the help of aerial photos and stereoscopic lenses. There are precious few places left on the planet where such a claim can be made. Many of the destinations mentioned in this book have not been fully explored.

■ FISHING By Fern Duperreault

Fishing remains an exciting activity, but its nature has changed over the years. The journals of the explorers yield fabulous tales of great numbers of large fish caught in record time, and even in the early 1980s fishing was a lot more productive than it is now. To protect this resource, regulations have become a lot stricter in the last few years, and the annual fishing guide should be read carefully as the rules do change. Much more of the fishing is now catch–and–release, and residents who wish to stock their freezers full of fish generally do not catch them here.

Lake fishing is popular both in summer and winter. Gwillim is a self–sustaining lake; most of the others are stocked annually. Gwillim Lake holds large Lake Trout as well as Northern Pike, Burbot, Rainbow Trout and Rocky Mountain Whitefish. Beware the many soft or open spots on this lake in winter due to underwater springs.

Boot Lake, Moose Lake and Quality Lake are stocked with Rainbow Trout and Brook Trout, and the Kinuseo Lakes (Greg Duke Memorial Recreation Area) have been stocked with Brook Trout. Bearhole Lake boasts Northern Pike, Yellow Perch, Rainbow Trout and Burbot, and Stony Lake has similar species. Pickerel are not found in the area. Restrictions on size, numbers and bait need to be heeded, for example single barbless hooks are mandatory at Bearhole Lake.

There are tales of large Cutthroat Trout in some of the subalpine lakes. In these and the alpine lakes fish take a very long time to mature, and the populations are easily fished out. This is one reason why air access in the provincial park alpine areas has been discontinued.

River fishing is possible on any of the major drainages and tributaries, but restrictions are even tighter than on the lakes. The season is closed from May 1 through June 30. Grayling are easy to catch and provide exciting fly–fishing, but size, amount and bait regulations are strict. The Bull Trout (known locally as Dolly Varden) has seen a drop in numbers and is now strictly catch–and–release only. The rivers may also yield Rainbow Trout, Northern Pike, Burbot (Ling Cod) and Rocky Mountain Whitefish. All river fishing demands single barbless hooks and no bait. River fish are most frequently found near logjams, rapids and tributaries.

Fishing licences may be purchased in town at Koals and Tags.

■ HARVESTING THE WILD

Annual rituals such as berry picking, mushroom harvesting, fishing and hunting have the potential to reaffirm for ourselves our place in and connections with the natural world. They also allow us to learn and to teach sustainability, the habit of taking just enough, and leaving enough behind to allow for a similar harvest in years to come.

Unfortunately many do not stick to these rules. Even with harvesting plants, it is possible to damage local populations by taking too much of one species. Yet sustainable use of these resources is practicable, and serves also to vary ones diet; many local plants are rich in essential vitamins and minerals. Their use over the ages to treat a variety of ailments represents a treasure trove of partially lost knowledge that begs better scientific investigation.

Before setting out to harvest plants, it is essential to know the toxic species first, such as Baneberry, Mountain Monkshood, and Death Camas. The Stone Corral Interpretive Hiking Trail describes some of the very toxic plants in the region, as well as detailing those preferably avoided. It is essential to use common species only; never harvest any portion of a plant you don't know, or one that is rare, and always take only a few leaves or berries from any one plant.

The commonest current uses to which plants are put in the area are leaves for teas, and berries for consumption. Labrador Tea, Raspberry Tea and Rosehip Tea are the most popular, with Spruce Tea and Pine Tea a distant second. Berry crops vary from year to year, and although they are abundant, do not reach the size of the coastal species. Strawberry, Raspberry, Cranberry, Blueberry, Saskatoon and Huckleberry are the most popular. A traditional ice cream is fun to make from Soopallallie berries.

Mushroom experts can harvest many species within a season, although over–harvesting is again a potential problem, and there are some highly toxic varieties out there such as Fly Agaric. The spring crop of Morels and the fall crop of Shaggy Mane Mushrooms are recognizable by most people. If harvested correctly, mushrooms can resprout.

■ HIKING

The easy access to many and varied hiking trails is one of the foremost attractions of Tumbler Ridge; there is truly something here for every age and level of expertise. A description of destinations forms the body of this book; this summary therefore simply seeks to categorize hikes for convenience. A weakness at present is inadequate disabled access to the trails, Kinuseo Falls being one of the few exceptions.

Half–day hikes:
The trail system around the fringes of town is deservedly popular, and is frequently being expanded. The TR Point trail is an old favorite, complemented now by the Linking Trail, the golf course trail, the

Flatbed Falls trail and the Upper Flatbed Trail (Kevin's Trail). For an aerial view of the town there is also the fairly steep Bald Spot Trail.

The trail to Quality Falls was built in 1996 and the Murray Canyon Overlook Trail in 2000. Both offer invigorating hiking off the Heritage Highway and the latter has the added benefit of an interpretive guide booklet available at the start.

The Babcock Creek valley and the Core Lodge area have great hiking potential. Here the Emperor's Challenge route up Roman Mountain is fully staked with rock cairns all the way so that it is virtually impossible to get lost no matter how severe the weather. Improvements are being made to the Babcock Falls trail, and trails to the summit of Quintette Mountain and to the Boulder Gardens are being built.

Off the road to Monkman Park are two unofficial trails to Nesbitt's Knee Falls and Barbour Falls, as well as the Greg Duke Memorial Recreation Area with trails to a series of lakes. Within the park are a number of trails around Kinuseo Falls as well as the highly recommended Stone Corral Trail, which includes two small caves and also has an interpretive booklet.

There are many other short hikes described within this book.

Day hikes:

The trail to Red Deer Falls usually takes a full long day. For those not fazed by thrashing up and down through the subalpine forest, Pinnacle Peak is a great destination. Bootski Lake is worth an excursion as a day-trip although many choose to camp overnight so as to explore the area further. An expedition up Mount Reesor also takes a full day if you want to reach the summit, and the flat summit of Mount Spieker is so expansive that most visitors spend a full day up there. The Albright Ridge is best suited to longer trips but its western end can be explored fairly easily in a day. Perhaps the ultimate peak–bagging day trip is the 27 kilometre Five Peak Circuit in the Core Lodge area.

Overnight and longer trips:

There is just about no end to the number of longer excursions that can be planned, varying in degree of difficulty. The easiest are the official long trails to Monkman Lake and Wapiti–Onion Lakes. Both are out and back trails and both deserve at least three days to allow for exploring and relaxation. The rough trail to Bootski Lake lends itself to a two–day trip or longer depending on one's climbing skills on the surrounding peaks.

All other long trips require at least some bushwhacking. If you are prepared for this discomfort you will be rewarded by true wilderness with a minimal chance of encountering any other humans. The Albright Ridge is a magnificent area worthy of three days, as is the Windfall Lake area. The Bat Lake area at the source of the Sukunka River can be explored in a long day but is better enjoyed by means of an overnight trip, and the series of lakes in the Sukunka Ridge north of the Table Tunnel probably requires three days. Expeditions to the Shark's Fin area and Mt Bulley require particularly good planning and preparation because of the remoteness and altitude.

For those who wish to follow in the footsteps of the pioneers and experience some of their hardships, two difficult cross–country traverses are possible, over Monkman Pass and Wapiti Pass respectively, with only game trails to guide you. The addition of the Limestone Lakes area to Monkman Provincial Park and the proclamation of Wapiti Provincial Park have made possible an interesting long–distance hiking trip, joining and almost entirely within these protected areas.

This summary just scratches the surface. There are many areas without any human footprints, and doubtless many new interesting undiscovered phenomena that await the explorer. This is a land that beckons.

■ ICE CLIMBING

Al Tattersall has pioneered this exciting winter sport, and has spearheaded first ascents on the fairly easily accessible icefalls in the region. One of his major obstacles has been the search for brave souls prepared to accompany him.

Climbs range from the beginner level in Martin Canyon to very challenging. Bullmoose Falls, for example, is 45 metres high and perfectly vertical. Intermediate in difficulty are Nesbitt's Knee Falls and Cowmoose Falls. Quality Canyon provides an area to hone ones skills close to town.

The highest icefall in the region is Bergeron Falls, just under 100 metres high. This climb is not quite as tough as one might suppose, as there are a few less than vertical patches in places that allow the climber a brief rest.

Naturally, the region's most famous waterfall, Kinuseo Falls, has been climbed. However, Tattersall claimed that this ascent was not challenging enough as these falls tumble in a series of inclined steps, rather than plummeting in a single drop.

Those seeking first ascents need not despair. The more remote falls in Monkman Park, including The Cascades, have not been climbed, and neither have a number of falls off the Murray Canyon.

■ JET BOATING By Don McPherson

The Murray River is a great jet boating river on Tumbler Ridge's doorstep. The best boat launch is at the Highway 29 bridge just outside of town; the launch at the next bridge upstream near the Quintette mine is not as good. Downstream the next boat launch is at East Pine.

There are therefore basically two directions to explore the river, up and down. Going upstream leads to Kinuseo Falls, an hour and a half away. At low water it is possible to get right to the base of the falls and touch the rock! Fishing is not permitted in this pool, but there are many other fishing holes and six camping areas on the way. This stretch of the river offers easy water and is good for first–time boaters and learners, with good scenery. More boaters are to be found here than downstream.

Heading down is more difficult, and is for more experienced boaters who are prepared to be cautious. There are many more sandbars, as well as large rock gardens, chutes and ledges. There are at least seven campsites on this stretch. Many of the side–creeks have waterfalls which can be explored, and there is more wildlife. Boating through the Painted Canyon offers the best scenery (three quarters of an hour down river). It has campsites at either end. Tepee Falls are visible from the river, a hiking trail may be built from the river past the falls to the highway one day. Next is Salt Creek, often with goats seen on the cliffs. Many years ago outfitters tried to set up a business here but could not get their horses down to the river.

Soon afterwards, the river spreads out wide and shallow, and boaters need to accelerate to get through. The Gwillim River then enters from the left, and a few kilometres later there is a collection of enormous rocks which have to be negotiated carefully. Soon there is another difficult section, where the river narrows right down into some chutes, with fast water and rocks on both sides, calling for experienced navigation. After a long easier stretch there are more rock gardens and then a series of ledges. It is best to descend these towards the left. Many boats get stuck up on the ledges and are difficult to get off. From here to East Pine the going is easier. It is a four hour trip from Tumbler Ridge to East Pine. Fewer jet boats are to be found on this section. Know what you are doing and let someone know when you will be back. The return trip, heading upstream, is usually easier.

Please remember always to be courteous to canoeists by slowing right down when you pass them, and help share this beautiful river.

Don operates a successful company, Murray River Adventure Tours, guiding tourists both up and down the river.

■ MOUNTAIN BIKING AND CYCLING By Kevin Sharman

The foothills terrain in and around Tumbler Ridge is tailor made for mountain biking. There are numerous old roads dating from the early development of the town that have reverted to double–track paths. These make good easy rides. More adventurous riding is found on trails like the Tumbler Point trail, with good views to the Flatbed and Murray valleys. One thing that off–road bikers will notice right away is the roots. Generally, the more traffic a forest trail has on it, the taller the roots are. A bike with suspension helps combat the jarring.

The Wolverine Trails to Lost Haven cabin, starting near the golf course, offer excellent forest riding on a fairly wide trail. The Loop Trail beyond the cabin is single–track.

Great single–track is found on horse trails that lead from the saddle club. Normally biking on horse trails means muddy, churned up stretches and horse–biker conflicts. Tumbler Ridge is lucky in this respect, with light use and a "share the trail" attitude among users.

Activities

Proper trail etiquette (watching for other users, dismounting for horses) will go a long way towards maintaining this cooperation.

Recently local riders have cleared some animal trails and created superb technical rides, like the Upper Flatbed trail★. Generations of deer, moose and elk have worn a single-track path that wends its way along the escarpment overlooking Flatbed Creek upstream from the falls. Deadfall removal has made this into a great extension to the Linking Trail that led from the falls down to the Lions campground. The most exciting part of this ride is the Razorback, a 30 cm wide path along a sharp ridge, with drop-offs on both sides.

Up in the mountains, trails from the coal exploration boom of the 1970's give access to the stunning scenery of the alpine areas. A good example of this is the Mt. Spieker trails. The rider can follow old exploration roads from the Perry Creek side across a large alpine bowl, over a high pass, and look forward to 800 metres elevation loss to the road at the Bullmoose mine. Bullmoose Mountain to the north has a network of similar trails.

A popular backcountry ride is the old road to Red Deer Falls. This 10 km trip passes through a 1988 burn. From the falls it is possible to cross the creek at low water and cycle on all the way up to Warner Lakes.

Road biking from town means climbing hills, whether on the Heritage Highway to Dawson Creek, Highway 29 towards Chetwynd, or the Boundary Road towards the Quintette mine.

★*The Upper Flatbed Trail is referred to in this book as "Kevin's Trail".*

■ ROAD TOURING

The roads around Tumbler Ridge do offer some experiences that are difficult to come by elsewhere, although they also are subject to certain frustrations. The main one is that so many are of necessity out-and-back trips. This is because of the rugged topography and also because many roads were built for exploration. There are just a few circular drives that break this pattern and they are not particularly interesting.

Expansion of the road network in the backcountry is one of the features of the last decade. It is something of a mixed blessing, giving access to previously remote areas, but having a significant environmental impact. Most valley floors are now accessible by road although the quality of the roads varies a lot.

Many of the attractions described in this book are at or near the roadside. For mountain scenery the upper reaches of the Sukunka Forest Service road, Wapiti Forest Service Road, Windfall Creek road and the upper reaches of the Wolverine Forest Service Road are suitable.

The best feature of the back roads is the excellent access they give to the subalpine and alpine, aided by the relatively low level of the treeline:

– the road up Perry Creek to Mount Spieker and Mount Reesor leads to just below the treeline beneath the summits of these big hills
– the drive into the catchment area of Babcock Creek to the Core Lodge and beyond takes motorists to the treeline on the slopes of Babcock Mountain and Quintette Mountain. In the summer this gives non–hikers a unique opportunity to appreciate the meadows, flowers, animals and birds of the tundra.

For the record, although neither is really recommended, the two circular routes in the area are:

– a circuit involving the Mast Creek road that joins the road to the Quintette Mine with the Wolverine Valley (distance 56 kilometres)
– a circuit incorporating the Boundary Road and the Hourglass Road, with stops at five pleasant forest service recreation sites along the route: Flatbed East, Stony Lake, Redwillow, Thunder Creek, Boot Lake (distance 183 kilometres, not feasible in wet conditions).

Activities

■ ROCK CLIMBING AND PEAK–BAGGING

The younger rocks close to Tumbler Ridge are not made for rock climbing, being soft and friable. In places they may be suitable for rappelling such as the Bergeron Cliffs. To find good climbing rock one needs to head further into the mountains. Many of the big peaks have unclimbed faces on solid rock, but access is difficult. The best wall for climbing that is readily accessible is just inside Monkman Provincial Park, well seen when driving in to Kinuseo Falls. It is less than a kilometre from the road to the base of the wall, which is 50 metres high.

One of the special attributes of the area is that almost all of the scores of summits to choose from can be ascended without technical gear. Some may prefer a rope to help with the rock scrambling on some of the ridges, but many find this unnecessary. Examples where ropes might be handy are Pyramid Peak, The Shark's Fin, Mt. Bulley, Paxton Peak, Mt. Crum and Mt. Becker. By contrast, most summits can be attained with no more than a good set of hiking boots.

Who made the first ascents of the summits is an intriguing question. Partly because they are not technical climbs, there are no records in the alpine journals. We do know that Frederick Vreeland climbed Ice Mountain and Mt. Vreeland in 1915. We know Fay's route and can guess at the peaks his party climbed, and know that the Albright Ridge and Pyramid Peak were explored. The same can be said of Gray's expeditions. Pioneers of the Monkman Pass recorded their climb up Forget Me Not Mountain. The Suska expedition of 1953 included the tops of Mts. Spieker, Reesor and Collier. The rest remains a mystery. Local residents who have climbed the big peaks like Mt. Bulley and the Shark's Fin report finding no rock cairns at the summits.

Has anyone climbed Mt . Vreeland or Ice Mountain since Vreeland's first ascents, or made it to the top of our highest peak at the head of the Bulley Glacier? Has anyone done a traverse of the Monkman–Parsnip–Vreeland Glacier system that straddles the Rocky Mountains? The only party I know of gave up long before reaching the glacier due to impenetrable forest. Who will be the first to climb the sheer faces of the Shark's Fin or Mt. Bulley? These are the challenges to spur on a new generation of explorers.

■ RUNNING

A convivial running group has sprung up in Tumbler Ridge, with regular weekend social runs, and annual running clinics are usually organized by the Northern Lights College. The trail system around the town is deservedly popular. There are few places that offer such excellent and beautiful training routes so close to a community. The Tumbler Point Trail, Linking Trail and Wolverine Trails seem to offer something new every day, and runners never tire of them.

The Murray Canyon Overlook trail has become a favorite of runners since its construction in 2000, offering a special "on the edge" sensation.

Yet it is the easy access to the beautiful alpine country that is the most special attribute of the area for runners. Mountain–runners are a distinctive breed who have forsaken the firmness and safety of the road to connect with their environment amidst the challenges of the hills, in conditions which are sometimes extreme but always exhilarating. Tumbler Ridge offers some of the finest wilderness running in the world, and has a good network of old exploration roads in many subalpine regions including Mount Spieker and the region around the Core Lodge.

Local runners of the Wolverine Nordic and Mountain Society, realizing this potential, have created a special phenomenon, the Emperor's Challenge Mountain Run, held each August. This is one of the most difficult half–marathons in the world, with its 800 metre vertical gain in altitude, and is without question one of the most beautiful, with its expansive views of the northern Rockies from the alpine expanses of Roman Mountain.

Around the same time these folks organize the Ridge Ramble Biathlon as another part of the Grizzly Valley Days celebrations. This event involves 20 KM cycling and 10 KM running.

■ SNOWMOBILING By Fred Banham

Tumbler Ridge offers a wide variety of sledding opportunities from serene trail rides to breath–taking alpine adventures to extreme mountain climbing. You can literally ride your sled from town in many different directions and experience only a few of the wonderful destination locations the Tumbler Ridge area has to offer.

The Ridge Riders Snowmobile Club has over the past fifteen years explored, mapped and signed over 300 kilometres of trails. The beauty of snowmobiling Tumbler Ridge is the wide variety of sledding destinations coupled with the relatively low ridership, that guarantees everyone a private outdoor experience, with access to untouched kilometres of fresh snow, open meadows and breathtaking scenery.

Using Tumbler Ridge as a home base there are many different and fascinating destinations. To the north is the Dawson Creek trail, south is the Core Lodge riding area, east is Bearhole Lake and Thunder Mountain, and to the west lie the Mt. Spieker, Bullmoose and Wolverine riding areas – all unique, all special and all easily accessible.

Tumbler Ridge is 820 metres (2800 feet) above sea level and most likely your low point. To get the best performance from your machine it is recommended to jet your carburettors for 1500 metres (5000 feet) although you can climb to above 2000 metres (6600 feet) in places. Mountain sleds are the most popular machines but short track sleds can tag along if they have modified tracks.

You will require warm clothing, a helmet, a reliable snowmobile, spare belt, spark plugs, tool kit, towrope, handsaw, shovel and probe. For safety it is highly recommended that you wear an avalanche transmitter, pack spare gloves, toque, a first aid kit, matches, fire starter and some energy bars. A few things that you might need for longer excursions are extra fuel, food and spare warm clothing. Always sled in groups, tell someone your destination and when you expect to return.

Start early in the day. Pack a lunch high in energy and carry plenty of fluids (non–alcoholic). Travel in groups, with each sledder being responsible for the sled coming behind. If you are the group leader, plan your route based upon the riding experience of your most novice rider. Wear your avalanche transmitter inside your winter clothing.

There are so many places to ride that there is no reason to compete for space with other outdoor enthusiasts. Cross–country ski trails, community schoolyards, parks, golf course and walking trails are no place for snowmobiles. Riding responsibly is mandatory in Tumbler Ridge. When you are out in the sledding areas around Tumbler Ridge you will encounter wildlife – stop, view and enjoy. Respect the animals and they will move off the trail and you can proceed.

The most popular sledding area is south of town around the Core Lodge. Donated to the Ridge Riders Snowmobile Club, the Core Lodge has been converted to a destination/start point for snowmobilers. You can drive to the Core Lodge, unload and start from here or you can ride from town and use the Core Lodge as your destination location. From the Core Lodge you can access many riding areas. Roman Mountain and Quintette Mountain are to the east. The Roman Mountain road offers a great high speed run to a well site just a few meters below the summit of Quintette Mountain.

Windy Ridge south of the Core Lodge is the site of the annual Windy Ridge Challenge Hillclimb. Its east face provides a 500 metre vertical climb that challenges the best machines built for hill climbing. On the front side of Windy Ridge you will find the Super Bowl and the Terminator. It is always playtime in the Super Bowl. Below Windy Ridge are the Summit Meadows and the Playpen, excellent family riding and a beginners paradise. Mr. Kostuik, Hidden Valley, and the three steeples, Eanny, Meany, and Meaner all are all accessed from the Core Lodge trail. Each has its own special and unique features.

One of the most popular destinations from the Core Lodge is the Back Meadows. A family climb takes you down Five Cabin Creek trail and then up into the alpine. At the top you are greeted with wide open meadows that sweep out in all directions with views over the Murray River and the Rocky Mountains.

Five Cabin Creek Trail gives access to Kinuseo Falls, Monkman Provincial Park and the Imperial Creek region. There are forestry roads that if not being used for active logging provide access to the remote backcountry. Visit the old Imperial Creek Sawmill site or venture up to the base of the Shark's Fin.

Activities

South of town on the Murray Forest Service road is the drop–off point for the run through Roger's Pass to the Wolverine Valley and Albright Ridge. Travelling west up the Wolverine Forest Service road gives access to the Wolverine riding area. The Snowmobile Club has constructed a warm–up cabin at kilometre 55 just below the Albright Ridge, always promising large accumulations of snow. In the heights of the Albright Ridge are three alpine lakes surrounded by steep climbing vertical. Check the snow for avalanche conditions before you play.

Mount Spieker is accessed from the Wolverine Forest Service road and has a warm–up shelter, "the Bus", located on the flats below Mount Reesor. You can often spot a herd of Caribou that reside in the winter alpine. While riding the windswept summit of Spieker there are hidden rocks and snowdrifts that can damage a sled and rider without warning.

From "the Bus", there are many cut blocks to play in, the Well Head trail and Gill's gulch to the south. One of my favorite rides is from town via the 350 Man Camp road to Mount Spieker and home: 85 kilometres of pure pleasure with some trail, pipeline, road, and alpine riding.

Behind Spieker Mountain is the Bullmoose riding area for the more advanced sledders that like to challenge the vertical. Avalanche hazard is high in the upper regions behind Bullmoose so be prepared.

The Westcoast pipeline passes to the west of town and is good riding from Tumbler Ridge to Gwillim Lake. BC Hydro also has its main power transmission line running parallel to the pipeline and provides its own challenging ride north toward Chetwynd. The moose like the delicate willow underbrush along both corridors.

North of Tumbler Ridge is the Dawson Creek trail signed all the way to Arras. There is a "Bus" warm–up shelter about 30 kilometres from town. The trailhead is at the Saddle Club corner on Highway 52. Starting from the same point riders can turn east on the Quality Lake road and head to Bearhole Lake. Ice fishing is good on both Quality Lake and Bearhole Lake. From Bearhole you can follow the trail over to Thunder Mountain with its great view of the Rockies.

For true adventure try the "100 Mile Run" from town to Quality Lake, Bearhole Lake, over Thunder Mountain to the old Kinuseo Road, up the Five Cabin Creek trail, over Babcock Mountain back to Tumbler Ridge, exactly 100 miles. This is a wonderful ride for the entire family.

For the advanced adventurer there is unlimited exploring about an hours drive south of Tumbler Ridge in the Red Deer Falls area. The spring sledding allows mountain sleds to traverse between valleys, saddles and ridges to gain access to unlimited, pristine snow. This riding area must be respected because extreme avalanche conditions abound and help is a long way away. This spectacular area is for the knowledgeable mountain sledder.

A group can come and sled Tumbler Ridge for weeks and never ride the same area twice or can find a favorite spot and spend lots of time there experiencing the scenic beauty, the wildlife, the fresh air and the great outdoors.

The Ridge Riders maintain frequently updated reports on snowmobiling conditions at the District of Tumbler Ridge website: www.district.tumbler-ridge.bc.ca

■ SNOWSHOEING By Mike Hunter

Snowshoeing has been an integral part of mobility in northern Canada for hundreds of years. Where horses flounder in open fields and skis get entangled in the woods, snowshoes are effective. Even today's snow machines cannot cover the territory selected by a determined individual on shoes. Depending on your skill and fitness to get home again from the untouched splendour of the winter environment is an empowering experience, and the Tumbler Ridge area offers some of the most exhilarating, most diverse snowshoeing to be found anywhere.

The best months are February to May, when temperatures are more moderate and days are longer. But you won't last long in the woods if you haven't prepared properly. Take a partner with you whenever possible, make sure someone at home knows where you are and when you'll be back, carry enough gear and emergency supplies.

The new lightweight alloys are significantly more expensive than the traditional wooden shoes, and have a smaller surface area, which obviously decreases your ability to stay 'afloat'.

My favorite quickly accessible area is the trail just above town and below the highway. There are ridges to scramble, twists and turns, ups and downs. It's great fun, great exercise and immediately accessible to everyone, with the added attraction of plentiful deer that you'll see in the woods in front of you before they turn tail and run.

The golf course, TR Point trail and the trail between them is another good area. Please remember to stay off the greens and avoid walking on the set ski–trails. Working your way up Flatbed Canyon above the Lions Campground is another exhilarating experience that you can make as easy or tough, short or long as you choose. The area behind the Saddle Club parallel to the highway to Dawson Creek is a good beginner area because help is fairly close at hand if necessary.

Bullmoose Falls can be visited on skis but make for a much better snowshoeing destination. This involves crossing the partially frozen Bullmoose Creek, then ascending a tributary to this spectacular site.

Another wild trip explores Quality Canyon and its falls. This little-known wonder so close to town is best explored in winter, and is not really suitable for anything except snowshoes. Start either at Albert's Point lookout or at the Quality Falls trailhead. This trip has many obstacles and is not advised for beginner snowshoers.

The same can be said for the Tower Trails, an area 15 kilometres from town off the highway to Chetwynd, initially developed as a possible cross–country ski area but subsequently abandoned for safety reasons. Parking can be a problem here; be sure to find a place to pull well off the road as the trucks carrying coal pass by frequently. Those who really want a challenge can hike right up to the radio repeater, a vertical gain of over 200 metres.

A bit further towards Chetwynd is Gwillim Lake Provincial Park. Beginners can amble through the campground trails while many more advanced options exist, combined with ice fishing and cross–country skiing or snowmobiling.

For anyone looking for even more adventure there is the Core Lodge area. Access is usually good and the peaks can be attained. One of the supreme challenges of the area is to complete the 21.1 kilometre Emperor's Challenge route over Roman Mountain on snowshoes (a rope is needed in places).

From a gentle walk on the golf course to the most challenging terrain anywhere, you are limited only by your imagination and your ability!

■ TRAIL RIDING

There is an active Saddle Club in town, always on the lookout for new members. A network of riding trails has been developed over the years, many of them leading north from the Saddle Club. Riding is encouraged on the Wolverine trail system in summer.

Although horses are no longer permitted in Monkman Provincial Park, much of the rest of the mountains lends itself to packing expeditions and trail riding. The trails and mountains around the Core Lodge are one favorite area, as is the Mt Spieker massif. Further south the Wapiti, Red Deer and Belcourt valleys offer excellent multi-day opportunities. Heading up into the alpine in these regions is truly following in the footsteps of the pioneers, who often were on horseback.

■ WATERFALL-BAGGING

Bluntly stated, there are just about no waterfalls for thousands of miles to the east. The Alaska Highway to the north has surprisingly few accessible waterfalls despite the mountainous terrain. Most of the interior plateau of British Columbia to the west of the mountains is fairly flat, with few falls. By contrast, the waterfalls of Tumbler Ridge are accessible, and will become more so as the trail system is expanded.

Kinuseo Falls is the big and famous one, but there are a couple of dozen others. The Cascades in Monkman Park are seven glorious waterfalls in succession, and are decidedly underrated and undervisited. The highest waterfall in the region is probably Bergeron Falls north of town, 100 metres high. Most of the tributaries of the Murray River downstream from town have canyons and falls, including Tepee Creek. Closer to town are the tinier Quality Falls and Flatbed Falls.

Up the Wolverine valley there are the hardly visited Wolverine Waterfalls, Upper and Lower Tunnel Falls and Perry Falls. Off the road to Kinuseo Falls are Nesbitt's Knee Falls and Barbour Falls. Sukunka Falls has its own provincial park, with Martin Falls up a tributary. To the south are Babcock Falls, Wapiti Falls, Red Deer Falls and Belcourt Falls.

Some of these have trails; others are wilderness destinations in the truest sense. Within this book, directions to thirty waterfalls are provided.

■ WILDLIFE WATCHING

The area is renowned for the relative ease with which large mammals can be observed. Elk populations are healthily high, although they cannot be found with the ease of those near Jasper. Likewise, moose are frequently seen, as well as both Mule Deer and White-tailed Deer. To find Caribou it is usually necessary to drive up to the subalpine or treeline. Hikers often encounter these graceful mammals in the alpine zone, and wilderness skiers and snowmobilers commonly encounter them here in winter as well.

There are no sheep populations in the area except sometimes in the far south (Wapiti River drainage). However there are few places anywhere that provide better opportunities for seeing Mountain Goat than the road that branches north off the Bullmoose Mine road and heads up between Bullmoose and Cowmoose Mountains. In summer, look high up on the slopes of Bullmoose Mountain. In fall, look lower down on the bluffs directly across the valley. Up to twenty goats have been seen at one time. Binoculars or a spotting scope are needed.

Beavers and Muskrats can be regularly found in the right environment. Amongst the carnivores, Coyote are a common sight, Wolves are not uncommon, and there have been a surprising number of Wolverine sightings. Bobcat and Cougar are sometimes seen; there have as yet been no attacks from the latter.

But in addition to the excitement of looking for all these animals, it is the presence of healthy bear populations that continues to enthrall residents and visitors. The ratio of Black Bear to Grizzly Bear is apparently about 10:1, and this is borne out in the relative frequency of Black Bear sightings. Of course, is it not possible to predict with accuracy where bears will be found, but there is a better than 50% chance that a drive to the Core Lodge in spring and summer will yield bear sightings.

Grizzly Bear are harder to find, and tend to occur at higher elevations. Virtually any subalpine area or near the treeline is appropriate territory. The Imperial Creek road has a good track record for Grizzly sightings, and stable populations have coexisted with the activity at the coal mines. Often it is best simply to check locally as to where recent sightings have occurred.

5 GEOLOGICAL HISTORY

Here as elsewhere, geology controls landforms, and has influenced climate, vegetation, industry and human settlement. Here the great northeastern plain, the remnant of a great inland sea, meets the former continental margin, now distorted and uplifted to form the Rocky Mountains. An accurate description of the monumental set of events which led to the creation of the current topography becomes complex and technical. Yet a simplification and summary of these events is possible, and leads to a fairly easy understanding of the natural features that we see around us.

The ancient rocks way below us (which are exposed in just a few places in the Rockies) are composed of granite and gneiss. On top of this, when our area was part of a continental shelf (similar to the current Grand Banks off Newfoundland) there was a slow, but very long (1.5 billion years) period of deposition of sediments. In time these sediments became sedimentary rock of various types. At roughly the same time ancient supercontinents formed and broke up. At times the rocks that we now see here were in the equatorial regions, and supported lush forests.

Relatively recently in geological time, about 175 million years ago, plate tectonics came into the picture. A collision of crustal plates caused the west–coast continental shelf to be pried loose of the underlying granite and gneiss, and be pushed in a northeasterly direction. Unimaginable forces caused these rocks to be bent and folded, and then to break into moving sheets of rock. These slid along and were stacked up in a giant wrinkling process that created great mountains.

Geological History

1–2 million years ago, most of the Rockies landscape was further sculpted by the great Pleistocene ice sheet, which covered some areas to a depth of two kilometres.

Because of the direction of the crustal movement, as a general rule, these sedimentary rocks are arranged in order of decreasing age from west to east. So the rocks of the foothills northeast of Tumbler Ridge, for example, are younger than the rocks of the mountains to the southwest of town. This is confirmed in the fossil record.

During the Devonian Period, around 400 million years ago, what is now western Canada lay near the equator. This is when the region's oil and gas reserves accumulated in reefs. These reefs were made up of giant colonies of sponges known as Stromatoporoids. Regional gas exploration has been fairly intense in the last decade, and a corridor identified in which many of these reserves can be found.

Closer to town (as on Mount Roman, Mount Babcock, Mount Spieker, and extending through Tumbler Ridge) are even younger rocks. These are usually sandstone, mudstone and shale, formed between 200 million years ago and 5 million years ago. These foothills were subjected to less upheaval and dissection, and are composed of softer, more easily eroded rock. The result is that their landscape is a lot less rugged.

Some of this rock was non–marine, i.e. it was deposited in fresh water. At other times an ocean extended up from what is now the Gulf of Mexico all the way along the eastern side of the mountains through our area to present–day Alaska, accounting for the many marine fossils.

This includes also the age in which the coal deposits accumulated, which led ultimately to the creation of Tumbler Ridge. These deposits are found in a relatively narrow band of this type of rock from Grande Cache through the Quintette and Bullmoose Mines towards Chetwynd and the Peace River, where they largely peter out. The presence of coal implies warmer climes and forests. We can imagine swampy forests, in which dinosaurs roamed, in the Cretaceous Period. The circumstances must have been just right for the creation of coal, with decaying plant matter quickly being buried, and an absence of oxygen. Heat and pressure from overlying sediments helped to remove water, leading to a kind of cooking process with the passage of time.

There is a spectrum of types of coal that may be formed, depending on the precise circumstances. It ranges from the impure lignite to the hotter–burning purer anthracite. Somewhere in the middle of that spectrum lies the coal of Tumbler Ridge, which is known as 'bituminous', and is suitable for conversion to coke, and use in the blast furnaces of the metallurgic industry, for the production of steel. This coal has low sulphur content, and when burned, would have a minimal acid–rain effect, compared with the coal burned in eastern North America.

A common question is why our mountains are less rugged than those to the south, as around the Banff and Jasper parks, or to the north in the Muskwa–Kechika area. The main reason is that massive quartzite and limestone formations underlie those mountains and are more resistant to erosion. Our deep rocks tend to be more shaly and do not have the thick cliff–forming formations found to the south.

The practical effect of this is clear. Whereas the seemingly more impressive scenery to the south and north lends itself to gawking at peaks and glaciers from the roadside, getting on top of those mountains is often only feasible for the few rock– and ice–climbing experts. The Tumbler Ridge mountains, by contrast, although not immediately as spectacular, offer a different and arguably more complete and enjoyable experience: they are a hiker's paradise, in which almost every summit can be ascended without technical gear. These are ranges to be appreciated from their summits and the lofty ridges that join them. The most distinctive peak on the Tumbler Ridge horizon is the descriptively named Shark's Fin, with its sheer 420 metre eastern face.

Much of the present topography relates to the effects of ice. The geologically more recent ice advances came from two different directions. Firstly, there was what is known as the "Stony Lake advance" over 100 000 years ago, coming from the Cordilleran ice sheet to the west. Expanding in a northeasterly direction, it spilled over the low passes, filled our upper valleys, and spread out to form lobes in the foothills. When this ice receded, it left behind large moraines and outwash deposits, which still cover substantial parts of the area.

Then there was the great continental (or Laurentide) ice sheet to the east, advancing in a southwesterly direction. It reached its maximum

Geological History

There are numerous interesting examples in the area of geological history, apart from the obvious examples of the fossil record and the dinosaur tracks.

- *The most irritating example is obvious to anyone who has tried to dig a vegetable garden in Tumbler Ridge. Inevitably, rocks of various sizes need to be pried loose, along with sand and stones. This was deposited with the melting of the great glaciers, and is known as glacial till.*
- *At Kinuseo Falls, the severe folding of the strata on the west bank of the Murray River can be seen in the form of a dramatic 'S' pattern. The southeastern face of Mount Crum displays equally impressive folding, and the subsidiary summit of Mount Becker has no equal in terms of symmetrical folding.*
- *The interpretive trail to the Stone Corral in Monkman Park passes below towering limestone cliffs with beautifully aligned and folded rock strata. The booklet covers some geological features.*
- *The dramatic series of waterfalls on Monkman Creek, known as The Cascades, represents a series of sharp fault lines intersecting the channel bed.*
- *The alpine caves occur in limestone, subject to dissolution over time, and the creation of subsurface drainage conduits. Springs like Hole in the Wall represent the resurgence of this underground flow.*
- *In the upper Kinuseo Creek – Flatbed Creek region are signs of the Stony Lake advance, with its moraine features, and Glacial Lake Peace, with its beaches and gravels.*
- *The interpretive Murray Canyon Overlook trail off the Heritage Highway between Tumbler Ridge and Dawson Creek practically explains some of the geomorphology of the region.*
- *Quality Falls, just east of Tumbler Ridge, is an example of a layer of sandstone which is more resistant to erosion than the underlying mudstone. Most of the other numerous waterfalls in the region are good places to study geological history.*
- *Wapiti Lake and Monkman Lake are examples of deep basins scooped by ice from softer sediments, with their depth increased by dams of glacial drift.*

extent about 30 kilometres northeast of Tumbler Ridge. Meltwater from the mountains flowing east was impounded against it to form a long narrow lake known as Glacial Lake Peace. An arm of the lake extended up the Murray, Wolverine and Flatbed valleys. The site of Tumbler Ridge was once submerged under this lake.

Eventually the lake drained and stream systems evolved. This lake would have made the area uninhabitable. Exactly when it disappeared is still open to some debate. But since then there has been an "ice-free corridor" to the east of the Rocky Mountains in this area, which has significant archaeological implications. Remains of mammoth, horse, camel and bison have been found in areas corresponding with the shore of the glacial lake.

An anecdotal account relates to the excavation of the area around the Tumbler Ridge sewage works and garbage dump. Large rocks were being crushed. Too late, the machine operator realised that he had just emptied not rocks, but two well preserved mammoth tusks into the crusher.

22 000 years ago ice came from the west through the passes again, terminating near Kinuseo Falls. Much of the meltwater flowed directly down the Murray, but a significant amount also drained through a large channel along Kinuseo Creek and then Flatbed Creek to the Murray. As this ice receded, Kinuseo Creek reversed its flow, and has since then flowed directly into the Murray, and carved itself a lower canyon.

In terms of much more recent history, evidence of bygone animal populations and distributions may accumulate through the discovery of old skeletons. One simple way to search for these is to discover new caves, then search the floors of these caves for evidence of bones. Given enough time, animals will fall into such caves, perhaps during a winter blizzard, and not be able to extricate themselves. Because of the preserving qualities of limestone, which is alkaline, bones discovered may be up to 40,000 years old. An example would be to determine how recently sheep inhabited this area. Collected samples have been sent to the Royal B.C. Museum for analysis and potential carbon dating.

Geological History

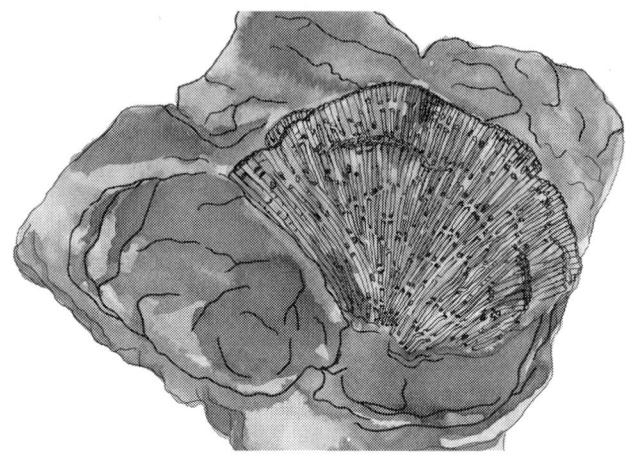

Plate 3: Coral fossil from the Stone Corral (actual fossil diameter 20 CM). Credit: Joan Zimmer

Plate 4: Fossilised coral – wristwatch in centre for scale.

6 PALAEONTOLOGY – THE FOSSIL HERITAGE OF TUMBLER RIDGE

The approximate ordering of the rocks from oldest in the southwest to youngest in the northeast helps us to understand the fossil record. In the distant reaches of Monkman Park in the Pioneer Range, for example, the quartzite rocks are 600 million years old and contain few and primitive fossils, often in the form of worm burrows.

Closer to Tumbler Ridge the fossils become much more interesting and numerous. There are four major strengths to the local fossil record, corresponding to different periods in geological time. These are

1) Corals, crinoids and trace fossils
2) The Triassic reptiles and fishes
3) Dinosaur prints and trackways
4) The Cretaceous plants.

Each of these is of great importance, and is readily accessible to the amateur and professional palaeontologist. However, there is a poor record in North America of vandalism of fossil sites, and of collectors damaging and cleaning out special sites for their own private use, to the eternal loss of those who come after them. For this reason, no exact sites are mentioned here unless they are already well known.

In addition to these four major groups, many other types of fossils have been found, including oysterbeds, ammonites and clams close to Tumbler Ridge, and trilobites in Monkman Provincial Park.

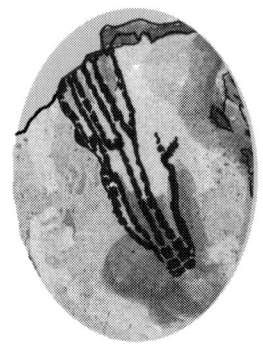
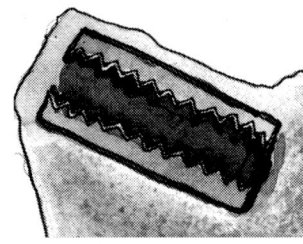

Plate 5: Crinoid fragments from the Stone Corral.
Credit: Joan Zimmer

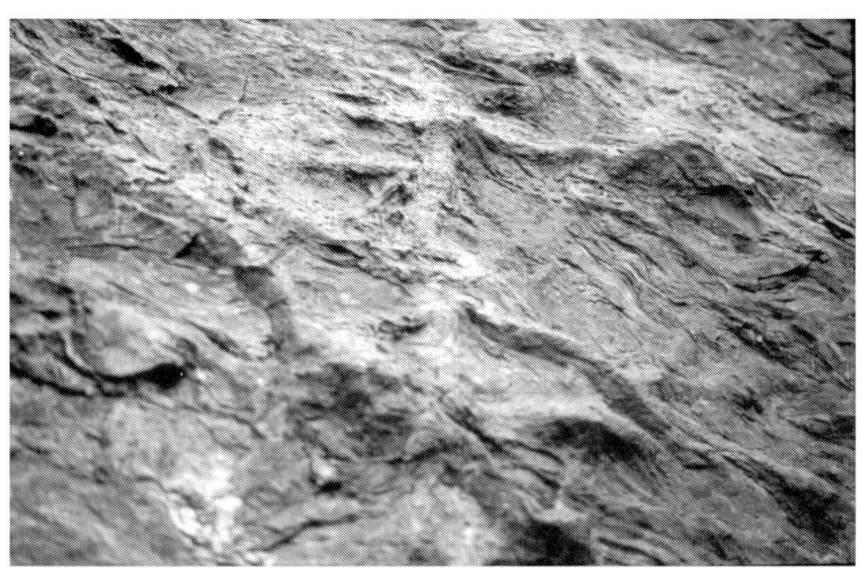

Plate 6: Detail from The Mural – a trace fossil site of crustacean burrows near the Stone Corral.

■ CORALS, CRINOIDS AND TRACE FOSSILS

Many of the ranges a short way into the mountains from Tumbler Ridge, for example Mt Crum, the Albright Ridge, Mt Watts, are formed of limestone and aged 300 – 400 million years. It is thought that minute lime particles were formed within innumerable tiny marine cyanobacteriae. With time these combined with coral and shell fragments to form limestone. In many parts of the world limestone is rich in fossils and the Tumbler Ridge area is no exception. It is possible to look up at cliffs near Wapiti Lake and Mt Becker and see long thick bands of paler rocks. Upon closer inspection these turn out to be fossilized coral reefs.

The interiors of some of the caves that have been discovered also harbour interesting coral and other fossils. In one cave the entire wall of a chamber comprises such formations. The typical coral fossils found in the area are either colonial or rugose (solitary). Walking along the alpine ranges, it sometimes seems that every single rock contains a fragment of fossilized coral (Plates 3, 4).

Brachiopods are also found, and so are crinoids (Plate 5), or sea–lilies. These relatives of the sea–stars were abundant when these rocks were formed, but the group has now almost become extinct, with only a few species surviving in the deep oceans.

The interpretive hiking trail to the Stone Corral in Monkman Provincial Park leads hikers to a crinoid and coral fossil site as well as to a remarkable feature known as The Mural (Plate 6), 335 million years old. Here a vertical rock wall, a single bedding plane, is crisscrossed by an intricate pattern that looks like fossilized seaweed, but is actually a large collection of interwoven crustacean burrows known as fucoids. Such fossils are known as trace fossils. Arrangements have been made for a trace fossil expert to visit and analyse this site.

Please note that no fossils may be removed from provincial parks.

Palaeontology

Plate 7: A fish fossil near the shore of the internationally significant Fossil Fish Lake. Credit: Kevin Sharman

Plate 8: The coelacanth *Whiteia* (50 CM long).
Credit: Mark Wilson, University of Alberta

■ THE TRIASSIC FISHES AND REPTILES

The area around Wapiti Lake in Wapiti Provincial Park is an internationally important site for the primitive reptiles and fishes of the Triassic Period. Over 200 million years ago, the present continents were united in the supercontinent Pangaea, surrounded in places by shallow seas with abundant fish and primitive reptile populations. A number of fossil sites from this period, representing different parts of this ancient coastline, show striking similarities, including Madagascar, Greenland, Spitsbergen, Banff and Wapiti Lake.

The fossil fishes and reptiles that have been discovered demonstrate a diverse fauna, filling a number of ecological niches similar to those observed in modern species. By 1992, twenty genera of fishes and ten of reptiles had been identified.

Before the Triassic Period there had been a great extinction of many species, including whole groups of fishes. Three main groups survived this mass–extinction, all of which are well represented near Wapiti Lake: the sharks, the ray–finned fishes, and the lobe–finned fishes.

The best–known example of lobe–finned fishes is the coelacanth, the "fish with legs", hundreds of which have been found at the site. The discovery of a live coelacanth off the coast of South Africa in 1938 revolutionized the study of fish worldwide, as this primitive creature had been thought to have become extinct 70 million years ago. The Wapiti Lake coelacanth, *Whiteia* (Plate 8), closely resembles this fish. All amphibians, reptiles, birds and mammals are derived from this kind of creature, which would stalk or lunge at its prey.

Amongst the ray–finned fishes *Albertonia* (Plate 9) is interesting because it has only been found at Wapiti Lake and a few other locations in western Canada, and because it quite possibly had differing male and female forms, like the modern suckers. Its extremely long pectoral fins initially caused some scientists to speculate that it was a flying fish. Another large fish from the Wapiti site is *Bobasatrania* (Plate 10), over a metre long, and related very distantly to the modern–day sturgeon.

There are also a number of predatory fish fossils, including the fearsome *Saurichthys* (Plate11), thin and long, with elongated jaws and sharp teeth. It would ambush smaller fish and swallow them whole.

Plate 9: The ray–finned fish *Albertonia* (35 CM long). Credit: Mark Wilson, University of Alberta.

Plate 10: The ray–finned fish *Bobasatrania* grew to a length of over a metre. Credit: Mark Wilson, University of Alberta.

Perhaps the most dramatic fossil yet found at the site is of such a fish that died with a smaller fish in its mouth.

The Triassic reptiles are no less interesting. Most of them are known as ichthyosaurs, primitive fish–like reptiles, and articulated skeletons of other creatures with fascinating names like thalattosaurs, *Myxosaurus* and *Utatsusaurus* have been discovered. Closer to Tumbler Ridge, a portion of the spine of an ichthyosaur was discovered in Flatbed Creek. (A recent find of an ichthyosaur near Pink Mountain, 200 kilometres to the north, has aroused great interest. Twenty–three metres long, it is the largest creature currently known to have existed.)

Perhaps the best–known and most enigmatic reptile discovery at the Wapiti site has been that of *Wapitisaurus problematicus*, a member of the group known as Weigeltisaurs. A single large skull was discovered. Preceding similar discoveries had been of small lizard–like fossils, and palaeontologists have struggled to work out exactly how this primitive reptile was related to other groups.

Research continues, and the Royal Tyrrell Museum of Palaeontology near Drumheller houses a special exhibit on the Wapiti Lake site, which will surely continue to yield discoveries of great scientific value.

■DINOSAUR PRINTS AND TRACKWAYS

While it is well–known that Alberta has yielded a precious heritage of dinosaur fossils, both in numbers and variety, it is not generally known that there are not that many dinosaur tracks in that province. By contrast, British Columbia can boast only a few known dinosaur fossil bones, but has tracks aplenty, in particular in the northeast.

There are good reasons for this apparent anomaly. During the ages when the dinosaurs thrived, much of what is now Alberta was an inland sea, whereas what is now British Columbia was mountainous even then. Rapid erosion resulted in deposition of large amounts of river–borne sediments in Alberta, enough to bury whole dinosaur carcasses, while the eroding areas in B.C. were not conducive to fossil preservation, even though the area was rich in dinosaurs. In addition, the groundwater in B.C. was acidic, which tends to dissolve bones but preserve plants.

Palaeontology

Plate 11: Head of the predatory fish *Saurichthys*, fossilised with a small fish in its mouth.
Credit: Mark Wilson, University of Alberta.

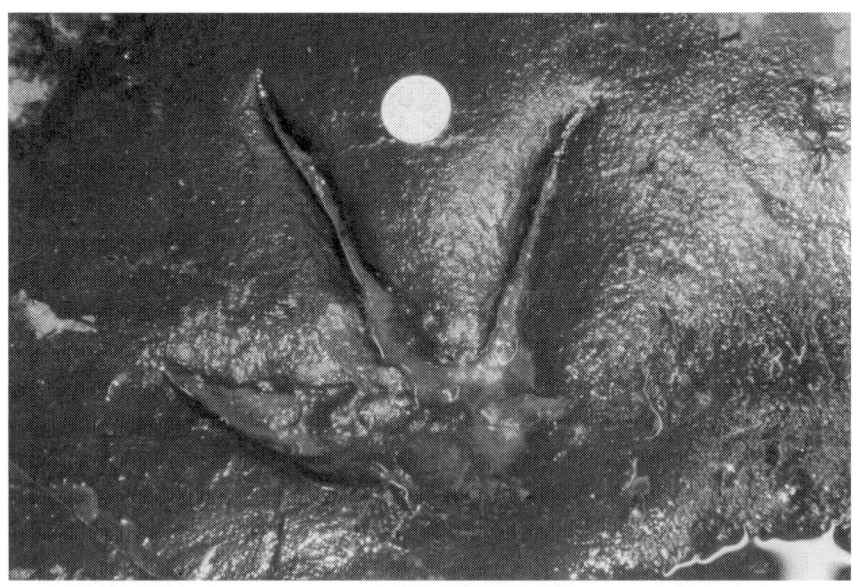

Plate 12: A print of *Irenichnites*, a small carnivorous dinosaur, found at Bullmoose Mine.
Note the quarter at top centre for scale.
Credit: David Tolmie.

By contrast, conditions required for preservation of footprints were quite different, and included wet mud and slow-moving water. Some parts of B.C. (including areas around Tumbler Ridge) were ideal for this process, and offer some fine trackways.

The region east of Tumbler Ridge close to the Alberta border resembles the Alberta plains, but is more thickly forested. On the Wapiti River a few miles east of the border is a site in a cliff that gets eroded every year by the spring flood, yielding new bones annually. Such sites may well exist in B.C. as well, concealed by the forest cover.

In many ways, trackways tell palaeontologists more about dinosaur behaviour than the actual fossilized skeletons. An understanding of the trackway potential around Tumbler Ridge requires a knowledge of what occurred until recently nearby. To the north, in the Peace River Canyon, upstream from Hudson's Hope, there were over 1700 world-class footprints that have been flooded by the Bennett Dam and the Peace Canyon Dam. To the south above the Narraway River, a southern tributary of the Wapiti, a near-vertical sandstone cliff contained over 200 prints, allowing deductions of interesting dinosaur behaviour. Soon after these were discovered, the entire rock-face slid down into the river and shattered!

The finds over the past few years near Tumbler Ridge have proven the potential of the region, with the probability of more exciting discoveries to come:

A beautifully preserved set of prints recovered during operations at the Bullmoose Mine was made by a small carnivorous dinosaur named *Irenichnites* (Plate 12).

In August 2000 two young Tumbler Ridge residents, Mark Turner and Daniel Helm, were tubing down Flatbed Creek when they spotted the distinctive form of a trackway (Plate 13). Their subsequent excavations at the site have progressed to the point where nine prints are now identifiable, with more to come, along with two much smaller prints, probably of a juvenile. It is believed that these tracks were made by bipedal Hadrosaurs, or "duck-billed dinosaurs", about 90 million years ago. The absence of a tail track substantiates the belief that these animals carried their tails high as they walked on their hind feet.

Palaeontology

Plate 13: The Flatbed Creek dinosaur trackway – made by the herbivorous *Hadrosaurus*.

In August 2000 Mark Turner and Daniel Helm were tubing down some rapids along Flatbed Creek when Mark fell off the tube and swam to shore. We were walking back along the shore and we noticed some depressions in the rock. We immediately thought they might be dinosaur tracks, then we called Daniel's dad and he agreed.

After this we called an expert named Peter Sherrington who had a look and agreed. Next we showed a palaeontologist named Mark Wilson who knew for sure we were right. Then we made e-mail contact with Rich McCrea. He is the dinosaur track expert in all of Canada.

We originally had five dinosaur footprints and had to use a crowbar to lift up the rocks to expose the next four, so now we have nine footprints, with maybe more to come. There are also two baby footprints beside the adult tracks. We watered down the tracks to make them clear and brushed the sediment away. Then we sprinkled baby powder into the tracks to show them off for our photos.

These were some of the measurements that were taken:

Footprint length: 30 CM
Footprint width: 35 CM
Stride length: 136 CM
Pace length: 79 CM
The baby prints were 21CM wide.

We sent this information with our photos to Mr McCrea, who did some calculations for us. We now know that this was a Hadrosaur (Duck-billed Dinosaur) which was walking on 2 legs and not dragging it's tail. It was 1.98 metres high at the hip level. It was walking at a speed of 2.1 kilometres per hour. This seems quite slow but is maybe because it was walking with its baby.

The dinosaur trackway is in a beautiful place with a creek and rocks in a canyon near a pool with a beach. Each time we visit it we have to wade through the icy river with our equipment. We are keeping the site a secret because we are worried about people vandalsing the tracks. Mr McCrea is coming in person next year to finish the excavation with us.

This has been an exciting project so far and we hope that there are more tracks in the area that we can discover.

By Mark Turner (age 11)and Daniel Helm (age 9)

Plate 14: The footprints on Roman Mountain of *Aquatilavipes*, a primitive bird distantly related to modern shorebirds.

Plate 15. Frond of the fern *Contopteris*. Credit: Zhihui Wan and James Basinger, University of Saskatchewan.

Nine prints on a rock near the summit of Roman Mountain were made by *Aquatilavipes* (Plate 14), a primitive bird distantly related to modern shorebirds. This represents one of the earliest examples of bird footprints in the world. Birds are the direct descendants of dinosaurs, in fact, an emerging body of opinion states that birds *are* dinosaurs.

A 2000 field trip by a group of palaeontologists from the University of Alberta in search of fossil fish incidentally located an eroded dinosaur track near the Murray Station just a few kilometres from Tumbler Ridge.

Dinosaur trackways in B.C. range from 90–150 million years in age. Dinosaurs became extinct about 65 million years ago. Searchers for trackways should therefore confine themselves to rocks of this approximate age and not head too far into the mountains.

■ THE CRETACEOUS PLANTS

The Early Cretaceous Period lasted from 140 – 97 million years ago, and the Late Cretaceous Period from 97 – 66 million years ago. During this time a great transformation occurred in the vegetation: initially the forests were dominated by cycads, conifers and ferns, but by the end of the Period these forms had been eclipsed by flowering plants.

The same forests that formed over time into B.C.'s northeast coal beds have also been preserved as fossils in the adjoining sandstone and siltstone rocks. The Tumbler Ridge area presents one of the best places to find traces of these great forests in which the dinosaurs roamed. The climate then was significantly warmer than nowadays, and wet and humid. Most of the trees were deciduous, in response more to short winter daylight hours than to cold temperatures.

The coal–bearing Gates Formation comprises rocks from the early Cretaceous period, and has delivered some wonderful plant fossils. The Quintette and Bullmoose mines are situated in this formation, and the mining activity has exposed numerous fossil beds. Younger rocks in the locally occurring Dunvegan Formation represent a largely uninvestigated fossil resource that should include more evidence of

Palaeontology

Plate 16: The redwood *Elatides*, a common conifer of the Cretaceous. Credit: Zhihui Wan and James Basinger, University of Saskatchewan.

Plate 17: *Pseudocycas*, a cycad from the Gates Formation. Credit: Zhihui Wan and James Basinger, University of Saskatchewan.

The Gates Formation was the subject of a 225 page doctoral thesis by Zhihui Wan of the University of Saskatchewan. He visited Tumbler Ridge in 1990 along with his supervisor, Dr Jim Basinger, and collected fossils from the mines. Later, specimens were obtained from other mines in the Gates Formation at Cadomin and Grande Cache. 52 species from 28 genera were found and described, including 15 new species.

Some of the fossil plant treasures so far discovered include ferns (Plate 15) and redwoods (Plate 16). Cycads (Plate 17), currently on the verge of extinction worldwide, have been found in a number of forms. The distinctive leaves of seed–ferns (Plate 18) are also common, interesting because a branch of these is thought to have been the source of all flowering plants. A fossil genus that will seem familiar to many is that of *Ginkgo* (Plate 19), the Maidenhair Tree. The present–day *Ginkgo biloba* that is commonly used medicinally is almost indistinguishable from some of these fossil specimens.

Among over 5000 specimens collected, there were just a couple of unidentifiable angiosperm leaves. These were some of the earliest flowering plants, and a hint of things to come.

Maybe one day in the future, when the coal mines have shut down, the rocks their workings have exposed will continue to be a treasure trove of fascinating fossils.

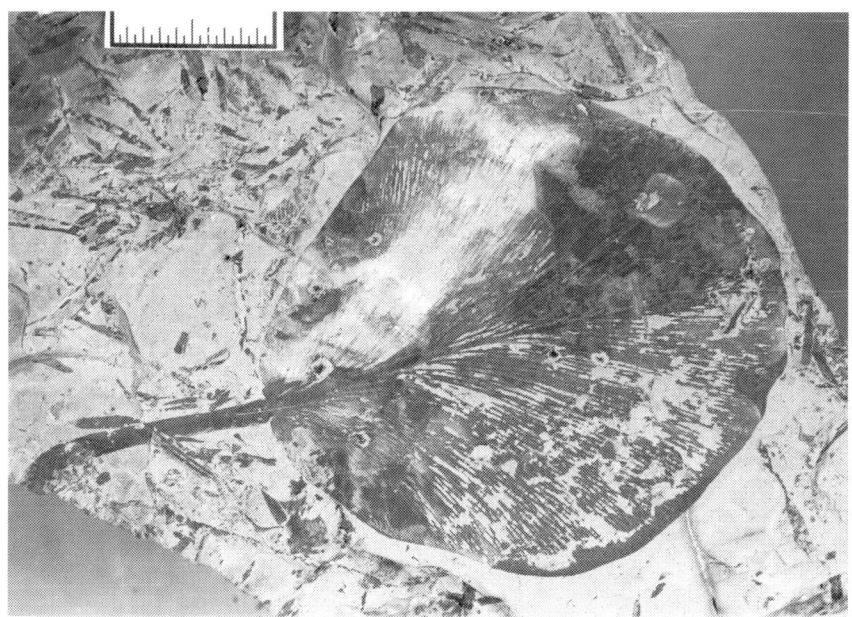

Plate 18: Leaf of the Seed–fern *Sagenopteris*.
Credit: Zhihui Wan and James Basinger, University of Saskatchewan.

Plate 19: Leaves of the Maidenhair Tree, *Ginkgo pluripartita*.
Credit: Zhihui Wan and James Basinger, University of Saskatchewan.

7 PREHISTORY

It is hardly disputed that humans spread to North and South America from Siberia, via the Bering land bridge. Exactly when this happened is still a matter of debate. Some evidence suggests that this was as much as 30 000 or even 100 000 years ago. Northeastern British Columbia is believed to be the route through which these populations came from Asia and colonised the continent. This hypothesis requires the presence of an ice–free corridor between the Rockies in the west, and the ice sheet overlying the prairies to the east. This would have allowed a migration route.

These first humans found different conditions from those of today, especially with regard to large mammals. There were camels and horses, giant bears, mammoths and mastodons, lions and sabre–toothed tigers. In an instant in geological time, between twelve and ten thousand years ago, 57 large mammal species became extinct, although most smaller mammals and plants were hardly affected. This period coincides with the emergence of the Clovis Culture of very successful plains–oriented hunters. What caused this mass extinction remains open to debate. Some scholars believe that overhunting was the cause, others that the intense climate change at the end of the Pleistocene was responsible. A new theory is that the bacteriae and viruses that the first humans in North America brought with them from Asia were responsible, once they had been transferred to the indigenous mammals. A combination of causes is also plausible.

The Peace River to the north, the Rocky Mountain Trench to the west, and plains to the east provided prehistoric human inhabitants with natural corridors of travel. The degree to which they penetrated the Tumbler Ridge area was only revealed in the past twenty–five years.

The Charlie Lake Cave and a site at Pink Mountain, both north of Fort St. John, are amongst the oldest regionally, dating back roughly 7 000 to 12 000 years. They were occupied by the Clovis Culture, hunting along the shores of Glacial Lake Peace. They may have penetrated the Tumbler Ridge area, but there is as yet no evidence for this.

The current distributions of caribou, goats and sheep are discontinuous, suggesting that at one time there must have been a more extensive and continuous belt of tundra and grassland. This most likely occurred roughly 4 000 to 7 000 years ago, when the climate was warmer and drier. Grassland and open habitats were more extensive in the mountains, with increased carrying capacity for animals, and more favourable conditions for human settlement.

Archaeological evidence reflects this in sites of the Mummy Cave people, also excavated in the Peace River area to the north. Their distinctive notched spear points represent improved weapon production. This was the time of greatest prehistoric human occupation. Some sites in the Tumbler Ridge area appear to be from this period, e.g. above Babcock Falls.

From 3 000 to 1 500 years ago there was a mini ice–age, or 'neoglaciation'. Its onset was relatively rapid. Forests and wetlands expanded, with a decreased carrying capacity of large mammals. Populations of caribou, sheep and goat were cut off from one another, and survived in the smaller areas of tundra. It is believed that elk arrived in the area as recently as 2 000 years ago. Further south, grasslands could be maintained by controlled burning, but in the north the changes were too extensive, and the Mummy Cave people probably retreated south.

Corresponding with these conditions, a new tool appears in the archaeological record: the microblade, a small, sharp cutting edge usually derived from obsidian. Bound to a handle, these made good knives. The microblade is a sign of a forest–adapted people, in this case known as the Late Oxbow Complex people. Microblades have been found near Gwillim Lake. Obsidian does not occur regionally, and is thought to have originated at Mt Edziza, in northwest B.C. This implies significant trade patterns. The Gwillim Lake site was radio-carbon dated to 3 447 years, give or take a hundred years or so.

From 1 500 years to 200 years ago, as the climate warmed, new cultures with distinctive tools emerged. Arrow points replaced spears as weapons. People lived in extended family groups, and hunted and fished in a pattern similar to the historic Beaver and Sekani peoples. These nomadic tribespeople travelled the foothills and eastern flanks of the Rockies.

An impressive total of sixty-two prehistoric sites has been discovered and excavated in the Tumbler Ridge area. Most of these were discovered through assessments prior to proposed mining, forestry, petrochemical or rail developments. Directions to sites are not given here, so as to prevent vandalism.

Most of these finds are what are termed "lithic scatters", which comprise fragments from the production of stone tools, or the tools themselves. Hearths and fire-scorched rock have been found at many sites. One basalt flake was found close to the rail bridge over the Murray River just outside of Tumbler Ridge. Some of the sites are on knolls which allow a panoramic view which would aid hunting. Others are on glacial terraces above streams or beaver dams, or near lakes. It will come as no surprise to those who know the area well, to discover that there are a number of sites near Hook Lake, as this lake was on a prehistoric trail connecting the Sukunka and Murray valleys. No rock art has been found.

Before the Quintette mine site was developed, archaeological reconnaissance was done. No alpine sites were found, but three prehistoric sites were found just upstream from Babcock Falls. These yielded some interesting artifacts and lithic scatters.

One of these sites yielded quartzite flakes and a side scraper. Similar findings in the mountains to the south suggest that this site may be over 3 000 years old. The absence of fire-cracked rock from any of these sites suggests that they may date back to before the mini ice-age, and may be as old as 5 000 years. It is thought that these sites represent small hunting camps, well situated for exploitation of the alpine areas above, with their herds of ungulates.

From studies of all these materials, a possible picture begins to emerge of a 'seasonal round' involving the Plains, the Foothills, and the Rocky Mountains. Wintering sites were typically in the grasslands near the Peace River, allowing hunting of bison and other game. A number of families would come together at these sites, which were probably reused annually for thousands of years. Depending on fish populations, winter camps could also be on the shores of larger lakes, such as Gwillim Lake.

By contrast, summer camps would be in the big mountain passes such as Monkman Pass or Wapiti Pass. These corresponded with the summer caribou range. Sites were not visited annually, maybe just every five or ten years, so that the stocks of caribou, sheep and goat were not unnecessarily diminished. Such a camp might comprise just one or two families.

In between these two extremes would be intermediate camps. These are the kind of sites that have predominantly been found in our area. The sites above Babcock Falls likely fall into this category, of spring or fall hunting camps, by people en route to or from the wintering areas. The area immediately below Tumbler Ridge, where the Flatbed, Murray and Wolverine valleys converge, was probably a preferred site, but only limited archaeological finds have occurred here.

The impact of the arrival of the first white explorers and the fur trade was enormous on the Beaver and Sekani people, whose ancestors had subsisted in the region for countless generations. Traditionally the Beaver had lived to the east, and the Sekani further west in the foothills. Small and large game (especially moose) were hunted, with bow and arrow, spears, deadfall and snares. Fishing was considered an inferior pursuit, resorted to only during lean times, with nets and harpoons. Ice fishing was also employed with hook and line. Conical lodges were made of spruce, covered with animal skins and bark. Both dugout canoes and bark canoes were used.

With the fur trade, there was increasing competition and friction between peoples who had previously co–existed relatively peacefully. There was disruption of social organisation and hunting practices, and tribal boundaries. The Cree westward expansion displaced the Beaver westwards, who in turn displaced the Sekani out of the area and to the west of the mountains. Meanwhile the Salteau settled to the north close to the Klin–Se–Za (Twin Sisters) area following a remarkable migration from Manitoba, following a vision of just such sacred peaks, and formed an affiliation with the Beaver people living there. Trapping became the major pursuit.

Currently, Beaver, Cree and Salteau First Nations peoples reside at Moberly Lake. Iroquois and Cree are found mixed with other local populations throughout the Peace River area. Although these groups may have penetrated the Tumbler Ridge area from time to time, there is no compelling evidence of a more permanent presence. The first European explorers felt as if they were entering a land almost untouched by human hands, although the Metis of Kelly Lake were already filling this void. The Lheidli T'enneh First Nation traditional territory includes an area on the eastern flanks of the mountains south of Tumbler Ridge, but current negotiations with the Ministry of Aboriginal Affairs do not involve this area.

In the course of archaeological research a number of historical (as opposed to prehistoric) sites have been discovered. These include a group of cabins on Hambrook Creek. One cabin in the Honeymoon Creek area, known for decades as the Monkman Cabin, but used by Dave Gray and trappers from Kelly Lake, was unfortunately torched by vandals in the 1970s.

Culturally modified trees, estimated to be 70 years old, have been found near local lakes. One site contains eight lodgepole pine trees, with their bark stripped, some of which have distinct knife cut marks. One interesting find is near the Tumbler Ridge townsite. A carved wooden face was found on a tree trunk. In front of it was a ring of stones. Nearby was a fallen tree trunk with another carving. This was thought to possibly represent an historic burial ground, from the days when Napoleon Thomas and his family lived near the current Lions Flatbed Campground.

8 THE EXPLORERS

Alexander Mackenzie, in his well known crossing of the Rockies via the Peace River in 1793, heralded the arrival of the fur trade. It is difficult to believe that he did not see the copious dinosaur tracks on the rocky riverbank, but he did not comment on them and thus escaped even more fame. Once through the mountains, Mackenzie ascended the Parsnip River valley, and passed along the western aspect of our mountains.

On a clear day he was able to see their summits, and described

> *"a valley which appears to be of very great depth, and is full of snow, that rises nearly to the height of the land, and forms a reservoir of itself sufficient to furnish a river, whenever there is a moderate degree of heat."*

This is the first written description of any geographical feature in the Tumbler Ridge area. The "valley full of snow" refers to the Parsnip Glacier and the "height of the land" refers to Mount Vreeland, which is the source of Monkman Creek.

Rocky Mountain Fort was built at the junction of the Peace and Moberly Rivers in 1794, Fort St John was built in 1797, Fort Nelson in 1800, and a trading post was established by Simon Fraser at Hudson's Hope in 1805. The first recorded crossing of the Pine Pass to the north (between present-day Chetwynd and Prince George) was by a group of deserters from Simon Fraser's party in 1806.

Yet there is virtually no written record during the entire nineteenth century of any activity in the Tumbler Ridge area. Eurocanadians were slow to penetrate the area. Dense forests, the ruggedness and remoteness of the mountain terrain and the lack of suitable water routes were responsible, and the early activities took the form of temporary exploratory intrusions.

One of the great tragedies in the history of the area is the loss of First Nations oral tradition and folklore. Contrast Mackenzie's expedition, in which he associated closely with the local population and assimilated their knowledge (which often proved life-saving to his party) with the expeditions of the early twentieth century described in this book. There was apparently no legend of the great falls deep into the foothills, no oral tradition of which passes were best for crossing the mountains, and the explorers felt they were entering an unexplored land and had the sensation that they were the first to discover its major features.

There are a number of possible reasons for this. One is the Cree westward expansion of the 19th century. Groups that had traditionally used the area and knew it most intimately were displaced westwards across the mountains. Second, many First Nations communities at this time were ravaged by diseases like smallpox, which could have caused both a loss of elders' knowledge and of young hunters to follow the traditional routes into the mountains. Third, there was a great fire that swept through the foothills east of the mountains in the late 1800s. Blowdown following this natural event obliterated all the traditional trails. Such events may have occurred every few centuries through the ages, and the trails would have been slowly rebuilt, but maybe the above factors precluded their re-establishment. Whatever the reasons, the region became virtually deserted once more and the First Nations group that established the main presence in the area was a newcomer: the Metis of Kelly Lake.

■ THE SEARCH FOR RAILWAY PASSES

The development and settling of the Peace River country, advertised as "The Last Great West", was inextricably bound with railways, and in the early 1900s it often seemed that the only topics of conversation in northern Alberta were grain prices and where the railways would go. Speculators bought land where they thought the tracks would lie one day, and fledgling communities formed, only to have to shift when these dreams were not realised. The talk at government and railway-company level was not only about routes into the Peace region, but also focused on the potential routes through the mountains to the ports.

It seems that a superior intellect is necessary to understand the ramifications of railway company development in the early twentieth century as companies formed, amalgamated, dissolved, changed plans and broke promises with wild abandon. And in a way it may seem irrelevant to the history of the Tumbler Ridge area, because nothing developed here from all those plans and rumours. Eventually the line that came to carry the coal away came through the mountains from the west, and the Pine Pass to the north ultimately became the conduit for the products of the northern prairies.

Yet it is important, not only because of the epic story of the Monkman Pass Highway but also because considerable exploration occurred along these valleys and over the passes, for tracks of steel that would never be laid. The Rocky Mountains were *the* great natural barrier, and because their height is greater in the south, it stood to reason that the easiest passes would be in the north. For this reason some of the earliest surveys were undertaken just to the south and north of the present Tumbler Ridge area.

The major player in the late 1800s was the Canadian Pacific Railway (CPR). To the south, in the winter of 1875 Jarvis and Hanington surveyed what came to be known as Jarvis Pass in the Kakwa area for the CPR. They concluded that the route was impractical for a railway.

To the north George Dawson surveyed the Pine Pass for the CPR. Dawson is remembered and respected not only for his scientific ability but also for the spirit with which he overcame a severe physical handicap that would have incapacitated most lesser humans. He left detailed observations which established the Pine Pass as a feasible route. He noted the Sukunka and Murray river valleys but did not explore them.

These surveys all missed the least steep, and potentially most suitable routes: Gray Pass and Monkman Pass.

However, the logic of a northern railway route was overridden by sovereignty issues, and the threat of expansionism in the American northwest brought political pressure into play for a more southerly route. The result was that the CPR line was eventually built over the Kicking Horse Pass west of Banff.

In the early 1900s the two new major companies looking at a line through the Peace area and the mountains were the Canadian Northern Railway (CNR) and Grand Trunk Pacific (GTP). Both surveyed the area for prospective passes, although the version they put out for public consumption was that they would proceed through the mountains via the Peace and Pine Passes. They certainly surveyed the Wapiti Pass in the first years after the turn of the century. Cautley in the Alberta – B.C. Boundary Commission Report describes coming across an old GTP survey trail heading towards the mountains south of the Redwillow River. When Alex Monkman identified Monkman Pass he found a GTP stake on the western side of the pass, and Frederick Vreeland, surveying in 1915, wrote that he "succeeded in tying up with the work of the Grand Trunk Pacific engineers on the eastern slope".

The Yellowhead route west of Jasper was the major alternative route, and cost studies done in 1907 estimated in the region of 42 million dollars for the Yellowhead, 45 million for the Wapiti, 46 million for the Peace-Pine route, and 48 million for the Peace Pass.

Soon there was a turnaround and these companies within a few years of one another announced their intention to proceed with the Yellowhead route, resulting in an incredible duplication of effort. These decisions were coloured to a large extent on how practical the Peace region was considered for agriculture and development, and expert opinion differed hugely on this issue.

This wholly unsatisfactory state of affairs from the perspective of the region formed the basis of the discontent amongst the farmers who settled. The identification of Monkman Pass as a suitable route in 1922 was a spur to action.

The GTP amalgamated with the CNR in 1919. A 1925 map by R.W. Jones, a surveyor for the GTP, provides excellent detail on many aspects of the local topography, but is remarkable for omitting Monkman Creek and Monkman Pass altogether, and instead showing a feasible route at the head of the Murray River (Upper Blue Lake to Limestone Lakes) where none exists.

In 1928 Gray and Dimsdale identified Gray Pass as a very suitable route. But Dimsdale was employed by a railway company that had not yet been absorbed into the CNR, and this pass was not mentioned in the 1929 report by the Joint Board of Engineers of the CPR and CNR. This report noted that Wapiti Pass was 900 feet higher than Monkman Pass, that its line would be twenty miles longer than the Monkman route, with no advantage in gradients or construction costs. However, they believed that although the Monkman Pass line was superior to the other regional passes, it would be very expensive to build. They favoured a route from Grande Prairie south to join the existing CNR line through the Yellowhead Pass.

The tracks went through the Yellowhead, and again the region had not obtained its desired outlet.

■ THE FIRST LOCAL EUROPEAN EXPLORERS

It is quite astonishing that while volumes could be written on the history of the southern Canadian Rockies in the nineteenth century, absolutely nothing is recorded about the Tumbler Ridge area during this time period. There are just unconfirmable reports of a group of miners working in the Bullmoose Creek – Murray River region in 1896, but no written records. The absence of records may be due to fear of competition amongst the early traders, trappers and prospectors.

There is one tantalising reference in the diary of Prentiss Gray:

> *"Wapiti Lake had been visited by Beau Gaetz in 1898 when he spent two winters trying to find a route to the Klondike."*

(Beau Gaetz was a resident of Red Deer, and he accompanied Prescott Fay on some of his earlier expeditions).

TUMBLER RIDGE *Enjoying its History, Trails & Wilderness*

An Englishman, Spencer Tuck, was one of the first white men to enter the Tumbler Ridge area. He recorded his travels in the form of a diary which he sent to his mother in England. He entered the region from the south, crossing the Wapiti Pass to Wapiti Lake in August–September 1907. He complained of the extremely difficult nature of the terrain, and the difficulties he had with his guide. He was an adventurer from Jasper, timber–cruising for a lumber company, and managed to stake out an enormous area. He and his guide eventually reached Grande Prairie on the verge of starvation and hypothermia.

Excerpts from Tuck's diary make for illuminating reading:

> *"We have been through some of the hardest traveling it was ever my lot to put in….. we came very near losing all our horses… we have been mixed up in the most awful confusion of mountains I ever saw….. one night we camped among the eternal snows, and mighty cold it was….. We have crossed two more mountain ranges and finally landed on the banks of the Wapiti River, tired and ragged, horses and men on the verge of collapse… we have very little grub left of any kind… having no map, we had to go entirely by compass and guess work…The (guide) who is with us says that no man ever before went through the mountains the way we came; I believe he is right - no-one else would be such a darn fool as to try."*

Mike Murtha, noted authority and historian for BC Parks, queries the urgency with which Tuck's exploration was conducted in seeking timber tenures. He speculates that Tuck's employer was trying to tie up timber rights along the potential future rail line through Wapiti Pass.

The lake at the summit of the Wapiti Pass is known as Tuck Lake. Tuck later became a prominent resident of Pouce Coupe.

The Explorers

Plate 20: Fay's party descended into the Red Deer Valley via a treacherous scree slope above Whatley Creek.

Plate 21: For 200 miles Fay and his team had to chop their way through deadfall to make a trail for their horses.
Both reproduced with permission from the Jasper–Yellowhead Museum and Archives.

■ PRESCOTT FAY – THE FIRST SCIENTIFIC EXPEDITION

The first formal exploration of the area was undertaken by Samuel Prescott Fay in 1914. Known to his friends as "Pete", this adventurer from Massachusetts had based himself in Jasper, and in 1912–13 began exploring the area to the north. In the process he recorded the highest peak in the Canadian Rockies north of Mt. Robson. It came to be known (at his suggestion) as Mt. Sir Alexander. In 1914 he planned a much more ambitious hunting expedition, from Jasper all the way north along the eastern flank of the Rockies to the Peace River. The U.S. Biological Survey heard of this, and proposed that the expedition be formally conducted on its behalf. It was particularly interested in the distribution of the various mountain sheep species, but asked him to collect as many other specimens of mammals and birds as possible, in his exploration of what they called a "blank space on the map".

Fay wrote a detailed 117 page journal of the very successful, but extremely difficult expedition. Fully published only in 1956, it contains numerous descriptions of the wildlife encountered, the weather, and the geography of the terrain. It contains some beautiful first descriptions of the natural features of the Tumbler Ridge area, as well as providing enormous insight into the limited human presence in the region.

The expedition comprised Fay, his U.S. friend Charles Robert Cross, the famous Jasper guide and outfitter Fred Brewster, with Jack Symes as cook and Bob Jones as packer. There were fifteen pack horses and five saddle horses. They set off from Jasper on 26 June 1914.

On 21 August they entered the Red Deer Creek drainage via a treacherous scree slope, made famous by a phenomenal photograph (Plate 20):

> *"We started the horses down an almost impossible steep slope of scree which formed a covering to the steep ledges – a misstep meant a roll of five hundred feet over rocks and cliffs and a dead horse without doubt – the most dangerous place we have yet taken horses – the sharp rocks cut their feet and they hated to come but they did and without mishap."*

Plate 22: Cross and Brewster map the way ahead for Fay's party.

Plate 23: The first photograph ever taken of Kinuseo Falls – Prescott Fay, 1914. Both reproduced with permission from the Jasper–Yellowhead Museum and Archives.

They found occasional signs of human trails about ten years old (which possibly represent the exploration trails for the railway pass) but often had to chop a trail for their horses with axes. A week later they passed Wapiti Lake (see page 307): Brewster went ahead to reconnoitre, and reported a valley running north that they could enter. They speculated correctly that it was one of the branches of the Pine River. The next day they climbed a mountain to scout the terrain ahead and make maps, then entered the Murray Valley through a low pass. Their detailed map allows the exact route to be plotted. There were absolutely no trails, and they had to laboriously chop one to proceed at a dismal rate of half a mile per hour (Plate 21).

This almost impenetrable section of the Murray was the toughest of their entire trip. Sixteen consecutive days of rain plagued the party. They found solace in catching fish, as their food supplies were low. On one occasion Fay caught forty-five Dolly Varden in three hours.

To allow two members of the party to explore the mountains (including what would come to be known as the Albright Ridge) in search of sheep, they made a camp near where Monkman Creek joins the Murray, and here found some traces of human presence. Fay speculated that a few outfits had been there, one in winter on the ice, and one in summer by boat, but more than ten years previously.

Proceeding down the river on 20 September, they were unaware that they were approaching one of North America's great waterfalls, to which Fay would in time give the name Kinuseo (Cree for fish) because of the number of trout above and below the falls. Prescott Fay was not the first to see these great falls, but he was the first to photograph them (Plate 23), and describe them in writing (see page 263).

Fay estimated that the previous party had been through about ten years previously, and this corresponds with an anecdotal report by Jim Dixon, who settled in the Beaverlodge area. Dixon told Janet Hartford that he had seen the falls in 1907.

Near where Kinuseo Creek enters the Murray, Fay's party found several meat racks, tipi poles, boats, campsites, a paddle, a log cache, and a blaze on a tree with Cree writing and the name "Issidore". Progressively more signs of hunting and trapping were found, but no indication of any previous horses. The absence of any trails made the

Plate 24: Prescott Fay, Robert Cross, Bob Jones, Jack Symes and Fred Brewster pose in Hudson's Hope after their 1914 expedition. Jasper–Yellowhead Museum and Archives.

Plate 25: Frederick Vreeland. Reproduced with permission of the Vreeland family.

going desperately slow, and at times they were forced to swim their horses in the river. In a final unsuccessful attempt to look for sheep they climbed the ridge of Pyramid Peak, and thought (incorrectly) that they saw Moberly Lake from its summit. They still did not know exactly which river they were descending, and thought it was probably the Sukunka.

On 1 October they climbed the flanks of a big hill, probably Babcock Mountain, and looked out onto the plains:

> *To the east lay level prairie country as far as the eye could reach. There within eyesight probably, yet too far off to be visible, stretched the last remaining piece of prairie that is being ploughed up for cultivation. There the country is being homesteaded and people are coming into it almost daily to take up their land. To think how near and yet how far we are from civilisation and the land of plenty, for it will be many weeks before we reach it."*

On 3 October they finally hit a horse trail and found a blaze on a tree, a cause for great celebration. They had covered over 200 trailless miles in two months, cutting trails almost all the way. On 5 October they reached "The Big Flat", the area just below present day Tumbler Ridge, where they noted both a creek from the west (Wolverine) and the southeast (Flatbed) joining the Murray. A trail led along the latter towards the Wapiti. They then realised that they had after all been on the Murray River, not the Sukunka, for the preceding month. Fay was ecstatic in describing the Big Flat (see page 145).

Camped out that night they heard the blows of an axe, and next morning encountered a lone trapper, Nelson, the first human they had encountered in three months. They asked him for news, and he told them about the war. They thought he meant that Mexico and the U.S.A. were at war, only to learn he was talking about Britain, Europe and Germany.

Nelson took them to his cabin on Rocky Mountain Lake (Gwillim Lake) and Fay in his familiar style wrote a fine first description of this lake (see page 169). It was twenty miles over the hills to the Sukunka, and it appears that Nelson incorrectly told them that this was the Pine

The Explorers

River, with the result that when they reached it they mistakenly traveled upstream. Only a chance encounter with another trapper saved them from a long trip back into the mountains. In the process they found and photographed Sukunka Falls (Plate 72) (see page 213).

The remainder of their trip led them past Moberly Lake to the Peace River at Hudson's Hope, which they reached on 16 October after sixteen weeks of constant travel over an incredible distance of 746 miles (Plate 24). They then returned to Jasper via Grande Prairie and Edson, and every single horse made it back safely.

Fay and Cross enlisted and soon found themselves assisting the Allies in ambulance work in France, where Cross was killed in action, helping to remove wounded soldiers from the trenches. Fay later successfully motivated to have one of the satellite peaks of Mt Sir Alexander named Mt. Cross in his honour. Cook Jack Symes was also killed in action at Ypres, in 1916, soon after receiving his commission. Fred Brewster became a major and was decorated with the Military Cross and Bar. Packer Bob Jones went on to become a respected park warden, before drowning east of Jasper in 1955.

The expedition and area left a permanent impression on S. Prescott Fay, and he continued corresponding with various authorities until well into the 1950s. From a biological point of view the expedition was a great success, although it suggested that there were no Bighorn Sheep north of the Wapiti River. The many specimens they obtained were meticulously kept and sent to Washington, along with a detailed report. The U.S Biological Survey congratulated him on having "cleared up one of the blank places on the map of North America". Fay produced a paper which was read to the American Alpine Club and published in the magazine Appalachia and the Journal of the Canadian Alpine Club. The map they made was the best yet produced.

In 1920 his application for the official name of Kinuseo Falls was accepted by the Geographical Board of Canada. In the March 1941 edition of the magazine "Natural History" he redescribed coming upon Kinuseo Falls. He was also responsible for the name "Kakwa Lake". He was thus involved in the naming of four major geographical features. After his epic journey he may have been a trifle surprised by a written comment from the Geographical Board of Canada that he was lucky in having these names accepted as "the Board generally looks with disfavour on names suggested by tourists."

He remained intrigued by Mt. Sir Alexander and in 1957 wrote a two–part article on it in the "The Beaver":

> "Major Fred Brewster (still at Jasper) was the most resourceful man I have ever met. You always had the most complete confidence in him, no matter how bad things ever got. As for C.R.Cross,.....I can say just as much. As a friend of mine back home in Boston, he had originally interested me in hunting and exploring in difficult and inaccessible parts of the Northwest...He and Fred Brewster were as perfect a pair as any man could want to be with in the wilderness. The three of us together worked out our plans, and every decision was in our hands jointly...We could always count on Symes and Jones...both were good companions, and no hardship or difficulty ever bothered them for long. It was altogether a fortunate group of men. Never once had there been any misunderstanding or unpleasantness between any of us during our five consecutive months in the bush, during three of which we saw no other human being."

Fay Lake, in the Kakwa area, was named after this heroic man who died aged 87 in 1971.

■ A MYSTERY PASS

Maybe there were a lot more folks in the mountains in those days than we know about. An example is a cryptic note passed on to me by historian Mike Murtha. Dated January 1915, it was written by a Henry Munroe to Luther Gunn, a well–known land surveyor in Prince George. He describes his trip to the eastern side of the mountains:

> "I have found another Pass aside of the one I went to look at.....believe me it is a good pass this one.... the top of the pass is timbered its entire length.....I broke the instrument before getting the elevation of this pass, I accidentally dropped the gun on it. I found an immense quantity of coal in that country, as to quality I don't know. Some road will eventually use this good pass."

Unfortunately the location of this pass remains a mystery.

■ VREELAND CLIMBS THE BIG PEAKS FROM THE WEST

While Fay was making the first recorded journey along the eastern flanks of the mountains, Frederick Vreeland (Plate 25) was exploring them from the west, doing topographic reconnaissance and mapping surveys. This able American inventor and manufacturer was already in his forties (he lived to be 90) and spent three successive summers exploring these mountains on a voluntary basis. He wrote:

> *"There is something about the great mountains that enlarges men's souls and inspires them to do great things."*

In 1915 he canoed up the Parsnip River and climbed its headwaters to reach the summit of what came to be known as Mt Vreeland. This great peak is the most northwesterly glaciated summit in the Hart Ranges, and gives rise to the only Rockies glacier described by Alexander Mackenzie, as well as being at the head of the Monkman Glacier and thus Monkman Creek.

Next he followed the historic Arctic Portage and ascended what he called the Great Ice Dome, now known as Ice Mountain. This ice-capped massif way to the south of Tumbler Ridge is a familiar sight to anyone who ascends into the high alpine. It is a sacred site for the Lheidli T'enneh First Nation.

Fay and Vreeland learned of one another's exploits, compared notes and communicated regularly. In recognition of his pioneering work, the Geographic Board of Canada proposed that the initial peak he climbed be named Mt Vreeland in his honour. If anything, he would have preferred that the name be given to Ice Mountain, for that ascent was a far greater achievement. But he tried to decline the honour, pointing out how it should have belonged to Mackenzie, who had described the peak first, and indicating that he disapproved of the habit of explorers giving their names to objects which had long been known. Despite his objections, the name Mt. Vreeland was approved.

■ FIRST DESCENT OF THE WAPITI

Donald "Curly" Phillips (Plate 26) was another of the legendary figures of the first half of the twentieth century that worked out of Jasper. Nicknamed for his curly shock of hair, this greatly respected guide and outfitter was born in 1884 in Ontario, and acquired trapping skills and backwoods knowledge at an early age. When the woods and waterways of eastern Canada became more populated and ceased to be an untamed frontier, he moved to the Rockies in 1908.

Although most of his exploits centered around Jasper, the exception is his 1918 expedition, with its death–defying descent down the swollen Wapiti River Canyon. Unusually for someone in his profession, he faithfully kept a diary, and passed it on to one of his distinguished clients, who became a famous mountain historian and preserved it.

Subsequently William C. Taylor, a retired professor of paediatrics at the University of Alberta, reviewed these priceless records and blended them into the inspiring book "Tracks Across my Trail", which has served to immortalise Curly Phillips.

Soon after he arrived in the west, he was involved in one of the most amazing annals in the history of mountaineering in North America, when he helped to outfit and guide Reverend Kinney up Mount Robson in 1909. Although he had no mountaineering experience at all, they came within ten metres of the summit (the highest peak in the Canadian Rockies) and what would have been an incredible first ascent. He rapidly built up a name for himself guiding leading scientists and mountaineers.

In 1915 he guided an enterprising pair to Mount Sir Alexander: Mary Jobe and Caroline Hinman. He and Mary became wilderness sweethearts for three summers, and Curly led members of this party to within 30 metres of the summit. Again, this was by far the highest anyone had climbed on this giant of the northern Rockies. It was eventually climbed only in 1929 by an expedition which Curly outfitted and guided – ironically he was not a member of the summit party.

In 1917 Curly Phillips and Mary Jobe led a party that ventured further north, in a 75 day packing trip beset by early winter snows. They built a cabin and left a cache on the Narraway River, just south of the Tumbler Ridge area. After this trip he never saw Jobe again, and she went on to enjoy a distinguished career in Africa's Belgian Congo.

One purpose of this expedition was the 1918 winter trip that Curly outfitted for Bill Rindsfoos, who worked for the Smithsonian Institute in Washington D.C. Rindsfoos' mission was winter big game photography, and the plan was to ascend the Wapiti drainage from Grande Prairie in February, and survive off the land for a couple of months. A third man joined the party, but proved lazy and a hindrance.

Dog teams were used for transportation, and the account of the expedition sometimes seems to be a sequence of one canine near-disaster following the next, including an attack by a bull moose. Suffering many tribulations caused by the severe winter, they nonetheless managed to reach the cabin up the Narraway River, do some exploring of Belcourt Creek and the surrounding alpine areas, obtain the necessary photographs, and hunt and trap successfully. Rindsfoos wrote:

> "Moose were on every bend and caribou on every hill, wolves were in every valley, and beaver, marten and fox were very plentiful."

Coming back out, they had a deadline to meet: Curly had been called up to serve in the Canadian forces in the First World War. The spring came early, food was scarce and travel was difficult in the deep slushy snow, so they chose to work their way along the ice along the edges of the rivers. Unfortunately it is not possible to know for certain which branch of the Wapiti River they descended. It makes no difference, for each of these is characterised by deep and fearsome canyons of white water which to this day command the respect of kayakers.

The trip has been given the recognition it deserves in Professor Taylor's book, which describes an epic struggle between the three ill-equipped man and the raging river:

> "At one point they had to portage everything across the rocks and lower their loads, dogs included, over an ice-covered face. In a half-mile stretch they had to build three bridges across side-streams in full flood. In many places they crept along the river bank.... covering only two or three miles a day...

> *On April 16 they were forced to abandon the toboggans, as there was no ice left along the shores of the river. They spent two days building a raft twenty foot long by six feet wide..."*

The raft often grounded, at other times they had to contend with logjams and icejams. Time after time they had to break up the raft, carry the logs over portages, and then reassemble it. They had to carefully judge the icejams, which would accumulate and then give way with a great roaring flood. Food supplies ran extremely low, but there was no time for hunting, such were the incessant demands of staying alive on the river:

> "They swept around a bluff...there was ice jammed on the left... and a logjam at the foot of the bluffs on the right...in the centre was a narrow area free of obstruction. But their luck was out...the raft swung sideways onto the logjam. The water rushed over the upstream side of the raft, forcing it under. The toboggans...were swept away, taking Rindsfoos with them..."

Once they had the raft in the water again, testing white water loomed, where the Wapiti River raced around a high cliff and where a ledge formed a waterfall. Curly wrote in his diary (and he was not one to exaggerate):

> "Out of the swells ahead there loomed up two jagged boulders right in our path...We bumped past the first, only to be hurled at the second. By good luck I got my pole against something on the bottom, and pushed with all my might and cleared the second rock, and on we went through a mad tumult of running ice and rough water for half a mile."

Beyond another logjam they struck a large rock, and lost the third man's outfit, their cooking kit, and all their remaining food except one piece of moose meat. Taylor continues:

The Explorers

> *"On and on they went, fighting the current, dodging rocks and never knowing what lay around the next bend. It was desperate and dangerous work. They were worn out, starved and chilled but they knew that their only chance of getting out of the woods alive was to reach the next food cache."*

Finally they reached the undisturbed cache, hit calmer waters, and drifted into Grande Prairie on May 6. Curly Phillips was just a few days late for his military call–up. He served only briefly, and was given an honourable discharge after being severely trampled by a horse.

He went on to become one of Jasper's most celebrated guides and entrepreneurs. In the 1930s there was an interest in recreational skiing, and he was one of the first to investigate its tourist possibilities. Engaged in this exciting new pursuit, he was tragically killed in an avalanche in 1938. Rindsfoos went on to become founder and president of a major bank. He died aged 78.

■ THE FIRST SURVEYORS FOR OIL AND GAS

A surveying expedition by J.C. Gwillim in 1919 helps to shed further light on the limited development of the area at that time. Gwillim was born in England and came to Canada aged 13. He was appointed professor of mining at Queen's University, Kingston, in 1903. He would spend his summers in the field, exploring for coal and oil, and his work was held in high esteem. His last field work was in 1919, when he represented the Geological Survey of Canada, and was sent to northeastern B.C. by the Department of Lands, to investigate oil and gas possibilities. The survey lasted almost three months, and was unsuccessful in the search for oil.

Gwillim's route took him up the Sukunka River, to Rocky Mountain Lake. Little did he know that subsequently its name would be changed to Gwillim Lake in his honour. He proceeded to Moose Lake, along Bullmoose Creek to the Wolverine Valley, and to Flatbed Creek and thus the site of present day Tumbler Ridge. He returned via Muskeg Lake, and crossed the Murray River where the Gwillim River entered it, and headed over the ridges to Lone Prairie.

He noted that *"the most desirable flats of wintering-places for stock and feed are already partly taken up by squatters...there are a few trapper settlements, squatters and absentees"* in the valley of the Murray River and at Flatbed Creek. He went on to recommend further geological exploration of the area, which led to Edmund Spieker's expedition the following year.

Gwillim was a meticulous recorder, and the map he drew of the area is a masterpiece, a huge improvement on anything that had existed before. However, it is only accurate for the features along Gwillim's route, and he admits to its vagueness elsewhere. It also lays to rest any questions that may remain as to exactly what, and where, the "Tumbler Ridge" was. Current maps mark the ridge above town, that includes The Bald Spot, as 'Tumbler Ridge'. But Gwillim's 1919 map clearly indicates the long ridge that parallels Bullmoose Creek, and ends in the southeast in Mount Bergeron, as 'Tumbler Range'. Spieker's party recorded being near this ridge, and Spieker had the distinction of coining the name Tumbler Ridge, as for some reason he disliked the name Tumbler Range.

The Department of Lands sent Spieker specifically to search for oil in the area recommended by Gwillim, from Hudson's Hope south to present day Tumbler Ridge. Spieker covered over 500 kilometres, on a route quite similar to Gwillim's. His search for oil was also fruitless. Mount Spieker, the great flat–topped mountain that forms much of the western horizon from Tumbler Ridge, is named after him.

Although gas seepages were found during the construction of the Monkman Pass Highway in 1937, it was not until the 1950s that the next detailed geological investigation of the region would take place.

■ THE BOUNDARY COMMISSION

The Imperial Act defined British Columbia as extending "...*from the Boundary of the United States northwards by the Rocky Mountains and the one hundred and twentieth Meridian of West Longitude...*". It was thus understood that the boundary between B.C. and Alberta would follow the divide between waters flowing to the Pacific Ocean and waters flowing elsewhere; where this divide intersected the 120th meridian, it would follow this directly north. No–one knew if the divide would cross the

The Explorers

Plate 26:
Donald "Curly" Phillips.
Reproduced with permission of Dr. W. Taylor.

Plate 27:
The Boundary Commission, cutting a swath along the 120th meridian.
Natural Resources Canada. Reproduced with the permission of the Minister of Public Works and Goverment Services Canada, 2001.

meridian more than once. If it did, then the northernmost crossing of the meridian would be the place where the boundary left the summit of the mountains and headed north. For years this boundary was drawn in every atlas and on every map of Canada without anyone knowing exactly where this mystical spot lay, while most of the actual boundary lay in unknown and unexplored territory.

Therefore a federal commission was appointed to survey, explore and define the boundary, and this work continued from 1917 until well into the 1920s. The two commissioners were A.O. Wheeler representing the Province of British Columbia, and R.W. Cautley, representing the Dominion and Alberta Governments. The section that involves the Tumbler Ridge area south to where the meridian meets the mountains was surveyed under the leadership of Cautley in 1920 and 1922, and the formal report was published in 1925.

First it was necessary to establish exactly where the 120th meridian was. Using a point of known longitude (Ottawa), the only telegraph line in the entire region, a telegraph station known to be roughly near the meridian (Pouce Coupe) and state of the art astronomical instruments, the exact longitude of Pouce Coupe was calculated in 1918, and the distance to the meridian then measured. Then the survey work could begin, again measuring distance and direction with great precision.

As the entire meridian section was forested, they cut a swath four metres wide the whole way (Plate 27), managing about two kilometres per day. They also set about building bronze–capped monuments on the most prominent points, like ridge–tops. Alberta was divided into "townships" and they numbered the monuments accordingly.

They found no trails of use to them whatsoever, and were plagued by immense amounts of windfallen timber. They commented on the small pieces of float–coal they found on the gravel bars of rivers like the Redwillow.

The amount of material that had to be transported is staggering. This included 22 000 lbs of cement for the monuments, 14 000 lbs of supplies, 4 000 lbs of camp outfit, and a further 40 000 lbs of gravel for the monuments. The absence of trails or navigable rivers meant that the entire 80 000 lbs would have to be carried by pack train. They offset this to some extent by placing caches close to the line by winter freighting.

Plate 28: A monument constructed by the Boundary Commission. Natural Resources Canada. Reproduced with the permission of the Minister of Public Works and Goverment Services Canada, 2001.

Plate 29: John Holzworth from: "Wild Grizzlies of Alaska."

The 1922 party comprised twenty men with a pack train of thirty-two horses. Working south, they had to cross major rivers and deep valleys like the Wapiti and Narraway, and crested many ridges before finally striking the mountains at what they called Torrens Mountain. On the return journey they worked on building concrete monuments. Altogether an astounding forty-nine concrete monuments and twenty-seven post monuments were constructed. Each day an average of two monuments would be built, and the two tops for the following day's monuments filled. This therefore meant that forms, gravel, cement and water had to be carried by packhorse to four monument sites kilometres apart each day. In twenty-nine days the job was finished.

Cautley described the country his party traversed in meticulous detail, produced a marvelous map, and the book detailing the expedition contains some wonderful photographs of river crossings and mountain views (usually with a monument in the foreground) (Plate 28). The party named many of the features it found, and a glance at a detailed map of the area today still shows a disproportionate number of names close to the boundary, a direct result of the work of the commission. Many of the original monuments remain, an interesting destination for the historically minded.

■ HOLZWORTH – ANOTHER ZOOLOGICAL EXPEDITION

In 1923 another expedition was arranged by the U.S. Biological Survey and was led by thirty-five year old John Holzworth (Plate 29). Holzworth was a lawyer, explorer and author. His task was to investigate further the distribution of mountain sheep and caribou in the area, and collect specimens. He helped establish that there are no sheep in the area except for the far south. He too wrote a fascinating journal.

He approached from the north, down the Peace Canyon, then over the mountains to reach the Sukunka, and recorded a camp where it is joined by Martin Creek. From the Burnt River region he approached the mountainous country around present day Tumbler Ridge. He described hunting by the lakelet in the pass between Windfall Creek and Bullmoose Creek, a site well-known nowadays to hikers, skiers and snowmobilers. Here he shot a caribou. He was spellbound by the beauty of the country and wrote ecstatically:

> "For sheer joy and contentment, I know of nothing like this; a hundred miles or two from any civilisation and no human being within miles…the spell of the mountains."

He followed the Wolverine River down to its junction with the Murray. A mile below this confluence, he found the cabin of the Peck trapping family, and was impressed by the indomitable Mrs Peck and took a photo of her at work in her cabin. Then on enquiry, he learned that because of the amount of downed timber, he would not be able to travel with his horses along the trail up Flatbed Creek to the Wapiti, and instead took the established trail to Pouce Coupe. On the way he skirted Muskeg Lake, and recorded a cabin and large log barn which had been in use years before, and the carcasses of a herd of cattle that had died of starvation. From Beaverlodge he superficially explored the Wapiti River drainage, including Belcourt Creek, where he obtained specimens of the northernmost population of bighorn sheep. In addition to his journal and report, he described this expedition in his book "Wild Grizzlies of Alaska".

■ THE FIRST PRENTISS GRAY EXPEDITION

In 1927 Prentiss Gray (Plate 30) led a party of twelve men from Hudson's Hope to the Fraser River near McBride, passing through what is now the Tumbler Ridge area. Although this expedition has been described as a duplication in reverse of the northern half of Fay's 1912 journey, this is not true. In only a few places did their routes cross, and for the most part they explored and described adjoining regions.

Known to his family and friends as "Prent", Gray was a remarkable and distinguished man. He was born in California in 1884 and developed a love of hunting at an early age. After graduating, he was actively successful in the family shipping business until a chance encounter on a street–car led him to Belgium in the First World War, where he supervised the provision of food to starving non–combatants behind the

German lines. For this unstinting work he received many decorations. After the war he became a highly successful banker in New York. He found increasing time for his passions of hunting and photography in remote wilderness settings. He was an avid member of the Boone and Crockett Club, conceived of the idea of the club's famous book "Records of North American Big Game", and was its first editor.

His two older sisters, envious of his many exciting escapades, requested that he provide them with detailed reports. Thus an enduring custom was established and by the time of his premature death in a boating accident in 1935 he had produced an astonishing twenty-one fascinating journals, describing hunting expeditions around the world. His son Sherman Gray lovingly preserved these priceless and beautifully illustrated treasures, which were bound in leather. Gray was a gifted writer and his journals make for entertaining reading.

The first collection, which includes ten of the thirteen North American journals, is entitled "From the Peace to the Fraser – Newly Discovered North American Hunting and Exploration Journals". This was published by the Boone and Crockett Club in 1993. The title reflects the fact that his expedition through what is now the Tumbler Ridge area was perhaps Gray's greatest achievement, as it explored some completely new territory and discovered "Gray Pass", a new route through the mountains. For this he received a fellowship in the Royal Geographic Society in London. Prentiss Gray's son Sherman, in addition to meticulously preserving his father's records, is himself an active member of the Boone and Crockett Club and plans a visit to retrace his father's footsteps.

The group Gray invited for the expedition contained some of the greatest names in big-game hunting of the century. Among these was Harry Snyder who devoted a chapter of "Snyder's Book of Big Game Hunting" to this trip. So did Elmer Keith, the cook, in his book "Hell, I was There!", which provides innumerable hunting anecdotes but nothing in the way of solid history. Three Calliou brothers from Jackfish Lake near Moberly Lake served as guides and scouts.

As opposed to some of the earlier expeditions in the area which involved official scientific pursuits, this one was purely for the love of the outdoors, hunting, photography and exploration. The ever-

The Explorers

Plate 30: Prentiss Gray.

Plate 31: Gray took the second photos of Kinuseo Falls in 1927.

Photographs reproduced with permission from Sherman Gray and the Boone and Crockett Club.

present issue of the distribution of sheep populations was once more a dominant question.

Snyder's group arrived at Hudson's Hope by boat via the Crooked River, Parsnip River and Peace River. Gray arrived by train from Edmonton to Grande Prairie, by car to Rolla and then by boat upriver to Hudson's Hope. Here he met and was duly impressed by Mrs. Peck.

Passing Moberly Lake and the area around present–day Chetwynd, they passed through Lone Prairie and then forded the Murray River. Soon they encountered the first of the muskeg and deadfall that would dishearten them over the next week as they traversed the Kiskatinaw Plateau.

Many travelers along the Heritage Highway between Tumbler Ridge and Dawson Creek enjoy the open meadows of the Salt Creek drainage, and Gray enthused about them too:

> *"Our course lay along the bank of Salt Creek, a beautiful stream that meandered through a wide valley.... The meadows through which we traveled were firm and smooth."*

The party passed Muskeg Lake and ascended the West Kiskatinaw River (then known as the west branch of the Cutbank River) supplementing their diet with fresh grayling and rainbow trout. Next they described and took the first recorded photograph of Bearhole Lake (Plate 79), which has recently been proclaimed a provincial park.

They followed the shore and found its outlet, then slowly ascended the ridge of what is now known as Thunder Mountain. Nowadays people drive the rough road to its summit on a clear day to enjoy the magnificent mountain view from the old fire tower. Gray was ecstatic about this great scene which gave him his first good look at the mountains (see page 300).

They camped on the upper reaches of Flatbed Creek (which they called Parsnip Creek and believed drained into the Kiskatinaw) and shot their first moose. Gray then decided to make a side trip with Snyder and Pete Calliou to Kinuseo Falls. The route they chose seems unconventional by today's standards but was designed to avoid muskeg as much as possible. It first took them south all the way to Onion Lake, which

The Explorers

Gray dutifully photographed (Plate 124) and described (see page 307). Onion Lake is now the destination for many hikers on the Wapiti Lake–Onion Lake hiking trail.

They circled around Bone Mountain to the west of the lake, looked down upon Wapiti Lake, then headed through difficult country until they entered the valley of the Murray. They commented on a "fair sized lake" that they called Dewing Lake after a member of the expedition. It is now known as Lower Blue Lake.

Pete Calliou told Gray about the existence of another lake higher up the valley (Upper Blue Lake). He had been in the area eight winters before, and they believed that his axe–cuttings on the trees were the only evidence of anyone having been there before. They did not know that from here down to their destination, Kinuseo Falls twenty–five kilometres downstream, they were struggling through the same deadfall that had so bothered the Fay expedition thirteen years earlier.

They had a torrid time and were forced to leave the horses behind and proceed on foot through endless downed timber at risk of serious injury, lugging their heavy camera equipment and rifles. What was planned as a day trip turned into a three–day rainy nightmare with dwindling provisions. They survived on a few sandwiches each and a couple of Oxo cubes until Gray shot a spruce grouse which they shared. But no tribulations could detract from their joy on arriving at the falls, which they described and photographed (Plate 31).

Gray recorded one precious fact. Whereas Fay had named the falls Kinuseo, there was also a mellifluous First Nations name: Kapaca Tignapy, meaning "falling water". Gray was aware of Fay's visit and first description and photographs. He correctly believed that his was the first movie taken of the falls. Most of the nitrate films perished in time, but miraculously one copy survived, was copied onto safety film and has been transferred to video format.

Gray shot a grizzly on the return trip to join the remainder of the party. He wrote:

> *"It was a cold but happy ride into camp. Happy because we had Kinoosao Falls in our camera box and a grizzly hide in a sack."*

Their route now took them past Wapiti Lake (see page 307). The main party was camped in Red Deer Creek to the southeast, and they made their way up a gentle valley to a pass. The descent was a stark contrast:

"*a terror, straight up and down in places.*"

Tumbler Ridge hikers who have hiked the standard route in to Fossil Fish Lake from the Red Deer Valley will sympathise, having endured the steep alder–covered slopes that reduce experienced backpackers to tears.

The next few days were spent hunting Bighorn Sheep, Mountain Goat and Caribou. They were heading into an area which the latest government map called "High Snow and Glacier Peaks – Unexplored Country". They explored the upper reaches of the Red Deer, Belcourt (Fish Creek) and Narraway (Sheep Creek) valleys and found the pass leading into Jarvis Creek and the Fraser drainage that still bears Gray's name. A few days later they arrived at the railroad near McBride, having covered 344 miles on horseback in thirty days. Prentiss Gray had satisfied his lifetime ambition of hunting Bighorn Sheep, but had not finished with the region.

■ GRAY'S FOLLOW–UP TRIP

Gray was obviously enchanted with what he had discovered, and longed over the ensuing winter to return and study the area in more detail, and fill in the remaining blanks on the map. He searched diligently and without success for any records of the new area, compiling data on the known exploration of the surrounding areas. His interest in photography had increased further, and he desperately wanted to take more moving pictures of Bighorn Sheep.

He teamed up with H.G. Dimsdale, a civil engineer from Edmonton who was working for a railway company that would in time be absorbed into the CNR. They assembled some of the same guides he had employed the previous year. The party of eight, with twenty–six pack–horses, was burdened with large amounts of cumbersome state of the art camera gear and surveying instruments (Plate 33).

The Explorers

Plate 32: Gray's party crosses the Wapiti River, 1928.
Plate 33: Prentiss Gray carried state of the art camera equipment into the mountains to produce some of the first quality moving pictures of wild animals.
Photographs reproduced with permission from Sherman Gray and the Boone and Crockett Club.

Their route lay further to the southeast than in 1927, and they approached the mountains via what they named Muinok Creek ("peaceful, placid and beautiful" in Cree), now known as Belcourt Creek. Existing maps had its couse incorrectly marked and failed to include the substantial Belcourt Lake in its course. They established a semi–permanent camp on its shores. Gray wrote:

> *"The lake was...surrounded by high rugged hills. The high ridge...was streaked with snow, and made a wonderful backdrop for the sheet of blue water before us. I put in the morning building a raft and after lunch we circumnavigated the lake, letting Dimsdale take shots with the transit at various points to determine the configuration of the shoreline."* (Plate 121).

The previous year Gray and his guide Pete Calliou had thought they had seen spray rising from a point in Red Deer Creek. They now determined to investigate this further. After a series of high passes and difficult deadfall they made camp on a flat at the head of the gorge where they suspected the waterfall had to be. Exploring in the morning their search was initially unsuccessful although they had a great view of the Red Deer Canyon. Finally they stumbled upon Red Deer Falls (Plate 126). Gray acknowledged that First Nations peoples may have seen the falls before him. His is certainly the first known description of this fine waterfall (see page 313).

The expedition filmed and hunted in the inspiring mountains, working their way south towards Gray Pass as they surveyed the headwaters of the Belcourt and Narraway drainages. Gray named the lakes on the eastern side of the pass Sherman Lakes after his son. They are now officially known as Dimsdale Lakes after Gray's companion, and are the source of the Narraway River. The lakes on the western side of the pass remain known as Barbara Lakes, after Prentiss Gray's daughter.

Gray and Dimsdale realised that they were surveying a potentially very suitable railway route through the mountains, either via Belcourt creek or the Narraway River. They showed that the slope on the Pacific side of the pass was not too steep, and celebrated over a bottle of scotch. They could not believe that all the money spent by the railway

Plate 34: William Sheldon.

Plate 35: Self portrait by Richard Borden. Both photographs by Richard Borden, reproduced with permission from Beatrice Borden.

engineers searching for a route to the Pacific had failed to find their ideal route, which was almost on a straight line between the existing railheads on either side of the Rockies. They were well aware of the Pine Pass and Monkman Pass, but dismissed these as costly and usable only as a last resort. They identified too the great need of the Peace Country for a rail outlet to the west.

Gray and Dimsdale did their homework well and proved the feasibility of this route, which would have traversed some of the finest scenery on the North American continent. But in the ensuing years the Monkman Pass route grabbed the attention and Gray Pass faded into obscurity. Even today it is visited only by the hardiest backpacker.

■ THE FIRST FORMAL EXPLORATION OF THE SUKUNKA

By the 1930s, the major drainages in the area had been formally explored, with the exception of the Sukunka. This was towards the end of the age of the official hunter–naturalists, who shot much of what they saw for the purpose of documentation, scientific research and museum collections. One of the most remarkable things about William (Bill) Sheldon (Plate 34) and Richard Borden (Plate 35), who thoroughly explored the Sukunka in 1932, was their age. Sheldon was just twenty, Borden two years older. Sheldon's father Charles was also a naturalist, and had instilled his values and knowledge in his son from an early age. By the time of his father's unexpected death in 1928, Sheldon was ready for the kind of adventure he had been prepared for, and soon identified the northern Canadian Rockies as the site of his exploration for the American Museum of Natural History.

Yet again, the subject of sheep distributions was one of the driving forces behind the venture, and in 1931 Sheldon and Borden enjoyed classic sheep hunting experiences in the Rocky Mountains northwest of Fort St. John. In 1932 they planned a trip further south, and realised that the Sukunka River, despite its size, had only perhaps been penetrated by a handful trappers on snowshoes at low elevations in winter. Jim Ross, who had outfitted both of Gray's expeditions, was their guide, on what turned out to be more of an exhilarating exploration than a hunting trip.

The Explorers

In 1981 Sheldon published a book of these travels. Only 1 000 copies were printed and the book has become very difficult to obtain. In the introduction he wrote:

> *"We were at that happy time of life when the body seemed never to tire. We loved what we were doing. The panoramic views, the smells of the woods, the sounds of the rushing rivers are still indelibly etched in my mind and I can play them back, like an old movie... We spent nearly 250 nights in the same small lean-to tent, often under trying conditions, and remained friends."*

They canoed from Summit Lake down the Crooked River, down the Peace to Hudson's Hope. As had so many travelers before them, they encountered the Peck family there, and met with veteran guide Pete Calliou at Moberly Lake. Heading up the Sukunka with Ross and a pack of horses, they had a great deal of difficulty penetrating the thickly forested valley bottom, and had time to comment only briefly on Sukunka Falls. As they approached the headwaters, they ventured up into the mountains on numerous side trips. Unfortunately it is virtually impossible to pinpoint their exact route, but they appear to have explored just about every bowl, creek, ridge and summit! Mention is made of a large lake in a valley bottom, which could well have been Hook Lake. They returned via the high country above Windfall Creek.

They found tantalising suggestions of sheep sign, including very convincing photographs of tracks, but no incontrovertible evidence. Yet they collected many other mammal and bird specimens. Sheldon's book makes interesting reading, of definite interest to the hunter who has an interest in a bygone era.

The two young explorers eventually went on to serve with distinction in World War II, followed by distinguished careers. Borden went on to become one of the most famous wildlife photographers. Sheldon obtained a doctorate in Vertebrate Zoology and became a renowned wildlife research scientist.

9 THE SETTLERS

■ THE FIRST PERMANENT SETTLEMENT

Kelly Lake is a Metis community east of Tumbler Ridge, just west of the B.C.– Alberta boundary. It represents the first permanent settlement in historic times.

Tracing their ancestry to Cree–speaking women and French Canadian voyageurs and traders of the North West Company, the adventuresome Metis moved westwards in a series of steps, from the Red River area. This was partly in response to a nomadic desire to explore and inhabit untouched territory, partly to changing circumstances such as the disappearance of the immense herds of bison. It also represented flight from the encroaching European culture and its government.

In the wake of the Riel Rebellion many Metis became fugitives from the expansionism that was occurring across the prairies. The trail took some from the Batoche region in Saskatchewan to Lac Ste Anne, a mission sixty kilometres west of Edmonton. Most of the original settlers of Kelly Lake were born in Lac Ste Anne, and to this day an annual pilgrimage is undertaken there by their descendants. Another move westwards around the beginning of the nineteenth century led to Flyingshot Lake, three kilometres southwest of present–day Grande Prairie. From here they began to establish traplines and hunt in the foothills and mountains to the west. Within years of their arrival at Flyingshot Lake, increasing numbers of settlers and farmers followed, and these Metis chose to move west again, to Kelly Lake, in search of a suitable homesteading area.

The Settlers

The exact date of arrival is unknown, but is likely around 1910. Narcisse Belcourt and St Pierre Gauthier were the first arrivals, followed by the Gladu, Calliou, Gray and Hamelin families. It is claimed that Monkman Pass was discovered by Gauthier.

A Syrian fur–trader soon established what seems to have been an unwholesome presence in the fledgling community, but was soon bought out by Jim Young, one of the heroes of the early days. Young established a store in 1922, traded furs, and was largely responsible for the establishment of the first school in 1923. He left Kelly Lake in 1927, became a regional celebrity in Rose Prairie, and lived to be ninety-three.

Gerry Andrews was the first schoolmaster from 1923-25. This was the beginning of a distinguished career. He went on to become British Columbia's Surveyor General and Director of Mapping. His mapping skills were invaluable to the Allies in World War II. His initial class contained 12 pupils, only one of whom could speak English, and initially Andrews knew no Cree. After two years, it is claimed, they spoke the best English in the district, as they never encountered any colloquial or incorrect versions.

Andrews wrote an absorbing and heart–warming book about Kelly Lake and his experiences there, entitled "Metis Outpost". He is lavish in his praise of the people of this tiny community. With the first permanent snow of winter, the men would head out to their trapping grounds, which included the drainages of the Murray, Flatbed, Kiskatinaw, Redwillow and Wapiti Rivers, in short, much of the area that now surrounds Tumbler Ridge. Dogs would pull their birchwood toboggans. The men would stay on the traplines all winter, except for a short Christmas break. The woman snared smaller animals locally. The hunting and trapping lifestyle was greatly favoured over agriculture.

The residents of Kelly Lake have continued to trap in this area ever since. The camp where Five Cabin Creek enters Kinuseo Creek was a favourite location. Dave Gray is one elder, well into his eighties, with a wealth of stories from decades of trapping, especially in the Bone Mountain, Onion Lake and Wapiti Lake region.

In the 1950s, maps were produced indicating all the area's traplines and their owners. Examining these provides an instant who's who of that time period: Albert Belcourt, Eddie and Joseph Calliou, Daniel Gauthier, Isidore Gladu, David Gray, Albert Hambler, Clarence and James Letendre, John Terry, Olna Warn, Louis Young. With the exception of Terry and Warn, these are all Kelly Lake names.

As Andrews pointed out, there is now no avenue of further retreat, although the area these people were the first to occupy in recent times has seen dramatic development. While the folks of Kelly Lake have proven themselves resilient and adaptable, the issue of whether the changes inflicted upon them have been adequately addressed politically has not been resolved.

■ THE CALLIOU FAMILY

There are a number of threads that run through the annals of early exploration of the area. One of these is how so many travelers met the Peck family. Another name that keeps cropping up is Jim Ross, who outfitted the expeditions from Hudson's Hope. But the name one probably encounters most frequently of all is Calliou (or Callao, or Callihoo).

Calliou is one of the esteemed names of the area in First Nations history. Louis "Karhiio" Kwarakwante was one of the two very first Iroquois to come west from Quebec as voyageurs for the Hudson's Bay Company, soon penetrating as far as Lesser Slave Lake. He is likely buried near Grande Cache. Many of his descendants took the name Calliou as their surname, and joined the Metis community at Lac St Anne. Much of the Calliou genealogy is available at www.compusmart.ab.ca/museum . Some of the very first Kelly Lake inhabitants were Callious, and Calliou Lake and Calliou Creek were named after the first arrival, William Calliou.

By the time Cautley of the Boundary Commission explored the area in the 1920s, the "Calliou Trail" was a known feature leading south from Kelly Lake. Cautley had hoped to use this trail, but found that it was a winter trail and not at all suitable for his summer expeditions as it passed through extensive swamp and muskeg.

Plate 36: Pete Calliou, veteran guide.

Plate 37: Bill Taylor, Johnny Napoleon and Pete Calliou carrying camera equipment for Gray's 1928 expedition.

Photographs reproduced with permission from Sherman Gray and the Boone and Crockett Club.

The second generation of Callious included three brothers, Joe, Pete (Plates 36, 37) and Sam. Then, as now, there was movement between the Kelly Lake First Nation and the Salteau First Nation at Moberly Lake, and these Callious settled near Moberly Lake.

All three brothers guided Prentiss Gray on his first expedition, and Pete and Joe were with him on the second expedition. The admiration Gray had for them is plainly evident in his journals, and the fact that he rehired them is a tribute to their skills. Interestingly, Pete Calliou believed that he was the first to have penetrated the upper reaches of the Murray River when trapping there in 1919. The brothers lugged Gray's heavy camera equipment all over the alpine, and assisted in the making of some of the first motion pictures of wild game in North America. Pete Calliou was with Gray when they came across Red Deer Falls for the first time.

When Sheldon and Borden passed through Moberly Lake in 1932, who should come out to greet them and give them valuable advice about the Sukunka River which they were going to explore, but Pete Calliou. The activities of the brothers can be traced through the decades by means of the B.C. annual report of the Provincial Game Commission, which contains a guide list. As late as 1947 the three brothers Joe, Pete and Sam were still listed as guides operating out of the Moberly Lake area, and must have been the foremost experts on much of the area at the time. Apparently their descendants are to be found in the Kelly Lake region.

Guide–outfitting became a family business in the 1940s for another branch of the family at Kelly Lake, led initially by Johnnie Calliou and then his sons Charlie and Cliff. They maintained up to forty pack–horses and developed a clientele from the U.S.A. and Europe, conducting circular trips three weeks long. Later 'Calliou Outfitters' arranged fly–in floatplane trips to Belcourt Lake, which served as a base for their trophy–hunting clients.

Plate 38: Kathleen Peck.
Courtesy of the Fort St. John North Peace Museum.

■ THE FIRST SETTLERS NEAR PRESENT–DAY TUMBLER RIDGE

Towards the end of the nineteenth century, the Klondike and Omineca gold rushes saw the passage of prospectors through the northern Peace country. Some stayed in the area to prospect on the gravel-bars of the Peace and Pine Rivers, and some began homesteading and trapping. In the early part of the twentieth century, settlement by Caucasians was also occurring in the Pouce Coupe area and agriculture was beginning. Pioneers amongst these settlers began trapping in the northern part of the area.

Possibly the earliest settler in the immediate vicinity of present–day Tumbler Ridge was Victor Peck. Born in Missouri in 1885, he came to Canada in 1906 and Pouce Coupe in 1910. He settled and built a cabin a mile downstream from the confluence of the Wolverine and Murray Rivers. In 1914 he married Kathleen Shepherd, an English nurse who had come to the Peace district to visit her parents. They raised four boys in this isolated spot, and he successfully established a trapline from Kinuseo Falls down to the Murray Canyon.

Mrs. Peck (Plate 38) seems to have made a habit of impressing important explorers. Holzworth visited in 1923, and wrote:

> "I found Mrs. Peck and three bright boys, the oldest six years. Mr Peck went out two weeks ago for operation….. Mrs. Peck was doing the buying, digging potatoes, caring for stock, shooting meat and fishing when required. A very bright cheerful woman and a wonder under the circumstances. Runs her own trapline in the winter. She has been here seven years and her husband three or four years before her – came on with nothing but a rifle and a bag of flour."

When their oldest son was ready for school, the Peck family moved to Hudson's Hope in 1924, where Victor became a forest ranger and later operated the ferry. Prentiss Gray met her there in 1927 at the start of his expedition, and arranged that she make five mosquito nets for his party, as she had the only sewing machine in town. His comments provide a vivid insight into the hardships of frontier life:

"Mrs. Peck was a fine type of frontierswoman who, when she found that I was eager to learn all I could about the country, welcomed the chance to talk. Her conversation, stored up during the many months of lonely life in the woods, poured out in overwhelming volume...She was at this time 37 years old.... In Pouce Coupe, which most people would consider the edge of civilization, she had married Peck and they decided they would really pioneer, taking up from the Government free land, as they had no money...they filed on a homestead on the (Murray) River where the nearest homestead was 40 miles away. They raised some cattle and enough hay to feed them. She and her husband each maintained a trapline over 50 miles long...sleeping at night when away from home in a brush lean-to. From their traps they earned the $500 a year necessary to buy clothes and such food as they could not raise on their farm. For seven years they kept up this struggle while four boys were born to them."

Yet another explorer to enjoy the Pecks' hospitality at Hudson's Hope and be favourably impressed was the twenty–year old Bill Sheldon in 1932, who remarked upon

"... one of the most delightful acquaintances one could make in the north. They got married and went to live for nine years on a homestead far off on the (Murray) River. In this wilderness home she gave birth to four sons. When the oldest was seven they moved to Hudson's Hope to give the children a better opportunity for education. I have never seen more attractive, healthier children in any backwoods settlement. Mrs. Peck was a woman of slight build and a very attractive personality, with a surprisingly broad and intelligent outlook on life. She grew so attached to her home on the (Murray) that she hated to leave, and she stated she was not as happy in Hudson's Hope as if she had been there in her self-supporting home. She told us of an unusual experience that Vic had. He had shot a moose and lay down to sleep on a moose trail near the carcass. In the night he was suddenly awakened by another moose who stepped directly over his head. He snatched up his rifle and shot the moose... Vic Peck was one of the most successful trappers in this country."

Kathleen died in 1954 and Victor in 1964. Their descendants still inhabit the Peace region. Peck sold his trapline to Frank Gesler, who drowned in the Murray River while crossing it on a raft in 1935. The trapline was passed on in turn to Art Skinner, Bill Warn and Bill Goodwin.

Bill Warn is one of the legendary old–timers of the area, born in 1907 in Swift Current, Saskatchewan. He recently wrote a book, "Trapping to Survive for 90 years". Written in anecdotal form, and concentrating on his trapline in the present–day Tumbler Ridge area, it allows understanding of the early trapping life, and sheds light on such interesting events as the 1939 flood that caused the drowning of a family of eight near the confluence of the Murray and the Pine, the immense logistics of rescue of injured fellow–trappers, as well as numerous bear encounters. Later he manned the Puggins Mountain fire lookout. Now into his nineties, he lives in Dawson Creek, and has recently remarried.

Settlement actually occurred before the land was officially surveyed, and the residents were consequently known as "squatters". Not all the citizens were apparently as solid as these worthy pioneers. As with most remote corners of the North American West, there are dark tales of murderers and cutthroats, of fugitives from justice who found sanctuary of a sort in these unpatrolled foothills and mountain fastnesses.

■ RANCHERS OF THE WOLVERINE VALLEY

While a number of early ranchers and trappers came and went, some of the best known, because of their incredible longevity, and connections with the recent past, are Kate Edwards (Plate 39) and John Terry (Plate 40) of the Wolverine Valley.

"Aunt Kate" Edwards was born as Katherine Coutts in Ontario in 1861. She married a widower with a family but had no children of her own. After she was widowed, she came to the new frontier, the Peace River Country, aged 51, in 1912. She chose the isolated Wolverine, 300 kilometres from the nearest railway and 160 kilometres from the nearest settlement of Pouce Coupe, for reasons she gave in an interview with the Toronto Star in 1926.

The Settlers

Plate 39: 'Aunt Kate' Edwards. Reproduced with permission from the South Peace Historical Society

Plate 40: John Terry
Credit: Darcy Jackson.

> "I wanted to get land somewhere near civilisation… But there's a rule which prevents people without dependants securing land in the block. We are always being bothered by silly laws made by people who know nothing what-so-ever of conditions in the west…It was impossible to get a grant of land near people unless I told a pack of lies."

This tribute was paid to her in "The History of the South Peace":

> "Aunt Kate dressed like a man, talked like a man, and smoked a pipe like a man, thereby scandalizing some of the 'well-brought-up' ladies…she was a rancher, she drove and rode horses like a ranch-hand. No hands were more gentle, coaxing a flicker of life into a tiny premature baby, nobody was more tender in caring for a wee mite too small or too weak to be carried, except on a pillow. Nobody could be more careful, stoking the fire, night and day, so that the wee occupant of a shoebox on the ovendoor could have exactly the right amount of extra heat, that is now provided in a hospital 'incubator'. No veterinarian could more firmly suture a gash in a horse - or a man. The lash of her tongue was the only anaesthetic needed if the latter didn't hold still. Some women disapproved of her, some men were afraid of her, but many of both sexes and all ages admired her - even loved her."

Up to three times a year she would drive her stock to the railhead, supported by shacks she had constructed every 70 kilometres. She was renowned as midwife, doctor and nurse to other trappers and their families in the area. This true pioneer stayed on her ranch into her seventies, until the authorities made her move to Dawson Creek, as she was thought to be too old to live independently. She died aged 97 years.

She summed up her feelings in the interview with the Toronto Star:

> "It's a great life and a great country; I wouldn't want to change it for the world."

In 1947 in Dawson Creek, she met John Terry. Terry was born in Melfort, Saskatchewan in 1912. He moved to farm in Alberta, married and raised a family there. He saw active service in World War II, then moved to Dawson Creek, where he started a shoe and harness business. Meeting "Aunt Kate" was a personal turning point for him. She persuaded him to take over her ranch which had been unoccupied for almost 15 years, and he spent the next half-century there ranching, guiding, and trapping. He guided many of the survey parties for Denison Mines in the late 1960s.

To get to Dawson Creek in the early days he would ride the trail down the Wolverine and across the Murray, then over the hills past Muskeg Lake and onto Fellers Heights. This trip would take up to ten days, and the river crossings were fraught with hazard. It could not have been easy for someone like John Terry to experience the encroaching development of his piece of paradise, with a forestry road and railway line virtually crossing his backyard. One of his many talents was writing poetry, and one of his poems ended with the following verse:

> *And when I'm old and weary,*
> *And my days on earth are still,*
> *Let my bones rest here in freedom*
> *By my cabin in these hills.*

His wish was granted. John Terry died in 2000, aged 88. Unlike Aunt Kate Edwards, it was possible for him to stay on his ranch virtually to the end, aided by his family and friends, and many caring Tumbler Ridge residents. Terry initially may have had doubts about the town that was springing up downstream, but in later life came to appreciate its people and the assistance they provided him.

Just two weeks before his death, he was asked how he would relive his life if he had the opportunity. His reply was typical:

> *"I'd live it right here, and twice as hard! There was a time in my life when my soul asked for a change. I am forever grateful to old Aunt Kate and the Wolverine for seeing what I needed and filling that need. I think everyone needs a valley, maybe not a literal valley like mine, but a quiet place where they can be alone long enough to know God. I don't believe a man has to shine his shoes and go to church every week to know God!"*

■ THE MONKMAN PASS EPIC

Just to the southeast, an epic adventure began unfolding in the late 1930s. The construction of the Monkman Pass Highway is a tale of bravado and dedication in the face of great odds, that was defeated eventually only by the outbreak of the Second World War.

Alex Monkman (Plate 41) is one of those credited with finding a route through Monkman Pass, one of the lowest passes through the Rockies at under 1 100 metres above sea level. Monkman was one of those on their way to the Klondike who had stayed to operate a trading store at Lake Saskatoon, between present–day Grande Prairie and Beaverlodge. He developed a trapline westwards into the mountains. In 1922 he met trappers on the Murray River who had come in over the mountains from the west. He then traveled over what came to be known as Monkman Pass and reached the Herrick River. There he found a 1904 Grand Trunk Pacific railway stake. The following year he guided an engineer over the pass.

Northwestern Alberta farmers were struggling because of impossibly inconvenient export routes for their products. Their products had to go via Edmonton and then the Yellowhead Pass. A 300 kilometre route through the mountains would allow access to the railhead at Hansard. They were faced with successive governments that showed no interest in their plight.

After years of unsuccessful petitioning for a railway, Monkman and a bunch of fellow–volunteers decided to take matters into their own hands and build the route across the pass themselves. They formed the Monkman Pass Highway Association and selflessly laboured over the next years to make this a reality.

In 1937 an advance group blazed the trail right through the mountains, while work crews followed and cut an eight–foot wide swath from Rio Grande in Alberta as far as Stony Lake. Before the next season they effectively mounted a publicity campaign, and in 1938 a group of four traveled the pass on horseback with a symbolic bag of grain.

A number of names became household words for a few years, then were forgotten for decades. Examples are the Big Spring (Plate 42) where water gushing out of the earth and falling off a cliff provided

Plate 41: Alex Monkman on horseback.
Reproduced with permission from Bev Whalen.

Plate 42: Ted Chambers bathing in the Big Spring – reproduced with permission from Dale Chambers and Joan Jones.

welcome relief to weary trailblazers, and Lake Joan, named by Ted Chambers after his infant daughter Joan who at the time fitted neatly into a shoebox. There was the Green Bowl, a beautiful rock–encircled meadow with excellent feed for horses, and Hell's Half Acre where a massive rockfall impeded easy passage.

The trail crew had extended the trail enough that it was considered feasible to try to get an automobile, the Pathfinder Car, over the pass. In a mood of increasing optimism and jubilation this vehicle was driven, coaxed, pushed and pulled with the help of horses and rope over a variety of obstacles.

Entrepreneurs were taking note, predicting 20 000 vehicles in the first season. There were applications for lots around Monkman Lake, and Monkman National Park was proposed. The Pathfinder Car was making eight kilometres a day when winter struck and reduced the rate of progress. Eventually the car bogged down within 28 miles of its destination. With one more good day of weather, it was claimed, they would have made it.

Increasing economic problems and the lack of cooperation from the B.C. government signaled difficulties, but in the summer of 1939 these pioneers persisted, and were within sight of victory. A photographer, Leake, had come to take the first quality photographs of the region's beauty spots, and his study of Kinuseo Falls (Plate 43) remains a classic. Euphemia McNaught had created its first paintings. (McNaught, now a centurion, became a famous artist, and still resides in Beaverlodge). Ted Chambers had recorded the epic in a fine photograph album. A movie camera had captured the first crossing of Monkman Pass by a brave group of women.

Then on 6 September the news came that Britain was at war, and Canada would follow. Some of those pioneers died in action. Monkman himself died on his farm in 1942, and after the war the B.C. government prohibited further work on the road and closed the pass area. The government then gave the citizens of Dawson Creek and Fort St John the choice between the longer Pine Pass to the north, or Monkman Pass. Despite their prior support for the Monkman Pass, the fact that it would not have passed through their communities swayed them, and thus the current road and rail route follows the Pine Pass.

The Settlers

Plate 43: Leake's 1939 photo of Kinuseo Falls. Reproduced with permission from Beaverlodge & District Historical Society.

Plate 44: Leake's 1939 photo of Brooks Falls. Reproduced with permission from Richard Brooks.

In the whole history of the Peace Country it is hard to match this co-operative act of heroism. Monkman Pass, the Albright Ridge, Chambers Ridge, Mt Watts, these names commemorate the names of that hardy band of pioneers. Their route took them through some outstanding scenery, notably past "The Cascades", a series of ten waterfalls on the way to Monkman Lake. Carl Brooks and Guy Moore were two legendary names in these endeavours, and with the help of their descendants, residents of Tumbler Ridge successfully submitted a proposal to the B.C. Geographical Names Commission to have the two most spectacular of the falls commemorate them.

Carl Brooks was recorded as the discoverer of the falls that now bear his name (Plate 44). He lost his life in an airplane crash in Kakwa in 1945, guiding a party of hunters. In 1999 the Brooks family congregated at Brooks Falls and constructed the following plaque set in concrete:

> *"Named after Carl Brooks who in 1937 with Ted Chambers and Shorty McGinnis led by Alex Monkman blazed a trail thru the Monkman Pass for the Monkman Pass Highway Association"*

Guy Moore went on to enjoy a distinguished career in government in Manitoba. But he never lost interest in the Monkman Pass area, and successfully campaigned to have many of the place names along the route officially accepted. In 1990, shortly before his death, he wrote in a letter that his own favourite falls were those below Brooks Falls. These are now officially named Moore Falls.

Near the summit of Monkman Pass, Moore and his companions had climbed a mountain filled with Forget Me Not flowers on a perfect summers day, now named Forget Me Not Mountain. Guy Moore's ashes were scattered on its summit by his family, in keeping with his wishes.

Tumbler Ridge matriarch Janet Hartford was a teenager at Kinuseo Falls in 1939, and terrified those who watched her ascend the cliff beside Kinuseo Falls. She was guided on horseback to Monkman Lake. Carl Brooks' son Richard was also on this trip, and 58 years later a reunion was coordinated in Tumbler Ridge between Janet and Richard. He is another of those who tasted something of the area in his youth, became entranced with it, and has never stopped returning.

The Settlers

Plate 45: A pioneer sits on the porch of one of the cabins at Kinuseo Falls, 1939. From Ted Chambers' photo album, reproduced with permission from Dale Chambers and Joan Jones.

Plate 46: Cliff Duke lights a gas seep, 1950. Credit: Cliff Rennie.

■ THE FIRST TOURISTS, AND ALMOST ANOTHER TOWN

Entrepreneurs were quick to take note of the development of the Monkman Pass Highway, at a time when the country was in the grip of a depression. Rudi Jacobs, a German immigrant, was one of the first of these. He noted how the route passed by the attractive expanse of Stony Lake (Plate 88), and realised that transportation and accommodation could be provided. So in 1938 he quickly built five cabins, a small store, and six boats, and employed a full time cook, Pearl Robinson, who served fare that focused on freshly caught fish from the lake. Jacobs Passenger Service advertised Stony Lake as the gateway to Kinuseo Falls and Monkman Pass, for swimming, motor–boating and fishing. Tourists were quick to respond, and one weekend in 1939 sixty people were camped at the cabins. (The ruins of these cabins can still be visited by canoe or motorboat.)

Jacobs also provided transport as far as the road had advanced, and tourists had to walk the remaining distance to Kinuseo Falls, unless Carl Brooks had been notified in advance, in which case he would be there with horses to meet them. Just above the falls Alec Watt and Bruce Albright had secured a land lease on 150 acres, and had constructed five 12 foot by 14 foot cabins (Plate 45) and a restaurant had been constructed. On one famous weekend there were no fewer than 200 visitors to the falls. Guests were offered an optional guided trip to Monkman Lake. (These cabins were subsequently vandalized beyond repair, and their ruins were removed during the development of Monkman Provincial Park)

One of the most interesting places along the Monkman Pass route was the Big Spring. There were many who assumed that the work would resume after the Second World War. They reasoned that such a long route would need supply communities. Because of the perennial and abundant supply of clean water, and the flat nature of the nearby terrain in the Kinuseo Creek valley, it was an obvious choice as a townsite. It was surveyed in 1941, with the spring at the southeast corner of the lot of 328 acres. However, it faded into oblivion when the highway did not materialize. The surveyed area has remained under private ownership ever since, an island in a sea of forested crown land.

10 DISCOVERY AND USE OF THE NATURAL RESOURCES

■ THE DISCOVERY OF THE FOSSIL FISHES

The end of the Second World War heralded a new era of exploration. The U.S. government retrained ex–servicemen in various fields. In 1947, as part of this program, Lowell Laudon led a group of geology students from the University of Kansas into the Wapiti Lake area, in search of new petroleum resources, and to "establish an island of geological knowledge" in the northern Rockies which were still virtually unknown from a scientific viewpoint. Instead they discovered a remarkable fossil site.

The party comprised Laudon, his wife, three sons and nine students. To fund the trip the Laudons mortgaged their home and purchased a Republic "Seebee" amphibian plane. They chose Wapiti Lake because its size offered a convenient landing site.

Unfortunately on one of the last trips in, the plane landed downwind and suffered damage to its hull. Basic repairs were done at the lake, and the plane managed to take off. For four days they waited in vain for the plane to return, then two members set off for Grande Prairie to investigate. Two hours before they arrived there, the plane left for Wapiti Lake, having had to go to Edmonton for full repairs and to await the arrival of a new bulkhead from the U.S.A. . This was the only real setback the expedition encountered, although they experienced almost two months of bad weather.

After the major geological work near their campsite just below the lake was done, they set off on a nine-day packing trip to explore the region. They made camp near a lakelet that would subsequently be called "Fossil Fish Lake".

Soon they discovered:

> "*excellently preserved specimens of ganoid fishes…a great number of Triassic fossil fish, many of them several feet long, weathered out and lying bare for our inspection.*"

They named the ridge of mountains the "Ganoid Range" after the type of fossil fish they had found.

Other parties soon followed their lead. Representatives of the National Museums of Canada, the Geological Survey of Canada, the American Museum of Natural History and various universities all visited the area to collect specimens, and in time important fossil reptile discoveries were also made.

Typically these expeditions would travel by pack train from Stony Lake and camp at Fossil Fish Lake. More recently scientists from the University of Alberta and the Royal Tyrrell Museum of Palaeontology have led the research, coming to collect specimens almost every year. Helicopters have replaced pack trains.

All in all thousands of specimens have been found and removed for research, averaging about ten specimens per person per day. This confirms the international importance of the site, which is now formally protected in Wapiti Provincial Park.

Visitors to the site today will be impressed by its remoteness and beautiful surroundings, but will be disappointed by the lack of obvious fossils.

■ NATURAL GAS

Most of the area relapsed into obscurity during the Second World War. But one important discovery during the Monkman Pass Highway construction ultimately had far reaching consequences.

One of the participants, Charles Mitchell, had discovered a gas seep in 1937, and he spent the war years trying to convince the government of the importance of this find. In 1948 the Geological Survey of Canada sent its first expedition, guided by Mitchell, to investigate further in the area around Stony Lake. The first well was soon drilled nearby at Lone Mountain.

In 1950 Mitchell went to Vancouver and managed to interest a consulting geologist and entrepreneur, Bert Nesbitt, in his find. Nesbitt canvassed the oil companies he knew, but found that he could not raise interest until he actually acquired licences for the area himself. Once he had done this, he had no problem dealing them off to the companies.

Nesbitt contracted the geological mapping of these licences, and later in 1950 he employed four geologists to investigate the Kinuseo Creek area. Party chief was Aaro Aho, who was later credited with the discovery of the Faro mine in the Yukon.

A young graduate geologist in the party was Cliff Rennie, who has provided a number of anecdotes of their expedition. The packer was Cliff Duke, a veteran of the Monkman Pass expeditions.

The party mapped traverses along Kinuseo Creek and Onion Creek (where they found coal) then headed over Quintette Mountain, down Flatbed Creek to its junction with the Murray, and up the Wolverine Valley. Rennie recalls finding an old cabin with a fenced grave near the site of the current Lions Flatbed Campground, along with cattle skulls, the remains of an unsuccessful ranching attempt during the 1930s.

They camped at this site for three weeks, and had some time to idle away. Rennie remembers how he and Aho used axes to carve two wooden faces on trees nearby. They painted these with ochre from a pulverised ironstone concretion.

In the Kinuseo Creek and Redwillow River areas they found a number of gas seeps. Grizzly tracks converged on these seeps. The grizzlies would dig them out, and the water coming up with the gas would form a pool. One way to find gas seeps was simply to follow grizzly tracks. Rennie speculated that the water and mud might have insecticidal properties which the grizzlies had discovered. Throwing a lit match onto such a pool would cause flames five feet high (Plate 46). He recalls putting a match down a hole where the water had evaporated, and causing an underground explosion.

■ FORESTRY

Compared with the other resources, the trees did not need to be 'discovered'. It was simply a matter of waiting until the commercial opportunities and technology were available to make use of this resource extraction. Operations were begun in the late 1950s, a time when more oil and gas exploration was also occurring and the first seismic lines were cut through the area. Fire towers were constructed at two sites: Puggins Mountain and Thunder Mountain. The former was broken down a few years ago and a new one erected in its place, but is very hard to reach nowadays. The Thunder Mountain tower is still operational and accessible, and provides an excellent view of the mountains. These towers were manned for months on end by dedicated individuals who did not mind working in isolation.

One argument that Tumbler Ridge residents have is the lack of ownership of this resource, reinforced by the daily sight of trucks of logs leaving the community with little if any discernible local economic benefit. The argument continues that a sense of ownership would increase healthy stewardship, and that local residents would be less likely to damage the resource on their doorstep than those from further afield.

■ COAL

In 1952 the B.C. Government formally allowed filing for oil and gas exploration permits in northeastern British Columbia. Deposits were 5 cents per acre, to be refunded if it could be shown that enough had been spent on mapping and exploration. Among the first to grasp this opportunity was the Polish–born team of Julian Suski and his daughter Madelaine Suska, who organised an expedition in the summer of 1953.

There were still no good accurate maps of the area, which was simply left blank on the provincial and federal maps, so they purchased aerial photographs and compiled these into the first photo–mosaics.

The expedition comprised Julian and Madelaine, four pack–horses, three saddle horses, and two guides. They surveyed two claim areas. One was in the Sukunka and Burnt River drainages. The other was an eight–mile by eight–mile area that included Mount Spieker, Mount Collier, and Mount Reesor. There were no trails whatsoever in the permit area, and they were told that they were the first to explore it.

Madelaine Suska relates how, in climbing Mt Collier (site of the present–day Bullmoose Mine) her clothes and face were dark with coal-dust by the time she reached the summit. They performed the first detailed geological analysis of this area, showing that the Cretaceous rocks possessed important coal sequences. They reported on the potential for oil and gas discoveries, and produced geological maps that were used as a reference for many others afterwards.

It had been known for a long time that the Peace District boasted coal resources. Alexander Mackenzie had noticed coal in the Peace River Canyon in 1793. A number of small private enterprises had sprung up near Dawson Creek and Beaverlodge in the early part of the century. But the thickness of the sequences in this area was something new. Ms Suska informed the BC Department of Mines of these thick coal seams, but it was maintained that coal mining in this region was economically unviable.

In the late 1960s, the global energy crisis loomed, and altered people's perceptions about what was feasible. It was announced that applications for exploring the coal resources would be accepted. Denison Mines was one of the successful applicants.

Exploration increased dramatically as mining exploration crews began surveying the region. By the late 1970s, fifteen coal deposits had been identified. The geographic isolation of the deposits was the next hurdle to overcome. The barrier of the Rocky Mountains, the distance to the ocean and the main Asian and European markets, and the lack of any local roads and infrastructure meant that any development would have to be vast in scope. Forty studies were commissioned by government to ascertain the viability of developing the resource and the development of the town of Tumbler Ridge. The Japanese Steel Industry was identified as the prime potential customer.

Finally in 1981, representatives of the Japanese Steel Industry, Denison Mines Ltd., Teck Corporation and the Government of British Columbia signed an agreement that allowed the Northeast Coal Development to proceed. Thousands of people were employed over the next three years to realise the plans.

The Quintette and Bullmoose Mines would be developed, with a combined projected annual capacity of over 8 million tonnes of coal. A paved road was built from Chetwynd to the site of Tumbler Ridge, and BC Hydro likewise had to build a transmission line from the Bennett Dam. BC Rail had to build a branch line right through the Rocky Mountains, through two massive rail tunnels, respectively nine and six kilometres long. The problems posed by these long tunnels demanded that the line be electrified. BC Rail also upgraded its line all the way to the intermediate destination of the coal: Ridley Island near Prince Rupert, where Ports Canada built a coal terminal capable of handling 12 million tonnes of coal annually. "1 000 Man Camp" and "350 Man Camp" were constructed near the Quintette minesite.

All this work continued at a frenetic pace for three years. Don Philips, the MLA for Peace River, and Minister for Economic Development, had been one of the project's greatest supporters, and he drove in "the last spike" on November 1, 1983, and the first shipment of coal was on its way from Bullmoose Mine to Ridley Island and ultimately Japan. In the summer of 1984 Stephen Roman (the head of Denison Mines) and Bill Bennett jointly pushed a plunger on a mountaintop near the Quintette mine, and detonated half a million kilograms of explosives. A lavish million dollar party ensued in Vancouver.

The Quintette Mine By Kevin Sharman

The systematic exploration of the coal fields in northeastern British Columbia began in 1969. The Quintette mine was developed by Denison Mines Ltd. The mine was designed to produce 6.3 million tones of coal per year. The Bullmoose Mine, also located in the northeastern coal fields, was developed during the same time frame as Quintette. The result was the largest single industrial undertaking in the history of the province. Investment by all parties to bring the mines into production was CDN$2.5 billion. Contrary to public perception, the mine never received subsidy payments or government bailouts. The mine operated from 1983 to 2000.

The mine survived through troubled times. World coal prices started to decline about the time the mine was built. Teck Corporation became the manager of Quintette in 1991 and an owner following completion of financial restructuring in 1992. The mine ran well until the expiry of the original 15 year contract in 1998. The coal price declined 5% in 1998 due to the Asian economic downturn, and a further decline of 18% in 1999 meant that the mine was uneconomic. It ceased production in August 2000.

Following this the already comprehensive reclamation process was expanded. At high elevation, all dumps are first helicopter seeded with a commercial alpine grass mix and fertilizer. Then seeds are collected from native plants on nearby mountains such as Babcock or Spieker, and the seeds are grown in a greenhouse. Seedlings are then transplanted to waste dumps in an island formation. Over time these native plants colonise the surrounding area. Mountain goats are attracted to the mine due to the escape terrain afforded by the pit walls and reclaimed dumps.

Revegetation programs at lower elevations include dumping of large, esker-like ridges which increase shelter for animals and provide windbreaks. Commercial grasses and legumes are planted, followed by native species, such as willow for ungulates and berry shrubs for bears. Perch sites, rock piles and woody debris piles are placed for raptors and carnivores. Then a conifer-planting program begins.

Air and water quality are assessed to ensure that the environmental impact of the mine is minimized. Water quality is protected by sediment ponds, which treat surface water runoff by settling out the sediment. Waste products generated by the mining process are collected and recycled.

Quintette Trivia By Kevin Sharman

- Period of operation: 1983 to 2000
- Coal production: 65 million tonnes
- Number of trainloads of coal (100 cars each): 6500
- Total rock moved: 567 million cubic meters (1.47 billion tonnes)
- Peak number of employees: 1600
- Total area disturbed: 3733 hectares
- Area reclaimed by the end of 2000: 1518 hectares
- Weight of largest mining shovel: 900 tonnes
- Cost of one tire for haul truck: $18,000
- Number of transplanted high elevation native seedlings by the end of 2000: 124 000
- Number of conifers planted by the end of 2000: 116 000
- The 13-kilometre overland conveyor generated power as it carried coal down from the pits to the plant.
- Highest temperature recorded at plantsite: 34 C^0
- Lowest temperature recorded at plantsite: -46 C^0
- Highest wind gust at summit: 121 km/hr
- The mine office for the Mesa and Wolverine pits was aptly named the Eagle's Nest. With its location high on a ridge above treeline, it saw its share of wind. In high winds, the walls of the building would flex several inches and water in the toilets would slosh around. One employee commented that it wasn't <u>really</u> windy until there were whitecaps in the toilets!

The town had to be built from scratch, and there are a number of "old–timers" full of war stories from the early days of the fledgling community. An entire separate book could be written about the people who have come and gone, and especially about those who have striven to make it what it is today. An obvious example is that of George and Janet Hartford. For these retired teachers, retirement is not the same thing as it is for ordinary mortals. Between them, there is hardly a committee or board they have not sat on, a good cause they have not supported, a volunteer position they have not filled. They serve as a timeless example, and have graciously agreed to provide a summary of the early days in Tumbler Ridge.

The Early Days in Tumbler Ridge
By George and Janet Hartford

Twenty years ago there wasn't much to see....just an idea really. However it was decided a short while earlier that a community should be built here to house the miners of the proposed coal-mines and a small group of people gathered to sign the requisite papers to define us.

For exact details of how it happened, contact Buck Wong, the only one of the original signatories still living in Tumbler Ridge. Even he was not here, but living in Calgary at the time.

While this was going on I was an alderman (name has been since changed to councillor) in Dawson Creek. We were asked, along with the other neighbouring communities, if we favoured a community near the mining facility, or did we prefer the miners to be sent to a camp on a shift basis? I felt it would be great to be part of the new town if that ever happened, so Janet and I opted to come out here if the opportunity presented itself.

We tried to find the place by following a logging road out here in 1981. We actually went too far and stopped approximately where the turn off to Quintette is. We had a bite to eat and went back to where the present entry to town is. There was a construction site there and we wended our way through a trail where a survey crew had started laying out the framework for the town. We were able to go down to the Flatbed where the present Lions Campground is and talk to a couple of people. As there were no bridges, and the road to Bullmoose was not yet built, we turned around filled with questions about where the town would actually be built, what it would look like, where the schools would be, etc.

In the spring of 1982 we had teaching positions in Dawson Creek, but by then the speculation was over and the construction had begun in earnest and we volunteered to go to Tumbler Ridge. By September there were construction crews coming in to get the various jobs done. One of these camps was at Quintette and, although living was a bit primitive, some of the crews brought in their families to the Kilborn construction site to live in trailers. The school district, a bit reluctantly, opened up a skid shack, with a bathroom, for elementary students. Shortly after it was apparent that a one-room classroom would not be enough.

I was sent off with the principal, who had no lodgings in Tumbler Ridge, to visit the schools in Williams Lake to see if their curriculum would meet our best-guess needs. We packaged many of the materials they had given us, and they languished in unopened containers after we arrived and opened the doors to the enlarged and very different clientele who descended on us. These were not the typical rancher, rural students from Williams Lake. They were a very mixed bag of students. My favourite student had spent the last year at home in Norway, but had done her Christmas Shopping in Kuwait! We later found she had been born in Fort St. John while her father was an engineer building the W.A.C. Bennett Dam in Hudson's Hope. One of the first students to enroll came to school every morning in his uncle's helicopter. Uncle was helping build the tunnels for the railroad.

My first accommodations were at the Thousand Man Camp built for the main workforce at Quintette. The secondary school (another secondary teacher and I) moved in to the original skid shack, now divided into two classrooms. The elementary school staff had grown to three plus a principal. The elementary school was put in the smart executive housing for the Japanese dignitaries.

By the fall of 1982, the layout of the town was obvious and although no houses had been completed, many were being constructed. No streets were paved so it was common to drive down Willow with two wheels on the sidewalk and two in the muddy potholes.

Our school arrived in pieces and it was quickly hammered together into a modest but practical building ready for our use by the end of October. At the same time Aspen Drive was the location for the first town employees: Fire Chief, Building Inspectors, etc. The school district used the same area to bring in trailers for the teachers and that is where we all spent the rest of the first year together.

We had recess every morning, and, when queried as to why some of the *girls were late returning to class, they excused themselves by informing us that there were the "cutest guys!" working on the first houses being constructed just a short block from the school!*

In November of 1982 a builder moved in to his new home on Birch – the only occupied house in TR. Most of the students were bussed from the Quintette Mine Site until the Pinewood Mobile Home Park was ready for occupancy. (At the beginning all those trailers were exactly the same). For Christmas 1982 everyone in town was invited to a party at Quadra Camp. A copy of the signatures of those attending is posted in the Library.

Miss Anderson's class kept a weekly total of the construction taking place and, by the end of 1982 their figures showed:

Apartments: six under construction – none occupied
Mobile homes: 60 on site – 38 occupied

Even in the start up phase we were all hooked to water, sewer, had propane service, and electricity. At first we had to go to the temporary telephone service at the first town centre at the turn off from the highway. This had postal service, bank, ambulance and town office, plus a few shops.

We had a community centre (now the New Life Assembly building, since moved from its original location adjacent to the portable school). We had TV – one channel – provided by Quadra Camp – that really focused on adult type entertainment until the TV Society decided it needed to be altered!

Oh yes, and we had fun!

11 THE RECENT PAST

■ LATTERDAY EXPLORERS

In contrast to the more touristed southern Canadian mountains, the Tumbler Ridge area has been explored only by few hardy souls in the last few decades. Some have completed adventures of epic proportions.

Chris Townsend walked the length of the Canadian Rockies in 1987. In many ways he found the Tumbler Ridge area the most difficult, as he got horribly lost in the eastern foothills until he bumped into an Alberta–B.C. boundary monument. Then he stumbled starving into the Redwillow campsite and was revived by two Tumbler Ridge hunters.

Peter Vacco took the concept a step further by hiking from Mexico to the Arctic, but spread this over many years. En route to Tumbler Ridge he almost drowned crossing the Narraway River. In town he was presented with a memento by the mayor, then became absorbed with the Monkman Pass concept, and followed in the footsteps of the pioneers. His description makes for sober reading. He described the summit of the pass as:

> "a joy to walk through, and the last enjoyable feature of the hike"

He considered the impenetrable forests of Fontoniko Creek the central node of plant life in North America. After five miserable days of bushwhacking he reached Hobi's Cabin exhausted. Then he did what the pioneers had done in 1938: he built a raft and floated down the Herrick River to civilisation. However he got sucked under a logjam and was fortunate to survive.

In 1999 Karsten Heuer and two companions in an epic 28 day ski–touring expedition along the Continental Divide, traveled from Jasper to Kinuseo Falls. They then canoed down the Murray River, all part of Heuer's Yellowstone–to–Yukon adventure to promote environmental awareness of the importance of the integrity of the Rocky Mountains.

The Wolverine Nordic and Mountain Society and the Ridge Riders Snowmobile Club continue a systematic exploration of the area.

■ THE EVOLUTION OF TUMBLER RIDGE

Tumbler Ridge developed into a model rural mining town, aided by its beautiful foothills setting and its inspired design. At its peak the town boasted a population of almost 5000. But the transience of much of its population, and the lack of comprehensive home–ownership policies caused it to be a stepping stone, rather than a permanent home, for many. The difficulties of competing on the world market, decreasing coal prices, the fluctuating value of the Canadian dollar, and the complex geology of the coal–bearing rock (which made extraction of the resource more difficult than anticipated) led to a series of workforce reductions. In 2000 the Quintette Mine closed down, with predictions that the Bullmoose Mine would cease production in 2003.

The community faced a crisis, and predictably both government and the media were prepared to write it off. They did not reckon with the determination of its residents and councillors, who expertly dealt with the perceived quagmire of obfuscation constructed by CMHC (Canadian Mortgage and Housing Corporation). This proved to be the key to future prosperity. Within weeks T.R. Housing Corporation was formed under the able leadership of Al Galbraith, the most experienced person in Canada in selling homes in remote communities. Around 500 homes were put on the market and within four months a staggering 98% of these were sold, with long waiting lists established for the next batch of homes for sale. The prophets of doom were forced to eat their words, and have been replaced by visionaries of a different kind who recognise opportunity and potential when they see it. Prepared to stay the course, they realise that they are privileged to live at a pivotal moment in the community's evolution.

12 MAPS

Discussion of the maps of the Tumbler Ridge area can be divided into two categories. First there is the fascinating issue of the maps of the pioneers and first surveyors, copies of which have been located, to be placed in the future Tumbler Ridge Museum and Archives. Second there is the practical issue of current maps, and which ones are the best to use for various activities.

■ HISTORIC MAPS

The early explorers mentioned a map made by Murray (after whom the Murray River was named) and Copley early in the century. Copley was still around when Prescott Fay met him in Hudson's Hope in 1915. This would be the one of the first maps of northeastern British Columbia. It would be interesting to see how much was marked 'Terra Incognita'. To date I have been unable to trace this map.

Prescott Fay's 1914 expedition broke new ground, and he was congratulated by the U.S. Biological Survey for "clearing up one of the blank spaces on the map of North America". It is not surprising then that the map his party produced is the oldest located map of the area. It is a beautiful work, remarkable for the small number of errors it contains. He produced both a route map and then a more detailed map of the area he had traversed.

At roughly the same time, Frederick K. Vreeland of New York was engaged in a topographic reconnaissance of the area on the southwestern flanks of these ranges, and he too produced a map from his studies of 1914, 1915 and 1916, which provides some information on the high mountain ranges. Fay and Vreeland corresponded, and Vreeland's map includes mention of Kinuseo Falls.

J.C. Gwillim working for the Geological Survey of Canada produced the next map following his unsuccessful exploration of the area for oil and gas. He was a meticulous recorder, and his map was masterly for the features along his route. Yet he admitted to its vagueness and inaccuracy for the areas he did not cover. Specifically, his map indicates precisely where the historic "Tumbler Range" was situated.

By the 1920s a number of other maps had been made, and both Holzworth and Prentiss Gray inserted their routes onto different maps of the region. Holzworth wrote:

> "A study of all the published maps of the Canadian Departments showed most of the country as unexplored. Such maps as there were showed the main waterways vaguely drawn and subsequent actual travelling of the country showed them to be mostly erroneously sketched."

In 1925 R.W. Jones, working for the C.N.R. and researching possible railway routes through the mountains, compiled a map that included data from all known existing maps. Its enhanced accuracy does not extend to the Monkman Pass, which had only been officially recorded in 1922. In fact it leaves out the sizeable Monkman Creek and Monkman Lake completely, and shows a totally unsuitable pass between Upper Blue Lake and Limestone Lakes. On the copy I possess, someone has erroneously gone and marked "Monkman Pass" through this fanciful feature.

Also by 1925 the Boundary Commission finished its work on the 120th meridian, and published a beautiful map. This map is very long and narrow, as it just covers the area on either side of the meridian.

Over the decades, improvements in technique and technology allowed for ever–improving map quality, but in 1953 the father–daughter expedition of Julian Suski and Madelaine Suska still could find no adequate maps of the areas they wished to explore, near the current Bullmoose Mine. Instead, they used aerial photographs and compiled the first photo–mosaics.

Later aerial photography had progressed to the point where the detailed 1:50 000 – and 1: 250 000 map series could be produced. Although the margin for error was much reduced, this method was by no means perfect, omitting features such as the Big Spring and Stone Corral.

■ CURRENT MAPS

The map you need is determined by what you are seeking to do in the area, and what degree of detail you require.

For purposes of driving and gaining an overall feel for the area, two maps can be recommended:

The Dawson Creek Forest District Recreation Map at a scale of 1 : 340 000 has good detail of the road system and shows drainages and forest service campsites. It is available at Travel Info Centres and from the Forest District Office in Dawson Creek – phone (250) 784 1200.

The Outdoor Recreation Map #16 – Peace-Liard Region is one in a series of similar maps of B.C. It is published by the Outdoor Recreation Council of B.C., scale 1: 250 000. It has contour lines, which the Forest District Map doesn't, but is quite dated as regards roads. It includes information on trails and other attractions in the entire Peace–Liard region. It is available at Travel Info Centres, or from the Outdoor Recreation Council – phone (604) 687 1600

For hiking, the *1: 50 000* maps remain a standard, although they suffer from being older, and therefore obsolete as regards roads and other man–made features. The new edition when produced will include many more official place names in the area. These used to be available from B.C. Government Agents across the province, but currently need to be obtained from private outlets. Most of these are available at

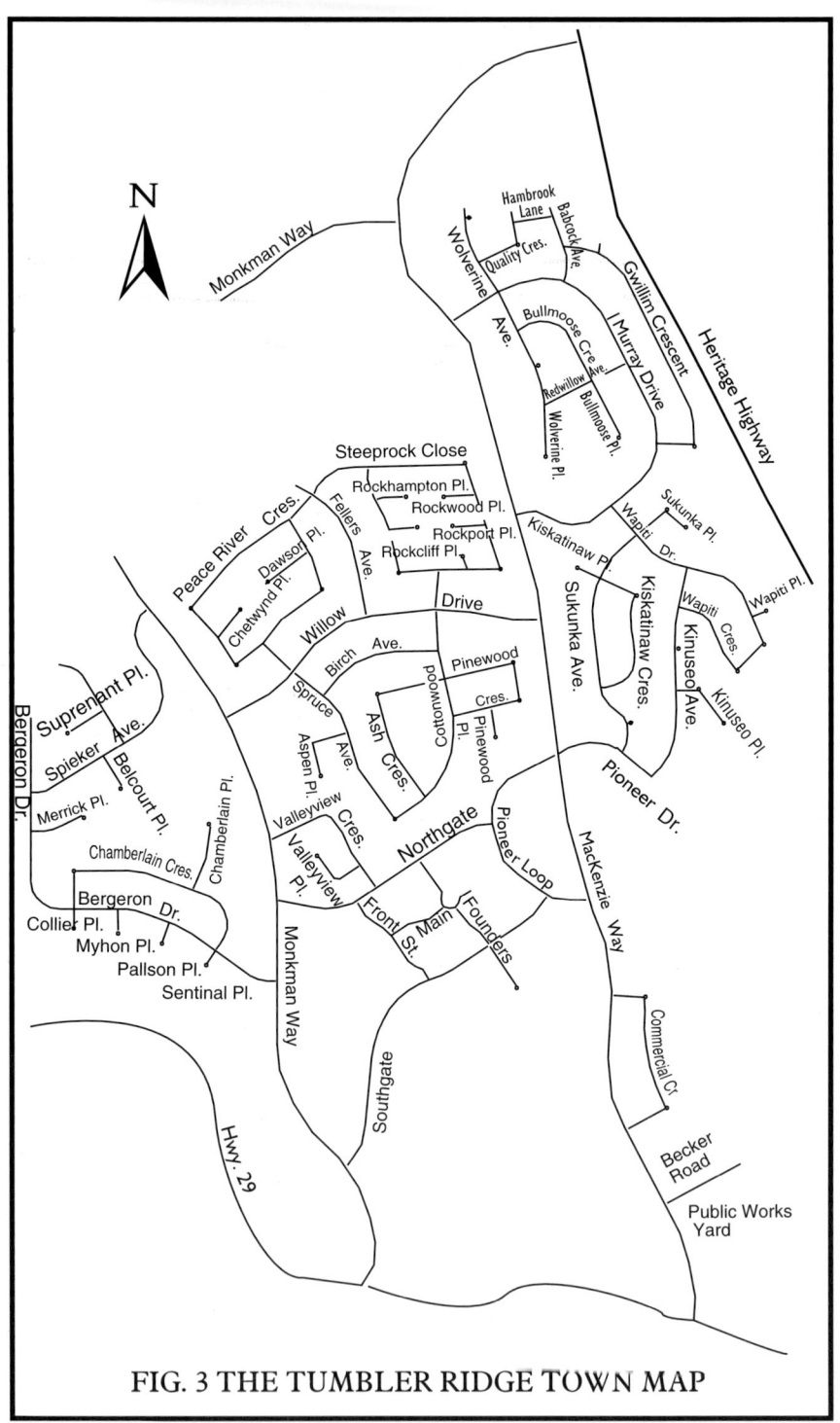

FIG. 3 THE TUMBLER RIDGE TOWN MAP

the Tumbler Ridge Travel Info Centre. They are also stocked by Corlanes in Dawson Creek and McElanney Associates in Fort St John. You usually need to specify the map number, which in the Tumbler Ridge area includes:

TUMBLER RIDGE AREA TOPOGRAPHIC MAPS		SCALE 1: 50 000	
Map Number	Location	Map Number	Location
93 P/7	Sundown Creek	93 P/6	Gwillim Lake
93 P/5	Burnt River	93 P/4	Sukunka River
93 P/3	Bullmoose Creek	93 P/2	Tumbler Ridge
93 P/1	Blackhawk Lake	93 I/16	South Redwillow River
93 I/15	Kinuseo Creek	93 I/14	Kinuseo Falls
93 I/13	Sentinel Peak	93 I/11	Monkman Pass
93 I/10	Wapiti Lake	93 I/9	Belcourt Creek
93 I/8	Belcourt Lake	93 I/7	Wapiti Pass

A recent addition is the set of **TRIM maps**, at a 1: 20 000 scale, in black and white. These show good detail and accurate contours, but are hard to obtain.

The Gold Standard in many respects is not a map at all, but *aerial photographs* viewed with stereoscopic glasses that show the land in incredible three–dimensional detail. These are held by Ministry of Forests in Dawson Creek, and can be inspected by prior appointment – call (250) 784 1200.

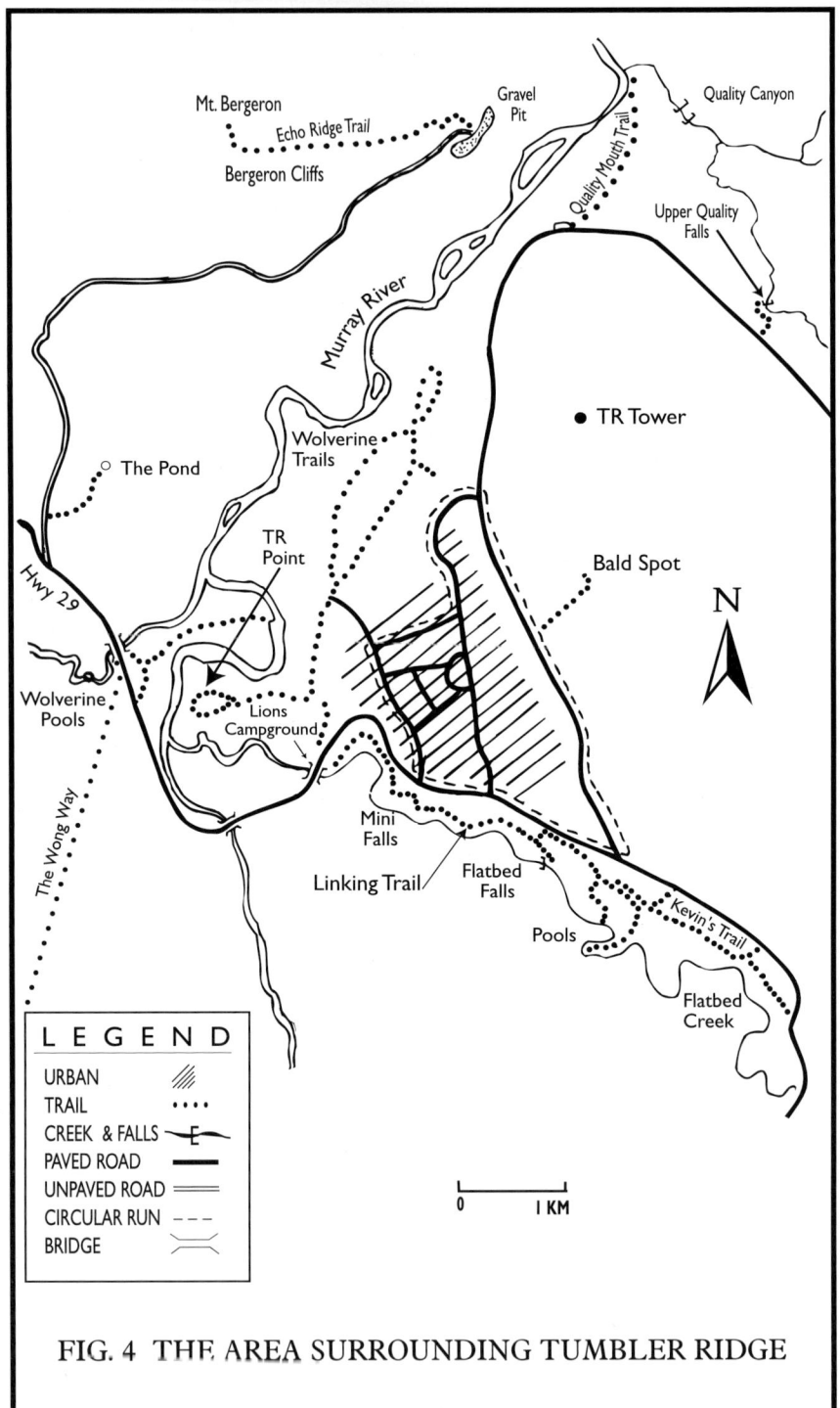

FIG. 4 THE AREA SURROUNDING TUMBLER RIDGE

13 THE DESTINATIONS

■ AROUND TUMBLER RIDGE

Tumbler Ridge has an inspired design, surrounded by foothills and forest. It comprises three tiers, centering on an accessible downtown core with business district, Community Centre and Health Centre. Enough woods are preserved within the town to maintain its rustic atmosphere, and there are many parks and walkways within town. Just outside the town limits there is a network of trails, some of which are official, others just favourite walks of residents that have evolved over the years. Between the Tumbler Point Trail, Flatbed Campground and the Linking Trail, the Wolverine Trails and the Bald Spot Trail, the town is surrounded on all sides by quality trails.

The Kids Triathlon

Every year in February the kids of Tumbler Ridge and surrounding communities have the opportunity to take part in a unique, fun-filled, healthy competitive event. The Kids Triathlon has 4-6, 7-9, 10-12, and 13–15 age categories, with individual and team entries for cross-country skiing, skating and swimming events. These events are held in close proximity to each other. The field is capped at sixty entries. Organised by volunteers who care for kids, this popular event is followed by a healthy lunch and prizegiving.

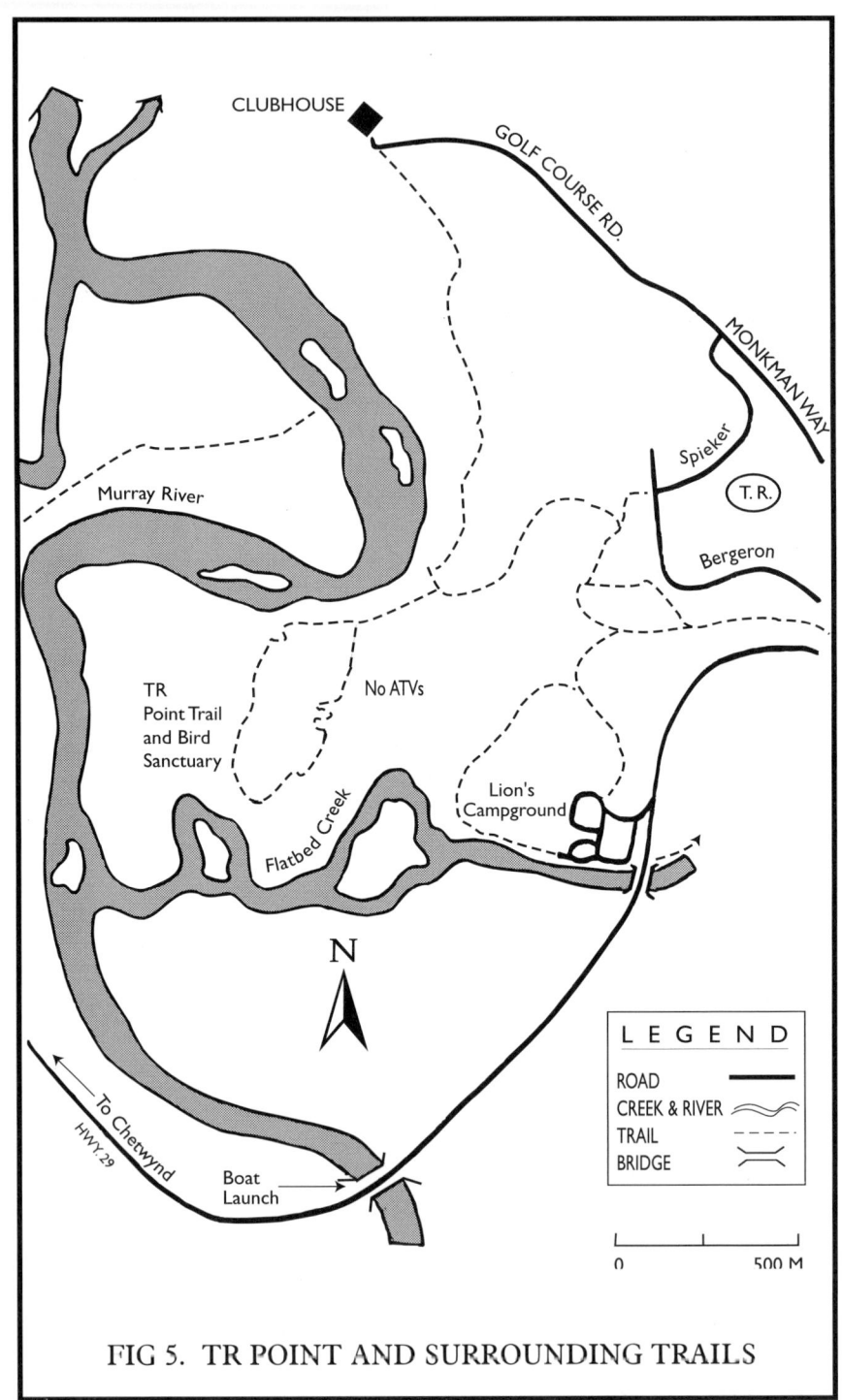

FIG 5. TR POINT AND SURROUNDING TRAILS

The easiest way to reach TR Point is to use the town map, and get to the bottom end of Bergeron Drive, near where Spieker Avenue enters it. Between #332 and #404 there is a walkway that leads west into the forest. Turn left at the T, the trail then curves to the right around a large ditch. Do not descend to the left, but head into the forest without losing elevation. You will see a large sign that introduces visitors to the Tumbler Point Bird Sanctuary. Some people walk the trail and complain that they did not see birds, not

DESTINATION #

NAME:
TR Point

FEATURE
Scenic Trail and Bird Sanctuary

ACCESS:
4 KM trail adjacent to Tumbler Ridge

realising that there is a favourable season and time to go birding. May and June are by far the best months, and the best time of day is undoubtedly early morning. The beauty of this trail is that it follows the edge of an escarpment for most of its 4 KM length, allowing a view down onto the forest canopy, which is where many birds are to be found. ATVs are prohibited on this trail.

After a few hundred metres in the forest, the trail reaches the escarpment and then hugs it faithfully, with a fine view of the Big Flat, the area of deciduous woodland below, leading the eye to the hills and mountains beyond. This was first described by Prescott Fay in 1914 after his monumental trip:

> *"This flat is at least a square mile and is covered with the best of grass and pea-vine but now all frosted and brown. In the summer it would easily be a sufficient range for two hundred head of horses. It is without doubt the finest flat I have ever seen in the foothills. Its edges are mostly fringed with poplar with here and there a clump of spruces. Tipi poles and meat racks were numerous. We forded the river here, and, thank God, we left it, with the hope of never seeing it again as for five weeks it has caused us considerable trouble, worry and work."*

A trail to the right provides a pleasant link with the golf course, two kilometres away. If you keep left, and stay on the escarpment, you will complete a small circuit including TR Point. I have some concerns about the long–term safety of this trail as some parts are prone to slides. Avoid the edge in spring thaw or very wet weather.

At two steep sections there are alternative sets of switchbacks. TR Point or Tumbler Point is a favourite lookout point. There are good views of Flatbed Creek below, near where it enters the Murray. Over the last few years there has been lots of natural change here. The old river course is plainly visible, and still fills up in times of flood, but was obstructed by a slide off the point in 2000, and you can see the new shortcut that the creek has taken. The views change to include the Murray River, which flows broadly by here in a majestic sweep.

You can return the way you came or take the trail to the golf course parking lot. It also follows the escarpment, and provides a couple of different views of the Murray River valley.

...

DESTINATION #2

NAME:
Lions Campground

FEATURE:
Riverside campground with trails

ACCESS:
Roadside

The Lions Flatbed Campground is situated just below town, one kilometre out on the road to Chetwynd. Apart from being a favourite picnic and swimming destination, it serves as a convenient trailhead.

It is situated in predominantly deciduous woodland, filled with mature aspen trees. This attracts a number of bird species not easily found elsewhere around Tumbler Ridge. The Philadelphia Vireo, for example, having migrated north and west for thousands of kilometres along the aspen belt, is confronted by coniferous forest when it reaches the foothills. So it travels along the fringes of deciduous forest along the banks of rivers like the Murray, in search of tracts of forest like this in which to breed. This bird is thus at the limit of its distribution here.

Trails lead from behind the campground that traverse part of this woodland, and an easy flat circular trail is possible. This is a good trail for forest flowers in summer. There is one moderately steep trail that leads up the slope to the lower level of Tumbler Ridge, and this forms the most convenient way to walk to the campground from town.

From the parking area next to the bridge over Flatbed Creek, a trail known as the Linking Trail (linking the campground and Flatbed Falls) leads upstream under the bridge. In summer there is a pleasant pool in Flatbed Creek here, at the base of the cliffs. Young kids swim here while their parents watch, older kids dam up the pool to create a chute down which they can tube, and teenagers living on the edge jump into the pool from a height. The latter cannot be recommended.

DESTINATION #3

NAME:
Linking Trail

FEATURE:
Scenic trail

ACCESS:
3 KM trail, roadside trailhead

The trail continues up the bank of the creek, climbing steeply in places, with nice views of the cliffs and creek below. For birders, this is the easiest and most reliable place to find Yellow–bellied Flycatcher in summer (listen for a plover like whistle emanating from the forest). There are some eroding areas with steep drop–offs where caution is needed, especially with children. Near the top the trail has been eroded alarmingly and it is essential to veer left into the forest up the newly built alternative trail, as the old trail is extremely dangerous. Despite these drawbacks this trail is very pleasant, and always seems to offer something different with each season.

Once it reaches the plateau (on the same level as the town) the Linking Trail levels out and continues to follow the valley edge. There is a turnoff left that leads to the highway. If you are coming from town and want to reach the Mini–Falls, you will use this access route. Refer to the map for directions as to where it starts.

DESTINATION #4

NAME:
Mini–Falls

FEATURE:
Cascades with pools

ACCESS:
Steep 300 M descent off Linking Trail

After a few hundred metres the trail to the Mini–Falls branches off steeply down to the right. Unfortunately this trail was made with an obsession for directness, and no thoughts as to erosion prevention. It descends mercilessly down a bare slope, and only flattens out a bit at the bottom. Serious consideration should be given to rebuilding this trail in a more sustainable fashion. That said, the Mini–Falls remains a

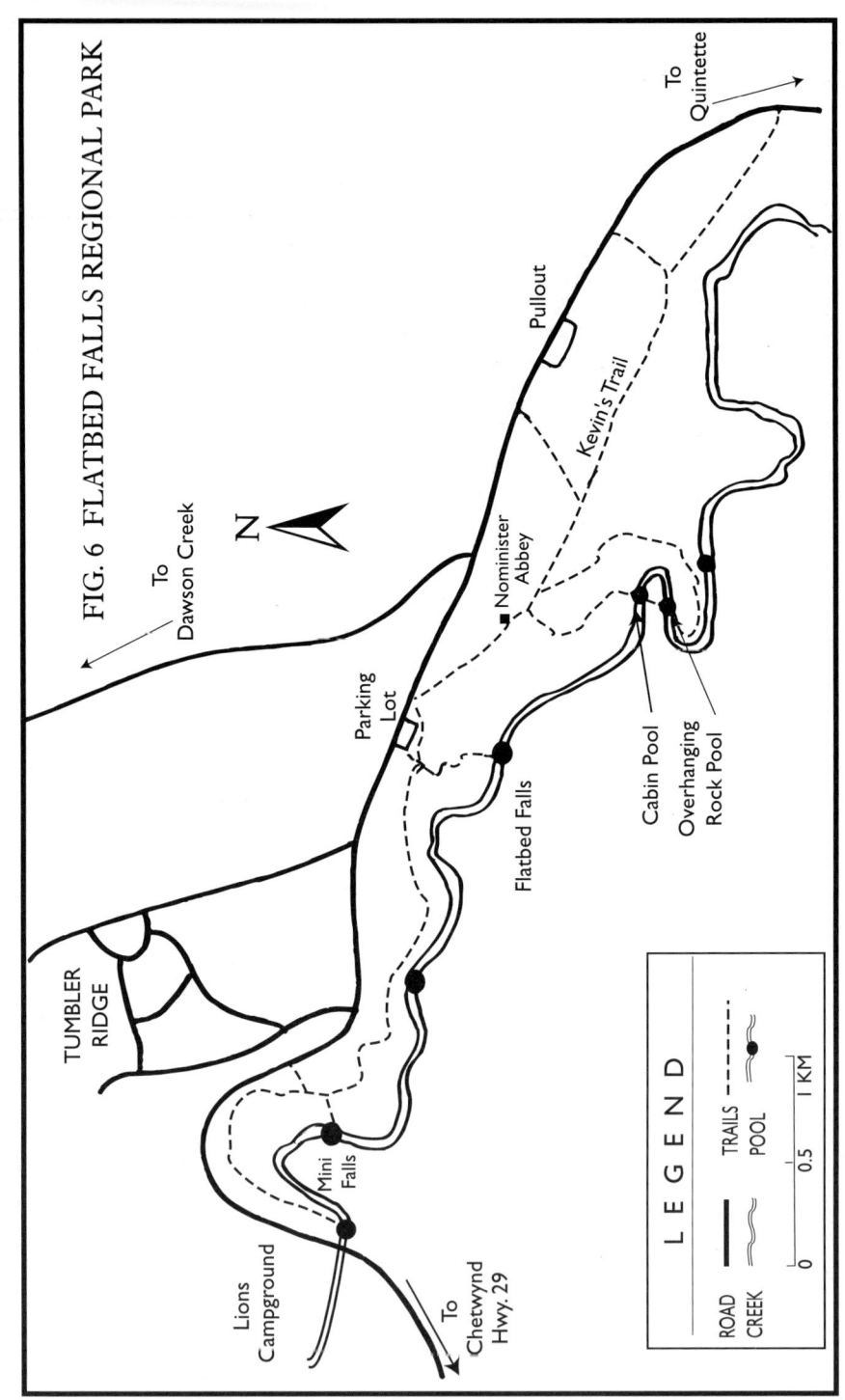

worthily popular destination. Here Flatbed Creek drops a few feet a few times in succession, forming delectable pools. The bottom pool is deep enough for safe jumping in most seasons, if you know where to aim as you fling yourself off the rock above, and climbing back out of the pool is facilitated by a natural rocky staircase. This is a great place to lounge away a summer's day on the rocks, and occasionally take a jump in the pool or cast a line into it. Always check the depth of the pool for submerged structures before jumping, and do not dive.

The Linking Trail continues along the valley edge through thick forest, with occasional clearer patches and views of the river below. After two more kilometres it joins the trail to Flatbed Falls. To access this trail from the highway, head out of town on the road to Quintette, and soon you will see the large parking area on the right with a big sign indicating "Flatbed Falls Regional Park". The trail starts at the right side of this area, and curves up to join the Linking Trail.

The trail to the falls makes a couple of steep S–curves down the incline (again, more thought could have been given to erosion prevention in its construction) and then flattens out where there is an old beaver dam on the left, and a large structure on the right that serves as an outdoor education centre. Beyond this, the trail crosses a small creek and then reaches the falls. Flatbed Falls (Plate 47) are moderately wide and not high, but their proximity to town, convenient access, rocks suitable for lazing about, and the pool at their base, have combined to make them an enduring favourite over the years. Again, jumping into the pool is not randomly advised, unless you have thoroughly plumbed the depths below; there are unexpected rocks in the pool, and each year there may be different submerged logs. A number of injuries have occurred here.

Every year, for a few weeks in spring thaw, the creek changes into a raging muddy torrent, and Flatbed Falls become a transient kayaking mecca. It is an incredible sight watching these experienced plyers of white water shoot off the edge of the falls, disappear

DESTINATION #5

NAME:
Flatbed Falls

FEATURE
Small falls near Tumbler Ridge

ACCESS:
1 KM hiking trail, steep in places, roadside trailhead

Plate 47: Flatbed Falls.

Plate 48: Kevin Sharman biking Kevin's Trail.
Credit: Birgit Sharman

into the foaming waters of the pool, and sometimes surface upright.

...

In recent years enterprising volunteers, notably Kevin Sharman, have taken it upon themselves to build a further extension to the Linking Trail, one that ends up on the highway over three kilometres away, near the upper bridge over Flatbed Creek. These trails have significantly increased the simple hiking and cycling opportunities close to town (Plate 48), and are known as the Upper Flatbed Trails or simply Kevin's Trail.

DESTINATION #6

NAME:
Kevin's Trail

FEATURE:
New trail near Tumbler Ridge

ACCESS:
3 KM trail, roadside trailhead

To access Kevin's Trail either follow a flagged extension from the beginning of the Flatbed Falls trail along a section known as the Missing Link, or walk next to the road for fifty meters from the parking lot until you reach the trail, or park at the pumphouse further up the hill, cross the road, and ascend the slope to gain the trail.

The first section of this extension is known as the Razorback, for obvious descriptive reasons. It seems incomprehensible that this was developed for mountain–biking purposes, and that cyclists will not inevitably hurtle down one side or the other of the knife edge. The trail then follows a beautiful escarpment edge, weaving in and out of the forest, before coming suddenly upon Nominister Abbey, a grandiose title for a wooden structure built in the early days of Tumbler Ridge, and recently cleaned up. One version is that a fugitive from justice hid out here for a whole summer before being apprehended.

Continuing past the Abbey, note a fork just below a steep section, where the trail passes through a gully. Straight ahead is the continuation of Kevin's Trail, which continues in much the same vein, complete with two shortcuts that allow access back to the highway. (These are flagged where they strike the road: one is just beyond the road to the next pumphouse on the right; the end of the trail is flagged just before the road descends to the creek crossing.)

The fork to the right leads to Cabin Pool on Flatbed Creek. The remains of a makeshift old cabin are situated just above the pool in the

Destinations

 # 7 DESTINATION

NAME:
Flatbed Rock Pools

FEATURE:
3 sunny pools on Flatbed Creek

ACCESS:
1 KM offshoots off Kevin's Trail

forest. This is an ideal spot for sunbathing, as the rocks that surround the pool and cascade are blessed with summer sun for over twelve hours a day. The pool has a sandy bottom, and there is a natural beach on the far shore. Like the other four sites on Flatbed Creek that are easily accessible, this pool is best enjoyed at relatively low water.

There is one more delightful portion of Flatbed Creek with pools that begs a visit. To reach it you must continue a short way further along Kevin's Trail, until it veers left away from the escarpment. Look for a side trail to the right which may be flagged. This hugs the escarpment, slowly curving to the right and leading down to a very tight S–bend in the creek. Here are two more lovely pools as well as an open stretch at the foot of a set of cliffs that has exciting rapids. A tubing option for kids is to start upstream at the pool, descend the rapids, and nip back over the narrow neck of the meander, to repeat the process. For younger kids adult supervision is essential at the two main rapids, and helmets and flotation devices are necessary for all. High water is unsuitable for kids, although this is when kayakers play in these rapids.

The lower pool has an interesting overhanging rock formation. If you wade through this pool just below this rock, and continue along a short stretch of trail, you will be surprised to find yourself at Cabin Pool, which you can cross to link up with the trail system there. Do not attempt to cross the creek at high water. A long–term plan envisages two 3–wire bridges across the creek, to create an exciting loop trail.

So much for Flatbed Creek in summer. In winter it provides excellent cross-country skiing, once the creek has had time to freeze up well, usually by January. Wolverine Nordic and Mountain Society members usually create the

DESTINATION 8

NAME:
Flatbed Creek

FEATURE:
Creekski near Tumbler Ridge

ACCESS:
Two road bridges 10 KM apart

trail upstream from the Lions Campground, and try hard to persuade snowmobilers and quadders not to ride over it for the next few months. It leads through beautiful winter scenery, through the Flatbed Canyon, and up to the falls, a return distance of 7 kilometres. There is usually a wealth of animal tracks in the snow to interpret. The falls have their own winter majesty, with a subdued sound of falling and churning water emanating from somewhere under the ice.

The usual backcountry skiing precautions apply, of avoiding the centre of the creek bed, and the areas immediately below the falls and cascades, and being extra–cautious after warm weather.

Another option is to park at the upper bridge and ski down past the falls to the lower bridge. This provides a much more varied ski, with different features, including the Overhanging Rock, a favourite stop for kids. When you reach the falls you need to detour to the right to get around them, and may need to remove your skis for a few metres.

The final two options for skiing on Flatbed Creek involve going further upstream or downstream. Upstream from the upper bridge leads along a route usually well–tracked by snowmobiles. Heading downstream from the Flatbed Campground leads past the cliffs below TR Point, where you can examine the slide of 2000 close up, to the junction of Flatbed Creek with the Murray River. Although the Murray is a popular snowmobiling route, it is not considered a safe skiing destination.

Directly above Tumbler Ridge the paved highway is little used, as most vehicular traffic from either the Heritage Highway or the Boundary Road tends to turn off into town. This makes this stretch of highway an ideal running and cycling route. It is a 10 kilometre circular route from downtown. This is the route used in the annual Ridge Ramble Biathlon. There is just enough elevation gain and loss to make this into a challenging racing or training route, with pleasant views of the Bergeron Cliffs and the mountains to sustain the tired soul. Near the highest point there is a

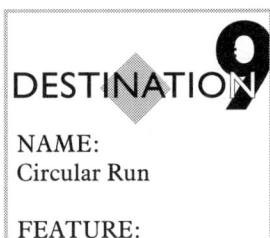

DESTINATION 9

NAME:
Circular Run

FEATURE:
Circular running route near Tumbler Ridge

ACCESS:
On pavement all the way

Plate 49: The Bald Spot offers a view of Tumbler Ridge and its surroundings. Credit: Birgit Sharman.

Plate 50: Lost Haven Cabin.

TUMBLER RIDGE *Enjoying its History, Trails & Wilderness*

small stream above the road, and athletes used to rehydrate themselves here. This can no longer be recommended, as there is an area upstream that has been thoughtlessly misused, and the quality of the water cannot be guaranteed.

> ### The Ridge Ramble Biathlon
>
> *Held on the Saturday at the end of the annual Grizzly Valley Days celebrations each August, the Ridge Ramble Biathlon draws runners and cyclists from the region. Individual and team events challenge competitors over a hilly course of 20 kms cycling and 10 kms running. Runners finish the course just before the parade, which guarantees streets lined with cheering spectators. For further details contact Wolverine Nordic and Mountain Society.*

Another attraction above the road is The Bald Spot (Plate 49), one of the most popular destinations close to town. The trailhead is signposted, adjacent to the gravel road that leads up to a reservoir. It is hard to enthuse about the trail, as it relentlessly follows a cutline uphill. Its only redeeming feature is that is serves as an excellent quadriceps–strengthening ground for masochistic runners preparing for the mountains of the Emperor's Challenge. It is steep and crumbly in places, and the occasional bench is a welcome break. You must take the fork left near the top, this is

DESTINATION #10

NAME:
The Bald Spot

FEATURE
Trail to viewsite above Tumbler Ridge

ACCESS:
Relentlessly steep trail, roadside trailhead

not signposted, and continuing along the cutline takes you nowhere. Many people have made this mistake, with the result that the trail straight ahead looks well used.

After all this negative stuff, the good news is that the view from the Bald Spot is magnificent and worth the effort. Tumbler Ridge is dwarfed below, and a favourite pastime for kids is to work out where they live. Its beautiful setting in the foothills of the Rocky Mountains is best appreciated from this vantage point.

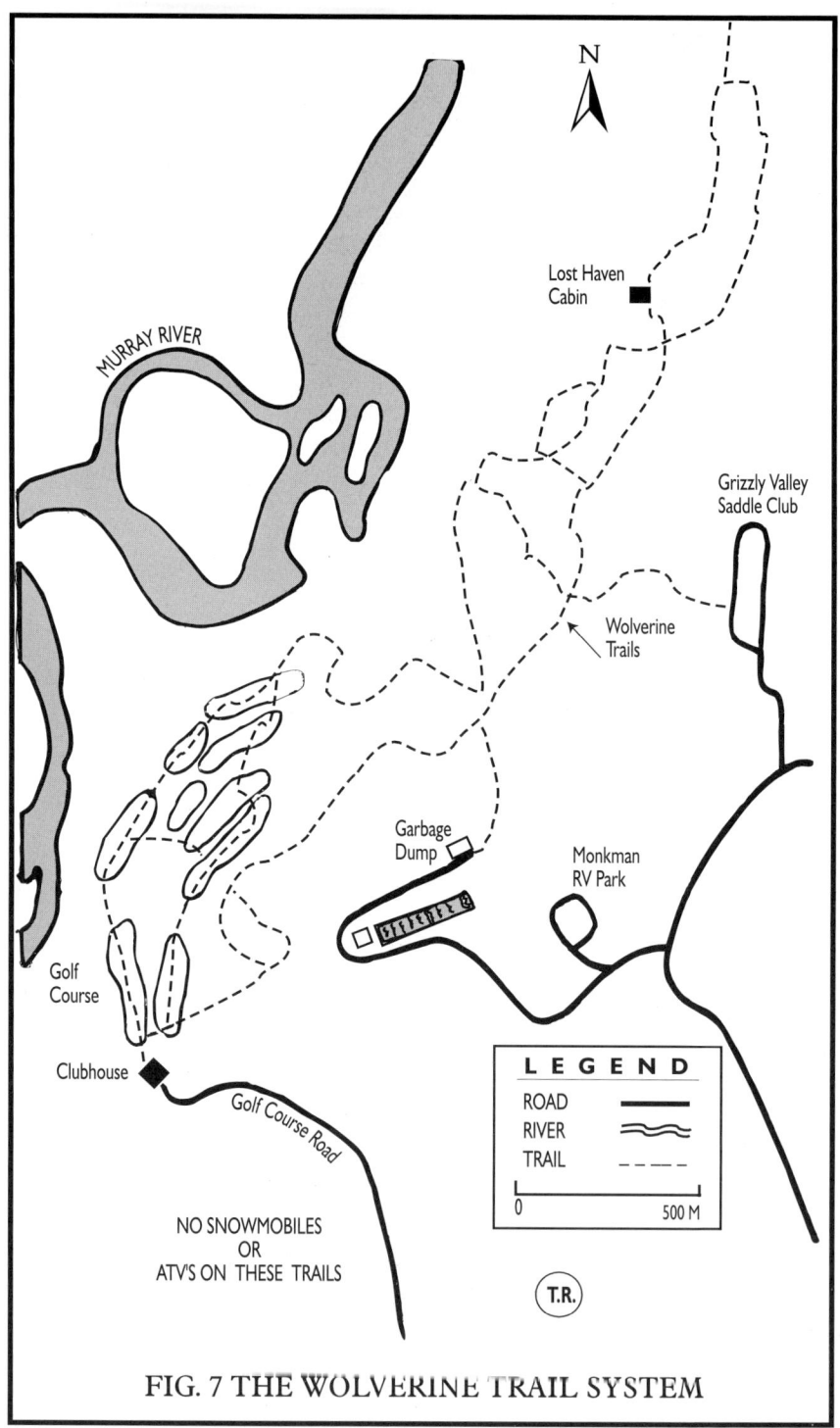

FIG. 7 THE WOLVERINE TRAIL SYSTEM

TUMBLER RIDGE *Enjoying its History, Trails & Wilderness*

Just to the north of town is another precious resource: the Wolverine ski trail system, which doubles up in summer as a great hiking, mountain biking, and horse riding area. The trail starts and finishes on Tumbler Ridge's exquisite golf course. Near the far end of the trails is the Lost Haven cabin (Plate 50), constructed in 1996 as a joint venture between Wolverine Nordic and Mountain Society, District of Tumbler Ridge, and Forest Renewal BC, with the help of the Northern Lights College and Ministry of Forests.

 # DESTINATION

NAME:
Wolverine Trails

FEATURE:
Network of trails past Lost Haven Cabin

ACCESS:
9 KM of trails starting at Golf Course

The Ridge Ramble Cross-country Ski Race
By Birgit Sharman

The Ridge Ramble Cross Country Ski Race is held on the second Saturday each February as part of the Tumbler Ridge Winter Carnival. It is hosted by the Wolverine Nordic and Mountain Society, and begins just below the golf course clubhouse. There are two categories for adults, with a "fun" distance of 6.7km and a "challenge yourself" distance of 20km. The route takes place on the groomed trails of the golf course fairways, and in the scenic woods beyond towards the Murray River. There are also two categories for children, with the Bunnies aged 7 and under skiing a 1.3km loop through the fairways, and the Jackrabbits aged 8-13 skiing this loop twice for 2.6km.

This is a fun event where all of the children take home a prize for their effort, with door prizes for adults The race usually draws 40 to 50 participants, half of whom are children. The golf course clubhouse is the headquarters, and provides a great view of the start/finish area.

The Lost Haven cabin is roomy, with a stove and firewood and a few benches and tables, and toilet outside. It has a large picture window looking out onto the Murray Valley with Mount Bergeron in the background. In winter this forms an ideal focus for a day on the ski trails; in summer the barbecue pit outside is an added attraction. The only drawback is that there is no running water at the cabin, although there is a long-term plan to pipe water from a nearby spring to a site near the cabin. Please be extra careful with your fires. Overnight use of the cabin area is possible only with prior permission of the Wolverine Nordic and Mountain Society. ATVs are prohibited on these trails.

There are two main ways to access the trail system. In winter the trackset ski trails begin at the golf course clubhouse, and leave the golf course at the 4th hole. The are signs at all intersections indicating where you are, and directing the way to the cabin. It is advisable to ski the trails in a clockwise direction.

Tumbler Ridge Golf and Country Club
By Linda Taylor

Registered as a non-profit society in 1986, and overseen by volunteer directors, this beautiful public 9 hole, par 36 golf course and 3 000 sq.ft. clubhouse was funded by a "Go BC" grant and built by dedicated volunteers. Generous donations and expertise were received from local corporate businesses and suppliers and the growing community of Tumbler Ridge.

The watered greens and fairways are tended to by a professional greenskeeper and they meander through the hills and valleys along the Murray River. An all day pass encourages golfers to challenge their skills on this quiet course which includes four elevated greens and one water hole. Fairways are separated by thinned bush and it is not unusual to have one or more trees ricochet an errant shot back onto the fairway.

Wildlife sightings are the norm. This is a beautiful afternoon walk even if your passion is not golf. Stay for lunch and enjoy the view of fairways 1 and 9 from the clubhouse dining room or sundeck. The golf course is open from May–September and has a restaurant, driving range, putting green, club rentals, golf cars and ample parking.

In summer golfers don't appreciate hikers on the golf course, so it is better to begin either at the dump or from the ninth hole of the golf course (see map for details).

In winter, tracksetting is done by the Wolverine Nordic and Mountain Society, and the trails are kept in tip–top shape. There are seven kilometres of tracked trails, and another three kilometres of wilderness trails. There is enough elevation gain to make these trails challenging and interesting, and increasing numbers of skiers come from further afield to test their skills here. The descent of the hill on the fourth hole is fun, as are a couple of steeper short sections and tight corners further along the trails.

The loop trail that starts at the cabin, although not trackset, is by far the most dramatic, as it provides some fine valley views as it follows a level bench that extends along the hillside. A picnic site is due to be built at the furthest point along the loop trail in future. In winter many skiers reach the cabin, light a safe fire in the stove, ski the loop trail, and return to a warm Lost Haven.

Sled Dog Races
By Mark Bernadet

Since 1999 the second weekend in February has become "Race Day" for the sled dogs of the South Peace, when Tumbler Ridge hosts its annual sprint race for both dog sleds and skijorers. Close to 100 dogs come to town to compete in the two to six dog races on a variety of trails. Although the races offer a small purse and prizes, they are very relaxed, characterized more by the friendly welcome than the competition.

Both main highways that leave Tumbler Ridge offer hiking opportunities close to town. The Heritage Highway to Dawson Creek leaves the north end of town, and at KM 6 (with the Visitor Info Centre as your KM 0 point) you come to Albert's Point, a pull out on the left with an expansive view down the Murray River. Into the forest from here, and unmarked, is a hiking and riding trail that leads down to the mouth of Quality Creek, a distance of under three kilometres.

Destinations

Plate 51:
Quality Canyon.

Plate 52:
Upper Quality Falls
Credit: Linda Helm

TUMBLER RIDGE *Enjoying its History, Trails & Wilderness*

Contact Wolverine Nordic and Mountain Society for precise directions if you wish to hike this trail. The rewards are a pleasant fishing spot where the creek enters the Murray River, and access to the lower reaches of Quality Canyon.

...

Quality Canyon (Plate 51) is a little–appreciated treasure close to Tumbler Ridge, a hundred metres deep with vertical friable rock walls. It is a closely guarded secret, in the sense that it is not easy to access. If you follow the creek up from the mouth you will see why. You reach a pool with a small waterfall above, and immediately above that the canyon begins. It is not easy climbing up through this first falls; the rocks are slippery, the canyon wall rocks are soft and break easily, and a slip or fall could be disastrous.

 # DESTINATION 12

NAME:
Quality Mouth Trail

FEATURE:
Hiking trail to Murray River

ACCESS:
Unmaintained 3 KM trail

There is sometimes a window of opportunity in late winter, when the snow is mostly off the ground, allowing hiking to this spot, but the creek is still frozen. Then you can make your way up the lowest falls and walk up the canyon with ease, just being careful to dodge the fragments of rock that fall into it from the magnificent rock walls above. After a sensational few hundred metres you reach the next falls, which are quite a bit higher, and here you need to turn round.

A great way to appreciate the canyon in its middle reaches is on snowshoes. Either access the creek from Upper Quality Falls, described below, or simply bushwhack down into the creek from along the highway. The creek goes through some tight slots, then descends into the canyon via a series of falls. Whenever heading into a steep–walled area like this, consider the avalanche danger and be prepared. The moderately easy section ends at a precipitous waterfall, which is just thirty meters from the waterfall which is accessed from the bottom end. The proximity of these features was an obvious challenge, and

 # DESTINATION 13

NAME:
Quality Canyon

FEATURE
Spectacular canyon

ACCESS:
Difficult seasonal access except on snowshoes

in 1996 the first full descent of Quality Canyon was performed, rappelling down the icefalls in succession. Although an exhilarating trip, this obviously is something that calls for considerable experience, as there are open pools at the bottom of some of the falls. The Quality Canyon trip remains a classic snowshoeing experience, one of the finest of its kind. It is too complex to recommend as a skiing outing.

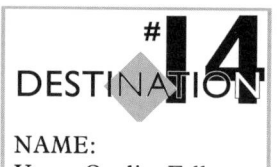

DESTINATION #14

NAME:
Upper Quality Falls

FEATURE:
Pretty small falls

ACCESS:
1 KM hiking trail

At KM 9 is the parking area and Upper Quality Falls (Plate 52) trailhead on the left. This pleasant trail was built in 1996 with the support of Forest Renewal BC. It leads through mature spruce forest for just over a kilometre, descending down a rustic staircase for the last bit. A view of the falls from the rim is reached first. There are barricades to prevent a fall, and a picnic site. It is worth descending further along the trail into the creek, then walking up the bank if the water level is not too high to the foot of the falls. The creek is not large and the falls just about ten metres high, but they have a peaceful ambience. Just be careful of flash floods after heavy rains.

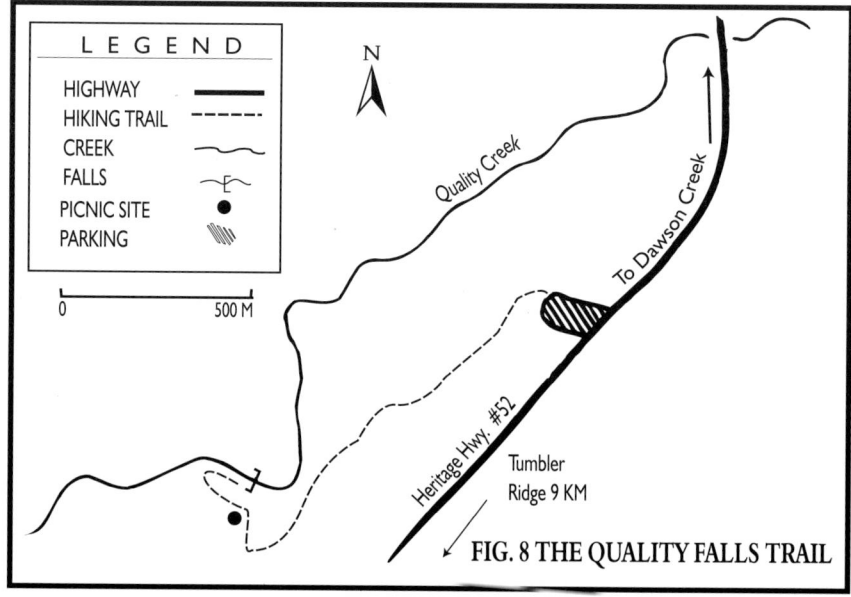

FIG. 8 THE QUALITY FALLS TRAIL

TUMBLER RIDGE *Enjoying its History, Trails & Wilderness*

The highway to Chetwynd also holds a number of nearby attractions. Immediately after crossing Flatbed Creek (KM 2.5 from the Visitor Info Centre) there is a steep road up on the left that leads to a gravel pit and a good training area for runners.

At KM 3.7 the highway crosses the Murray River. Just beyond the bridge on the right is the boat–launch. The road then parallels the river for a short stretch with a few nice views. It passes the Murray railway station and then some small cliffs on the left. This is another site for dinosaur tracks although they are of inferior quality and poorly preserved. Opposite these cliffs is a turnoff on the right at KM 5.7, descending down towards the Murray and Wolverine Rivers. A number of tracks enter the beautiful mature predominantly deciduous forest from here. The Wolverine River and Murray River approach to within 100 metres of one another here, then part and only join up a few kilometres downstream. The isthmus thus created provides enjoyable flat hiking with a wealth of birdlife and some good fishing sites. The first left fork brings one back to below the high bridge over the Wolverine. This is the site of a huge colony of Cliff Swallows which nest here each summer.

Proceeding under the bridge leads to two options. The track is actually the bottom of the Wong Way, a ski trip or biking trip described later. It is long and relentless enough that it is almost always done downhill, and is not recommended as an uphill excursion.

When the water level in the Wolverine River is low, it is feasible to head upstream to the Wolverine Pools, a good summer or early fall destination when the water is warm enough to wade through and swim in. In spring this is a favourite kayaking area (Plate 53). The Wolverine passes through a narrow canyon here, creating some interesting topography with rock pools and good flat rocks for soaking up the sun. Although the distance covered is less than a kilometre, some river crossings are mandatory and children may have trouble with this. A sturdy stick should always be used for support when crossing a river of this size.

DESTINATION 15

NAME:
Wolverine Pools

FEATURE:
Pools and cascades

ACCESS:
500 M wading along river at low water

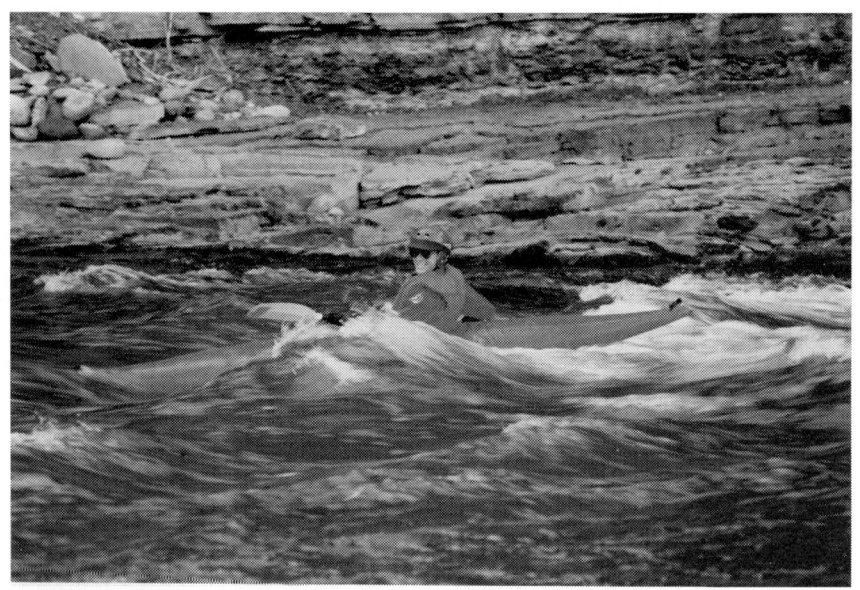

Plate 53: Kayaking the Wolverine Pools. Credit: Birgit Sharman.

Plate 54: Bergeron Cliffs on the Echo Ridge Trail.

The highway continues through a cutting. After this look for a road ascending steeply on the right. This leads to a number of destinations. The first is a peaceful pond, reached by turning right immediately upon reaching the hill summit. The track gets wet and full of pools at times and it is better, and healthier, to walk rather than drive. After a few hundred metres a T–junction is reached. The right turn leads a short way to a clearing with a view over the valley. The left turn leads on through the woods for another few hundred metres to The Pond, an attractive circular sunken feature which usually holds a few pairs of breeding ducks in summer. This is a quiet spot in beautiful mature mixed forest, ideal for a short family walk.

DESTINATION #16

NAME:
The Pond

FEATURE:
Small lakelet

ACCESS:
Rough drive or short hike

If you carry on straight along the road from the top of the hill, you pass through some old logged areas and two turnoffs to the right. These lead down to two private ranches, including Sanctuary Ranch. After eight attractive kilometres under the Bergeron Cliffs, the road ends at a large old gravel pit. This is the trailhead for the Echo Ridge hike. The Tumbler Ridge ecotourism group has done great work here in recent years opening up this old trail, which leads up in a series of steps to emerge above the Bergeron Cliffs (Plate 54). But an unseasonal snowfall in August 2000 damaged this trail, so check for current information before attempting it. In a sensational hike where children will need to be watched with particular attention, the trail leads gently up the cliff edge. Apart from being a fine site for rappelling, this trail provides outstanding views of the valley, Tumbler Ridge and the mountains in the distance. Where the trail reaches the site of an old burn in the forest, an extension leads up the steep open slopes high on Mt. Bergeron to reach the forested summit.

DESTINATION #17

NAME:
Echo Ridge Trail
(Bergeron Cliffs)

FEATURE:
Cliff–edge hike

ACCESS:
6 KM rough trail

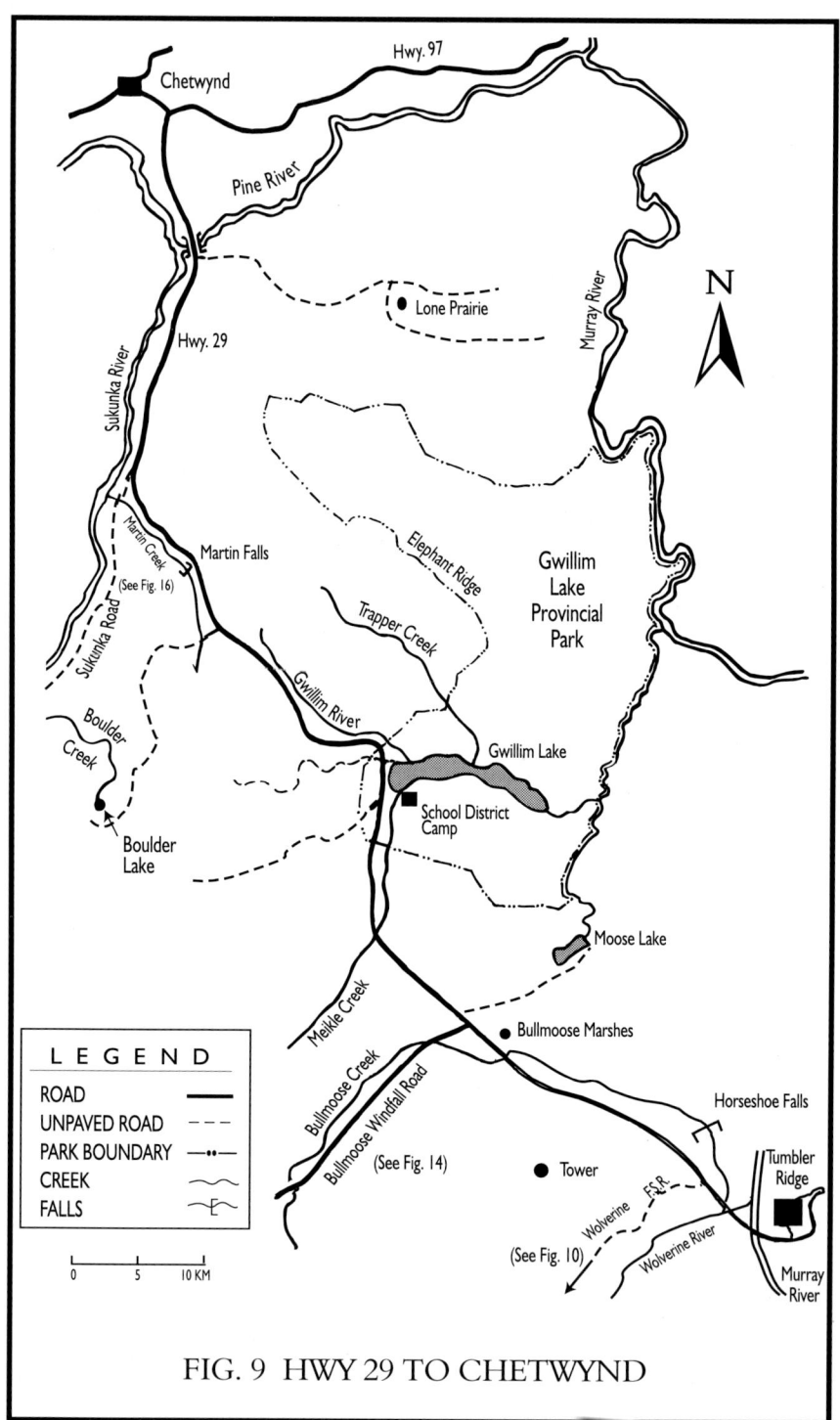

FIG. 9 HWY 29 TO CHETWYND

TUMBLER RIDGE *Enjoying its History, Trails & Wilderness*

■ HIGHWAY 29 TO CHETWYND

The first few kilometres of this highway have been described in the preceding section. Assume that KM 0 is the Visitor Info Centre.

Eight kilometres from town the road crosses Bullmoose Creek via a high bridge. In winter, Bullmoose Creek offers classic wilderness cross–country skiing. Knowledgeable skiers rate this amongst the finest creek skis around. Pull well off the road on the right (north) side before (east of) the bridge. There is an old track that descends, then parallels the road and enters the creek. Snowmobiles will sometimes have made a basic track part way or

#**18** DESTINATION

NAME:
Horseshoe Falls

FEATURE:
Falls up Bullmoose Creek

ACCESS:
18 KM return ski up creek to falls

all the way up to Horseshoe Falls, which is the usual destination, a round trip distance of 18 kilometres. On the way the creek makes some sharp hairpin bends beneath cliffs and passes some hoodoos. Depending on weather conditions, portions of the creek flood over at times. Upstream, the rock scenery becomes more spectacular, and there are a couple of as yet unclimbed ice walls. Finally Horseshoe Falls is reached. This is just four metres high, but beautifully wide and symmetrical, with a special character.

Returning naturally offers a slight, but perceptible downhill grade, and you'll be following your own tracks, making for much faster skiing. The usual precautions for backcountry creek skiing apply. The falls are difficult to reach in summer.

...

The highway climbs a steep hill out of the Bullmoose Valley, then passes a junction. The road to the left leads to the Bullmoose loadout and the long Wolverine Forest Service Road (see page 175). The road climbs steadily and 15 kilometres from Tumbler Ridge passes the old cross–country ski trailhead. The Tower Trail system was built in the early 1990s but discontinued due to parking and safety issues. The trails form a popular snowshoeing excursion; check locally before trying this as the trails are not maintained.

Destinations

DESTINATION #19

NAME:
Bullmoose Marshes

FEATURE:
Roadside ponds

ACCESS:
Roadside birding site

A sign proclaims the summit of the road, 1 126 metres above sea level. The road then descends back into the Bullmoose valley, and recrosses the creek known here as Bullmoose Flats. Soon after the bridge, look for a turnoff to the right, which leads to the Bullmoose Marshes. There are a number of pleasant primitive campsites here, and the area is good for birding due to the diversity of habitats.

Back on the road there is a major turnoff at KM 25 to the Bullmoose Mine. This road ultimately leads past the mine and into Windfall Creek (see page 197). Two kilometres past this junction is the turnoff on the right to Moose Lake. Moose Lake is a favourite camping and fishing lake with locals, nestling in the forested hills at just under 1000 metres above sea level. Canoeing and windsurfing are possible here, but as with most foothills lakes, the winds tend to be gusty.

...

As the highway continues, it makes an S–bend and then crosses Meikle Creek. There is a good creek–ski from here downstream through Meikle Canyon past some interesting hoodoos. You need to turn around where you exit the last canyon, as this is the boundary of the school district camp.

As the road descends towards Gwillim Lake, there is a turnoff to the right to the beautifully maintained School District #59 camp. A locked gate and a sign make it clear that organized groups only can visit the camp. The camp comprises a grand central cooking area and lounge, with six well–designed cabins and a sauna. The absence of electric power

DESTINATION #20

NAME:
Moose Lake

FEATURE:
Subalpine Lake

ACCESS:
Forestry road leads to lake

DESTINATION #21

NAME:
Meikle Canyon

FEATURE:
Canyon with Hoodoos

ACCESS:
Creek crosses Hwy. 29, 10 KM return ski trip

TUMBLER RIDGE *Enjoying its History, Trails & Wilderness*

lends it a delectable old–time atmosphere. A full time supervisor is in attendance. The location is well chosen, at the mouth of Meikle Creek with an expansive view of Gwillim Lake. There is a network of hiking trails and cross–country ski trails. Adults usually only get to appreciate these attractions as part of an official school group.

Back on the highway, there are two roads that lead off to the left and one to the right within the next few kilometres. First left at KM 41 leads up Smokehouse Creek, a pleasant drive, but with no particular destination. The second left climbs high to an old gas well with a good view of the foothills and Gwillim Lake. The right turnoff at KM 45 leads to Gwillim Lake Provincial Park (Plate 55), another local and regional favourite. Prescott Fay wrote the first description of this lake in 1914:

> "We came to the Rocky Mountain Lake and the cabin belonging to Nelson and his four partners. The lake was a pleasant surprise, not its existence of which Nelson had told us, but its beauty, and seen in the morning light it was certainly a lovely spot; the kind of lake you read about and such a place as you would pick out to build a house and live. It was about twelve miles long, set in a big depression of the foothills which rose quite abruptly from its shores. Its outline was irregular and here and there a point…extended into the lake. Not a breath of air stirred and the surface mirrored the surrounding hills."

The Provincial Park is open officially from May to October and offers good camping and boat launch facilities. The access road leaves the highway and passes a picnic area with a good view of the lake, with a mountain backdrop. Although there are 49 campsites, the park is often full to overflowing on long weekends. A short lakeside trail leads east from the boat launch.

The overgrown remains of an old road can be followed east to the crossing of Trapper Creek. There are reports of a pretty set of falls far up this creek. There are a few tongues of land that intrude into the lake, which form

DESTINATION #22

NAME:
Gwillim Lake

FEATURE:
Large lake, provincial park

ACCESS:
Paved road into provincial park

Plate 55: Gwillim Lake Provincial Park

backcountry campsites. They were also favoured by prehistoric inhabitants, as evidenced by the archaeological record. There are many documented archaeological sites around the lake. The prehistoric inhabitants must have had good taste because these sites are idyllically situated. Some of the material was radiocarbon dated to around 3 447 years before present.

The east end of the lake is shallower, and favoured by fishing enthusiasts. From here the Gwillim River exits the lake and flows into the Murray River.

One of the exciting developments in recent years has been the addition of a sizeable area of land, 22 461 hectares, to the park, following the Dawson Creek Land Resource Management Plan process. This includes the enormous Elephant Ridge north of the lake and a small southern extension. It remains to be seen how recreational opportunities will unfold and broaden following this proclamation.

One word of caution is in order about use of the lake in winter. Many parts of it are spring–fed, and there are horrific anecdotal accounts of loss of life through the ice, skiing and ice–fishing. It is advisable in winter only to head out onto the lake with someone who knows it well.

...

The highway continues northwest, over a pass, and descends into the Martin Creek drainage. At the bottom of a long hill (KM 60) there is a dirt road to the south. This leads for 18 winding kilometres through the Kwoen Hills. Boulder Lake, a forestry recreation site, is the destination. At the end of the main road, at a gas well, there is a steep 400 metre descent to the right, and at the bottom of this the signposted trail begins.

Boulder Lake is different from any other lake in the region. It has a near perfect rectangular shape, over a kilometre long and just 100 metres wide. It is the source of Boulder Creek, which exits near the northwestern end. It appears to occupy a trough, as it is hemmed in by attractive low rocks and small cliffs for most of its shoreline.

DESTINATION #23

NAME:
Boulder Lake

FEATURE:
Rocky fishing lake

ACCESS:
Forestry road, need to carry boat or canoe final 500 M.

Plate 56: Martin Falls drop into Martin Canyon.

TUMBLER RIDGE *Enjoying its History, Trails & Wilderness*

Boats or canoes need to be portaged 500 metres to the shore of the lake from the parking area, something that is well worth the effort. This isolated lake is usually peaceful and undisturbed, and offers some good trout fishing.

...

The main highway, descending further into the Martin Creek drainage, passes an open field on the left, then crosses a tributary creek. Soon after this at KM 66 there is an old dirt road on the left. Turning onto this leads to a berm after just a hundred meters. This forms the parking point for the exploration of Martin Canyon and Martin Falls.

Martin Canyon in its descent to the Sukunka River tumbles over at least four small falls, and rushes over many rapids through a big canyon. Although the canyon lies close to the highway, its existence is unknown to most travelers.

To reach the beautiful upper falls, it is necessary to bushwhack down from the berm. If you head down too sharply to the left, you will end up above the falls and have to traverse around. Shallow bluffs line this part of the canyon, and there is only one obvious point of weakness which forms the descent. Even so,

DESTINATION #24

NAME:
Martin Canyon

FEATURE:
Dramatic canyon with waterfalls

ACCESS:
Short, steep bushwhack from near Hwy. 29

some simple rock scrambling is necessary. The falls are not very high, just about ten metres, but are very picturesque (Plate 56).

A short walk downstream leads to another two sets of falls. It is not possible to descend these, and they need to be viewed from above. The rocks at these falls can be dangerously slippery, so anyone who makes it to the upper falls with kids should ensure that they do not go off exploring downstream unaccompanied.

It is best to return to your vehicle by the same route. From here it is a short walk back to the highway. Walk downhill in the ditch for a few hundred meters until the trees on the left thin out a bit. This is the indication that the canyon rim is close. Head left immediately after this feature, and gain a small trail that follows the canyon rim. This is sometimes overgrown, but affords excellent views of Martin Canyon and Lower Martin Falls.

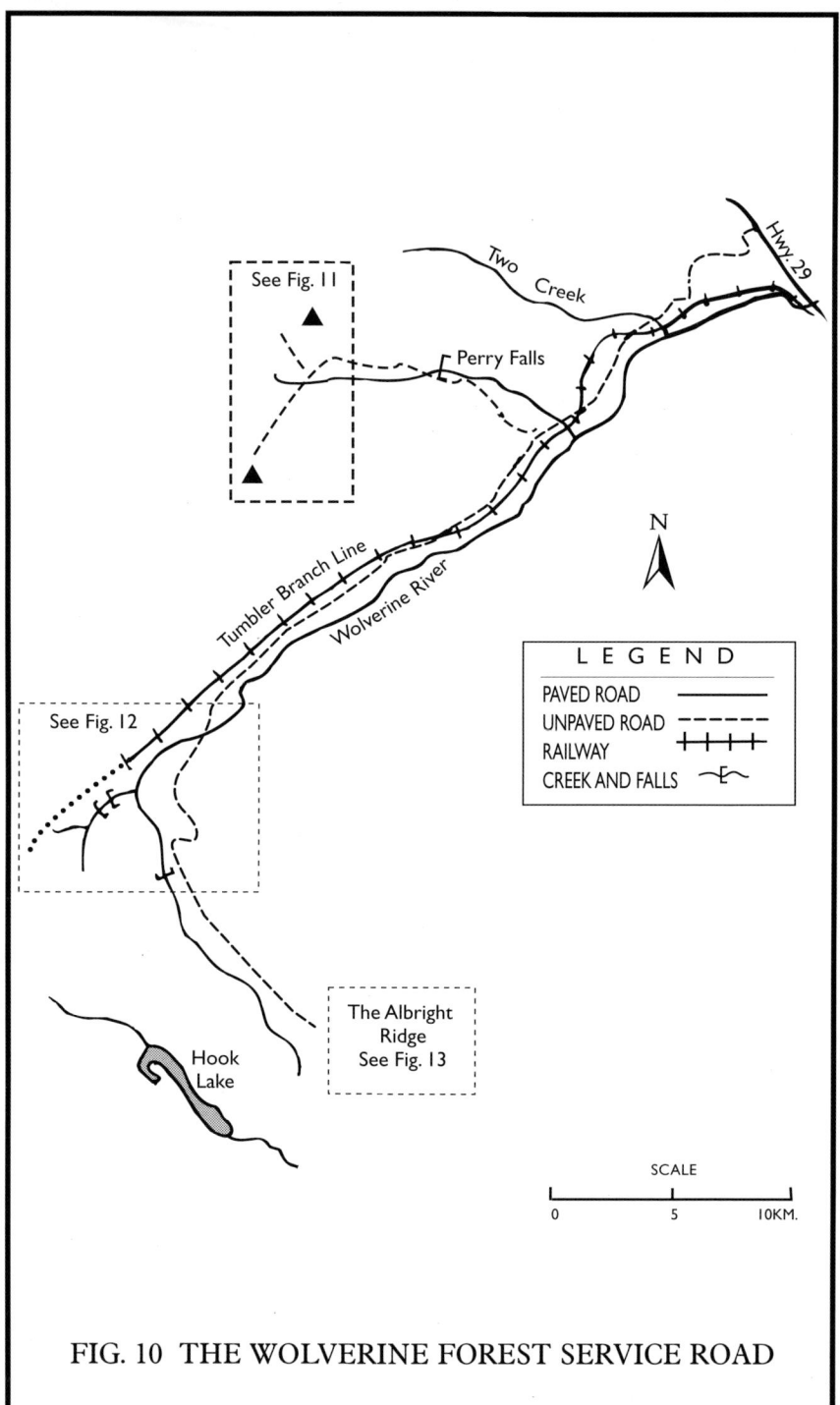

FIG. 10 THE WOLVERINE FOREST SERVICE ROAD

The highway continues downhill into the Sukunka Valley, and soon passes an important road on the left at KM 69, the Sukunka Forest Service Road (see page 213). The highway then more or less follows the river downstream, before crossing it just below its junction with the West Pine River. Canoeists should take note that while the Sukunka River offers excellent training, it does have a bunch of fearsome rapids and falls, and has seen its share of fatalities. In particular, the Pine River below this bridge is to be avoided by all but the most experienced canoeists, as the river accelerates through a dramatic canyon with large diagonal waves and no means of exit.

This area has another interesting destination: the regionally ancient and fascinating community of Lone Prairie, basking beneath the flat summit of Tuskoola Mountain. The road begins on the right just before the bridge over the Pine River. However, it is so close geographically to Chetwynd that it is not described further in this book. It has one particular feature that endears it to Tumbler Ridge residents: it offers an alternative exit from the Murray River canoe trip, and can save half a day's paddling for those with a constrained schedule.

From the bridge, the highway climbs over a sizeable hill, the despair of runners each September in the Chetwynd half marathon. It then joins the Hart Highway before entering the town of Chetwynd just over ninety kilometres from Tumbler Ridge.

■ THE WOLVERINE FOREST SERVICE ROAD

The Wolverine Forest Service Road provides good access to this lovely valley, although it is normally not plowed in winter past the first few kilometres. After turning off the main Tumbler Ridge–Chetwynd Highway #29, you need to turn immediately right (continuing straight on the paved road leads down to the Bullmoose loadout, where the coal from the Bullmoose Mine gets loaded onto the trains). Set your trip meter to zero here. The first kilometre is usually rough. After KM 3 a side road to the right leads to a hill with a tower, and a now disused series of cross–country ski trails built in the early 1990s. It is a long rough drive, and the view from the tower is not adequate to justify the effort.

Plate 57: Perry Falls.

Plate 58: The Caribou Highway on the trail up Mt. Reesor.

TUMBLER RIDGE *Enjoying its History, Trails & Wilderness*

Around KM 5 there is a very sharp corner to the right, which is particularly hazardous in the return direction. Soon the road crosses Two Creek and then crosses the railway line, which runs up the valley before entering the Wolverine Tunnel though the mountains. The first good view of the river is obtained at a junction after KM 8. The side-road to the left, across the bridge, leads up the valley of Mast Creek, and eventually reaches the road to the Quintette Mine, which makes for one of the area's few circular drives.

At the bridge is a pleasant picnic and fishing site, and a track leads down the north bank to another fishing spot. At KM 12 the road crosses Perry Creek. It is difficult to explore in summer, but if access is possible in winter, this creek forms a good backcountry cross–country ski destination. It winds up beneath a series of interesting rocky bluffs, and after three kilometres it narrows and an immense logjam is reached, quite a challenge to climb though while holding on to your skis. Above this obstruction, one pristine view unfolds after the next, but higher up, be on the lookout for avalanche chutes and dangers. Although it is possible to ski up to Perry Falls, the going gets rough and most skiers return the way they came before reaching the falls.

...

Soon after you cross the Perry Creek bridge, a lesser road branches off on the right. This leads up to one of the great Tumbler Ridge recreational areas: the massifs of Mt. Spieker and Mt. Reesor, which are potentially one of the best eagle–watching sites. Every year this road seems to get a bit rougher, every year a washout threatens its continued existence, but miraculously it remains drivable.

It climbs steadily for over seven kilometres, then as it begins the short descent to the bridge over Perry Creek, watch for a small flat cleared area to the right. This is the place to park to descend to Perry Falls (Plate 57). There may be some flagging, and the trail is faint and steep, and there is only one way down through the precipitous bluffs that line Perry Canyon. If you reach vertical cliffs with no obvious way

DESTINATION #25

NAME:
Perry Falls

FEATURE:
Wild waterfall

ACCESS:
Steep bushwhack of 500 M

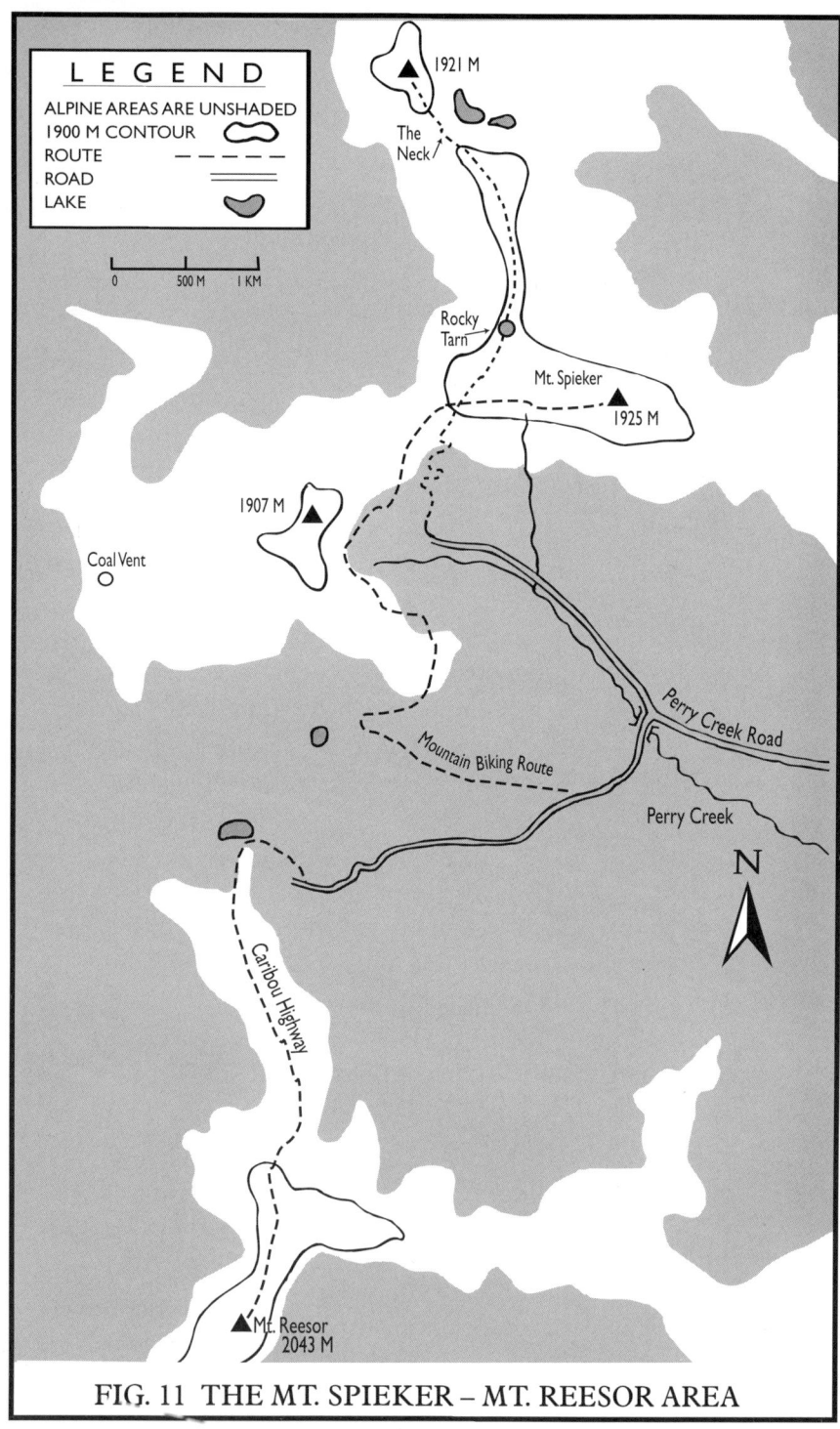

FIG. 11 THE MT. SPIEKER – MT. REESOR AREA

down, you are not on the trail, and should avoid descending further at all costs. However, the effort is well worth it, for the falls are wild and beautiful, with a moss–fringed pool suitable for swimming.

On the north bank is a steady spring that trickles down the cliffs. In winter it is worth skiing down the creek from the bridge above simply to see the magnificent ice formations that form. They have a reddish tinge due to high iron content. Skiers should be very careful when they approach the falls from above, and leave the creek bed to view the great icicles. The falls are almost impossible to view safely in winter.

This is the northernmost recorded site in the world for Black Swifts, which almost certainly breed here. These amazing birds make their nests in wet cool canyons such as this, in crevices in the rocks, and feed their young approximately once a day. The young apparently survive on this meagre diet because they are almost in a state of torpor in the cold microenvironment. Proving that they breed here will require rappelling down the cliffs in a number of places, or else waiting possibly a whole day to see the parent fly in once for a few seconds.

Back on the road, take a look down into the canyon to the left a short way after the bridge. There is an attractive small waterfall. On the left rear the rock–strewn flanks of Fortress Mountain. Proceeding up the road, ignore a turnoff to the left and one to the right. The crucial junction in the road is where the left fork immediately crosses the creek. This road leads to Mt. Reesor, the right fork leads to Mt. Spieker, whose bulky flat–topped form already looms ahead.

The road to Mt. Reesor should be followed to its end. There is just one side road to the right that quickly gets rough and is not recommended without 4WD (it leads up onto a shoulder of Mt. Spieker and provides good mountain biking). The whole area is good for grizzly bear sightings. You know you have reached the end when you come upon a big flat grassy area. The Ridge Riders Snowmobile Club has left a school bus parked here for a warm–up shelter, as the whole Reesor–Spieker area offers excellent snowmobiling in winter.

Ahead lies the ridge that forms the ascent of Mount Reesor, but the best way to gain it is to descend first from the parking area, towards the swampy area to the north. A rough trail leads west, skirting the southern flank of this swamp, which boasts beautiful meadows of wildflowers in summer. After a few hundred meters you pass a rock outcrop. This is actually the lowest point of the ridge, and immediately after passing it, look for an excellent game trail up to the left. Easy ascending and scrambling brings you up above the treeline with little effort, amidst increasingly dramatic views of a seemingly endless succession of alpine summits.

DESTINATION #26

NAME:
Mt. Reesor

FEATURE:
Alpine Summit

ACCESS:
8 KM return hike with 500 M elevation change

Once the top of the ridge is crested, a unique trail is encountered, known locally as the Caribou Highway (Plate 58). This is an appropriate name for this is a caribou migration path, and tracks are easily found, and this is one of the best localities for viewing these graceful animals, or finding their antlers. The "Highway" is about twenty metres wide, and a kilometre long and dead straight and devoid of vegetation, although stunted krummholtz grows to either side. Wind exposure and the high iron sulphide content of the shale probably lead to its barren nature, but to the hiker it presents an unusual sensation of alpine luxury, as it leads towards the beckoning conical summit of Mt. Reesor.

On the way there is, unfortunately, a col in the ridge into which one must laboriously descend, then regain the precious lost elevation. Looking way to the east, the town of Tumbler Ridge can be seen nestling in its valley. Conversely, this ridge is the furthest point that can be seen from the confines of the town. The last hundred meters to the summit are over fairly steep scree, but do not present a problem if approached with caution. The summit is 2 043 metres above sea level, and the view is unforgettable. It is best to return along the same route. Most people ascend Mt. Reesor as a day hike, but it is quite feasible to descend its western flank and continue along the Reesor Ridge over a succession of summits, possibly forever….hikes further along this ridge are accessed via the Windfall Creek Road.

Back at the fork, keeping right leads to the trailhead for Mt. Spieker, a unique and huge mountain, that seen from the air seems to comprise three arms, or giant spokes of a wheel. The old exploration track that switchbacks up from the parking area at the gas well leads past the treeline to a col which is pretty much at the center of this wheel. From the col the first views of the Bullmoose Valley and Bullmoose Mountain are obtained. All three arms are worth exploring. The western arm leads quickly up a caribou track to a summit with good views, which include the Bullmoose Mine. Workers at the mine sometimes noted a plume of steam emanating from the western flanks of Mount Spieker on extremely cold, clear winter days. Al Tattersall investigated this and after diligent searching found the source: an eerie hole of scorched rock where an underground smouldering coal seam found an escape.

The southeastern arm can be explored via the remains of exploration roads, and leads to the official summit of Mount Spieker at an elevation of 1925 metres above sea level. However, the entire mountain, because of its flat alpine terrain, has the feeling of a summit. There are small tarns, fields of wildflowers in season, ptarmigan, caribou, marmots and other wildlife. This is renowned grizzly country.

One of the unique features of Mt. Spieker is its rock formations. Not only is it defended on many sides by vertical cliffs, but what seems from a distance to be just a flat summit plateau is actually in many places a labyrinth of sandstone boulders, sedimentary rock strata, cracks, small sandstone caves, and rock walls. This is literally a playground, not just for kids but for adult kids too. One would take days to explore every nook and cranny (Plate 59).

DESTINATION #27

NAME:
Mt. Spieker

FEATURE
Alpine tabletop summit

ACCESS:
2-8 KM of alpine hiking, 300 M elevation change

These formations are at their most impressive along the northeastern arm. There are few exploration roads here, but the rocky terrain lends itself easily to hiking. A favourite wilderness campsite is at Rocky Tarn. This comes equipped with a sunken grassy area surrounded by rocks a few feet high, from which kids up to a certain age will not be able to extricate themselves unaided. It is nicknamed The Playpen, for obvious reasons.

It is well worth hiking on until finally stopped by vertical cliffs below. To the east stretches a view of another alpine lakelet, potentially

Destinations

Plate 59: Mt. Spieker is a family destination for all ages.

Plate 60: The rocky flat summit of Mt. Spieker.

another good campsite, with Tumbler Ridge far in the distance.. But the big surprise comes near the end of this arm. Before reaching a subsidiary summit, the ridge narrows down to a feature known as The Neck, where sandstone pavement (a delight to walk on) just seven metres wide drops abruptly on either side down imposing sheer cliffs. A striking pattern of deep cracks has formed in this rock.

Mt. Spieker is the kind of place that would attract tens of thousands of visitors annually if it were near a large center. Instead, its wilderness qualities can still be enjoyed and appreciated in virtual isolation. This may not always be so, as the area is rich in coal and future mining is a possibility.

...

Back on the Wolverine Forest Service Road, a ranch can be seen on the left. This has been occupied almost continuously for close on 80 years, first by Kate Edwards and then by John Terry. Terry's family has exciting plans to develop the ranch into an historic site, which may welcome visitors.

The next twenty kilometres pass through pleasant valley scenery, but without specific features. Then the road crosses to the south bank of the river, and just over three kilometres from this bridge there is an important junction. (Keeping left leads to the Wolverine Waterfalls and the Albright Ridge). The right fork leads to Upper and Lower Tunnel Falls, first crossing the Wolverine, then leading up to a parking area beside the railway line. It is then necessary to walk beside the tracks, heading west (upstream). Watch out for trains!

Directions to Lower Tunnel Falls (Plate 61) are fairly vague. After half a kilometre along the tracks, the clue is to listen for the faint sounds of the falls in the unnamed creek below. The best place to descend is just after the railway crosses a tiny tributary stream. It is under a hundred metres of steep bushwhacking down to the falls, which are wide and attractive, with a swimming hole at their base.

DESTINATION **28**

NAME:
Lower Tunnel Falls

FEATURE
Waterfall

ACCESS:
2 KM return hike, steep sections

Golden Eagle Migration in the Tumbler Ridge Area
By Peter Sherrington

Every year something in the order of six thousand Golden Eagles migrate northwards through the Tumbler Ridge area in the spring. Each fall most of the same birds return together with juvenile birds fledged on this population's low-Arctic breeding grounds. To date, however, observers in the area have seen only a fraction of this marvellous movement. How then do we know that they are here?

About 650 km to the southeast of Tumbler Ridge is Mount Lorette, an hour's drive west of Calgary. It was here on March 20th 1992 that Golden Eagles were first discovered to be migrating in large numbers. That first day over one hundred eagles passed to the northwest. Since that day 1,320 days have been spent at the site, and 75,365 migratory birds of prey have been counted, of which an astounding 83% have been Golden Eagles.

The spring migration starts surprisingly early with small numbers of birds moving north in mid-February, and peaks in the latter part of March. During this period an average of about 200 birds passes daily, with the highest spring total being 849 on March 25th 1993. In some years a few immature birds are still migrating north as late as May 25th. The difference in this timing is that the adult birds, anxious to migrate north to breed, are moving from their wintering grounds which are mainly in the eastern Great Plains of the United States. The young birds, that generally don't join the breeding population until their 5th year, have no urge to migrate early and are usually coming from far farther south.

The autumn migration sometimes starts as early as the end of August, but usually doesn't get into full swing until late September. On October 8 2000 a single day count yielded 1071 birds. In most years movement is fairly steady throughout November, and birds have been seen moving south as late as 17 December. Golden Eagles are therefore migrating over the Mount Lorette site for up to seven months of the year!

Movement can start at first light and not cease until the first stars are twinkling in the sky. The birds mainly move passively through the Front Ranges of the Rocky Mountains: that is, they rarely flap their wings. Instead they use wind and thermal energy to gain elevation through soaring, and wind and gravity to progress through gliding. Under ideal conditions glide speeds in excess of 120 km/hr have been calculated. As a result the birds move near or above the peaks and ridges, and are almost never seen in the valleys. This is probably the reason that this spectacular phenomenon remained unknown for so long.

Through satellite telemetry work we can follow the progress of juvenile birds as they move south to as far as Mexico in the fall, and back again in the spring. And most of the birds can be seen to pass over or close to the Tumbler Ridge area.

There are few places in the Rockies that offer such potentially good eagle viewing opportunities, but the best sites and preferred ridges have not yet been determined. So where should one look?

One obvious place to watch is the Tumbler Ridge itself, which forms part of a long, narrow, continuous ridge system ideally suited to the migration of eagles and other birds of prey. A good place to watch is Albert's Point, the roadside pullout on the Heritage Highway just north of town. There may be a tendency for the centre of the fall migration corridor to be farther east than it is in the fall. The Murray Canyon Overlook Trail affords a spectacular panorama and eagles migrating anywhere in the vicinity should be visible to observers with binoculars. It is west of the town where most eagles are likely to be found. Good viewing sites are easily accessible between Bullmoose Mountain and Mount Spieker, and on the southern flanks of Mount Spieker. There have been a number of interesting spring eagle sightings here. The mountains around the Core Lodge are also easily accessible and promising sightings have been recorded here too.

Remember that you are exploring and be prepared to spend quite a bit of time seeing relatively little. Finally, remember to take good notes of what you see, when and where and under what weather conditions, and share them with interested members of the community and with the Rocky Mountain Eagle Research Foundation. Good hunting!

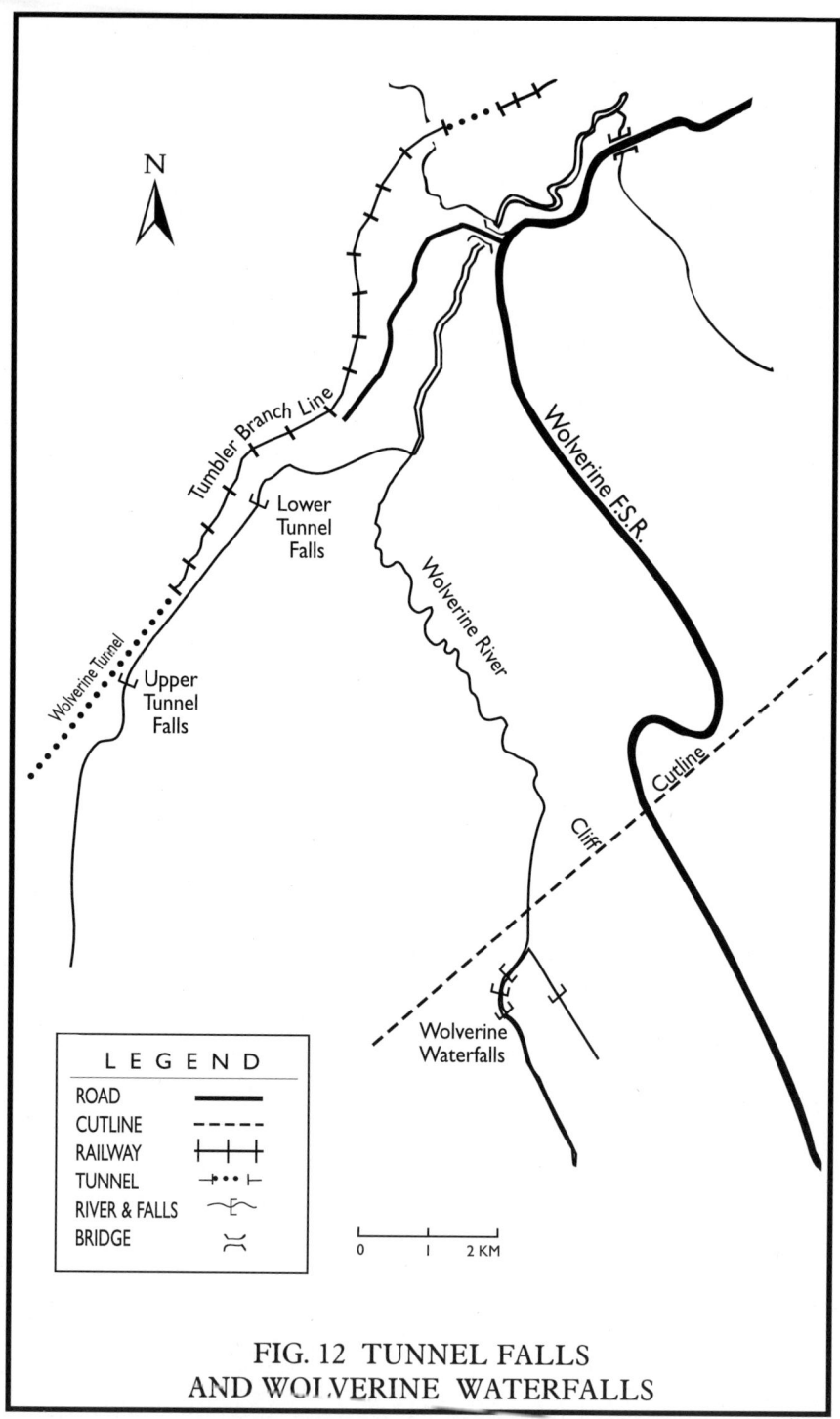

FIG. 12 TUNNEL FALLS AND WOLVERINE WATERFALLS

To reach Upper Tunnel Falls, proceed beside the railway to the entrance to the Wolverine Tunnel, which is about a kilometre and a half from the parking area. Entering the tunnel is not permitted by BC Rail. The creek here is almost at the level of the tunnel entrance. It is possible to follow game trails and bushwhack on the north bank of the creek for another 750 meters. The valley narrows down into an impressive box canyon, and at the far end of this canyon, the stately Upper Tunnel Falls drop into it from the south. Return along the same route.

DESTINATION #29

NAME:
Upper Tunnel Falls

FEATURE
Waterfall

ACCESS:
4 KM return hike with rough sections

...

Back at the forest service road, continuing left takes you further up the Wolverine Valley, which here makes a 90–degree bend to the southeast. The road climbs and makes a big S–curve, and the mountain scenery improves. Look for a cutline on the far western slope across the valley that climbs high into the mountains. You need to align yourself perfectly with this cutline, for where it intersects the road is the beginning of the hike to the Wolverine Waterfalls. You simply need to follow this cutline down into the valley, over humps, down cliffs and through marshes, as it forges its way ahead without respect for physical features.

The first stretch leads through a selectively logged area, which can be slightly distracting. Soon the waterfalls can be viewed below in the distance, a nice encouragement to proceed, irrespective of what lies in between. At one point the cutline reaches some cliffs. Although it is possible to scramble down these, or work your way around them, it is better to take a fixed rope, and use it to descend in safety, then re–use it on the way back. 30 metres is more than enough rope, and there are good trees above the cliffs for anchor points.

DESTINATION #30

NAME:
Wolverine Waterfalls

FEATURE
Spectacular waterfalls

ACCESS:
8 KM return hike, rope necessary, river crossings

Plate 61: Lower Tunnel Falls.

Plate 62: One of the Wolverine Waterfalls.

TUMBLER RIDGE *Enjoying its History, Trails & Wilderness*

After a number of ups and downs, the cutline brings you to the Wolverine River. Proceed upstream, and be prepared to make a couple of crossings. Do not attempt this trail if the river is in flood or in heavy rain. The rewards are great. The limestone scenery is invigorating and there are three waterfalls to explore. Before you reach the main falls, a subsidiary creek joins the river from the south. Heading up this creek a few hundred metres leads to a pretty falls.

The main falls (Plate 62) form an idyllic site, with plenty of rocks for relaxing and picnicking, a perfect swimming hole at their base, and the inspiration of the vertical simplicity of the single drop. Those with a thirst for more adventure may wish to find a way to scramble up the banks a way downstream, so as to gain access to the upper falls, which are more braided, but also higher.

This is another out–and–back trail, and you'll need to recollect that rope.

...

The main road continues towards the headwaters of the Wolverine River, passing a substantial cutting on the left, which caused the road-builders a lot of headaches due to slides. The goal is the magnificent Albright Ridge, which slowly comes into view. It is possible to visit part of the Ridge in a long day, but infinitely preferable to devote an entire weekend or longer to exploring this alpine jewel.

The starting point has tended to vary over the past few years. The road was only constructed in 1995, and some logging has actually facilitated access. Then again, the forestry road may be deactivated one day, and hikers may be forced to seek difficult access via Club Creek to the east again. Essentially, drive as far as you can and then choose the most convenient way onto the ridge! There are no constructed trails here, but the understory of the forest is not too thick and there are numerous game trails.

One route of access involves gaining the westernmost end of the Albright Ridge. This means ascending onto a subsidiary ridge on the

DESTINATION #31

NAME:
Albright Ridge

FEATURE
Alpine wilderness area, peaks and lakes

ACCESS:
Wilderness travel from end of forestry road

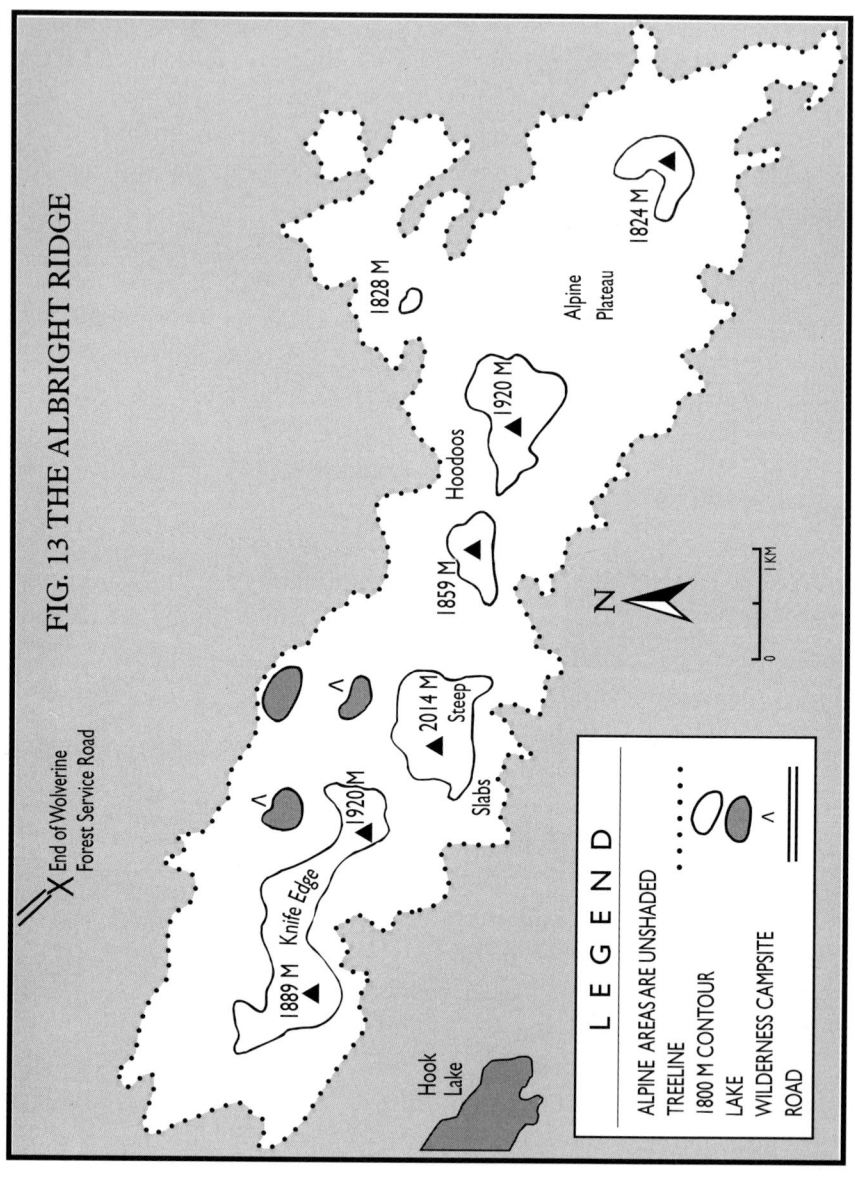

south bank of the creek that leads up in a southerly direction. This heads directly to an interesting karst and caving area, and then to the western summit.

Another access route involves ascending up the westernmost valley that drains the Ridge, until it crosses some prominent rock strata. Proceeding left (east) along this rocky ridge gives an easy route above the treeline. Where this band intersects a north–south ridge, you will have a view of the first of three opalescent lakes that form the heart of the Albright Ridge. Descending to the north shore of the lake brings you to an excellent campsite.

So what makes the Albright Ridge (Plate 63) something to rave about? It comprises a pristine series of six separate, but easily attained summits, joined by a ridge walk that in some places narrows to a sensational knife–edge. It has semi–permanent snowfields on its northern flanks, and the only bit of the ridge walk that has problematic rock scrambling lends itself when snow conditions are right to taking a deep breath, throwing your backpack down ahead of you, then launching yourself down a steep incline of snow and hurtling down 200 metres. If you are good you can call this glissading. Ordinary mortals just spin and tumble down, but mercifully the grade evens out gently at the bottom and you will have chosen in advance a fall line with no rocky obstacles.

On the ridge walk, (Plate 64) most of the cols between the peaks gradually lead down valleys or karstic landscapes on their northern aspects, from which it is possible to double back to the best campsites, which are at one of the two upper lakes. Towards the eastern limit of the Albright Ridge is a large plateau, filled with depressions and karst features and one small known cave. It is an alpine landscape like no other in the area.

Four valleys drain the northern flanks. From west to east, the first has no lake and is used for the one access route. The second and third hold the most beautiful lakes. The fourth has no lake but is graced by the most impressive rock towers and hoodoos in the entire region (Plate 65). The lakes are turquoise, surrounded on three sides by great rock cliffs and scenery, providing exquisite morning reflections. Substantial ice floes remain on the lakes well into August, and on a warm day it is

Plate 63: View from the top of the Albright Ridge.

Plate 64: Ridge–walking, Albright Ridge. Credit: Birgit Sharman.

Plate 65: Hoodoos on the Albright Ridge. Credit: Peter Andrews

Plate 66: Sunbathing on the Albright Ridge.

Plate 67: Jogging on the Albright Ridge.

possible to swim out onto a floe to sunbathe or go for a jog (Plates 66, 67).

There is just enough krummholtz on the northern shores to provide for fine campsites. But beware, this is grizzly country, and there is one dismal tale about a hiker running into camp with his pants around his knees, having been mock–charged by a grizzly during his morning ablutions. Directly below the eastern lake is the third lake, but this is surrounded by forest, and is not as attractive to hikers or wilderness campers.

The southwestern shoreline of the eastern lake is formed by another large snowfield. A suggested activity here is to bring a sheet of plastic with you, climb this, and slide down it into the lake (Plate 68). After a few runs over the same trail, friction is decreased, providing for an even more exhilarating and splashy entry into the lake. Obviously you should select an entry point devoid of shallow rocks, and clearly this is an activity more suitable after a long hot day's hike, than as a pre–breakfast excursion.

The Albright Ridge is also a caving area (Plate 69). There are some enormous sinkholes, and from the caving perspective, there is much to be discovered. There are some known deep holes that have yet to see a decently equipped expedition. Some of the caves harbour stalactites and cave bacon formations.

There is more. The southern slopes offer the finest set of stone slabs in the region. As yet these are unclimbed, but would make for an interesting friction–climbing experience. And the view from the ridge walk is unsurpassed, looking down onto the peculiar formation of Hook Lake to the west, Pyramid Peak to the north, and the alpine country of Monkman Park to the south.

In winter the Albright Ridge becomes preferred terrain for snow-mobilers, who find ideal conditions on its slopes and in its bowls. The Ridge Riders have constructed a shelter at the base of the ridge.

The ridge is named after Bruce Albright, a pioneer at Kinuseo Falls in the late 1930s who lost his life flying in the Second World War. As with any alpine travel, winter can occur at any season. Be prepared for any emergencies and be sure to carry good navigational equipment.

Plate 68: Relaxing after a long, hot day's hiking on the Albright Ridge. Credit: Ivor Byren.

Plate 69: Entrance to Goatbone Grotto, Albright Ridge.

■ TO BULLMOOSE MINE AND BEYOND: THE BULLMOOSE – WINDFALL CREEK ROAD

The excellent paved road leads up the valley of Bullmoose Creek, flanked by the cliffs of Bullmoose Mountain and then Cowmoose Mountain to the north, and Mount Spieker to the south. Access to Mount Spieker from this valley is possible, but so much more difficult than from the Wolverine Valley, that it is not described further here.

Sixteen kilometres from the start of the road, there is a tall stack of a gas plant on the left. Opposite this on the right is a dirt road, which can be followed as it climbs into the valley between Bullmoose Mountain and Cowmoose Mountain. Vertical bluffs characterise this valley, and these provide the easiest and most convenient site for mountain goat viewing, especially in the fall. Binoculars are essential. In summer scan the higher slopes of Bullmoose Mountain. In fall and early winter, the goats descend, and can best be seen on the cliffs directly across the valley. There is also a Golden Eagle nest high up on the cliffs which makes for good viewing.

This area is a favourite for ice-climbers in winter, as the Cowmoose Step Falls (Plate 70) lie just above the road. Look carefully for the lip of the falls; it can just be seen from the road. A trail is thrashed out of the snow each year. There are three successive vertical falls, surrounded by interesting rock formations.

Higher up, the road is barred, but it is possible to park and bash up through the subalpine vegetation, to emerge with a bit of difficulty at the treeline, where some old exploration roads may be reached. These give access ultimately to the slopes of Bullmoose Mountain. The slog up this

DESTINATION #32

NAME:
Bullmoose Cliffs

FEATURE
Mountain goat viewing site

ACCESS:
Roadside

DESTINATION #33

NAME:
Cowmoose Step Falls

FEATURE
Icefall

ACCESS:
200 M from road

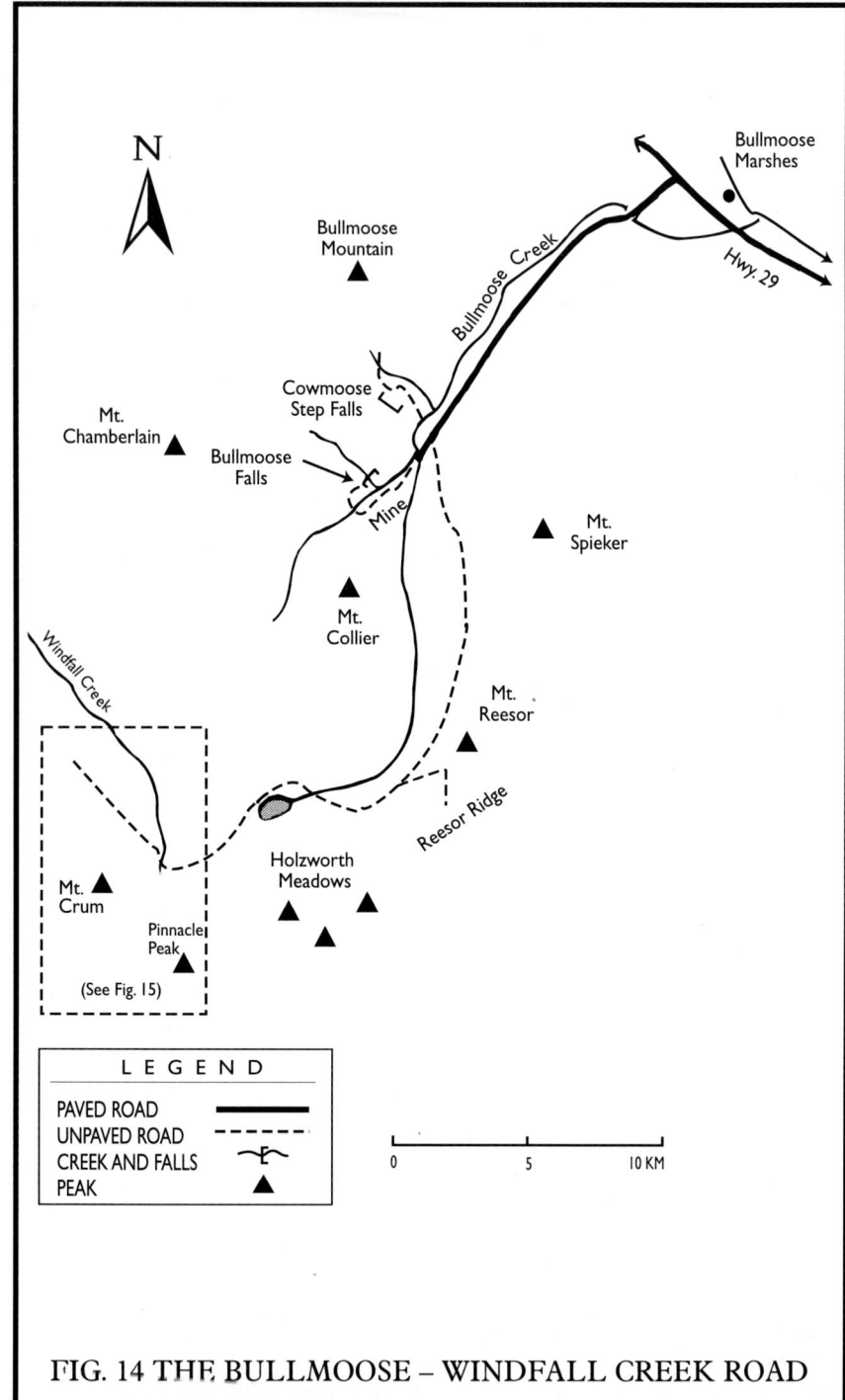

FIG. 14 THE BULLMOOSE – WINDFALL CREEK ROAD

mountain to the towers at its summit is long, but it makes for a stupendous view.

A traverse is also feasible via some interesting alpine tarns to Mount Chamberlain, overlooking the Sukunka Valley. This is more choice goat and caribou country, and the hiking is flat and easy on a large high plateau.

From Mount Chamberlain it is possible to descend via old exploration and forestry roads to Bullmoose Falls and the Bullmoose Mine, providing for a challenging one way trip, provided vehicles are left at both ends.

DESTINATION #34

NAME:
Bullmoose Mountain

FEATURE
Alpine summit

ACCESS:
10 KM return hike, some bushwhacking

...

The paved road continues straight towards the Bullmoose Mine. Permission usually needs to be obtained at the gatehouse to turn right along a sometimes muddy dirt road, past the sedimentation ponds, to reach Bullmoose Falls. The lip of these falls is visible from some distance as they drop into an impressive amphitheatre.

In both winter and summer conditions, there are two ways to access the falls. Having passed the sedimentation ponds, the road crosses a tiny tributary creek, then climbs. Just before the top of this hill, park, and head north down through a clearing towards the main creek. This bushwhacking is not too hard once you get used to it.

The creek needs to be crossed, via wading, logjams or snowbridges. The falls are on the tributary creek that flows in from the north, and it is necessary to ascend this. In summer it is fairly easy, in winter this can be done on skis, but snowshoes will be easier. Soon the walls of the amphitheatre appear, and the vertical falls.

DESTINATION #35

NAME:
Bullmoose Falls

FEATURE
40 M waterfall, icefall

ACCESS:
1 KM bushwhacking, creek crossing

In late summer they dwindle to a trickle, but are very impressive in spring and after rain. They form an ideal ice climbing location in winter and early spring, for experienced ice climbers. The 40 metre high vertical pitch was first climbed by Al Tattersall in 1995.

Plate 70: Ice climbing lesson on Cowmoose Step Falls.

TUMBLER RIDGE *Enjoying its History, Trails & Wilderness*

Even for non–climbers, the falls are sensational in winter. Because they are free–standing, it is possible to climb up to the base, crawl right behind the frozen columns, and emerge on the other side (Plate 71). Clearly the ice and weather conditions need to be checked before embarking on this little circuit, because at some time in the spring parts of the icefall come crashing down. In the right conditions this in an unforgettable experience.

The other way to access the falls is by continuing on the road to a bridge, turning right, and then walking back on the old exploration road until it passes close to the lip of the falls. Take a peek over the edge, or work your way to the far (northeastern) aspect for a fine view of the falls. The drop–offs are enormous and there are no safety features so please be careful. Continuing up the exploration road leads to Mount Chamberlain, described above.

...

The Windfall Creek Forest Service Road starts near the Bullmoose Mine and provides access to some of the most spectacular alpine scenery in the region. It leaves the paved road on the left a kilometre before the mine gatehouse at the electrical substation, and heads up the southern fork of Bullmoose Creek. It yields good views of the mine, as it passes between Mt. Spieker and Mt. Collier. Mt. Collier being the site of a coal mine is purely coincidental: it was named after Private Wilfred Collier of Gundy, killed in action in 1944.

Ahead lies Mt. Reesor, and a switchback road can be seen ascending its western flanks to a gas–well. After about eight kilometres there is a junction. The left fork leads up this switchback, the right fork continues towards Windfall Creek. Taking the left fork allows rapid altitude gain to a gas site at the treeline in an impressive bowl. It is then a simple matter to climb up into the bowl and gain the long ridge that stretches southwest of Mt. Reesor. From here Mt. Reesor can be climbed, or else the ridge can be explored in the opposite direction. The views are magnificent (Plate 72).

DESTINATION #36

NAME:
Reesor Ridge

FEATURE
Alpine ridge

ACCESS:
Steep road leads to treeline and alpine access

Plate 71: Backcountry ski trip to Bullmoose Falls.

TUMBLER RIDGE *Enjoying its History, Trails & Wilderness*

Returning to the junction, the right fork climbs towards the headwaters of Bullmoose Creek. Look carefully for a curve to the right after crossing a bridge about thirteen kilometres from the Bullmoose mine. Just after the curve, scan the forest on the left for a cutline that heads up from the road. This may be flagged. It is the key to gaining access to the Holzworth meadows, a recommended half–day or full–day excursion, with limitless opportunities for peak–bagging.

The route leads up the cutline, ascending gradually until the krummholtz is reached, and meadows filled with summer flowers. This is an easy place to find Willow Ptarmigan, while the White-tailed Ptarmigan are to be found on the summits above. Upon entering the meadows, keep to precisely the same direction, as the cutline does continue through the brush and following it makes for easier travel. Note your position carefully, for it can be harder to find the trail on the return trip.

Once above the treeline, there are many options. You can continue up the ridge straight ahead, which leads to a summit, or you can turn left (south) into a bowl, and choose which of the three peaks you want to climb. None are named, and all are spectacular. The Holzworth Meadows are named after John Holzworth, explorer and hunter, who was one of the first to travel through this area in 1923. He explored these meadows and wrote passionately about them in his journal.

From either of the two southerly peaks (the two peaks on the right as you face up the bowl) it is possible to follow the ridge further to the southwest onto the next peak. This is remarkable for a blunt knife edge section on the way up the last peak, with great views all along. From that summit you either return all the way you came, or some hikers prefer to descend directly back towards the road. The problem is that you will have to bushwhack a bit to reach the road, and you will hit it about 8 KM from your vehicle.

Access to the Holzworth meadows is different in winter, for purposes of skiing (Plate 73) and snowmobiling. These meadows

DESTINATION #37

NAME:
Holzworth Meadows

FEATURE
Alpine meadows and peaks

ACCESS:
2 KM trails to meadows, then multiple alpine routes

203

Destinations

Plate 72: Hiking the Reesor Ridge.

Plate 73: Skiing the Holzworth Meadows.

TUMBLER RIDGE *Enjoying its History, Trails & Wilderness*

and passes form the easiest winter alpine access in the area, provided the road has been plowed. You don't park at the start of the cutline, but carry on along the road for another kilometre, to a point where you are above the lakelet that lies in the pass between Bullmoose Creek and Windfall Creek. You should see evidence of the snowmobile and ski tracks that descend to the lakelet, cross it, and then follow a cut trail through the timber up into the alpine. This is potentially the best wilderness cross–country skiing area in the region. Consider skiing into the pass in the ridge, removing your skis, donning your hiking boots and climbing the windswept peaks.

Continuing on the Windfall Creek Road, after the pass is crested, spectacular mountain scenery continues. The most obviously impressive peak is Mount Crum. It is worth scouting out the right horizon of Mount Crum, which is the northeast ridge, because this forms a sensational ascent. From a distance this looks just about impossible, but is just feasible without technical gear, provided you have a good head for heights. Most will prefer a rope. The most striking feature of the mountain from this aspect is the incredible rock folding on its southeastern face, with what appears to be a cave in the apex of the folding. This is an illusion; the dark spot is just a big overhang, not a true cave.

To reach the start of this ascent you must turn left after crossing the headwaters of Windfall Creek. This side road also gives access to Pinnacle Peak, Windfall Lake, Tunnel Mountain, and many caves.

To climb Mt. Crum you need to bushwhack up on the right until you gain the ridge. Then simply follow the ridge for one breathtaking metre after the next all the way to the summit. Mount Crum stands separate from the main ridge, and is the highest peak in the immediate region (2 118 metres above sea level) so the summit views are very good. Mt. Crum can be climbed more easily from the west but access routes are much longer. This peak also makes for a five–star ski mountaineering ascent for those with the expertise and equipment (Plate 74).

DESTINATION #38

NAME:
Mt. Crum

FEATURE
Spectacular alpine summit

ACCESS:
Ridge ascent, ropes advisable, 850 M elevation gain

Destinations

Plate 74: Final steps to the top of Mt. Crum. Credit: Kevin Sharman.

Plate 75: Hiking up Pinnacle Peak.

Continuing up the side road you cross the headwaters of Windfall Creek again (the starting point for the Windfall Lake hike), then the road switchbacks up a clearcut. The top of the switchback is the starting point for the Pinnacle Peak excursion. This is wilderness hiking in the true sense of the word, and is for experienced hikers only.

The route to Pinnacle Peak first leads straight up south through a difficult steep brushy alder slope, probably an avalanche chute. Simple rock scrambling is necessary in places. After a lot of sweat you reach the treeline and continue up the ridge. Notice your landmarks, for it is advisable to return the same way after completing a circuit on top.

Continue up the ridge through improving scenery, until the jagged summit of Pinnacle Peak is seen ahead. From here it should be possible to plot a route. The shortest is to do a circuit, sticking to the ridge on your right, climbing up the peak, descending via the ridge to the left, crossing the bowl and creek, and returning to near where you are standing, then descending the way you came. The alternatives are all much longer, and involve proceeding from the summit of Pinnacle Peak to the mountains beyond in a southwesterly or southeasterly direction. If you head southwest, you can keep on going endlessly above the treeline.

DESTINATION #39

NAME:
Pinnacle Peak

FEATURE
Spectacular alpine summit

ACCESS:
7 KM return, steep hard initial bushwhacking, elevation gain 550 M

Reaching the summit of Pinnacle Peak is exciting. From a distance it appears that this could be a tricky ascent, but once begun, there are no particular difficulties. The sedimentary layers are stacked at a steep angle, and the rock scenery is superb, with a number of jagged castellated ridges leading off, forming a fine foreground for photography of the distant mountain scenery (Plate 75). A sixty-seven year old gentleman recently climbed it, could not believe he had succeeded, and proclaimed that it was the best day of his life (Plate 76).

...

The trailhead for Windfall Lake is currently near the bridge across the creek. This trip can be done as a long day hike, but there is more than enough to see to justify a few nights in a tent. The first part of the

Destinations

Plate 76: Hiking up Pinnacle Peak.

Plate 77: Windfall Lake.

TUMBLER RIDGE *Enjoying its History, Trails & Wilderness*

hike may be logged, which will facilitate access. At present game trails need to be followed for the first few kilometres. It is wise to stay near the creek to avoid the misery of hiking through the overgrown avalanche chutes above. There is no one correct trail, and as long as you are using a map and compass, heading south–southwest, and slowly ascending, you will eventually reach the lake after some inspiring thrashing through the undergrowth. The prize is that you will have the area to yourself. The better line of attack is to turn south–southeast up a good game trail up a

DESTINATION #40

NAME:
Windfall Lake area

FEATURE
Alpine wilderness area of caves and ridges

ACCESS:
8 KM return of bushwhacking to lake, then endless alpine routes

draw, when you are about a kilometre from the lake on your map. You may even find a few flags here to confirm your choice. This bypasses the worst forest and cliffs, and leads easily into a pass and the alpine. (This is the main pass between the Wolverine Valley and Windfall Creek, something the animals obviously realise). Just before the pass, traverse west to reach the lake.

Windfall Lake is pristine, untouched, lovely, surrounded by lofty ranges (Plate 77). Once you reach its shores, you may need to choose a campsite. Head to the end of the lake under the very imposing high sandstone and mudstone cliffs. This is the driest bit of shoreline; much of the rest is characterised by the toxic hellebore plant. This forms an excellent base camp. There are three directions for exploration. Immediately to the southeast above the first ridge is a large flattish alpine area, with an attractive sunken lake (you may have seen this already if you approached Windfall Lake via the traverse from the pass).

The topography here is obviously karst, and a few small caves can be found and explored. The Windfall Lake area has yielded some of the most interesting cave discoveries in the region. Sausage Cave, discovered in 1998, was the first true ice–cave known in B.C. An initial ten–metre rappel leads into a chamber from which descends a perfectly round tube filled with a permanent core of ice. Ice had to be chipped away to allow entry to the lowest chamber past an unexpected underground icefall. Ice chokes off the passage 45 metres underground.

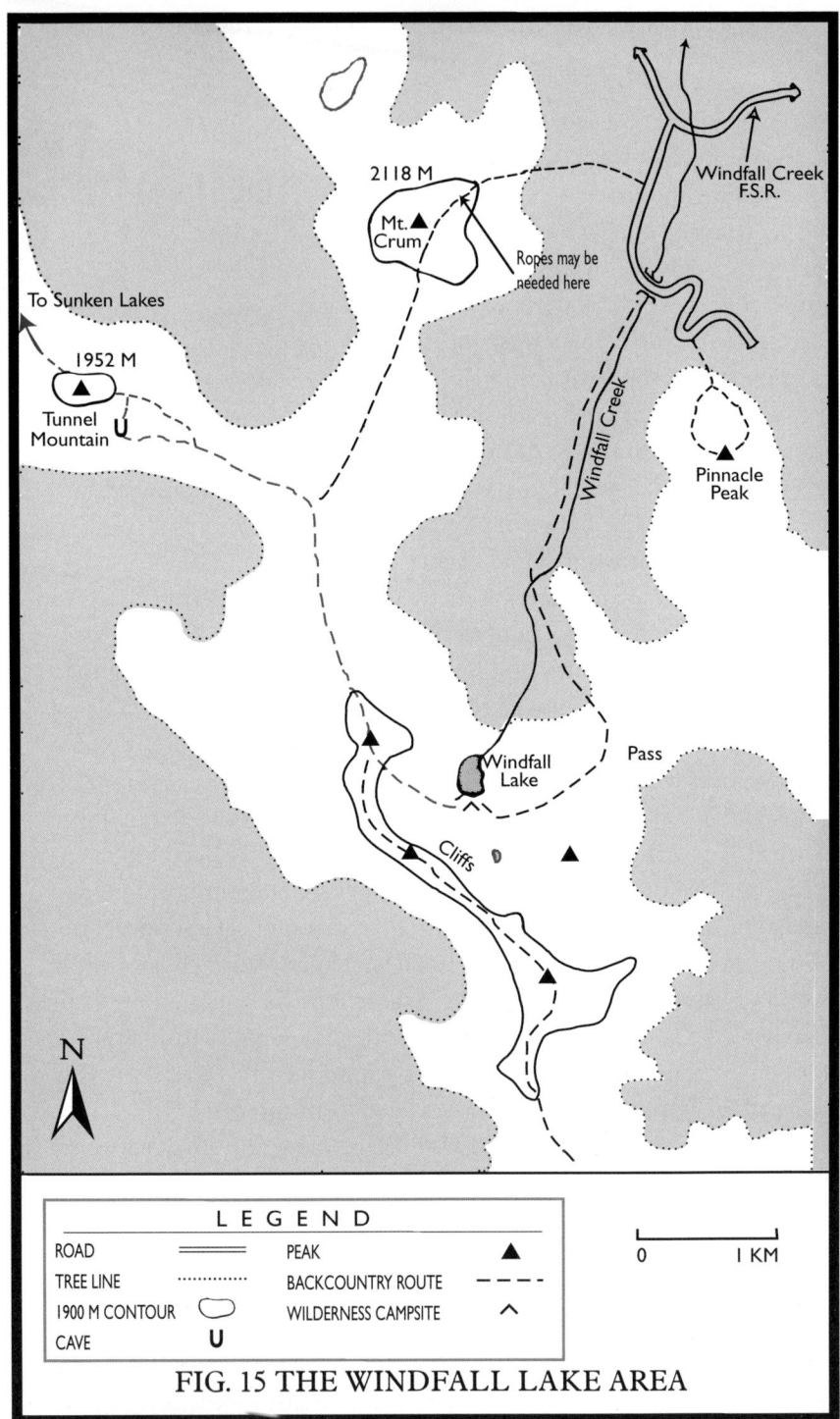
FIG. 15 THE WINDFALL LAKE AREA

Caribou Cave is a gash in the surface of the alpine. Rappelling into it allows exploration of four smaller caverns. There are also two unexplored caves. One is at the bottom of an enormous sinkhole, and hasn't been entered because of concerns about stability. The other is a small entrance leading to a vertical drop of 60 metres. A stone dropped into this abyss keeps on bouncing for a long time. Truly, there is much in the Tumbler Ridge area just waiting to be investigated by the intrepid. No excuse is made for not giving directions to these entrances. Only well–equipped caving parties should tackle such caves.

The other trips that can be done from Windfall Lake both demand first ascending the high steep ridge behind (southwest of) the lake. The western ascent is much easier, following a line of vegetation all the way up. The southern ascent is not recommended, as it involves negotiating steep cliffs. Some climbers have come unstuck trying to take a short cut up the cliffs. So go up the grassy western slope, even if it takes a little longer. You emerge on a minor summit. From here the options are obvious: you can hike northwest or southeast, in either case along the ridge. Both directions are worthwhile.

The ridge continues indefinitely if you head southeast. An occasional stunted fir–bush covered with mountain goat hair interrupts the tundra, as you walk the top of the steep ridge over a succession of peaks. This is ridge walking at its finest.

The northwest direction yields interesting rock scenery and a few surprises. Another karst area boasts an unexpected lakelet right on top of the ridge in a col. Proceeding past this lakelet in the same direction, some side–hilling is required. It is also possible to divert and climb Mount Crum from this aspect, but straight ahead looms the bulk of Tunnel Mountain (Plate 78). It is perfectly feasible to climb this via the ridge, but this is considered boring, because there is a much more interesting route!

From quite a distance, a dark blob can be seen directly below the summit, about a quarter of the way down the mountain. This is your destination. Traverse off the ridge along

#41 DESTINATION

NAME:
Tunnel Mountain

FEATURE
Mountain with Tunnel Cave

ACCESS:
5 KM alpine NW of Windfall Lake

Plate 78: Tunnel Mountain – Xs mark tunnel exits.

Plate 79: Looking out of Tunnel Cave onto the Sukunka Valley.

the steep scree slope to reach it. Yes, it is the entrance to the tunnel of Tunnel Mountain. You ascend 40 metres right through this sizeable tunnel (no need to crawl), and emerge a lot nearer the summit than you thought. "Climbing through the mountain" is a very different experience (Plate 79).

Continuing northwest along the ridge leads to a series of sunken lakes, another area with obvious karst potential. It is possible to bushwhack from these lakes to join the extension of the Windfall Creek road. Otherwise you return to Windfall Lake, grit your teeth and head back into the bush to eventually reach your vehicle.

■ THE SUKUNKA VALLEY

This reasonably maintained Sukunka Forest Service Road can be followed upstream for almost 100 kilometres to the source, deep in the mountains, of this major tributary of the Pine and Peace Rivers. Drive with great caution on this road and use the radio frequency if possible. Set your tripmeter to zero where the road leaves Highway 29.

The Sukunka River is a challenge to experienced canoeists, but novices should not be fooled by its seemingly placid nature at the roadside; this river has seen its share of canoeing fatalities. For the first few kilometres the road passes through farmland, and crosses Martin Creek. It then passes through beautiful mature aspen forest, with excellent chances of moose, elk and deer sightings, and some lovely river views. This is also one of the few places in the region where a herd of wild wood bison roams.

Sukunka Falls Provincial Park, despite its grandiose name, is not always signposted. It protects the wildest stretch of the Sukunka River, incorporating a series of rapids and falls (Plate 80), along with the riparian forest and the Sukunka–Burnt River confluence. Prescott Fay's 1914 description still applies:

> *"At this point the river goes through a rocky canyon, above which are a series of very pretty cascades and small, symmetrical falls, so much so as to be almost artificial looking."*

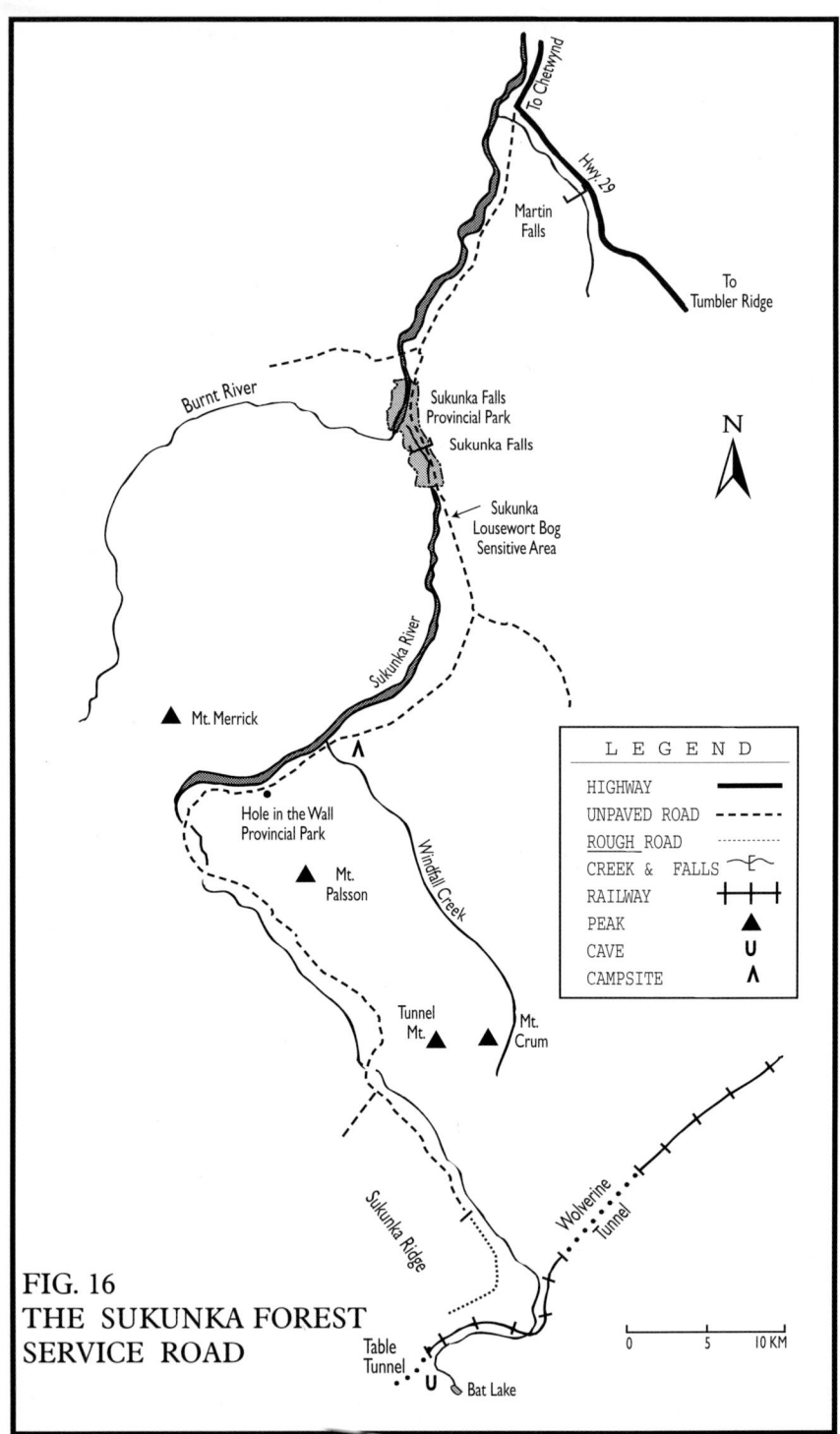

FIG. 16
THE SUKUNKA FOREST SERVICE ROAD

To find the falls if they are not sign-posted, watch for a pullout on the right around 21KM from the start of the road. This affords a fine view of the falls and rapids. The best time to view this scene is in the fall, when the aspen forests in the sunlight provide a fiery frame to the rushing white water. To hike down to the falls, proceed on to the second roadside pullout, from where a recently improved trail leads right down to the falls, a great place for kids and adults alike. It is possible to scramble along the rocky ridge above the falls, and be surrounded on three sides by roaring water. Great caution is needed here, as a slip could have dire consequences. Even without this breath-taking scramble, there are plenty of nooks, rocks, cliffs and overhangs to explore. The overhanging cliffs, nurtured by the moisturizing spray from the falls, are a botanist's delight, supporting numerous ferns and other shade-loving plants. A pleasant surprise is the small sandy beach just below the falls, flanked by cliffs on one side, a great logjam on another, and the falls ahead.

DESTINATION #42

NAME:
Sukunka Falls

FEATURE
Waterfall, provincial park

ACCESS:
Roadside, short trail down to falls

Just a few kilometres further upstream there is another set of rapids within the park, but there is no adequate vantage point.

...

The road passes an established 556 hectare "sensitive area", the Sukunka Lousewort Bog. This protects an isolated population of a red-listed plant, the Swamp Lousewort, of interest to botanists.

Where the road crosses Windfall Creek near KM 45, there is a forest service campsite, often full in fall with hunting parties. About five kilometres beyond this is the next feature of interest: Hole in the Wall (Plate 81), a recently proclaimed small provincial park of 140 hectares. Look for a substantial clear stream flowing beneath the road, without an obvious catchment area and valley upstream. This is a telltale feature of a resurgence spring, of which Hole in the Wall is an outstanding example. The mountains are substantially composed of limestone, characterized by subsurface water drainage.

Plate 80: Prescott Fay took the first recorded photo of Sukunka Falls in 1914. Credit: Jasper–Yellowhead Museum & Archives

Plate 81: Hole in the Wall.

This water typically emerges many hundreds of meters lower as a resurgence spring. In this case the spring is a mere 40 meters from the road, and accessed by a short trail. What makes Hole in the Wall special is that the spring flows from the base of a vertical wall of dark blue–gray limestone. Unfortunately in the past graffiti artists have defaced this unique phenomenon, but lichens are reclaiming the rock and making this eyesore less visible. The flow of water does change with the seasons, being greatest in spring, but even late in the fall, an impressive flow jets out of the rock.

DESTINATION #43

NAME:
Hole in the Wall

FEATURE
Resurgence spring

ACCESS:
Very short trail from roadside

Cave diving is a highly complex and potentially dangerous activity, best left to experts. Hole in the Wall certainly is a site with cave diving potential in the fall, and the experts are aware of it but have not to date mounted an expedition to northeastern B.C.

Proceeding up the road, there are further turnoffs, leading up the Burnt River (at KM 51) and Upper Burnt River valleys to the west. In this region is the Burnt River Cave, a walk–in cave with a large bat population. As with other cave locations, the site is not mentioned here, but dedicated cavers may approach the Wolverine Nordic and Mountain Society for details of expeditions to this cave.

The road crosses and recrosses the Sukunka River three times, with some primitive campsites. After the third crossing, the road climbs a hill, then swings right. Look for a fainter road straight ahead at this turn, and keep to it. This is the road that leads to the source of the Sukunka, and was initially used in the construction of the railway tunnels that enabled the coal to leave Tumbler Ridge. The quality of the road surface deteriorates, and a number of bridges have been broken or eroded, so that four–wheel drive with high clearance is mandatory. But the mountain scenery steadily improves, as the road heads up a valley between two parallel ridges and a succession of alpine summits (one of these on the east ridge is Tunnel Mountain). Eventually the site of the construction camps for the tunnels is reached (KM 95), and the roads to both tunnels can be explored. These roads are suitable for mountain bikes.

The east tunnel is the Wolverine Tunnel, six kilometres long. The west tunnel at the end of the road is the Table Tunnel, nine kilometres long.

Although the mountains above this tunnel are the crest of the Rocky Mountains, they are not the continental divide, because the waters on the far side drain into the Parsnip River, which also feeds the Peace River. The Divide here is an inconspicuous ridge further to the west best seen at Summit Lake north of Prince George.

The mountains here are rugged and the scenery impressive. A considerable volume of water can be seeing issuing forth from the Table Tunnel. During its construction, a water–filled cave was entered, which drained. The creek that flows nearby is the headwaters of the Sukunka, and a good series of game trails can be followed upstream near the west bank. Unexplored cave entrances can be seen on the limestone cliffs on all sides. After a few kilometres an open grassy gully is reached. Ascending this forms the easiest route to the alpine. There are no formal trails, and topographic maps and compass are essential, but a magnificent area is reached, centering on Bat Lake. It is so named because of a distinctive pattern of snow that clings to the vertical rock face to the south of the lake, which resembles a giant resting bat. Because of its elevation Bat Lake remains frozen well into the summer, and late in the year its southern shore is still a steep snowfield.

This prime wilderness location is located at the treeline, and its meadows blossom into a wonderful profusion of colours in July. It is also the center of an exciting and little explored caving area. Consolation Cave was explored in 1996. It is over 70 metres deep and is decorated with interesting formations. The walls of one chamber above the level of the main passage are composed almost entirely of coral and other fossils. In the alpine are beautiful examples of rinkelkarst, a type of eroded limestone pavement, and there is one deep vertical cave shaft of 60 metres that has yet to be entered. The fossils on the surface rocks are also amongst the best in the region.

One of Bat Lake's special attractions is that there are at least a dozen separate peaks that

#44 DESTINATION

NAME:
Bat Lake area

FEATURE
Alpine wilderness area of lakes, peaks and caves

ACCESS:
4 KM bushwhacking to the lake, than many alpine

can be accessed from a base camp at the lake over a period of days. None require technical gear, and as this is a virgin area, the intrepid adventurer will doubtless make exciting discoveries. Not surprisingly, the shores of Bat Lake have been selected as a potential site for an alpine hut. Nearby are the interesting Showerbath Falls.

Another great hiking area nearby is the Sukunka Ridge. Actually, this area is so little explored that the ridge has no name, and is simply called Sukunka Ridge in this book for identification purposes! It refers to the twelve kilometre–long ridge north of the Table Tunnel. The ridge itself is an enervating hike, but its eastern flanks are graced with a series of five bowls. Four of these are hold glistening alpine lakes, which are a delight to the hiker and camper. Only a few parties have ever been into this pristine area.

DESTINATION #45

NAME:
Sukunka Ridge

FEATURE
Alpine ridge with lakes

ACCESS:
Steep wilderness travel up from Sukunka Forest Service Road

...

A final interesting feature in the area is Hook Lake. Access remains difficult to this majestic big mountain lake, although this is likely to change with increasing road construction. At present there is a rough trail in from the head of the Sukunka Valley, and snowmobile access is feasible in winter. Access up Hook Creek from near Kinuseo Falls is not recommended, as a burn some twenty years ago has made subsequent travel very difficult.

In prehistoric times it formed the natural corridor of travel between the Sukunka and Murray valleys, as there is virtually no height of land between them here. Not unexpectedly, a number of archaeological sites have been discovered on its shores. The area is rich in waterfalls and is another potential caving area. It used to be called Avalanche Lake, but its name was changed to the descriptive Hook Lake because of its particular distinctive shape, obvious to air travelers.

DESTINATION #46

NAME:
Hook Lake

FEATURE
Remote large lake

ACCESS:
Difficult by land, float plane feasible

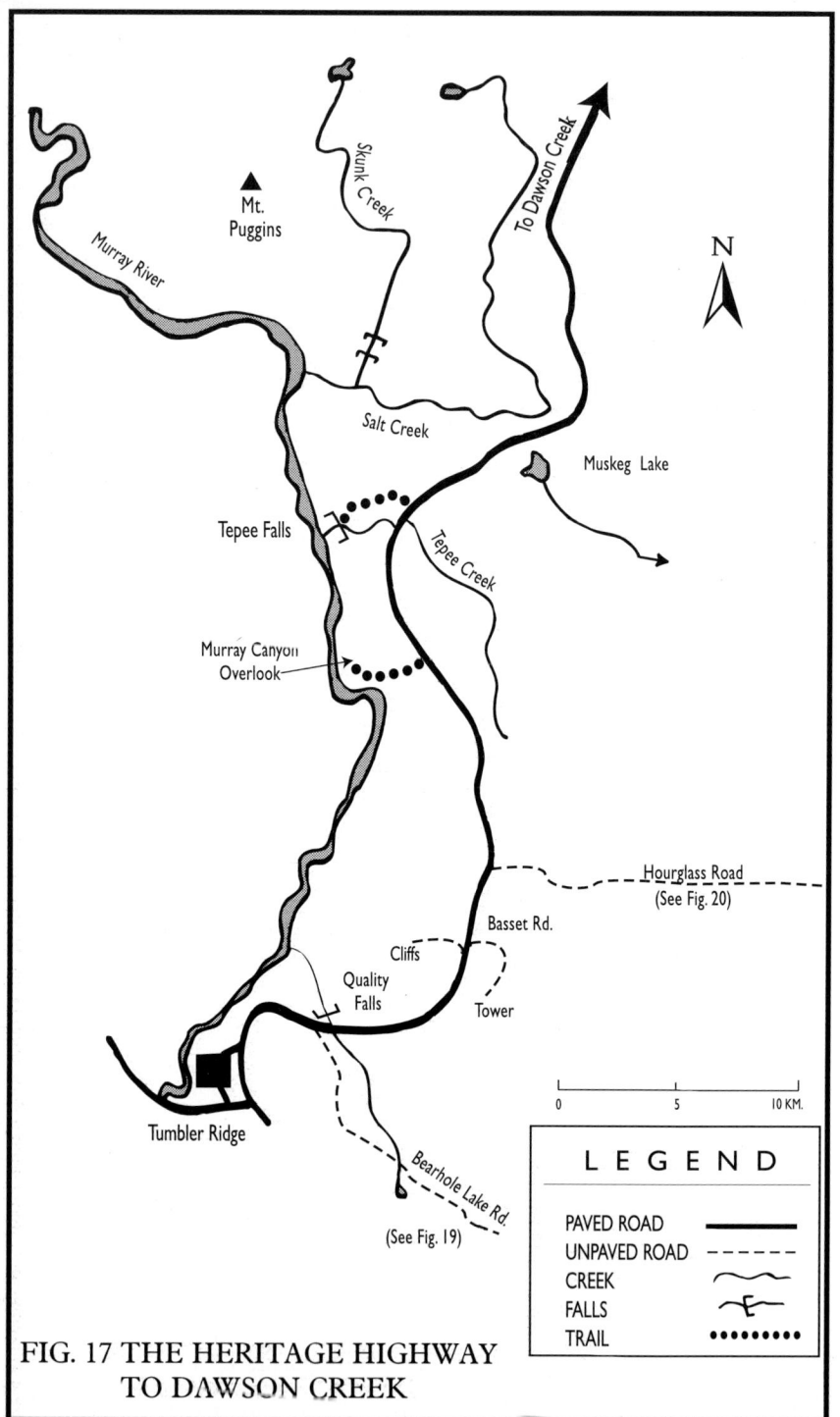

FIG. 17 THE HERITAGE HIGHWAY TO DAWSON CREEK

■ THE HERITAGE HIGHWAY TO DAWSON CREEK

The first nine kilometres of this road (also known as the Fellers Heights road) are described in the section 'around Tumbler Ridge'. Just a few hundred metres further is a forest service road on the right, which leads to Quality Lake and Bearhole Lake Provincial Park (see page 227).

The road then climbs Happy Face Hill. Note a hill with a tower on top. It is possible to drive to this tower via the Basset Road. In years gone by this gave a great view of the mountains and plateaus, but as the forest is regenerating, it is beginning to obstruct the view, unless you have something like a van with a roof to climb onto. To reach it take the first road right after the top of the hill (KM 16 from Tumbler Ridge), take first right again after 700 metres, then turn sharp right after another kilometre. The last bit is rough and overgrown and not advised for brand new vehicles with intact paint. Maybe one day someone will repair the road and build a viewing tower at the top.

Just before the point where this road left the highway (KM 16), turning left (west) may allow you to find with difficulty some eroded bluffs with a good view. Simply drive as far as you can, then walk ahead until you reach a slightly cleared area on the left. Swing 90 degrees to the left. You may or may not find the trail, but if you don't just bushwhack a hundred meters or two and you will stumble upon the top of the cliffs. It is fun traversing both the top rim of the cliffs in both directions to their limits, and descending to scramble along the bottom.

Back on the highway, there is a pullout with a view (KM 17), then look for the wooden tripod at KM 18.5 that signals the start of the Hourglass Road (see page 229). Soon afterwards the summit of the Heritage Highway is crested, with a sign indicating height above sea level (1 264 metres). This is a windswept spot that catches a lot of snow in winter, with interesting formations forming on one side of the wind–battered trees. The road then descends in a series of steps.

If you are driving this road in the other direction, coming from Dawson Creek, you have good views on a clear day of the northern Rockies. At one stage the road is aligned directly with the imposing peak of the Shark's Fin. Few are not impressed by this sight, which suggests the wilderness that lies just beyond Tumbler Ridge.

Destinations

Plate 82: Murray Canyon Overlook Hiking Trail.

Plate 83: Murray Canyon Overlook. Credit: Darcy Jackson

TUMBLER RIDGE *Enjoying its History, Trails & Wilderness*

Thirty kilometres from Tumbler Ridge (and sixty-seven kilometres from the T junction with the Hart Highway if traveling towards Tumbler Ridge) is the signposted trailhead for the Murray Canyon Overlook hiking trail. For those with an hour or two to spare, this is a highly recommended excursion. Minimum worthwhile distance is three kilometres return. The full trail is six kilometres return. At the start is a box with interpretive booklets which explain interesting sites.

DESTINATION #47

NAME:
Murray Canyon Overlook

FEATURE
Interpretive hiking trail

ACCESS:
3 KM trail,
highway trailhead

The Murray Canyon Overlook trail leads initially through pine forest. Then it gently climbs a small ridge and bigger spruce trees dominate. The trail slowly climbs with no hint of what is to come. Then suddenly a ridge is crested, and the trail, now a widened game trail, breaks into the open with a spellbinding view of the valley of the Murray River below, with the mountains beyond. The trail

FIG. 18 THE MURRAY CANYON OVERLOOK HIKING TRAIL

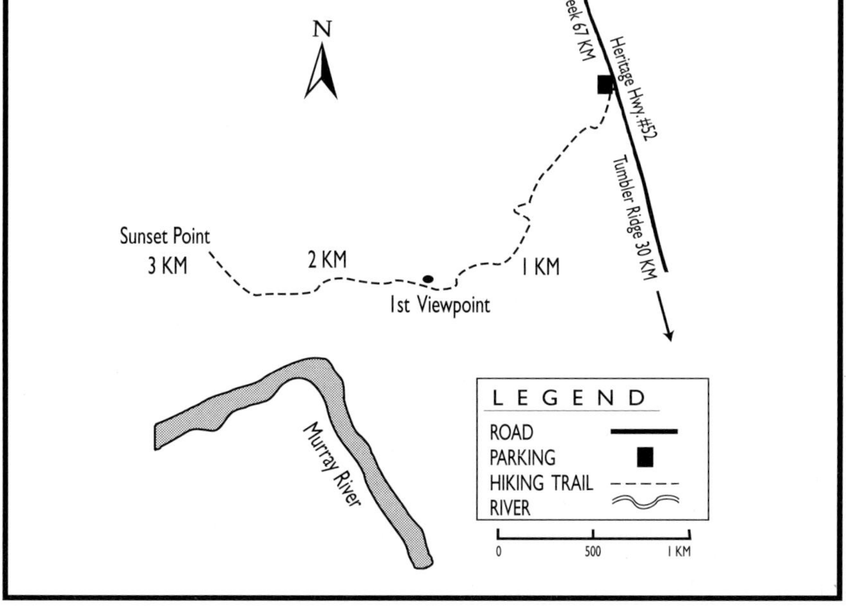

Destinations

Plate 84:
Tepee Falls.
Credit: Ruth Walkley.

Plate 85:
Prentiss Gray took the first photo of Bearhole Lake in 1927. Reproduced with permission from Sherman Gray and the Boone and Crockett Club.

descends a few metres and begins a delectable traverse (Plate 82). Again, this is an improved game trail, but it now traverses the top of a 300 metre high steep, grassy slope. A fall here will not lead to a vertical plummet, but could maybe cause an accelerating roll until terminated by a tree. Be careful and heed the signs.

The changing panorama, the differing aspects of the busy river below, a glimpse into its Painted Canyon, and finally, a long vista downstream provide a memorable experience, aided by the grassy bearberry-covered slopes which are devoid of obstructing trees. After 1.5 kilometres of traversing, the trail reaches an obvious terminus at Sunset Point. Return the way you came and savour the Murray Canyon again.

Understandably this trail has become a favourite running route with an on–the–edge feel to it. ATVs are prohibited and it is not suitable for skiing. It is recommended also for birders and wildflower enthusiasts.

...

Continuing on the Heritage Highway, Tepee Creek is crossed at KM 35, a seemingly insignificant trickle. But as it flows towards the Murray River, it changes character, first filling a delightful valley, then cascading over a small falls with a pleasant pool at their base, then suddenly leaping off a cliff–edge into the space of Tepee Canyon and dropping twenty metres (Plate 84). It lands in a hundred metre high steep chute of giant boulders and noisily struggles to thread its way through them in an inspiring display of white water. Then it curves around a sharp ridge before discharging itself into the Murray unnoticed, a spent force.

Hikers can view much of this drama, but trails are not developed yet, and bushwhacking along a sometimes–flagged game trail with a compass is currently necessary. The falls and canyon need to be viewed from the north rim. It is best to ask for detailed local advice on getting to Tepee Falls. One further word of caution: the drop–offs at the canyon rim are considerable, of the order of a sheer sixty metres. Great care is needed in approaching the rim, and this is not a place for kids unless expertly supervised.

DESTINATION #48

NAME:
Tepee Falls

FEATURE
Falls and canyon

ACCESS:
3 KM from highway along game trail

Destinations

Just the top of the falls is visible from the Murray River. There are plans to build a trail from the highway past the falls and canyon all the way down to the river. This would allow an interesting excursion, combining hiking with a return to Tumbler Ridge by jet boat.

Forty–three kilometres from Tumbler Ridge you can just see Muskeg Lake on the right. It holds Trumpeter Swans and a large Black Tern colony, but is privately owned, with no trespassing permitted. This stretch of highway is good for spotting owls. Old exploration roads lead west soon after Muskeg Lake, leading to the Salt Creek and Skunk Creek valleys with their waterfalls, and eventually to Mt. Puggins. This remote area is best explored by ATV or snowmobile.

The drive on to Dawson Creek is not unpleasant, but has few specific features worthy of mention. It passes through the scrub flats of Salt Creek, then descends off the Kiskatinaw Plateau, and climbs up and down through a series of attractive valleys sprinkled with farms, before joining the Hart Highway at a point 96.5 kilometres from Tumbler Ridge and 21.5 kilometres from the Mile 0 post in Dawson Creek.

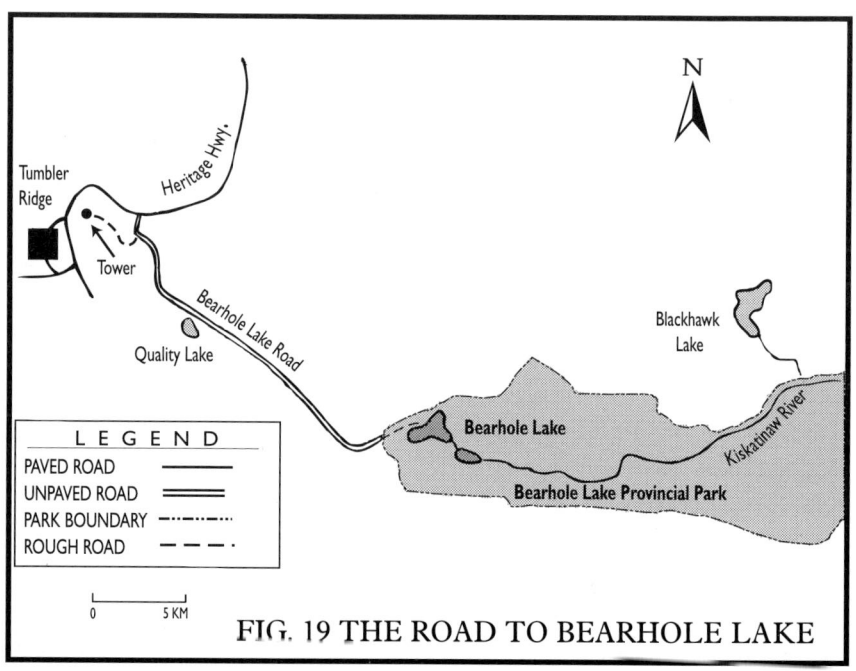

FIG. 19 THE ROAD TO BEARHOLE LAKE

TUMBLER RIDGE *Enjoying its History, Trails & Wilderness*

■ THE ROAD TO BEARHOLE LAKE

For a bird's eye view of the town, it may be worthwhile turning right after just one kilometre on this road. A track leads up for seven kilometres through uninteresting scenery to a communications tower on the top of the ridge. The town lies spread below, with the Shark's Fin and surrounding mountains forming a fine backdrop. For those unable or unwilling to hike to more remote destinations, this is a good way to get an overall feel for the town and its surroundings. However, this road was damaged by a 2000 unseasonal snowfall.

DESTINATION #49

NAME:
Tumbler Ridge Tower

FEATURE
View of Tumbler Ridge and area

ACCESS:
7 KM rough road

Driving up the forestry road leads to Quality Lake after just under seven kilometres. When Tumbler Ridge was built, the headwaters of Quality Creek were dammed and the resulting lake stocked with trout. It remains a popular fishing lake, and is good for cross–country skiing when the trails nearer town are beginning to melt. It is reached by a short trail to the right just after the bridge.

DESTINATION #50

NAME:
Quality Lake

FEATURE
Small lake close to Tumbler Ridge

ACCESS:
Short trail off forestry road

The forestry road continues to Bearhole Lake (Plate 85), a recently proclaimed provincial park of 18 257 hectares. You know you are within a few hundred meters of the lake when the road deteriorates into a rutted mess. It is not as bad as it looks, and most vehicles with fair clearance don't get stuck. The park preserves critical habitat for breeding Trumpeter Swans, and is the wintering location for caribou herds. The lake is big enough to attract a variety of birds, and the waters hold northern pike and perch. One reason it is a good canoeing lake is the channel at the east end, that leads into a second, more swampy lake.

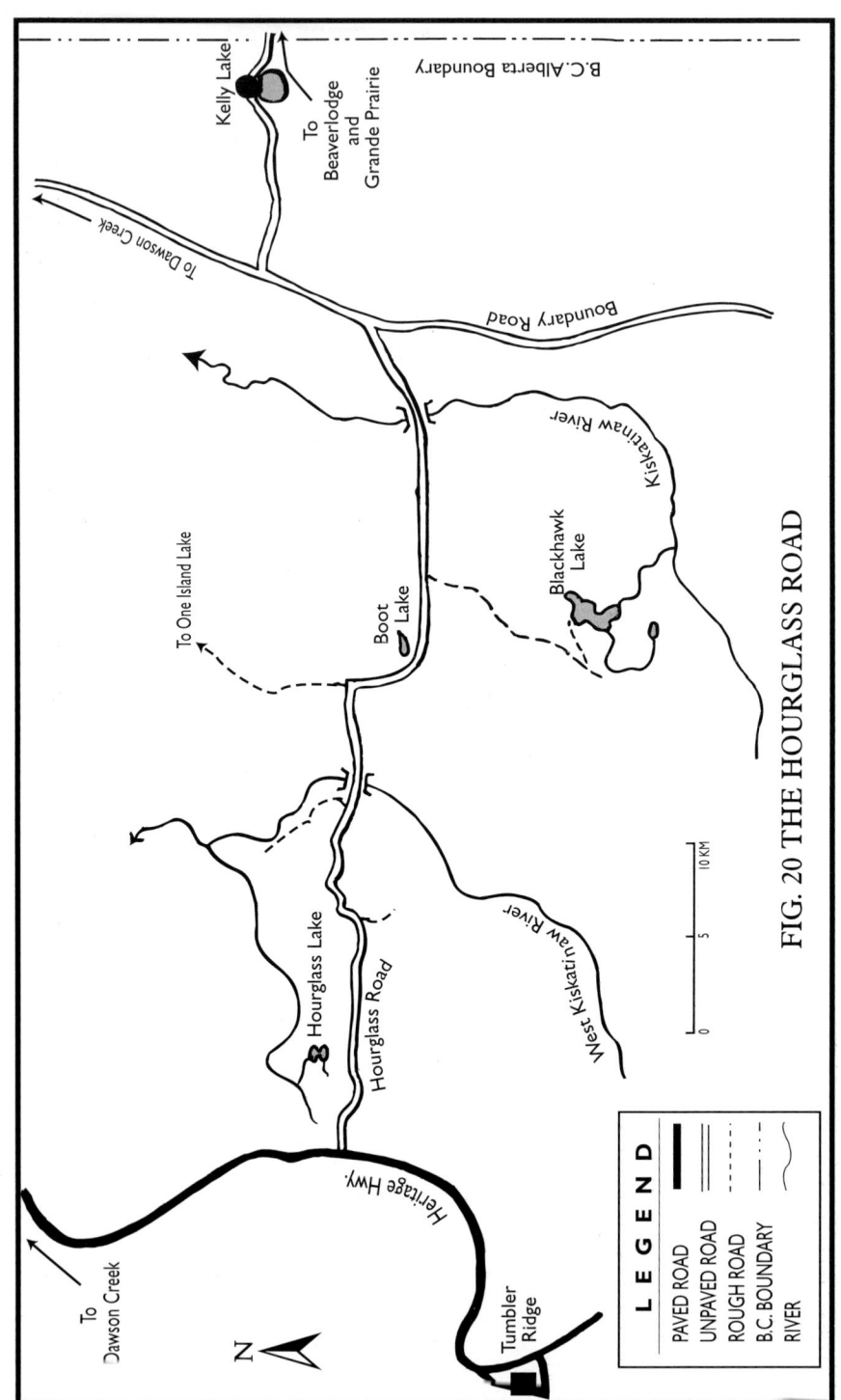

FIG. 20 THE HOURGLASS ROAD

There is also an island in the lake, but it burned down a decade ago when a campfire got out of control. In winter Bearhole Lake is a popular dog-sledding and snowmobiling destination.

Prentiss Gray provided the first description of this lake in 1927:

> "Bear Hole Lake…. does not appear on any map…but is a sizeable bit of water about two miles long and averaging over a half-mile wide, with a little island… the lake is located on a high plateau surrounded by dense jack-pine and spruce woods so that it is not visible for more than 200 yards from its edge…. there is no commanding hill near it from which it can be seen and it is not surprising that the government surveyors, in making a topographical survey of this country, missed it."

DESTINATION #51

NAME:
Bearhole Lake

FEATURE
Large lake

ACCESS:
Forestry road, last kilometre is rough and wet

■ THE HOURGLASS ROAD

The Hourglass Road leaves the Heritage Highway 18.5 kilometres from Tumbler Ridge. It provides the shortest route to Grande Prairie, saving about 100 kilometres in distance, but there are a number of caveats.

First, the initial part of the road is the roughest, and passes through a number of clearcuts. Here snowdrifts can block the road in winter. So driving it from east to west can have miserable consequences if you are forced to beat a long retreat, just a few kilometres from pavement. Second, this is a dry weather road, as part of it is muddy gumbo, and even tough four–wheel drive vehicles have had loads of trouble getting unstuck. Third, it has been known to contain a humongous pothole or two. Fourth, it has minimal signage and a few unmarked intersections and many have become lost. However, if driven with caution, with adequate directions, in dry, non–blizzard conditions it does provide an interesting alternative to the pavement, and leads to some lakes as it traverses the scenically unimpressive Kiskatinaw Plateau.

Destinations

After a few kilometres it is crossed by the Tumbler Ridge –Dawson Creek snowmobile trail. After this Hourglass Lake is to the left. It can be reached off the snowmobiling trail or via a rough cross–country ski trail, but this is difficult to find. The road bores through a long stretch of muskeg, climbs a hill, and then reaches a junction, at which it is imperative to follow the curve to the left. After some winding it descends into the West Kiskatinaw Valley, with a pleasant campsite just after the bridge (KM 42 from Tumbler Ridge). Continuing on, a T–junction is reached (KM 47 from Tumbler Ridge). Here you must turn right – the left road leads to One Island Lake Provincial Park, nearer Dawson Creek.

After some more winding, the road reaches the Boot Lake Forest Service Campsite on the left (KM 51). Boot Lake is a favourite fishing site, and a number of rare bird sightings have been made here. It makes for pleasant short flat–water canoeing, although there is not much variety.

A much larger and more attractive lake is Blackhawk Lake, although it is apparently devoid of edible fish. The road begins five kilometres east of Boot Lake (KM 56 from TR) and the lake is ten kilometres to the south. Pass a turnoff to the right, then turn sharp left at a T–junction where the right branch is disused. At the next intersection turn left and pass a gas installation. Then look carefully for a rough road to the right, which leads to the lakeshore.

Someone has had the devotion to build a little staircase down into the lake, which here has a rocky bottom. Blackhawk Lake is over three kilometres long, and hosts a substantial bird population, including two pairs of Trumpeter Swans.

This is a nice lake for a canoe to explore, perhaps with a small motor. The surrounding

DESTINATION

NAME:
Boot Lake

FEATURE
Fishing lake

ACCESS:
Roadside but road not recommended in wet conditions

DESTINATION

NAME:
Blackhawk Lake

FEATURE
Large remote lake

ACCESS:
Roadside but road not recommended in wet conditions

plateau is so flat that it is easy to imagine you are somewhere in northern Saskatchewan or Manitoba.

...

From the turnoff to Blackhawk Lake, the main road continues east, slowly losing elevation, and crosses the Kiskatinaw River (KM 64). There is a very pleasant primitive campsite on the east bank, with some short walks. Further on, the road joins the Boundary Road (KM 69). (It is possible to make a long loop back to Tumbler Ridge by turning right here). Turning left and then taking first right after six kilometres takes you through the historic Metis community of Kelly Lake. Soon you cross the B.C.–Alberta border (KM 86). Next you pass the tiny prairie community of Goodfare. From here the road heads directly east and is paved to the highway, which it reaches six kilometres north of Beaverlodge (KM 104).

Grande Prairie is then just less than fifty kilometres away.

■ THE BOUNDARY ROAD

Leaving Tumbler Ridge, the Boundary Road passes the Flatbed Falls trailhead and Kevin's Trail. It is joined by the highway from Dawson Creek, then makes some sharp turns, which deserve driving caution, as there have been a number of serious road accidents here. The road then descends to cross Flatbed Creek (KM 6 from Visitor Info Centre), the starting point for ski trips up and down the creek. It crests a hill and descends past the industrial park (KM 11.5). Ahead lies the distinctive rounded summit of Mount Babcock, with the notched summit of Roman Mountain to the left, and the five heads of Quintette Mountain still further to the left.

The road curves around Quintail Slough on the left (KM 13), where members of the Tumbler Ridge Ornithology Group have placed some pallets as a viewing platform in the spring, when large numbers of waterfowl are to be seen. Then at KM 14 there is an important intersection, where the Boundary Road continues straight, and becomes a gravel road. The turnoff to the right remains paved at first, and leads to the Quintette mine, Kinuseo Falls, and Monkman Park (see page 239).

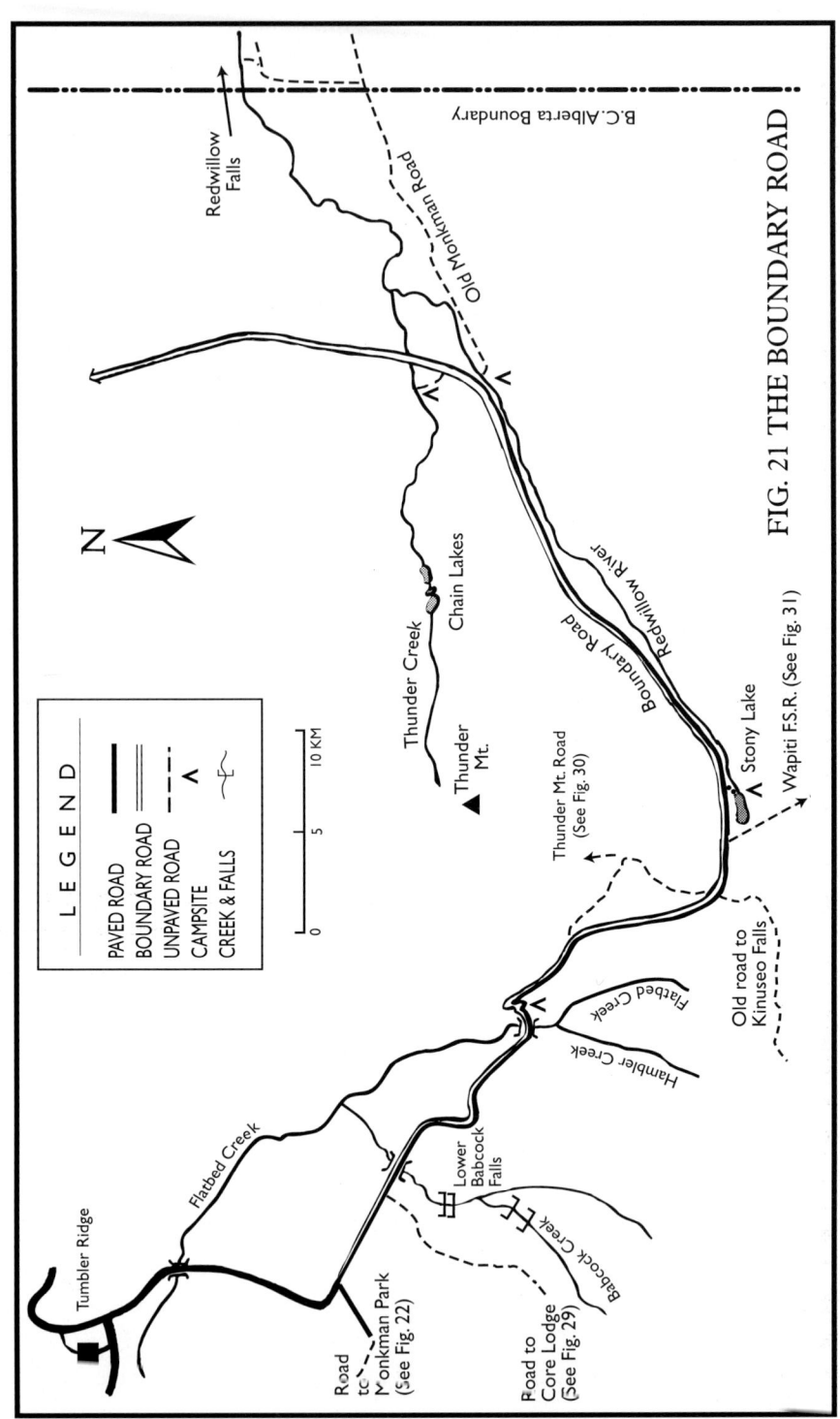

FIG. 21 THE BOUNDARY ROAD

The Boundary Road can be rough in wet weather, and often has soft spots which can be nasty. Soon the turnoff to the Tumbler Ridge airport is passed on the left, then a long stretch brings you to another important junction at KM 21: the turnoff to the Core Lodge and the circle of mountains that surround it: Mt. Babcock, Mt. Kostuik, The Terminator, Roman and Quintette Mountains (see page 285).

The Boundary Road then crosses Babcock Creek. Just before the creek crossing is a parking area on the right. In winter this is the trailhead for skiing up Babcock Creek. This is a beautiful ski route that leads past Lower Babcock Falls after four kilometres. There are actually two falls in quick succession; neither is high but both are wide and symmetrical. You may wish to look for one of B.C.'s northernmost known American Dipper nests below the top falls. Beware the deep pools below the falls which partially freeze over. Stay close to the rock walls and don't venture out towards the pool. A few hundred meters below the falls the rock scenery is good, with vertical walls decorated with icicles (Plate 86).

If you take off your skis and bushwhack around the falls, you will be rewarded with many more kilometres of delectable creek skiing through fine scenery. 3.5 kilometres beyond Lower Babcock Falls the river forks. The left fork is unnamed and is quite skiable, but probably no–one has ever skied up more than a kilometre. The map shows the creek passing through a canyon, just asking to be explored. The right fork continues as Babcock Creek. Within the first kilometre it narrows and climbs. At the top end are small falls in a slot canyon. It is sometimes possible to climb up these with care, avoiding the pool. Beyond the creek opens out until the next falls, which are broad and higher than the others (ten kilometres one way from the Boundary Road).

DESTINATION 54

NAME:
Lower Babcock Falls

FEATURE
Series of falls up Babcock Creek

ACCESS:
Up to 10 KM creek ski from roadside parking area

It is possible to bypass these on the right, towards the next canyon which looks big on the map. But I don't know anyone who has skied past these falls, and snowmobilers cannot use this creek. The only definite evidence of anyone ever having been here before is an ancient

Destinations

Plate 86: Skiing Babcock Creek.

Plate 87: Rappelling lesson above Upper Flatbed Creek.

archaeological site on a knoll above the creek. Can the creek be skied all the way up to the Core Lodge, and how many more falls and canyons lie in the way? Here is another opportunity for the adventurous. As with all backcountry skiing, it is advisable to gain proficiency on tracked trails first, initially to head onto the wilderness trails with someone experienced, and to avoid any potentially thin ice.

...

From Babcock Creek it is thirteen nondescript kilometres to the upper crossing of Flatbed Creek (KM 34). Just before the bridge is a turnoff to the right. This leads past a cabin to a picnic site on the banks of Hambler Creek.

After the bridge across Flatbed Creek, there is another turnoff to the right. This leads down to the Flatbed East Forest Recreation Site, where there are a few campsites near the creek. Someone has built a swing between two tall trees near the creek. Although the safety of this feature has to be checked each time before using it, kids that have enjoyed it proclaim that it is one of the great swings of the world, as it has a long period. There is a 500 metre walk between this site and the Hambler Creek site. An old historic trail leads from here all the way up to the Quintette Lakes.

Most folks just stay at the recreation site, but a very pleasant excursion is possible upstream, the Upper Flatbed Canoe Trip. What prevents this from being well-known is the first hundred metres, which are awkward in a canoe, where a beaverdam and deadfall have to be negotiated. Beyond this point the going is easy, as the creek widens and flattens, and provides flat-water canoeing for almost two kilometres. There is a lot of wildlife to be seen on the way, especially birdlife. The creek also passes beneath two sets of small cliffs. Both provide interesting short hiking opportunities, and the first is a suitable easy rappelling site for beginners and families (Plate 87). There is one short rocky section where the canoe is best pulled through, then there is another flat section. Still further upstream, near the source of the creek,

DESTINATION #55

NAME:
Flatbed East

FEATURE
Camping area with canoe route

ACCESS:
Roadside

Plate 88: Euphemia McNaught captured the beauty of Stony Lake in the winter, 1938. Credit: Euphemia McNaught.

Plate 89: Skiing M20 Creek.

a number of prehistoric sites have been discovered, but are not accessible. In poor snowfall years this creek provides excellent wilderness ski-skating.

...

From the recreation site the Boundary Road switchbacks up the hill, and after five kilometres (KM 39) there is a roadside pullout adjacent to Sora Slough, a small lake, which offers birding opportunities. Soon after wards there is a turnoff to the left, which leads to Thunder Mountain, Gibson Lake and Gap Lake (see page 299). It is then eight kilometres to where the other arm of the Thunder Mountain Road rejoins it.

After another kilometre (KM 48) there is a road to the right. This was the old access road to Kinuseo Falls, and some of it traces the old Monkman Pass Highway route. It leads an initial tortuous course, then straightens out and crosses Honeymoon Creek and the headwaters of Kinuseo Creek. There is a pleasant remote campsite at the bridge over Kinuseo Creek, which at this point has rocky banks. It is no longer possible to drive this road all the way to Kinuseo Falls, due to a substantial washaway near Five Cabin Creek, where Kinuseo Creek has cut right into the road. Further on, the bridge across Kinuseo Creek has also been washed out or broken. But the road does provide access for those hardy souls who wish to visit the beautiful Quintette Lakes by ATV or snowmobile. It also provides access to the historic Monkman Cabin, which was unfortunately torched by vandals in the 1970s. This whole area was thoroughly researched from an archaeological standpoint for the proposed Monkman Coal Project, and numerous sites were discovered, as well as more recent Culturally Modified Trees.

...

The Boundary Road continues to another important junction at KM 50 with the Wapiti Forest Service Road to the right (see page 301). This leads to Wapiti Lake, Wapiti Provincial Park, Bootski Lake, the Red Deer and Belcourt Valleys, and much more. The main road then passes two turnoffs to the Stony Lake forestry cabin which is not open to the public. Next there is a turnoff (KM 55) to the right which leads to the Stony Lake Forest Recreation Site. The lake has an interesting history, and the campsites are in a good place from which to appreciate it.

Destinations

DESTINATION #56

NAME:
Stony Lake

FEATURE
Large Lake

ACCESS:
1 KM by road off Boundary Road

To reach the site of the old cabins, which were a prominent tourist destination in the 1930s, it is necessary to canoe or boat directly across the short stretch of water opposite the boat launch. A few cut steps, cleared areas, and odds and ends are all that remain. The roadway from the cabins to the Monkman Pass Highway can be traced. The highway used to run along the south shore of the lake, and this provides one of the best places to trace its course, and find remains of the bridges that the pioneers built.

Stony Lake is a popular fishing lake, and there are impressive tales of the size of the fish caught in the early days. Canoeists and boaters should note that it is subject to sudden strong winds and consequent very rough water. Canoeing east (left) from the boat launch leads through excellent birding and wildlife country to a beaver dam after a kilometre. Stony Lake is big enough to attract unexpected birds. The view of the distant mountains, reflected in the waters of the lake, entranced the pioneers, and was beautifully depicted by Euphemia McNaught in one of her paintings (Plate 88).

The Boundary Road then becomes rather dull, and the next significant turnoff (KM 79) is at the Redwillow Forestry Recreation Site, set in the forest off to the right. You are leaving the mountains behind, and the scenery becomes progressively less appealing. By following the side road past the recreation site, over the bridge, and left at the fork, you are driving the historic Monkman Pass Highway route, which can take you all the way into Alberta, near Rio Grande, then Elmworth and Beaverlodge. Four kilometres from the Boundary Road look for a track on the left, to a primitive campsite above the Little Prairie Lakes, in mature aspen forest. After another six kilometres, the road crosses Hiding Creek, where there is a primitive

DESTINATION #57

NAME:
Monkman Highway

FEATURE
Historic Route

ACCESS:
Dry weather road

campsite on the right. From here it is ten kilometres to the border. This stretch of the road can become tricky after wet weather. It crosses Lattice Creek just downstream from Gunn Lake, which used to be called The Big Slough, prominently mentioned in the book "People of the Pass". Efforts are underway to preserve the forest alongside this road, in recognition of the historic value of this stretch of roadway and that it is the southernmost habitat in B.C. for the Connecticut Warbler. At the border there is a turnoff to the left which follows the boundary. This is one way to reach Redwillow Falls, just inside Alberta.

...

Back at the Redwillow Junction, the Boundary Road swings north, and soon there is a turnoff to the left to the Thunder Creek Recreation Site, a favourite in hunting season, on the banks of the creek. Other than this site, the rest of the Boundary Road is uninteresting. At KM 111 it is joined on the left by the Hourglass – Boot Lake Road, then by the road to Kelly Lake on the right, which provides the shortcut to Grande Prairie. Continuing straight on the Boundary Road leads to a turnoff to One Island Lake Provincial Park, and ultimately the road joins the main highway (#2) near Swan Lake.

■ THE ROAD TO MONKMAN PARK AND KINUSEO FALLS

When the pavement turns to gravel on the Boundary Road, turn to the right. This road leads past the Quintette mine, up the Murray River, to Kinuseo Falls and Monkman Provincial Park. There are a number of other attractions en route and beyond.

The first part of the road is paved, as far as the plantsite of the Quintette mine. It passes through two short tunnels under mining roads (which will vanish with the reclamation process) then winds down to the crossing over the Murray River. After the wide bridge, there is a large parking area and boat launch on the right. Murray River canoeists call this "the third bridge".

...

Soon after, note a small road leading off to the right. This parallels the river downstream for a few kilometres. It leads to a favourite winter destination, M20 Creek (Plate 89), which it crosses after a kilometre.

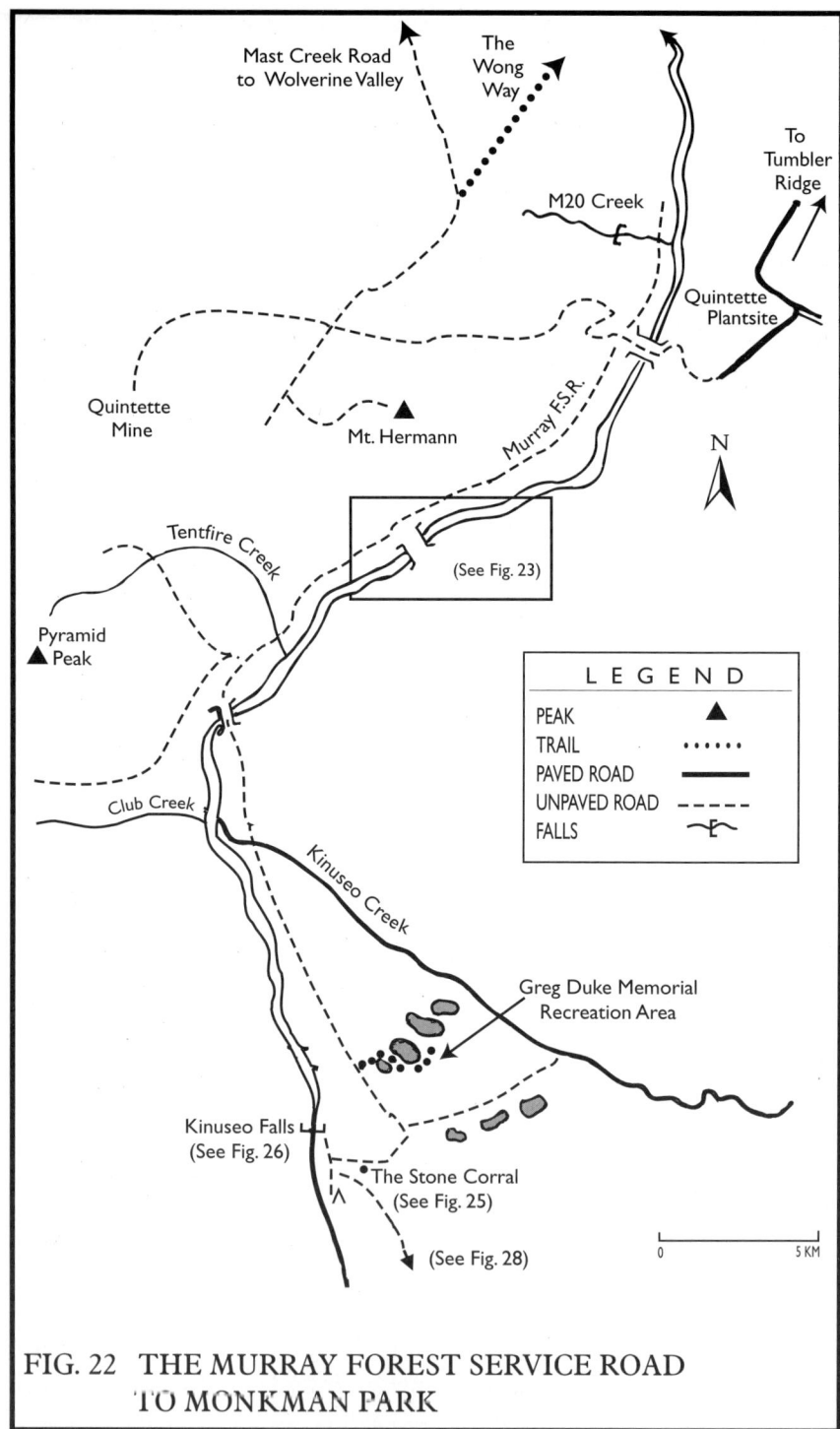

FIG. 22 THE MURRAY FOREST SERVICE ROAD TO MONKMAN PARK

TUMBLER RIDGE *Enjoying its History, Trails & Wilderness*

These creeks were given names that sound like freeways by the surveyors. In winter park your vehicle here, haul out the skis or snowshoes, and head upstream. Soon the creek narrows down into a beautiful cliff–lined canyon. At one point there is a small frozen waterfall, about six feet high. Do not venture over the pool at its base. Rather angle around on the right beneath the rocks, take off your skis, scramble up, walk the next bit alongside what is a long narrow chute in summer, and then put on your skis again.

DESTINATION #58

NAME:
M20 Creek Falls

FEATURE
Canyon and falls

ACCESS:
2 KM up creek from road

The winding canyon continues, through increasingly spectacular scenery, until a bigger waterfall is reached, usually with an open pool of water at its base. Intrepid skiers have climbed up the snow wall adjacent to the falls, and proceeded even further upstream, but this activity cannot be recommended; one false step, and the consequence is a fall into the pool. In winter this is clearly a bad thing.

…

Back on the main road, just after the turnoff to M20, an important junction is reached. The left fork is the beginning of the Murray Forest Service Road, and kilometre signs starting at zero are sometimes erratically present from here on. This is the road to Kinuseo Falls.

The right fork switchbacks up steeply, and leads to the Mesa Pit of the Quintette Mine. After three kilometres of climbing, where the road is crossed by overhead wires, look left for an Osprey nest on a pole. This has been used annually for over a decade. After nine kilometres on this road, there is a road to the left that leads up Hermann Mountain. This is a pleasant side trip, especially in summer when it is famous for its wild flower meadows. The road climbs rapidly, passes under the conveyor, and when almost on top, reaches a fork. Keep left (the right fork just leads to a gas well). The road doubles back past a "rocket", and climbs some more to the treeline. You can continue driving from here on a rougher road to the summit, or you can begin walking. Hermann Mountain contains an unexpected tarn, with the interesting backdrop of the mining operations. There are a number of rocky ridges to walk on

Destinations

DESTINATION

NAME:
Hermann Mountain

FEATURE
Subalpine summit

ACCESS:
Drive (some rough sections) then hike ridges

and explore, and fields and fields of summer flowers to identify and appreciate. There is a good view of the mountains and plains. Hermann Mountain also offers convenient early and late season skiing.

...

Back on the Quintette mine road, immediately after the Hermann Mountain turnoff, there is another junction. Straight ahead leads to the mine. Turning right provides a circular drive, a rarity in the area, as it leads eventually down Mast Creek and joins up with the Wolverine Forest Service Road.

After crossing a couple of bridges on this road (the headwaters of M20 Creek and Mast Creek) a large open area is found on the right. This was the site of 350 Man Camp, a relic of the early mining days. For present enjoyment, this is the start of the Wong Way, an exciting trip that leads all the way down towards Tumbler Ridge, emerging at the bridge over the Wolverine River on the highway to Chetwynd. The Wong Way is named after Buck Wong, who designed the road, which was to be the direct access from town to the mine. A number of slides presented an unanticipated hazard, and the route was changed. But the remains of the road are there, for the enjoyment of snowmobilers, mountain–bikers, and cross–country skiers. Before the descent begins, there is a small lakelet on the left of the trail.

The elevation loss is 400 metres. On cross–country skis, this amounts to one hair–raising descent after the next. But there is one caveat. About halfway down, trenches have been cut across the road. Crossing one of these at speed will likely result in a fractured pair of tibias, or worse. So be very aware of this potential hazard. As this road is not maintained it may well become overgrown and impassable with time.

DESTINATION

NAME:
The Wong Way

FEATURE
Old exploration road

ACCESS:
Leave a vehicle at each end, 400 M elevation loss

Murray Forest Service Road leads up the valley past a couple of roads that lead off to the right. These climb quite high, to near the treeline, but are not always maintained well. The next important junction is at KM 12 from the start of the road. Here a road leads left to a gas exploration area, and soon crosses the Murray River (the "second bridge"). It leads to an interesting area, with three waterfalls. However, because this is a gas area, there are warning signs about H_2S exposure. Exploration of the area cannot be unreservedly recommended and is clearly at your own risk (read the section on Hazards, page 13).

After a kilometre on this side road you reach a fork. Keep left to get to Nesbitt's Knee Falls, and to get to Barbour Falls in winter. Turn right to access Barbour Falls in summer, and to get to Folded Falls.

If you turn left, note how the road straightens out after a few hundred metres. This was an old airstrip. At the end of this strip, look closely to the right; you should be able to see the banks of Barbour Creek through the trees. This is where winter skiing and snowshoeing access begins. Get onto the frozen creekbed and head upstream. Before

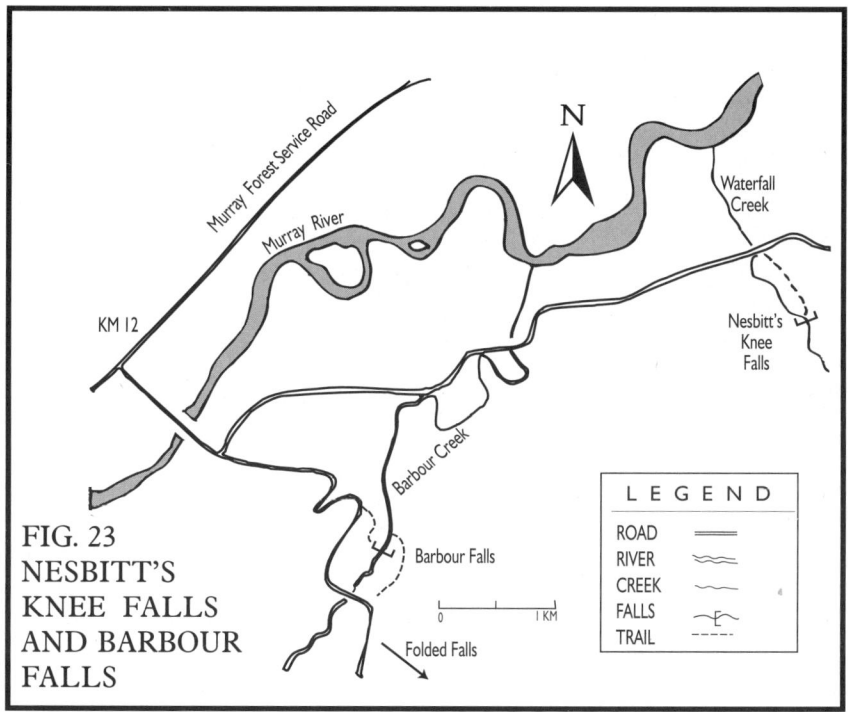

FIG. 23 NESBITT'S KNEE FALLS AND BARBOUR FALLS

Plate 90: Barbour Falls.

Plate 91: Skiing to Nesbitt's Knee Falls.

long you enter an impressive rock canyon, with interesting cliff formations on the left. After another kilometre and a few places where care is needed not to get wet, the box canyon reaches its end at the falls (Plate 90). Avoid crossing the pool at the base of the falls.

In summer, access to Barbour Falls is quite different. Keep right at the fork, and up a switchback. One trailhead is at the next sharp bend to the right. Park here and follow the rough trail, heading in a southeasterly direction. This is lined by deadfall to mark the way. Soon the lip of the canyon is reached. Follow it upstream, with occasional tangential views of the falls ahead. The trail descends to the top of the falls. It is an impressive place, but unfortunately a really good view of the falls in never forthcoming, and it is not possible to descend into the creek bed.

DESTINATION #61

NAME:
Barbour Falls

FEATURE
Waterfall

ACCESS:
Two 1 KM game trails, or creek ski

An alternative is to keep driving along the road past this trailhead to the bridge over the creek. On the far side, you can pick up a game trail heading downstream parallel to the creek. After a rough kilometre, with some side trails down to swimming holes, the falls can be seen better.

For both these trailheads, make sure you park well off the road, because large trucks use it at speed and do not anticipate finding vehicles parked on it.

...

DESTINATION #62

NAME:
Folded Falls

FEATURE
Remote waterfall

ACCESS:
2 KM bushwhacking

Folded Falls is very seldom visited. It is a destination for the purist waterfall–bagger. It is best visited in winter. Continue on past the above–mentioned bridge for under two kilometres to a tiny creek crossing (if you reach the next bridge over Barbour Creek you have gone too far). Put on old skis or snowshoes and whack through the forest and along the creek for under two kilometres, until the valley narrows, and a pretty, small waterfall is reached, named for the rock folding.

Plate 92: Nesbitt's Knee Falls in spring flood.

Plate 93: Summit scrambling, Pyramid Peak. Credit: Kevin Sharman.

TUMBLER RIDGE *Enjoying its History, Trails & Wilderness*

By contrast, Nesbitt's Knee Falls is a popular ice–climbing and summer destination. Take the left fork, past the Barbour Falls winter trailhead, and over the Barbour Creek bridge. Continue for another three kilometres to the smaller bridge over Waterfall Creek. Park on the right where the road widens just after the bridge, and away from the gas plant.

DESTINATION #63

NAME:
Nesbitt's Knee Falls

FEATURE
Waterfall, icefalls

ACCESS:
1 KM trail or 1 KM up creek

In winter, simply use old skis or snowshoes and head up the creek over, under, round and through a variety of obstacles that will irritate you. The falls are reached after a kilometre, at the head of a deep canyon (Plate 91). In winter the seep on the cliff left of the falls makes for a more challenging ice–climbing experience, but the frozen falls are good too.

In summer, the trail starts where you parked. It climbs up a ridge, then follows the edge of the valley rim through pine forest. After a few hundred metres the first views of the falls are obtained, very impressive in spring run–off before the aspen leaves have a chance to obscure the view (Plate 92).

Where the trail reaches the cliff–face at the head of the canyon, it is possible to scramble down the steep slope to swim in the pool at the base of the falls. This is a bracing experience, as the creek is fed by snows and the pool does not receive sunlight.

The trail continues, joins an old exploration road for a short distance, then a faint track leaves it to the right, where there is a view of the canyon from above. There are no safety features – caution is needed. It ends at a pool above the falls. This is a pretty place, but not one to let kids swim in unattended. Nesbitt's Knee Falls was named after a prominent local resident who sustained a knee injury at the base of the falls.

...

From the KM 12 turnoff, the Murray Forest Service road continues upriver. At KM 19 from the start of the Murray Forest Service Road it crosses Tentfire Creek, a raging torrent in spring, a dry creek bed for much of the rest of the year. If it is possible to reach this point in winter, if the road has been plowed, an ascent of Tentfire Creek on skis or

DESTINATION #64

NAME:
Tentfire Canyon

FEATURE
Deep canyon

ACCESS:
Canyon starts 1 KM upstream from road crossing

snowshoes is an enthralling experience. This is not a good beginner ski trip. After a kilometre in the open, the creek bed narrows into a mighty impressive canyon. From here on the creek is mostly unfrozen, and great care must be taken not to fall in, and there are a number of obstacles to bypass. The rewards are great: winter canyon scenery at its finest, big icefalls coming in from the side, fascinating rocks etc. I don't know of anyone who has descended the canyon in summer; this would certainly make for an interesting exploratory trip.

...

Just after the bridge across Tentfire Creek, there is a turnoff on the right. Soon this road forks: straight ahead leads up into the Tentfire Creek basin; left leads into Club Creek along a rough road. The Tentfire Creek road crosses the creek after a few kilometres, where there is a hunters' campsite. Further on the road was at one time broken at a bridge. This has complicated access up into the impressive mountains above, and the ascent of Pyramid Peak.

You need to work your way through the woods and brush up the steep slopes on the far (south) aspect of the creek, to get onto the ridge. Once on the ridge, head right (west) and up. The climb looks intimidating from a distance, but has only one area where scrambling is needed (Plate 93). Ropes may be needed. Pyramid Peak is another isolated summit, the highest in its area, and thus provides magnificent views on a clear day, including onto the alpine lakes of the Albright Ridge.

DESTINATION #65

NAME:
Pyramid Peak

FEATURE
Alpine summit

ACCESS:
Initial bushwhacking and then ridge walk and climb

Ridge Riders Snowmobile Club has forged a challenging route from Tentfire Creek through to the Wolverine Valley via Roger's Pass, named after the irrepressible Roger Ball.

The Murray Forest Service Road then crosses the river (the "first bridge" for canoeists), where there is a pleasant campsite, prone to flooding at times of very high water. There are occasional views from the road of the big mountains, like Castle Mountain and The Shark's Fin. It crosses the sizeable Kinuseo Creek. Nine kilometres after this crossing look for a small parking area on the left, with a sign in the bush. This is the trailhead for the Greg Duke Memorial Recreation Area, developed by the Dawson Creek Forest District in commemoration of a highly esteemed forester. This trail leads past a series of lakes, the Kinuseo Lakes. The trail is being extended, and eventually will lead to five lakes. There is a pleasant picnic spot at Irene Lake, just half a kilometre from the trailhead.

DESTINATION #66

NAME:
Greg Duke Trail

FEATURE
Forestry trail to fishing lakes

ACCESS:
2 KM one way, trail is being lengthened

...

There is a big sign welcoming the visitor to Monkman Provincial Park. Just before this sign, note a road to the left. This was the old access road to Kinuseo Falls, and also more or less follows the route of the old Monkman Pass Highway of the 1930s. Currently it only leads seven kilometres to the crossing of Kinuseo Creek, where the bridge has been deactivated. It is still an interesting road, although it is rough.

First it winds close to the shore of the appropriately named Serpent Lake. Then it climbs, and parallels Serpent Creek. There are two more lakes in this valley, one of which is Lake Joan. This name was given by one of the Monkman Pass epic figures, Ted Chambers, after his infant daughter Joan, now Joan Jones of Beaverlodge.

The hills on the far (south) side of the creek hold a number of creeks, most of which have waterfalls. Some of these are difficult to access; others have been visited by snowmobilers. Canary Falls is on Canary Creek, which enters the lake visible about five kilometres down the road. It is also hard to reach, and is worth the arduous access trek only in spring, as it dries up later in the year.

Plate 94: The Stone Corral. Credit: Joan Zimmer.

Plate 95: Looking out of Corral Cave, Stone Corral Hiking Trail.

TUMBLER RIDGE *Enjoying its History, Trails & Wilderness*

DESTINATION #67

NAME:
Kinuseo Creek

FEATURE
Birding site

ACCESS:
Roadside

There is one important warning about this road. There is a washout which is not easily visible in advance unless you are looking for it. Vehicles with a long wheelbase or low clearance will have trouble here; all vehicles need to negotiate it slowly.

The end of the road is a compulsory stop, but also an interesting one. This is one of the very best birding localities in the region, especially in spring migration. Kinuseo Creek is also known as the Contrary River, because it seems to flow into the mountains. The east–west orientation of the valley makes it a very convenient migration route.

There is a quad track from the washed out bridge leading upstream, past where Serpent Creek enters Kinuseo Creek via an almighty beaver dam. There is also a basic campsite at the end of the road.

...

This is historic ground. A prehistoric site was discovered near the washed out bridge in the 1970s. In the 1930s the nearby Big Spring was a favourite resting place for the builders of the Monkman Pass Highway, who would refresh themselves here and drink from it. This was a planned townsite. After the outbreak of World War II, it was quietly forgotten, known only to a handful of trappers and hunters, and the owners of the adjoining land. The Big Spring lies on private property and access is therefore not permitted.

As you drive back the way you came, ponder also the width of the valley you are passing through, relative to the small creek that occupies it. This used to be the path of a great glacier, coming from over the mountains, flowing east. After it melted, Kinuseo Creek used to flow the other way, into Flatbed Creek. Subsequent geological events have caused Kinuseo Creek to reverse its flow, and cut itself the lower canyon that starts just downstream from the end of the road.

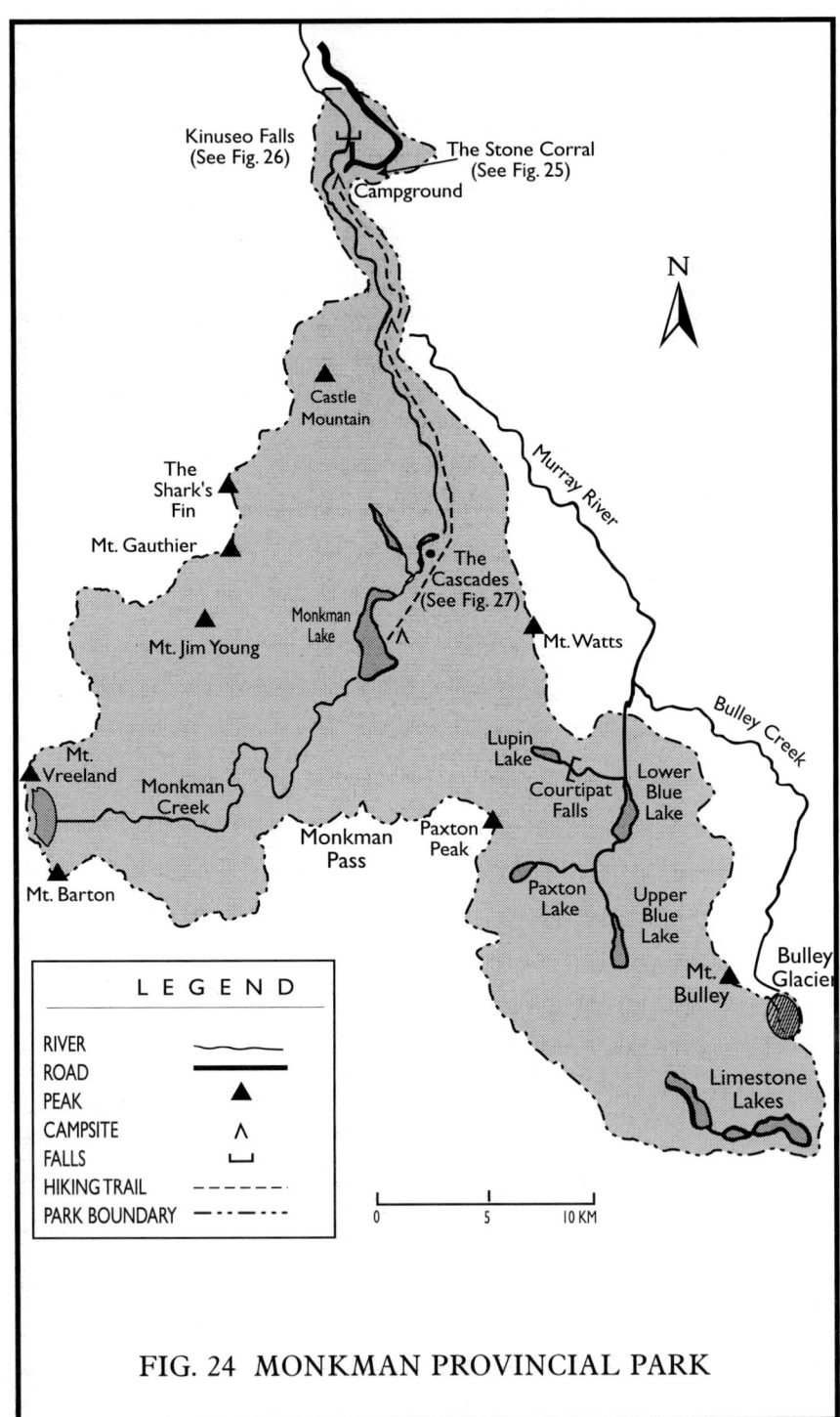

FIG. 24 MONKMAN PROVINCIAL PARK

■ MONKMAN PROVINCIAL PARK

A large roadside sign welcomes you to Monkman Park, which is officially open from May to October. This is one of the jewels of the region. It used to comprise two separate units, but a connecting segment was added in 2000, along with the two more units: the Stone Corral and the large Limestone Lakes area in the south. Besides preserving important habitat for Grizzly Bear and other wildlife, the park contains outstanding scenery, from Kinuseo Falls and the Stone Corral in the front country, to the less visited Cascades and Monkman Lake, to a vast alpine area of peaks, lakes and glaciers.

Drive with caution: the road narrows a bit, and logging trucks still share it with visitors' vehicles, as the road also leads to the Bulley Creek drainage, which has been quite heavily logged. Note a limestone rock wall straight ahead after you round a bend. This offers some of the best rock climbing in the region. After a few kilometres the green waters of Jade Lake can be seen below through the trees on the right, then the road winds down to cross Jade Creek. Just before it, on the left, is the trailhead of a regional highlight: the highly recommended hike around the Green Bowl to the Stone Corral.

...

It is worth spending at least half a day on this unique excursion, although it can be done in two hours. The trail around the Green Bowl is fairly easy, with just a few short steep sections, whereas the trail to the Stone Corral involves more elevation change and steep areas. Be sure to take some flashlights to explore the caves. This is an interpretive self–guiding trail, with brochures at the trailhead. The first part of the trail leads along the eastern shore of a lakelet. A fork to the right leads down to a series of beaver dams. Above these, the body of water is known as the Green Bowl, nestling amongst rocky cliffs. This is more historic ground. The builders of the Monkman Pass Highway found that this offered the very best feed for horses. In the late 1930s either the beavers were not active, or their dams had broken, for the area was not submerged then, and there are photographs of horses gently grazing the lush grasses. The trail negotiates some ridges, then descends to reach a bridge across Monkeyflower Creek that feeds the Green Bowl. You will

Plate 96: Icicles in Corral Cave in spring, Stone Corral Hiking Trail.

Plate 97: Cliff scenery, Stone Corral Hiking Trail.

have noticed by now that the feel of the land is different here, with strange looking ridges ahead, and outcrops of limestone rocks appearing in many places. You are entering a fascinating karst area.

Recent explorers noted that this creek flowed strongly throughout the year, and that on the maps it has no significant catchment area. The temperature of the water, even in winter, was noted to be a surprising $8C^0$. They followed the creek a hundred metres upstream, as you will do, to find its source in a sizeable spring, where the beavers have again been active, damming it so that its crystal clarity can be fully appreciated. Springs like this imply large underground drainage patterns, and the ridge ahead, Chambers Ridge, provided the obvious source for this water. The explorers then turned their attention to aerial photographs of the area, with stereoscopic 3D glasses (a standard cave-finding technique) and were not too surprised to find a number of large sinkholes in the ridge, and one enormous one. Amazingly, despite the proximity to Kinuseo Falls, no one was aware of these features, and in November 1999 the first exploration of the ridge began and was immediately successful, yielding the Stone Corral and Corral Cave. Subsequent exploration when the snow was off the ground focused on sinkholes and yielded the tiny, but exciting Porcupine Cave, as well as a few other caves. Exploration of the area continues in a methodical fashion, and is likely to yield more finds of interest.

Follow the trail up the creek and enjoy the spring. Then the trail climbs steeply up a much used game trail now converted into a staircase, to reach a notch in the ridge. The trail winds around a pond. On the opposite side of the pond note a deeper area at the foot of some cliffs; this is another spring. A pattern begins to emerge: a series of springs at different levels, connected by underground channels, with no surface drainage except in times of exceptionally high rainfall. The rock scenery becomes magnificent, with some faces and tall cracks suitable for climbing.

DESTINATION #68

NAME:
The Stone Corral Trail
FEATURE
Interpretive hiking trail, caves, scenery
ACCESS:
4 KM return trail, some elevation change, steep and exposed sections, take flashlight for caves

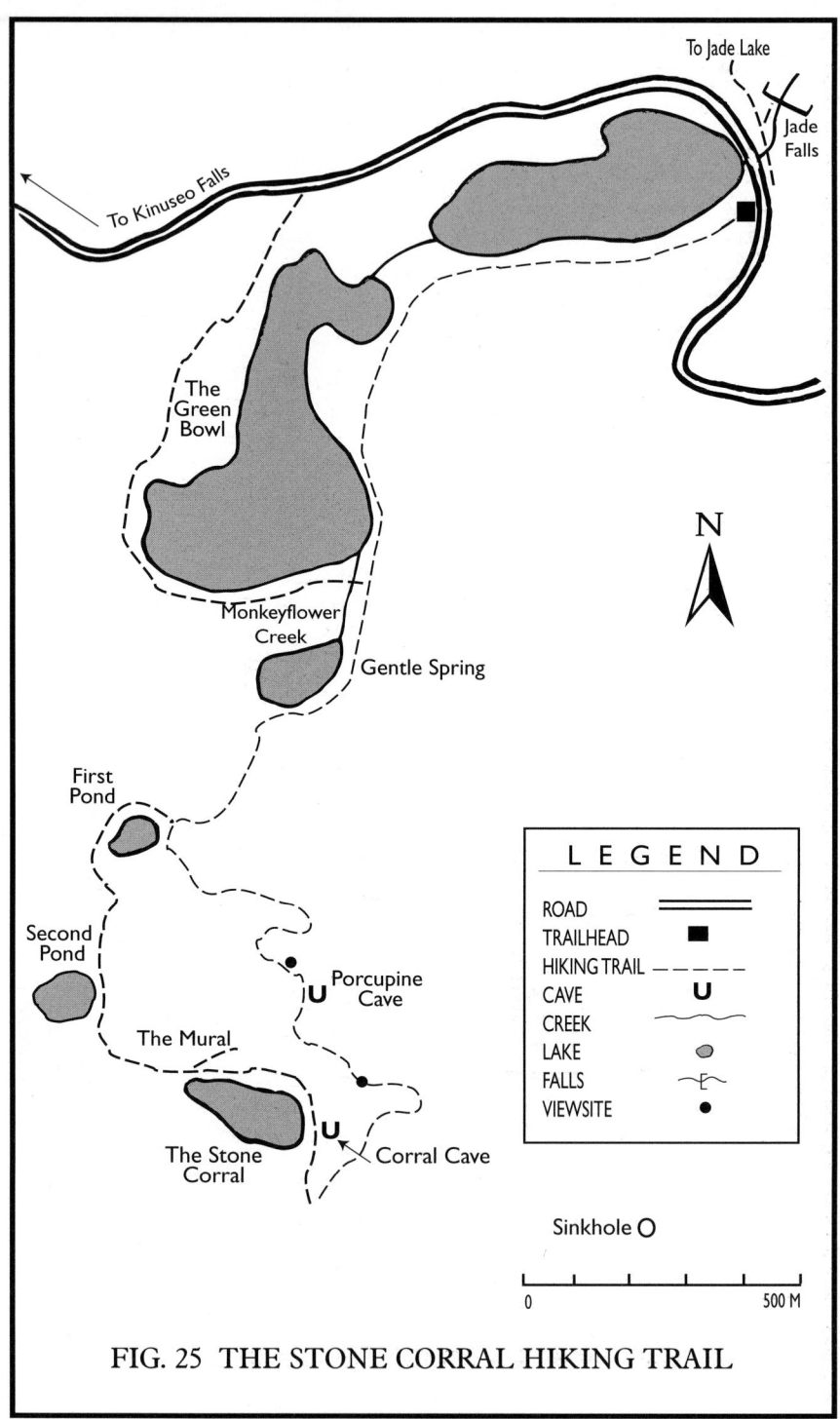

FIG. 25 THE STONE CORRAL HIKING TRAIL

The trail ascends through Devil's Club and ferns to reach another large pond, also cliff–encircled. This is as far as earlier explorers got. It is easy to see how the Stone Corral was missed, as reaching it requires turning left at a right angle from this pond, something that would seem improbable without the knowledge gleaned from the aerial photos.

Climbing again, the trail crosses a lip and enters the Stone Corral. Most visitors are immediately surprised by the tranquility of the scene (Plate 94): a dark lakelet with no discernible inflow or outflow, surrounded almost completely by towering limestone cliffs. It seems tempting to climb the cliffs on the right and jump in, but scuba diving has shown that appearances are deceptive, and the maximum depth is eight metres. The area beneath the cliffs has submerged rocks, and jumping or diving is strongly discouraged.

The area is rich in fossils, and up on the wall to the left is "The Mural" (Plate 6) an unusual fossil feature twenty metres square, where a bedding plane has been tilted almost to the vertical, and subsequently exposed. It gives the appearance of a forest of seaweed, but actually is a mass of trace fossils, the burrows of numerous crustaceans.

Proceed up to the head of the Stone Corral, and take the side trail up to Corral Cave. This cave is only twenty metres deep, but is quite safe and is full of interesting features. It is a walk–in cave (Plate 95), dipping gently in the beginning, with high walls and a high ceiling. On the way in, note a perfectly round tubal orifice leading off to the left. This is a typical phreatic tube, an indicator of how the cave initially formed when filled with water. The mid–section of the cave is wet, with dripping off the ceiling. In spring and early summer this is festooned with giant icicles that have to be negotiated (Plate 96).

At the far end the cave suddenly ends, but looking on and up, a distinctive white tongue of material can be seen on the left wall, with more of the same material on the ceiling. This is moonmilk, a fascinating substance, part organic, part calcite. It contains *Actinomyces,* a kind of fungus which has antibacterial properties. This may explain the successful use of moonmilk in the Middle Ages in Europe as a wound dressing agent.

Note also the impressive walls of flowstone, and if you look up to where the dripping originates, you will see a bunch of tiny stalactites.

Plate 98: Kids in Porcupine Cave, Stone Corral Hiking Trail

Plate 99: Exiting Porcupine Cave, Stone Corral Hiking Trail

Other cave discoveries in the Tumbler Ridge area have either been too sensitive or too dangerous to open to the public, but it is believed that the educational and recreational opportunities provided by the Stone Corral outweigh the minimal risks to this cave. One would have to be quite dedicated to wreck these formations, which are well out of reach.

The trail continues up an interesting gap in the cliffs, then breaks out on top and ascends slowly, close to the cliff edge, until the top of the highest cliffs is reached. Throughout this section one of the commonest plants is the Mountain Death Camas, a member of the lily family and closely related to the edible onions. It is said that eating as few as two of the bulbs has been fatal to humans. Watch for their long leaves and green flowers in July.

For those with energy and time to spare, leaving the trail to bash further up the ridge in line with the Stone Corral is very interesting, with another enormous sinkhole a few hundred metres higher up.

As you continue on the trail, the rock scenery becomes fascinating, with sheer vertical strata. There is a great example of rock folding to admire (Plate 97), then the trail follows a flat section along the cliff–top, with a picnic bench dedicated to pioneer cavers. The views of the surrounding peaks and valleys and Monkman Park are magnificent, and the view down into the Corral quite breathtaking. Creep to the edge and stick your nose and eyes over the edge, or look down one of the cracks that periodically intersect the cliff. This is an area where caution is needed with kids as a slip off the edge would be catastrophic. One adult should be present for every child.

The trail then leads away from the cliffs through a gully, and reaches Porcupine Cave. This is actually a ten metre long tunnel between two adjacent sinkholes. Believe it or not, even these small sinkholes could be identified on the aerial photos, so that this spot was an early target for cavers. Although this is a small cave, it too has interesting features, and is a wonderful introductory cave for kids. The challenge is to enter at one end and leave by the other exit. This is much easier if you start at the bigger entrance. In the middle there is a small chamber (Plate 98) in which adults can stand, then there is a tight squeeze for non–obese adults and an uphill crawl to emerge in daylight again (Plate 99). You may emerge with your skin lightly pierced in places by porcupine quills, and will have enjoyed the primordial pleasure of floundering in old porcupine poop. Kids obviously seem to fit through much better, and the challenge for their parents usually is to get them to leave this place. Non–lean adults should not attempt this crawl–through. Rescue would be difficult and expensive.

When in the central chamber, look up at the ceiling and note a tiny stalactite and a beautiful coral fossil. On the roof and some of the walls are also some classic cave popcorn formations. In these and other northern caves, speleothem formation is very slow, and not usually dramatic, compared with the enormous features often found in the subtropics and tropics.

The trail passes a second viewpoint, descends to another sinkhole at the bottom of a sheer limestone cliff, then descends sharply to emerge near the first pond. Turn right, and you will be returning down the staircase the way you came. When you reach the bridge over Monkeyflower Creek at the Green Bowl, you may turn left so as to complete the trail around the bowl. It leads past more fossils, and down beside the cliffs to the water's edge in places, allowing perhaps for a refreshing swim in the shallow bowl after the toil of the preceding hours. The trail finally emerges on the road; turn right and walk along the road to reach your vehicle at the trailhead.

DESTINATION #69

NAME:
Jade Falls and Jade Lake

FEATURE
Falls and lake trail

ACCESS:
3 KM return on new trail

Jade Creek does not freeze over in winter. Just downstream from the road, it plunges over a cliff as Jade Falls, then flows into the beautifully–coloured Jade Lake, a favourite place for wildlife watching. A new trail is being built down to the shores of the lake (still rough at present). A whole network of new trails is being built in this front–country section of the park, linking the campground, Kinuseo Falls, Jade Lake and the Green Bowl.

...

Continuing on the road, after another few kilometres there is a turnoff to the right to Kinuseo Falls; continuing straight ahead leads to the campground and day use area. The road to the falls leads for under a kilometre to the parking and picnic area.

On the way it follows the shores of the Murray River, a good birding site, and the most reliable site in the region for finding Harlequin Duck. The view upstream is beautiful, with the bulk of Castle Mountain in the background.

Few don't feel a mounting sense of excitement as they approach the viewing area for the first time, knowing that one of the world's great falls lies ahead. Imagine then, the ecstasy that must have been aroused in the hearts of Samuel Prescott Fay and his party in 1914, when they stumbled upon the falls in the latter part of their epic exploration of what was a blank spot on the map, from Jasper to Hudson's Hope. Fay took the first photos of the falls and provided the first written description:

DESTINATION #70

NAME: Kinuseo Falls

FEATURE Great waterfall on Murray River

ACCESS: Short trails to viewpoints from parking area; some disabled access

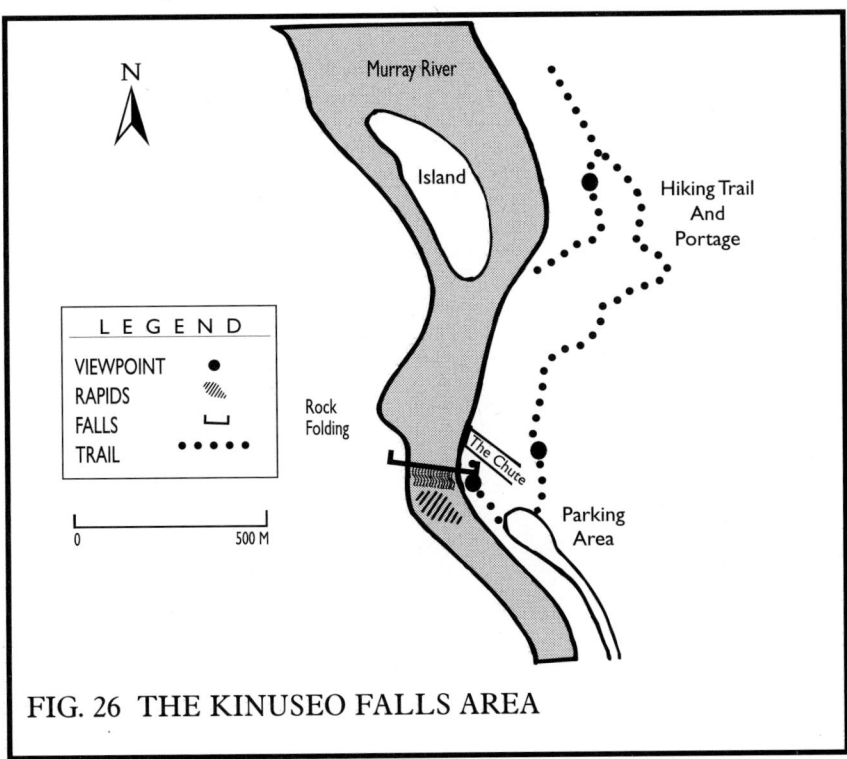

FIG. 26 THE KINUSEO FALLS AREA

Plate 100: Kinuseo Falls.

> "There were some big falls roaring ahead and a canyon below... they had a drop of about 250 feet and were very magnificent. Such a thing as a big falls was certainly an unexpected sight. Here we found lots of chopping, indicating that the last outfit up here had portaged over the ridge and hauled their boat up this steep hill, which must have been quite an undertaking... The falls were magnificent without any question... they cascade over the rocks and are extremely beautiful. In one place there is a big, fan-shaped cascade, while on the right is a little fall by itself falling fully a hundred feet sheer to the pool below... It gave me an inspired sensation as I stood there alone at the foot of the falls, covered with spray, to think that only two or three parties had ever beheld this magnificent sight. They are fine enough if they were accessible, to be a sight such as tourists would travel a long distance to see. These falls and our Mt. (Sir) Alexander are the two scenic wonders of the trip and they in themselves are worth it."

One European, a man named Dixon, described having seen them seven years earlier. However, the falls were certainly known to prehistoric peoples, and archaeological sites have been discovered a few kilometres upstream.

The next recorded visitor was Prentiss Gray in 1927. He too took photos and enthused wildly about the falls and their beauty:

> "What a sight met us! A great river.... poured over a series of shale ledges that extended across the river bed.. Then it made a sudden drop 235 feet to a deep pool. Perpendicular from this pool on both sides rose black cliffs that seemed to frown down on the river for having escaped their iron grasp. From the pool the river took up its peaceful way, dividing into two channels and leaving an island directly in front of the falls... It was raining all the time we were working with the cameras but we took two dozen rolls and 200 feet of moving picture film."

Incidentally Fay got to learn about Prentiss Gray's expedition, and in his 1941 letter to Natural History magazine, he wrote:

Plate 101: Al Tattersall leads the first winter ascent of Kinuseo Falls. Credit: Ed Hillary.

TUMBLER RIDGE *Enjoying its History, Trails & Wilderness*

"The only other person whom I know definitely to have seen the falls was Prentiss N. Gray, whose curiosity, aroused by an article which I published in Appalachia…caused him to make a hurried trip through the eastern area…."

In the late 1930s, as more tourists came to know of the falls, and the Monkman Pass Highway passed close by, a number of enterprising individuals built cabins for tourists at the site of the current parking area. World War II put an end to this, and the cabins were vandalised beyond repair in the 1970s, and destroyed with the creation of Monkman Park. A plaque commemorates Bruce Albright, one of the heroes of those days, who was killed in action.

There are a number of ways to explore the falls. The easiest is to simply walk to the Lower Viewpoint. This provides the only disabled access. From the large platform there is a commanding view. The waters of the Murray are seen to accelerate and contort themselves over a diagonal series of rock strata before leaping off the lip, and cascading down in an ever–enthralling pattern, to enter the great pool below in a huge cloud of spray and a thundering roar. If you are lucky you will see an Osprey fishing in the pool. Across the river are strata with a classic S–shape. Interpretive signs at the platform explain this and the formation of the falls.

Another way to see the falls is to take the trail from the parking lot to the Upper Viewpoint, which allows a profile view. Fairy–slippers (Calypso Orchids) are found here in substantial numbers in May, which is when the falls are often at their most impressive with the spring run–off. Continuing on along this trail will lead you to the shores of the river after 1.5 kilometres, a pleasant winding walk. At one spot you emerge onto the edge of a drop–off, and there is a great view upstream to the falls (Plate 100). If you are prepared to leave the trail and proceed downstream for a few hundred meters along the rim of the valley, the views become even better; this is the site from which the most enduring photographs of the falls have been taken.

The final way to appreciate the falls from the ground is currently not feasible and is prohibited by BC Parks, as it makes use of The Chute, a steep and eroding gully that is regarded as a safety hazard. It is

Plate 102: The Monkman Lake Trail.
Credit: Don Nesbitt

Plate 103: Monkman Lake.

to be hoped that funds become available for the construction of a staircase down this route, for the rewards are ample. You end up at the great pool with the spray in your nose and the roar echoing all around you. Giant logs whirl about, and sculpted wood lines the shore. From here you look up at the falling mass of water, a true in–your–face experience. Just downstream there is a small overhang called Honeymoon Cave by the pioneers of the 1930s; it is not visible from above.... An overhanging branch above the trail down The Chute was the site of a Rufous Hummingbird nest for four consecutive years. Excitement mounted, as another year would have established a B.C. record. Unfortunately, the nest was discovered by some thoughtless and ignorant hiker who removed it as a supposed keepsake.

The main road continues towards the campground, passing a big bend in the river, site of a tragic drowning in 1995. Just before it reaches the campground, note the turnoff on the left, the Bulley Creek Forest Service Road. The campground has 42 sites with ample room and a number of pull–through sites. The best sites are at the far right, as they are closest to the shores of the Murray River. In previous years tourists would sometimes complain that there was not enough for them to do once they had reached the campground and seen the falls, as the only other advertised attraction was the long hike in to Monkman Lake. With the construction of the Stone Corral and Jade Lake trails that has all changed, and a couple of nights can be fruitfully spent here, while exploring the trails by day.

Look for Stream Violets in the campground in May, and Queen's Cup Lilies in the surrounding forest.

...

The trail in to Monkman Lake is becoming increasingly popular. But at 24 kilometres one way, its distance still puts off some would–be hikers. One solution would be to build a short cut from the Bulley Creek Road to the swing bridge at KM 7. This would effectively lop six relatively uninteresting kilometres off the distance, and make the destinations of Monkman Lake and the Cascades more readily accessible.

Currently the trail starts at the far end of the campground and follows the bank of the river. Just when you thought you were entering the wilderness, you cross the Imperial Creek Forest Service Road after

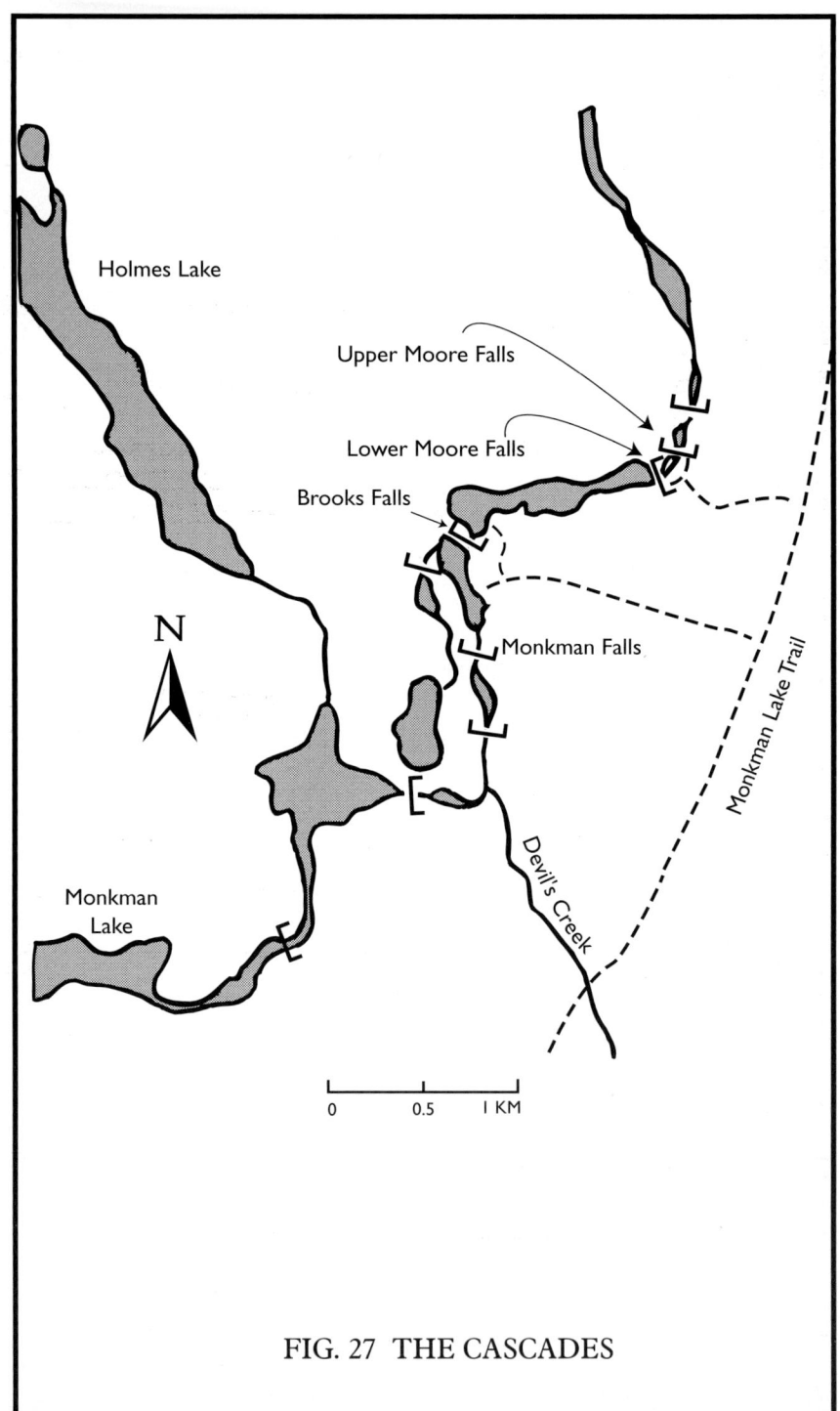

FIG. 27 THE CASCADES

one kilometre. Then you continue for another six kilometres to the swing bridge across the Murray, a lovely structure (Plate 102). In the days of the Monkman Pass Highway, this was called the Slate River, and the crossing here was always on horseback and often quite a challenge. Just across the bridge there is a primitive campsite, with bear–caches for your food. (There is another primitive campsite at KM 13 on the trail. Mountain bikes are only allowed as far as KM 12, and horses and llamas are no longer permitted in the park.)

Soon afterwards, a more interesting section of the trail begins, as you slowly gain the top of a long limestone ridge that the route follows for the next five kilometres. In places the forest thins out and the views of the mountains improve steadily. Looking across the valley, note Horsetail Falls. Closer to your feet, note the formation known as The Whale, a large, long piece of limestone bedrock that you walk over, complete with blowhole.

At the far end of the ridge, with Mt. Watts directly ahead, the trail descends to the right, and leads through thick forest for a fairly featureless few kilometres. The next point of interest may be audible below and to the right. The Cascades were rightly regarded by the Monkman Pass pioneers as a fantastic phenomenon. Here the waters of Monkman Creek fall and fall again, ten times in all, in the space of just a few kilometres. In between the river widens out into placid cliff–lined pools. Nearby are enormous sinkholes, and a number of lakes feed the river (in few parts of the world would a river like this be called 'Creek').

Three of the biggest of the falls are named: Moore Falls, Brooks Falls and Monkman Falls. The first trail leads down to Moore Falls. After about a kilometre you emerge between the Upper (Plate 106) and Lower (Plate 109) Moore Falls. Both are impressive. From the lower falls, if you look downstream, you can see another fall, the last of The Cascades. Some of the best photographs of Moore Falls have been taken from the cliff-top, but at present no formal trail leads there, and bushwhacking is required.

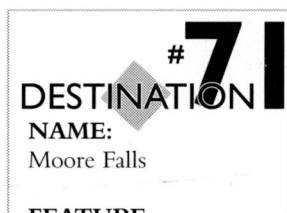

 # 71
DESTINATION
NAME:
Moore Falls

FEATURE
Two falls on Monkman Creek

ACCESS:
1 KM side trail off Monkman Lake Trail at about KM 17

Destinations

The Cascades

Plate 104: (Above left) Unnamed.
Plate 105: (Above) Unnamed.
Plate 106: (Left) Upper Moore Falls.
Plate 107: (Below) Unnamed.

TUMBLER RIDGE *Enjoying its History, Trails & Wilderness*

The Cascades

Plate 108: (Left) Brooks Falls.
Plate 109: (Above) Lower Moore Falls.
Plate 110: (Below) Monkman Falls.

Guy Moore was one of the legendary Monkman Pass pioneers. He retained a keen interest in the area, and the summers he spent here remained a highlight of his life. He was responsible for the naming of many features along the pass, and kept its history alive and vibrant. Shortly before his death he wrote of how these falls were his personal favourite, and they were subsequently officially named after him. His ashes were scattered on Forget Me Not Mountain on the far side of Monkman Pass, in keeping with his wishes.

...

The next trail leads down to Monkman and Brooks Falls. This is a longer side trail and descends down slopes of bedrock where cairns are used to indicate the route. Monkman Falls, the further upstream of the two, is reached first. Monkman Creek splits into three just above the falls, so that a beautiful triple cascade results, emptying into a lake–like widening of the river (Plate 110). This is one of the most gorgeous sights in the park.

Just a few hundred metres below, the waters of Monkman Creek plunge again over Brooks Falls (Plate 44, Plate 108). This is the highest of the ten Cascades, a single impressive leap into another cliff–lined lake in the river. Look for the trail downstream from near the Monkman Falls viewsite. Unfortunately some visitors have not realised that Brooks Falls are so near, and have returned to the main trail without seeing them, a real shame. These falls can be appreciated from a number of angles: either from the chute directly above, from near the lip, or from the cliffs above, which is the most frequently photographed view. It is possible to clamber down the rocks to the pool at the base, but they are very slippery sometimes and care is needed.

DESTINATION #72

NAME:
Monkman Falls

FEATURE
Triple falls on Monkman Creek

ACCESS:
1.5 KM side trail off MonkmanLake Trail at about KM 18

DESTINATION #73

NAME:
Brooks Falls

FEATURE
Highest of the Cascade Waterfalls

ACCESS:
Another 200 M beyond Monkman Falls

Carl Brooks was another of the pioneers. He lost his life in a plane crash in Kakwa in the 1940s. His family has taken a keen interest in the region ever since and were delighted when the falls that he discovered in 1937 were named after him in 1995. In 1999 they gathered from across Canada, and erected an impressive plaque commemorating him on the cliff above the falls.

Most visitors will return to the main trail after seeing these great falls, but for the adventurous there is more to see. In the long term BC Parks plans a hiking trail along the length of the Cascades. For now one needs to do some route finding, heading upstream from Monkman Falls. This is a very rocky area, with many cliffs and a large sinkhole. It is fascinating but not the easiest territory to traverse. But the rewards are substantial as the beauty of the seldom–visited upper Cascades is revealed. At the unnamed Cascade (Plate 105) above Monkman Falls, the whole river is compressed into a narrow channel and hurtles down a vertical drop.

A kilometre upstream from here and just before the next waterfall (Plate 104), look for Devil's Creek, a tributary entering from the east. If you are heading for Monkman Lake, it is reasonable to head up this creek until you reach the main trail, rather than retracing your steps all the way back via Monkman Falls.

An interesting feature on the main trail is Hell's Half Acre, where it emerges from the forest into a jumble of enormous boulders. These were the result of a large landslide off Mount Watts. Hell's Half Acre was one of the major obstacles to the pioneers who built the Monkman Highway. How they coaxed the Pathfinder Car through this rocky chaos defies imagination, described in the book "People of the Pass".

The trail flattens out through some marshy areas before reaching the campsite on the shores of the lake, 24 kilometres from the trailhead. There are a number of tentsites here and the usual cache in which to protect your food against the bears.

...

Monkman Lake (Plate 103) was likened to Lake Louise in the 1930s, and Monkman National Park was proposed. Some visitors to the lake today expect the precipitous scenery of Banff National Park and end up disappointed. Monkman Lake is a beautiful pristine body of water,

Plate 111: Glacier view from Paxton Peak. Ice Mountain is in the centre in the distance. Credit: Paul Jurgens.

Plate 112: Summit view from Paxton Peak. Credit: Nigel Myers.

surrounded by attractive mountains, but it is not Lake Louise, and such comparisons are odious. It needs to be appreciated on its own terms as an enchanting place to connect with nature away from the crowds and commercialism that unfortunately distinguish so many mountain lakes like it.

Despite its size, Monkman Lake is shallow, and its inaccessible upstream regions form a very important regional wetland. Marshes here support a great variety of breeding waterfowl and other birds.

DESTINATION #74

NAME:
Monkman Lake

FEATURE
Beautiful lake in Monkman Provincial Park

ACCESS:
24 KM hiking trail

Above this, the high mountains remain fairly inaccessible, a land of peaks, cirques, moraines, tarns, icefields and flowers. It used to be possible to charter float–planes or helicopters into the alpine areas, but this has now been forbidden by BC Parks, primarily as a strategy to protect the grizzly bears and to prevent the small lakes from over–exploitation. The result is that a magnificent wilderness area is accessible only to the hardiest adventurers.

...

DESTINATION #75

NAME:
Lupin Lake area

FEATURE
Alpine lake, peaks, waterfall

ACCESS:
Very vague trail up from Monkman Lake

There is a rough trail up from the lake into the alpine areas surrounding Lupin Lake. It is hard to follow and some parties have given up in frustration. Lupin Lake is a superb alpine jewel, just above the treeline. It is the highest of the four large lakes that characterise the southeastern section of the park. It drains via a very impressive waterfall, Courtipat Falls, into Lower Blue Lake.

Lower and Upper Blue Lakes form part of the headwaters of the Murray River. Situated well below the treeline, they are seldom visited. Although the Bulley Creek Forest Service Road extends close to Lower Blue Lake, BC Parks does not encourage visitors in this section of the park, and the crossing of Bulley Creek can be difficult.

The fourth lake is Paxton Lake, another unspoiled piece of paradise. It is situated at the head of a box canyon and is visited occasionally by snowmobilers and hardly ever in summer. It is another destination for the truly adventurous.

Hiking further up into the Monkman Tarns area from Lupin Lake gives access to another splendid wilderness region. Obviously, there are no formal trails here and parties need to be experienced and fully equipped for all wilderness misfortunes. Also known as The Playground, this area of numerous tarns and lakes above the treeline lends itself to days of summer exploration. It also gives access to one of the easily climbed major peaks of the area, Paxton Peak. Some rock scrambling is needed to gain the summit, but technical gear is not mandatory. The view from this summit is hard to beat (Plate 112). Paxton Lake is visible below in its box canyon. Far to the east lies the Monkman Glacier (Plate 1), the source of Monkman Creek, held in place by the ramparts of Mt. Vreeland to the right and Mt. Barton to the left. To the south lies the great ice–mass on the relatively flat–topped Ice Mountain massif (Plate 111), a sacred site for the Lheidli T'enneh First Nation.

DESTINATION #76

NAME:
Paxton Peak

FEATURE
Remote alpine summit

ACCESS:
Lengthy wilderness travel

...

Paxton Peak is a choice destination for the true lover of the northern Rocky Mountains. Only a select few have stood on its summit, and a well–planned expedition is needed to reach it nowadays.

For those that reach Lupin Lake, a return to the main trail via the Mt. Watts traverse is an option. This is more untracked wilderness, but the bulk of Mt. Watts provides easy alpine hiking. It has an enormous sheer east face, and is a significant fossil site. With the use of a topographical map and compass it is possible to descend down its north ridge, bushwhack through the forest, and rejoin the main trail close to where it leaves the rocky ridge.

...

A very welcome recent addition to the extreme southeastern region of the park is the Limestone Lakes section. Although it is a long way from Tumbler Ridge, traverses to it are just feasible via the Monkman Tarns or possibly from above Upper Blue Lake. Another lengthy access route is from Wapiti Lake via the Wapiti Pass.

It remains to be seen what the BC Parks approach to this area is and whether floatplane access is allowed. However, all who have visited this area rave about its special qualities: a relatively unexplored alpine karst landscape where creeks disappear seemingly at random, to reappear further down as waterfalls and springs, all amidst towering peaks.

DESTINATION #77

NAME:
Limestone Lakes

FEATURE
Limestone lakes recently added to Monkman Park

ACCESS:
Very remote alpine destination

...

The natural question that occurs to those who visit the park and have taken the trouble to learn about the pioneers who tried to build the Monkman Pass Highway in the 1930s is: "Can I hike over the pass and end up in Prince George?"

Well, the answer depends on the amount of suffering you are prepared to subject yourself to. It has been done on at least two occasions in the last decade by enterprising individuals and groups inspired to follow in the footsteps of the pioneers. But they tell tales of misfortune and misery, of impenetrable forests and unavoidable swims in chilly canyons, of a daily distance of five kilometres of thwacking through dreadful deadfall.

For most of us at the present moment, this remains a trip to enjoy in our dreams. However, the long term potential for reopening this route as a Heritage Trail is promising, and interest has been expressed in such a concept by various groups.

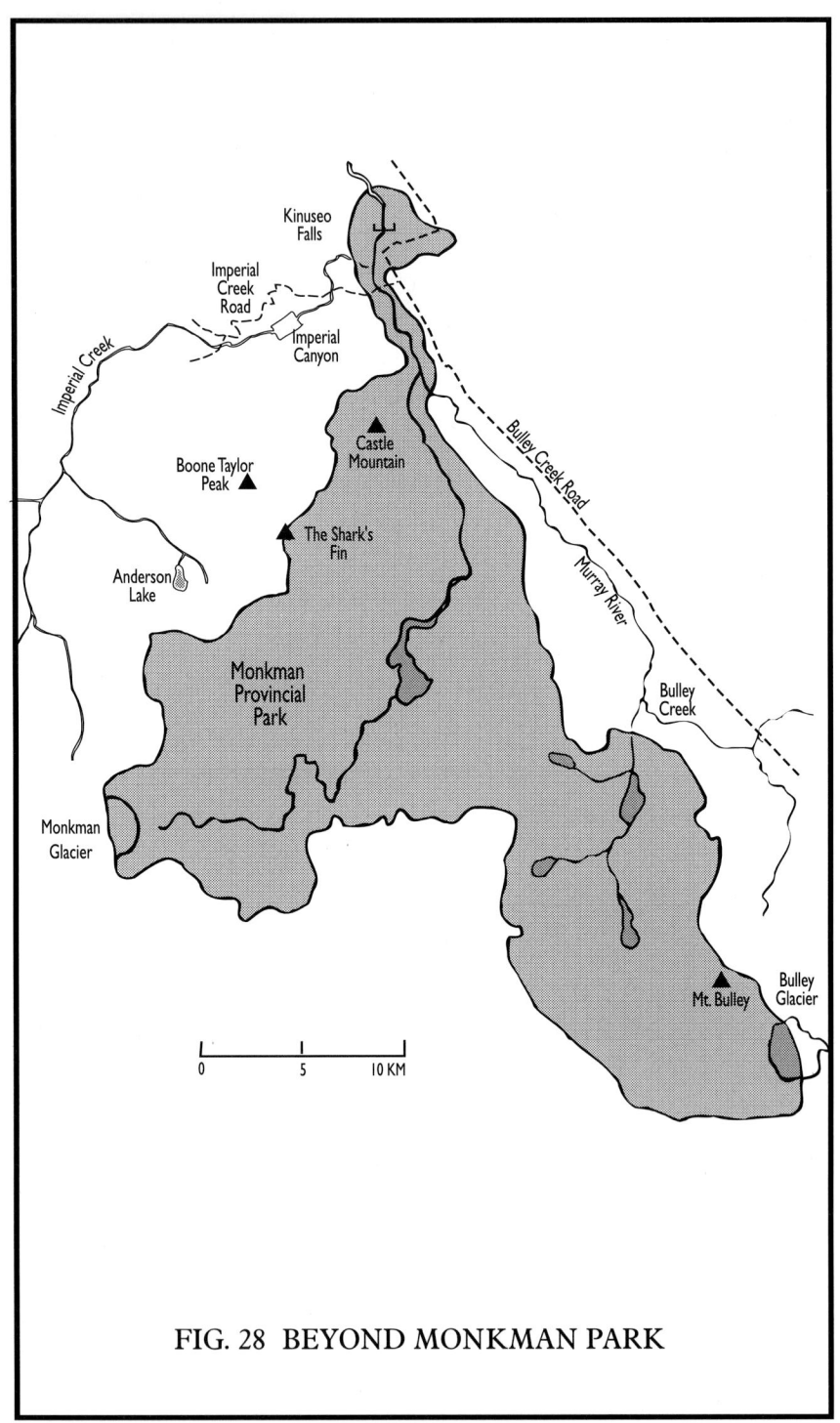

FIG. 28 BEYOND MONKMAN PARK

■ BEYOND MONKMAN PARK

The area just outside the park is no less appealing, and in some ways is more accessible. The key to reaching these areas is the road that branches left (east) just before you reach the main campground in the park. Known as the Bulley Creek Forest Service Road, it splits after just over a kilometre, with the turnoff to the right being the Imperial Creek Forest Service Road. Both roads lead to interesting areas.

The Bulley Creek road extends for over forty kilometres and may be extended still further in future. This valley has been quite extensively logged. Irrespective of one's views on clearcutting, the point made by those who seek a diversified economy for Tumbler Ridge seems justified: that a precious local natural resource has been exploited with absolutely minimal economic benefit to the local community, as the contracts were dished out years ago to companies that have no stake in Tumbler Ridge's future.

The road leads mainly near the valley floor, but there are some good mountain views. Initially Castle Mountain is prominent to the right, with the Albright Ridge way off to its right. Further along the road, the towering spike of Mt. Bulley dominates at the head of the valley. The route by which Fay's party entered the Murray valley has been confirmed – they chose the line of least resistance from north of Wapiti Lake. The deadfall in the area you are driving through was one of their worst obstacles.

For the experienced backpacker in search of a new challenge, the Mt. Bulley excursion is recommended. It involves a difficult crossing of a frequently flooded Bulley Creek, then an ascent through tough forest where an occasional game trail relieves the monotony of relentless bushwhacking. One route leads up a ridge, another past some lakes at the treeline. Once the alpine is reached, the going remains difficult as a lot of side–hilling is required, along with careful route selection using map and compass or GPS. You pass a

DESTINATION #78

NAME:
Mt. Bulley

FEATURE
Remote high summit

ACCESS:
3 day wilderness expedition, elevation gain 1 100 metres

tiny lake and glacier at the foot of the north face. Finally the slopes of Mt. Bulley need to be ascended. They are steep but can be survived without technical apparatus, although a rope may prove useful.

The reward is a great view of the northern Rockies from one of the highest regional summits, including unsurpassed views of the Bulley Glacier. A Tumbler Ridge group that made this ascent in 1999 may well have been the first ever to tread upon these few square feet of flat rock with the land falling away precipitously in all directions.

The sheer east face is definitely unclimbed and remains one of the big mountaineering challenges of the area. A trip up Mt. Bulley is at least a three-day excursion, not to be undertaken lightly.

...

For even more adventure, consider bushwhacking upstream from the very end of the Bulley Creek road. At least three days should be planned for this trip. Eventually you will emerge at the treeline below the large Bulley Glacier (Plate 2). It is possible to zig-zag up to the Divide to the west, avoiding any glacier travel. 1200 metres above tower the cliffs of Mt. Bulley.

Experts in glacier travel may wish to cross the Bulley Glacier and ascend the peak at its head, which can be considered the true source of the Murray River. This unnamed summit is the highest in the Tumbler Ridge area at 2 630 metres above sea level. This whole area offers the most dramatic relief to be found anywhere in the region. No one has left records of ascending this peak. Enough said!

#79 DESTINATION

NAME:
Bulley Glacier

FEATURE
Remote glacier

ACCESS:
Lengthy wilderness travel, glacier travel optional

...

The Imperial Creek Forest Service Road has more to offer the recreational driver, as well as leading to some choice wilderness destinations. However, it is sometimes gated, either at the start or at the Murray crossing. From where it leaves the Bulley Creek road, it descends through a logged area, then crosses the Murray River. It swings right to parallel the river in a downstream direction, then crosses the impressive torrent of Imperial Creek.

TUMBLER RIDGE *Enjoying its History, Trails & Wilderness*

Just after the bridge look for a track leading off on the right. This descends a few hundred metres to a beautiful rustic site on the banks of the creek, ideal for picnicking or camping, as well as birding. Look for American Dippers which nest under the remains of an old bridge here. Nearby are the remains of an old lumber operation dating back to the 1970s when the area was logged. Two archaeological sites were discovered nearby, complete with prehistoric stone artifacts.

As the road continues it becomes more interesting. Many of the valleys in the region are covered with glacial till. Imperial Creek is an exception, as here the limestone bedrock is on or close to the surface, and as the road ascends it winds around some of these impressive limestone ridges. This road is one of the more reliable grizzly bear sites.

After just a few kilometres the mountain scenery becomes increasingly spectacular, with good views back towards the Murray River with the foothills beyond, and the north faces of Castle Mountain to the south. The limestone ridges lead up above the road, and provide relatively user–friendly trailless hiking for those so inclined.

The road descends to recross Imperial Creek. It is steadily being expanded, with potential access to further remote regions for the backpacker. Apart from the scenic qualities alluded to, it gives improved access to two specific destinations: Imperial Canyon and The Shark's Fin.

Imperial Canyon lies in between the two road bridges mentioned above. It was rediscovered in 1999 by a party of visiting cavers. Using aerial photos they identified the terrain where the creek cuts through the ridges of limestone bedrock as an area of high cave potential.

They bushwhacked down to it and found an enticing blue rope leading off a cliff–edge to an overhang at the foot of the canyon. Clearly some unknown explorer had been there before them. They reported a magnificent canyon, over a kilometre long, similar to some of the famous tourist attractions of the national parks to the south. No–one has been there since. Imperial Canyon beckons the explorer with the lure of unknown surprises.

DESTINATION #80

NAME:
Imperial Canyon

FEATURE
Remote canyon

ACCESS:
2 KM bushwhacking to canyon

Plate 113:
The Shark's Fin.
Credit: Kevin Sharman

Plate 114:
The unclimbed face of
The Shark's Fin.
Credit: Kevin Sharman.

The Shark's Fin remains arguably the ultimate prize for those with a passion for this area. From a great distance it stands unchallenged on the horizon as a beacon and a symbol of the untapped beauty of the backcountry. Few will have driven the Heritage Highway towards Tumbler Ridge on a fair day, seen this dominant and unusually shaped peak (Plate 113), and not felt a yearning deep inside to be transported onto its summit.

DESTINATION

NAME:
The Shark's Fin

FEATURE
Prominent remote alpine summit

ACCESS:
3 day wilderness expedition, elevation gain 1 200 metres

In the tradition of a great mountain, it has bastions which need to be overcome. The weather is one. Swirling mists often engulf the peak, and the rainfall and snowfall here is more than double that in Tumbler Ridge. Although the Imperial Creek road has removed the need for a canoe crossing of the Murray River, an epic bushwhack through difficult forest remains. A long side–hill section follows into a high pass. From here the summit ascent can be attempted.

The sheer northeast and southeast faces are unclimbed (Plate 114), but the south and west ridges are climbable. Some scrambling is involved but there is no great technical difficulty. From the summit another unbeatable mountain view unfolds when the weather is clear. A local party found no cairn at the summit in 1990, and chose not to build one themselves. They repeated the ascent a decade later and found the summit still unmarked.

Although the Shark's Fin itself is regarded as the prize, and a trip to the summit and back can just be performed in three days, a lengthier expedition will allow access to a magnificent wilderness area. This exceptional region offers numerous further alpine ascents, such as Boone Taylor Peak (the prominent summit to the right of the Shark's Fin as seen from near Tumbler Ridge), a host of tarns and flower–filled meadows, and Anderson Lake.

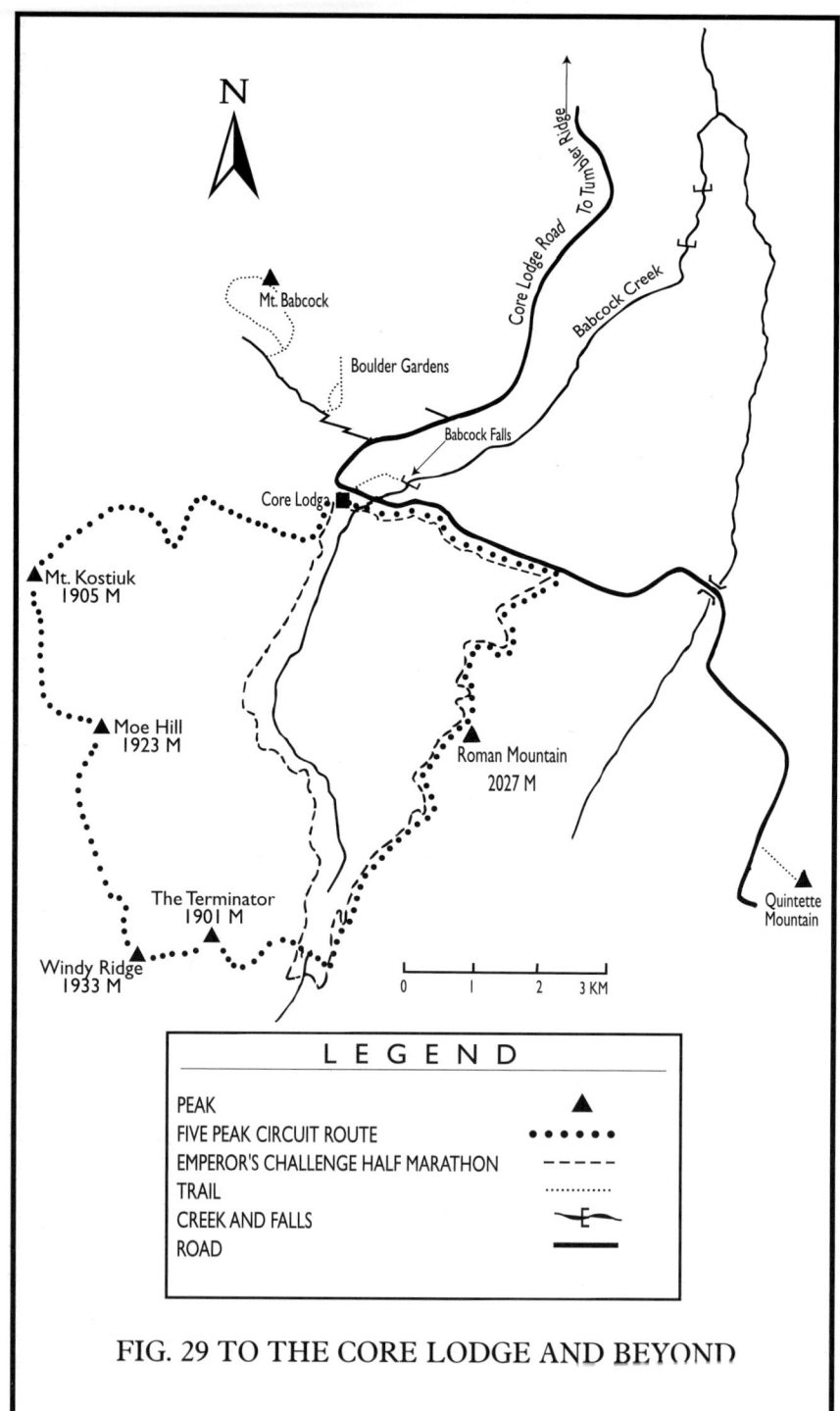

FIG. 29 TO THE CORE LODGE AND BEYOND

■ TO THE CORE LODGE AND BEYOND

The road to the Core Lodge leaves the Boundary Road 21 kilometres from Tumbler Ridge, just before the Boundary Road crosses Babcock Creek. It climbs slowly over the next 10 kilometres, finding its way into the upper Babcock Creek drainage. This is one of the best places to see Black and Grizzly Bear from the safety of your vehicle, especially around dawn and dusk, when the probability of a sighting approaches 70%. You curve around the flanks of Babcock Mountain, until a view of the valley and surrounding peaks is obtained. It is worth noting the features from here. On the left lie the "five heads" of Quintette Mountain, with some towers on the highest point. Straight ahead is the ridged bulk of Roman Mountain. Then clockwise are the two summits of The Terminator, Windy Ridge, Moe Hill and Mount Kostuik. Babcock Mountain lies behind you to the right. Below you in the valley lie Babcock Falls. Each of these is a destination in its own right. Together, they form a fine recreation area for residents and visitors.

A side road is passed to the right (KM 33 from Tumbler Ridge) that leads nowhere interesting. The next fork (KM 34) is important, for the right turn provides access to the Boulder Gardens and Babcock Mountain, discussed below. Keeping left leads to the Core Lodge. You pass a turnoff to the right to a gaswell, then cross a creek. On the left (KM 35) is the road that leads to Roman Mountain and Quintette Mountain. Immediately afterwards is another left turn, to the Core Lodge.

The Core Lodge was built for exploration purposes. Its name refers to the core samples that were drilled. It was donated to the Ridge Riders Snowmobile Club, and serves as one of the headquarters of this dedicated group who have consistently promoted responsible use of the outdoors. In winter the lodge is a buzz of activity, with trails extending in all directions. They have also generously allowed it to be used as the start and finish of the Emperor's Challenge Mountain Half Marathon. The area also lends itself well to exploration on horseback.

For summer destinations, first let's consider the road up to the Boulder Gardens and Mount Babcock. From the KM 34 fork it climbs steadily up switchbacks. After the second set of switchbacks note the rock scenery just above the road. Park here at the beginning of an old

Plate 115: The Boulder Gardens.

Plate 116: Training for the Emperor's Challenge – runners crest a ridge near the Roman Mountain summit.

exploration track. There are plans to build a formal trail here. Until then, be content with these directions. Walk east along the overgrown exploration road for 100 metres, then turn left (north) and find the easiest way to gain the top of the rock cliffs through simple scrambling.

Once up, you enter a surreal landscape (Plate 115), unlike any other. Below you lies a "valley" which has no stream at its bottom. Rather, it represents a line where the rocks on the right have broken away from the mountain, over a length of a kilometre. Rocks are strewn everywhere, in chaotic abandon, and cracks, crevices, and climbable cliffs abound. A series of eerie depressions fills the valley floor. You can follow the rim of the ridge or walk up through the valley, or make it into a circular route. Below on the eastern side of the ridge is a charming tarn among the rocks.

DESTINATION #82

NAME:
The Boulder Gardens

FEATURE
Interesting rock formations

ACCESS:
1.5 KM walk, some scrambling, many crevices and pits, trail planned

After a few hundred metres you will have absorbed the ambience of this awe–inspiring place, guarded by sentinel black ravens, and filled with flowers between the boulders in season. The area is characterised by innumerable small caves, hollows, depressions, steep dropoffs and an alarming selection of deep pits and crevices. A fall into one of these would lead to death or serious injury. If you watch where you walk and are careful, this need not happen. Please heed this warning and be especially careful with children.

...

The road continues up Mount Babcock until it reaches a gas well near some rock tower formations. Don't go as far as this well. The easiest ascent of Mount Babcock is probably from a few hundred metres before the end of the road, where another old exploration track joins it. By following this and switchbacking uphill, you avoid the steeper sections. It is possible to follow the remains of exploration roads almost all the way to the top, thus protecting the fragile tundra from damage by too many different trails.

Mount Babcock is full of surprises. From a distance it looks as if an ascent will be a boring slog. But you will find a number of beautiful

The Core Lodge By Dan McNeil

The Babcock exploration camp was built in 1975 as part of the development of the North East Coalfield, and was used as the base for exploring Roman, Quintette and Babcock Mountains. While it was active, the camp consisted of fifteen trailers and prefabricated buildings and two large metal storage sheds. One of these was used to analyse and store the drill core, which was being recovered in the area. The front part of this shed was insulated for working in and the back was filled with core storage racks. The camp was abandoned in 1980 when the decision was made to mine Babcock later, and only this shed remains, now known as the Core Lodge.

Many of the miners from T.R. were snowmobilers and they quickly discovered how beautiful and challenging the riding was. In 1986 the T.R. Ridge Riders snowmobile club was formed and one of their first projects was to build a clubhouse. Quintette Coal agreed to turn the shed over to the club in 1987.

The first step was to clean out the shed, which included seven years worth of garbage as well as the tons of core, boxes and the racks on which they were stacked. The core boxes were stacked carefully outside for later use and then the racks were dismantled. All the rough wood and iron rebar was removed. The rebar was later donated to the T. R. Aquatic Centre for use in the construction of the pool. The remaining steel beams and timbers were used to build the floor frame over the existing dirt floor. The drill core was then carried back into the building and most of it was dumped on the ground to fill the space below the floor. The long pieces of conglomerate core were saved and used to build the hearth around the central fireplace. The central fireplace was built using a Wemco basket as the fire pit, with a large tin cone and insulated pipe for the chimney. A wooden sign officially identified the building as The Core Lodge.

Most of this work was done in three months in 1987 by fifteen club members. The first annual Windy Ridge Hillclimb was held soon afterwards, and since then there have been tens of thousands of visitors, with a peak of 900 visitors on one day.

TUMBLER RIDGE *Enjoying its History, Trails & Wilderness*

alpine tarns on the ascent, and then just when you think you are reaching the summit, you will be confronted by a wide valley that bisects the peak. Go down through this and up the other side to reach the true summit, with its view down onto the Quintette Mine in one direction, and the expanse of the Hart Ranges in the other. Then follow the summit valley westwards, to where it holds a few small lakes. If the weather is good, start circling anti-clockwise, staying near the edge of the cliffs, until you end up somewhere above your vehicle. The Quintette Mine pushed far up the slopes of Mount Babcock, and parts of the mountain were off limits for a few years, but the route described is considered safe. This is a good site from which to view the mine, getting greener every year as reclamation takes hold.

DESTINATION #83

NAME:
Mt. Babcock

FEATURE
Alpine summit close to Tumbler Ridge

ACCESS:
Gentle alpine summit, 3 KM hike, elevation gain 300 metres

...

One of the most interesting roads to explore in this area is the Roman Mountain road, which leads ultimately to Quintette Mountain. It descends from near the Core Lodge to cross Babcock Creek. Just upstream from the bridge is a pleasant rock pool, ideal for swimming in on a hot summer's day. The road then climbs the flanks of Roman Mountain. 3.5 kilometres from the Core Lodge the road reaches its highest point, and right here there is a track leading up to the right. This leads all the way to the summit of Roman Mountain (Plate 116), an exhilarating and highly recommended hike.

DESTINATION #84

NAME:
Roman Mountain

FEATURE
Alpine summit, scene of Emperor's Challenge

ACCESS:
Well marked 3.5 KM trail to summit, elevation gain 600 metres

Thanks to the efforts of the Wolverine Nordic and Mountain Society in flagging the route for the Emperor's Challenge Mountain Half–Marathon, you can now follow this route with virtual impunity in any weather condition except deep snow, without fear of getting lost. In mid–August hardy mountain runners descend this route in droves in what

The Emperor's Challenge Mountain Half-Marathon

THE EMPEROR'S CHALLENGE… *the name conjures up images of Roman legions seizing new territory in some far-flung corner of the empire, or of gladiators locked in mortal combat. Today's challenge seems hardly less daunting for the intrepid mountain-runners who brave the elements in what is one of the world's most gruelling and most beautiful half-marathons. They need to haul their bodies up a net height of 2 331 feet to the 6 651-foot high summit of Roman Mountain, then return to the starting point via an awe-inspiring circular route.*

In 1997 a visitor from England mentioned to Al Tattersall, president of the Wolverine Nordic and Mountain Society, how the area reminded him of the England Lake District, and how popular fell-running events had become there.

Tattersall explains: "I was convinced, and soon we had a committed group that wanted to create a unique mountain run. We hoped to share these mountains that we enjoy so much with others. There is a sub-group of runners on the lookout to expand their running horizons, and out for running adventure."

The first formal running of this event was held in August 1999, and attracted a field of 39 starters. 2000 saw a field of 66, and in 2001 the race became part of the Jump-BC Circuit. The Men's record is 1-44-18, held by local athlete Kris Swanson. The Women's record is 2-12-30, held by Marlene Corcoran of Grande Prairie.

The mountain is named after Stephen Roman, a business tycoon. The organisers enjoy playing on the imperial Roman theme. Male and female winners are crowned Roman Emperors. All finishers receive a Gladiator Award. Landmarks along the route include The Roman Road and the Via Appia, and some runners dress up in togas or as gladiators.

"Run with the goats…cruise with the caribou…rise to the Challenge!" is the slogan of the race. Less speedy runners simply "trot with the ptarmigan".

The Tumbler Ridge Search and Rescue Organisation operates feeding

> *and first-aid stations on the mountain. A one kilometre kids race parallels the last part of the course, and provides these young competitors with their own hill to climb. A guided hike to nearby Babcock Falls is arranged just after the kids race. Telescopes are set up for spectators at the Core Lodge, trained on the summit and the descent, so that runners' progress can be visually monitored. Volunteer massage therapists set up their tables in a clearing in the subalpine forest, with a view of the recently conquered peak for exhausted runners, who can also swim in a pool in Babcock Creek*
>
> *This website has more information and entry forms: www.pris.bc.ca/wnms*

is arguably the world's toughest and most beautiful half marathon. The way is marked by painted stakes in the initial forested areas. Then, as you ascend above the treeline, the stakes become more frequent, at approximately twenty–metre intervals, and each has a line of stones leading from it, indicating the direction to the next stake. In misty conditions, they remain visible. Don't be surprised to see XVII marked on a rock…Roman numerals indicate kilometre marks.

As you ascend into the tundra, note the damage inflicted by ATVs, This is clear evidence of the need for regulations prohibiting use above the treeline. These scars will take many years to heal. The north aspect of Roman Mountain is a series of cliffs. The route dexterously avoids all major obstacles, and there are just a few places where some simple scrambling is needed. You climb a diagonal grassy slope, called the Via Appia, then ascend onto the minor summit. From here there is a virtually continuous line of stones and stakes to the summit ridge. This is a unique sight in North America; it is reminiscent more of the moors and highlands of England. Many visitors have remarked that this area bears an uncanny resemblance to the English Lake District.

The actual summit is just a few feet east (left) of the half-marathon route. At 2 027 metres (6 651 feet) above sea level, this is the highest point of land for many miles, and the views are predictably amazing on a good day. You are virtually guaranteed sightings of marmot and White-tailed Ptarmigan here, and caribou are most often seen on the southern alpine slopes (just continue following the line of stones and stakes for

Destinations

Plate 117: The flat summit of Quintette Mountain.

Plate 118: Babcock Falls.

another kilometre or so, and you will get a good feel for this part of the mountain too). This is also where a fossil trackway has been found, of a series of footprints in one of the sandstone rocks. These were made by *Aquatilavipes*, a primitive bird distantly related to modern shorebirds (Plate 14).

Your options are to return the way you came, or to continue following the Emperor's Challenge route in reverse and making this into a circular 21 kilometre hike.

In winter some snowshoers prefer to ascend Roman Mountain via the long deep valley that leads to the col between the main and minor summits. This route is subject to an avalanche hazard, so check conditions out carefully. An extreme snowshoeing day involves completing the entire Emperor's Challenge course. A rope is advisable.

...

To reach Quintette Mountain, you simply continue past the Roman Mountain trailhead. The road descends into a deep valley, one of the headwaters of Babcock Creek. The bridge over this creek bears close safety inspection before crossing, as it is deteriorating. Hopefully it will be maintained for years to come, because this easy alpine access should not be lost. Check locally before driving this road. From the bridge the road climbs steadily, very steeply in places, but at no stage is four wheel drive needed in good weather. It ends at a large flat cleared area close to the treeline 48 kilometres from Tumbler Ridge at the site of a gas–drilling operation. Don't go as far as this, stop about a kilometre before the end of the road, where it crosses below the long rocky ridge that leads to the summit.

Although Quintette Mountain is not immediately as dramatic as some of the other mountains in the region, the very fact that one can drive to treeline, and that the five hills are not that far above the road, appeals to many (Plate 117). The alpine flowers are magnificent from late June through July, and this forms one of the easiest places to study them. The birdlife of the treeline and alpine zones is also easily examined here, and with patience the

DESTINATION #85

NAME:
Quintette Mountain

FEATURE
Alpine summit close to Tumbler Ridge

ACCESS:
Steep road to tree line, then ridge walk to summit

songs of five sparrow species, the Water Pipit, the Horned Lark, and two thrushes can be identified.

The highest summit is capped by a couple of towers. Simply walk straight up the hill up the gentle angle until you reach the towers. Walk a little way south so as to be able to appreciate the view down to the Quintette Lakes. Caribou are often seen here. This is one of the few places from which these remote lakes can be seen. Use binoculars to identify the white specks on the lakes that are Trumpeter Swans.

...

Back at the Core Lodge, Babcock Falls are a fairly quick and easy destination. Start by turning left halfway down the first hill of the road that leads to Roman Mountain, just 200 metres from the Core Lodge. The trail is hard to pick out at first, but it immediately crosses a small creek and joins an old exploration road. Follow this for under a kilometre, roughly paralleling Babcock Creek, a few hundred metres away from it. When the exploration track peters out, the trail dips down to the right, and proceeds through meadows filled with bog-orchids in summer, to the top viewpoint of the falls, which are very pretty. They drop into a deep pool surrounded by rocks, ideal for swimming (Plate 118).

DESTINATION #86

NAME:
Babcock Falls

FEATURE
Waterfall

ACCESS:
1 KM trail to the falls, to be upgraded

To get down to the falls, work your way along downstream along the top of the cliffs, until an easy scrambling route becomes apparent in the large rocks. Look for an overhang with a tree growing in front of it. This provides an excellent shelter if the weather is foul, and gives a good view of the falls. The swimming hole is deep and inviting, but it is also worthwhile to carefully clamber over the slippery rocks to get right to the base of the falls and behind them. This trail is also earmarked for upgrading.

...

If you follow the road south from the Core Lodge, after a few hundred metres you will notice a trail leading off on the right. This leads up Mount Kostuik, the first of the five-peak circuit. Alternatively, it can be a lovely mountain to climb in its own right.

Because you are starting at a relatively low level, there is lots of forest to climb through, and the trail is hard to find in places. Leaving the road, it enters a big cleared area. It is vital that you do not head up to the far end of this area, but right away, look for the vestige of an old road traversing on the right. Follow this a short way, and look for a track up on the left, which is the one you must get onto (if you don't take this you'd end up on an overgrown track that takes you only partway up the mountain).

DESTINATION

NAME:
Mt. Kostuik

FEATURE
Alpine summit

ACCESS:
unmarked trail to treeline, then ridge walk to alpine summit

Assuming you have found the correct track, it will lead you up a long ridge. Where it eventually peters out, keep heading in the same direction for a hundred metres until you emerge onto another old track, which traverses along the flanks of the mountain.

You need to be up on the bigger ridge above you on the left, and where you encounter a track leading off onto this ridge, grab the opportunity. Once on the ridge, the trees peter out, and the views improve. Once at the upper end of this ridge, you can start aiming for the main summit, staying as high as you can all the way. Bands of rock intersect the length of the mountain, and you cross one after the next. The rocks become progressively more interesting as you reach the top, and some simple scrambling is necessary amongst the ptarmigan. From here you either return, or attempt the Five Peak Circuit.

The road that leads south from the Core Lodge passes the Kostuik Mountain turnoff, then after just over a kilometre, there is a washout. From time to time the ford is repaired, and the road ahead becomes accessible to 4WD traffic, but more often than not you need to park here. Close by are archaeological diggings that identified three prehistoric sites. Don't bother to look for them; they are impossible to find.

The route ahead leads to Five Cabin Pass, six kilometres away. This is the route followed by the Emperor's Challenge Mountain Half-

Marathon, and by snowmobilers on their way to The Hillclimb, the premier annual event of the Ridge Riders Snowmobile Club. This has consistently drawn hundreds of machines and riders into the area for an action–packed day. On the way, there are signs indicating the many trails that the Snowmobile Club has built over the years with enticing names like the Hidden Valley Trail, Johnson Creek Trail and Summit Meadows. The road is a good cycling area as well, although you should consider that bears don't have as much warning of your approach on a bicycle. When you reach the pass, you see the tortuous switchbacks of the Roman Road snaking up Roman Mountain across the valley. The mountain on your right is The Terminator. Its very name is a challenge to the intrepid riders who push their skills and their luck to the limits in challenging its steepening grade.

Windy Ridge Challenge Hillclimb
By Fred Banham

The Tumbler Ridge Ridge Riders annually host the Windy Ridge Hillclimb the first Saturday in March of each year. This BC Snowmobile Federation sanctioned event is one of the longest running as well as most challenging events in the Hillcimb racing circuit.

Competitors from BC, Alberta and the United States tune their stock, improved stock and modified snowmobiles to race from the Summit Meadows to the top of Windy Ridge. The racecourse is a simple slalom course followed by a hill-shot straight up Windy Ridge.

A 370 metre change in elevation is realised in just less than 1 500 meters distance that can take some of the big sleds less than a minute to cover. Going up is the easy part, most of the excitement and thrills occur on the way down.

The Hillclimb is a great spectator event with crowds of 600 snowmobile enthusiasts situated across the Summit Meadows, below the racecourse. Racers attempt more than 100 runs up Windy Ridge through the day with top prize money going to the "King of the Hill" at the end of the day.

The story at the end of the day is always the one that didn't make it!

TUMBLER RIDGE *Enjoying its History, Trails & Wilderness*

At the highest point on the pass, there is a cutline up to the right up the slopes of The Terminator. Although this is initially steep, it allows quick access to an alpine ridge. Note where the trail reaches this ridge, to facilitate your return route. Follow the ridge up until you emerge on the lesser Terminator summit. Below on the right is a big bowl backed by vertical cliffs, a favourite haunt of mountain goats. Between the minor summit and the main summit, you follow a very impressive pebbly knife–edge ridge, with great views to either side.

> **DESTINATION #88**
> **NAME:** The Terminator
> **FEATURE** Alpine summit
> **ACCESS:** 7 KM on exploration road, (sometimes driveable with 4WD) 2 KM hike up cutline into alpine, then ridge walk to summit

From Five Cabin Pass, the road used to continue down the valley of Five Cabin Creek to its junction with Kinuseo Creek. This remains a snowmobiling trail to get to Kinuseo Falls from the Core Lodge. A more interesting route for hikers is to continue on the Emperor's Challenge route up Roman Mountain, following the familiar pattern of stakes and stones. Again, it is virtually impossible to get lost provided you stick to this trail, which leads through preferred caribou territory to the summit. From the pass to the summit is six kilometres.

...

Having considered all these bits and pieces, you may be tempted simply to go for gold and bag them all in one day, the Five Peak Circuit of 27 kilometres. This sounds arduous, but the elite few who have done this regard it as a highlight in their lives. You start at the Core Lodge, climb Mt. Kostuik as already described. From its summit you descend into a col, then climb Moe Hill, the next summit… then down the southern ridge of Moe Hill, and up the long and aptly named Windy Ridge to its summit…. off this, turning east, and over the summits of The Terminator… down the cutline already described into Five Cabin Pass, then up the Roman Road and

> **DESTINATION #89**
> **NAME:** The Five Peak Circuit
> **FEATURE** Five peaks in a single day
> **ACCESS:** 27 KM of mostly trackless alpine hiking from the Core Lodge

over the top of Roman Mountain... down Roman via the route described... then walk back along the road to the Core Lodge, stopping to swim in Babcock Creek first.

Good clear weather is a prerequisite, as most of the circuit is ridge–top walking without any trails. One important route–finding spot is when you come down the ridge off The Terminator. When you encounter the first small trees, start looking carefully for the cutline on the right that leads steeply down to the pass. If you are really well organised, you will have a seconding party ready for you here with refreshments, although the drawback of such preparation is that it may be tempting to call it quits at this point.

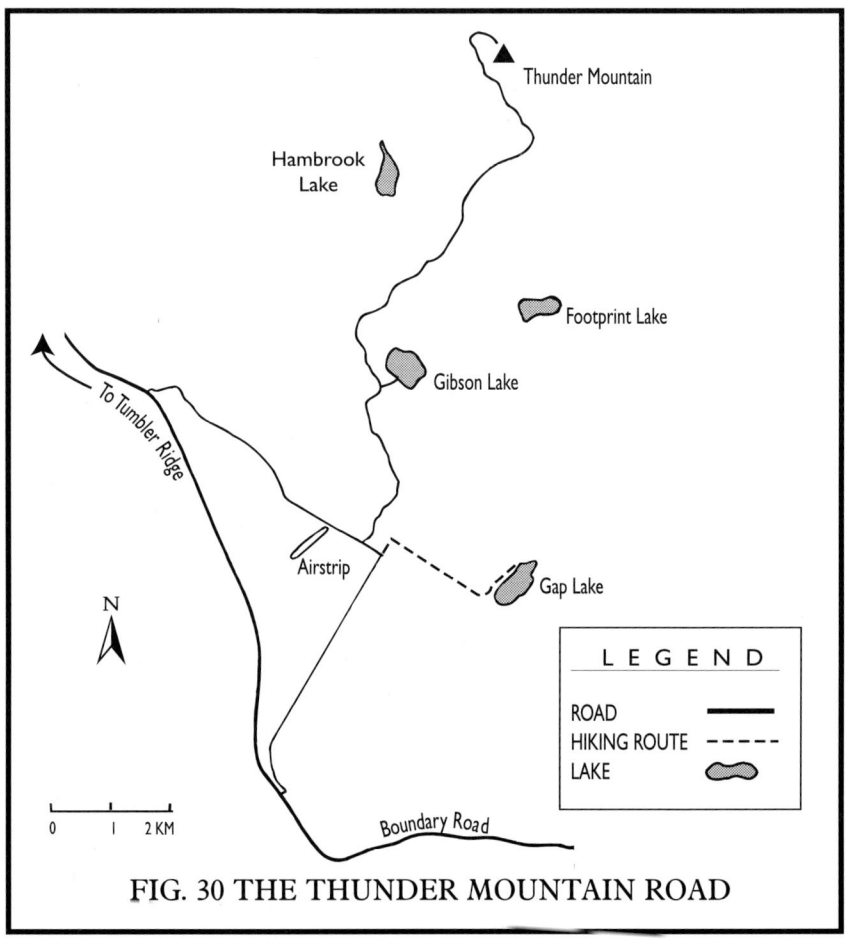

FIG. 30 THE THUNDER MOUNTAIN ROAD

TUMBLER RIDGE *Enjoying its History, Trails & Wilderness*

■ THE ROAD TO THUNDER MOUNTAIN

There are two roads that leave the Boundary Road for Thunder Mountain. The first of these leaves at KM 39 at Sora Slough and passes the Grizzly Valley camp and an airstrip. After five kilometres turn sharp left, as continuing straight leads you back to the Boundary Road after another five kilometres. Turning left leads to Gibson Lake and Thunder Mountain. The road is rutted in places, and careful slow driving is needed, but 4WD is not necessary. The turnoff to Gibson Lake is reached after another 3.5 kilometres. The ruts are worse here but the track is passable, or you may choose to walk down.

Gibson Lake is typical of many of the lakes in the upper Thunder Creek drainage. These have achieved some fame, as almost every one has a pair of breeding Trumpeter Swans each year. But Gibson Lake is the only easily accessible lake. There is a sign educating visitors about loons. The swans are most often seen on the left (north) shore, often partially concealed in the shoreline vegetation. There is a simple picnic area at the end of the road.

The road to Thunder Mountain continues slowly upward. Avoid side roads (one to the left, then one to the right) and stick to the road that leads up the west flank of the "mountain" which is more accurately a big hill. After a kilometre of climbing, the road angles sharply right to climb fairly steeply to the summit. On top is a forestry lookout tower and a couple of dilapidated dwellings. Forestry towers have a limited half–life, and no guarantees can be given as to this one's

DESTINATION #90

NAME:
Gibson Lake

FEATURE
Birding lake

ACCESS:
Roadside; last 500 M is rough

DESTINATION #91

NAME:
Thunder Mountain

FEATURE
Impressive viewsite

ACCESS:
Rough road to fire tower on summit

safety, but climbing it to the viewing platform does present a magnificent view of the Hart Ranges of the Rocky Mountains. Thunder Mountain is a lone hill some distance away from the main ranges, and thus it offers an unsurpassed panorama, all the way to Mt Ida in the south. Below to the south is Footprint Lake, and binoculars usually reveal a pair Trumpeter Swans on this lake as well. Off to the east are the Chain Lakes, an important wetland area. To the north is the Kiskatinaw Plateau, and it is possible to work out where Tumbler Ridge is situated. This is one of the finest views in the area, and was aptly described by Prentiss Gray during his 1927 expedition:

> *"We had our first view of the promised land to the south. Bold and clear rose the Fortress with its black sides beyond the sharp-pointed Mt Ida. Running across the southern horizon and then stretching north was the crown of the Rockies. The peaks were all snow-covered.... the sight cheered our hearts and... we all felt very happy to be at least in sight of hunting country. More important, the high mountains gave promise that we were out of the land of muskeg."*

You return via the same road. When you reach the T-junction you can return to the Boundary Road either way. If you turn left, the road soon takes a 90° turn to the right. This is the starting point for the walk or ski to Gap Lake. Simply follow the cutline northeast for a few hundred metres, then turn 90° right at the intersection with a bigger cutline. You follow this line for just over two kilometres, negotiating the occasional swampy area on the way, then follow a track slightly to the left to reach Gap Lake. The origin of the name is obvious, as the lake fills a gap in the substantial ridge. This site was well known to the ancients, and prehistoric sites have been discovered on its shores. A track leads along its western shore, where there is also a barbecue site. The area has a network of snowmobile and quad routes. Gap Lake has its own beauty, seldom visited and pristine. Return the way you came.

DESTINATION #92

NAME:
Gap Lake

FEATURE
Seldom visited lake

ACCESS:
3 KM one way along cutlines to lakeshore

■ TO THE WAPITI, RED DEER AND BELCOURT VALLEYS

The Wapiti Forest Service Road is the key to exploration of this area. It leaves the Boundary Road in a southerly direction 50 kilometres from Tumbler Ridge. The area that it services gets quite heavy recreational use from the Alberta side including lots of quad activity, and those seeking a pristine uninterrupted wilderness experience might find this disquieting unless they head further into the backcountry or into Wapiti Provincial Park. It remains the quickest way to drive into the really big mountains from Tumbler Ridge.

The first seven kilometres are absolutely straight. Somewhere along this stretch is a clear spring of bubbling cold soda water, discovered many years ago by Cliff Rennie. He cannot recall its exact location, and no one else has found it since. The road then swings southwest, through the valleys of Fearless Creek and Dokken Creek. The Bone Mountain massif looms closer on the right, then the road enters the Wapiti River Valley.

After 24 kilometres on this road there is an important fork. The left turn known rather misleadingly as the Red Deer Forest Service Road leads on through the foothills to give access to Belcourt Creek. Keeping right leads on much closer to the mountains, giving access to Wapiti Provincial Park, Red Deer Falls and more.

If you take the left turn, you descend the hill to emerge after a kilometre at the Wapiti East Recreation Site, with a number of campsites just above the crossing over the Wapiti River. This site is often full, and is particularly popular amongst the four–wheeling fraternity. There is a nice pull–off just before the bridge, to appreciate the river. The road climbs up the far side and winds through the foothills. It passes a very attractive unnamed small lake with a cabin on its shore (42 kilometres from the Boundary Road, 18 kilometres from the fork) before descending to cross Red Deer Creek. This is seemingly a bigger volume of water than the Wapiti River. Here there is another primitive pullout with opportunities to enjoy the creek and ignore the senseless graffiti on the bridge.

Once again the road climbs into the hills before descending into the Belcourt Creek drainage. Twelve kilometres from the Red Deer

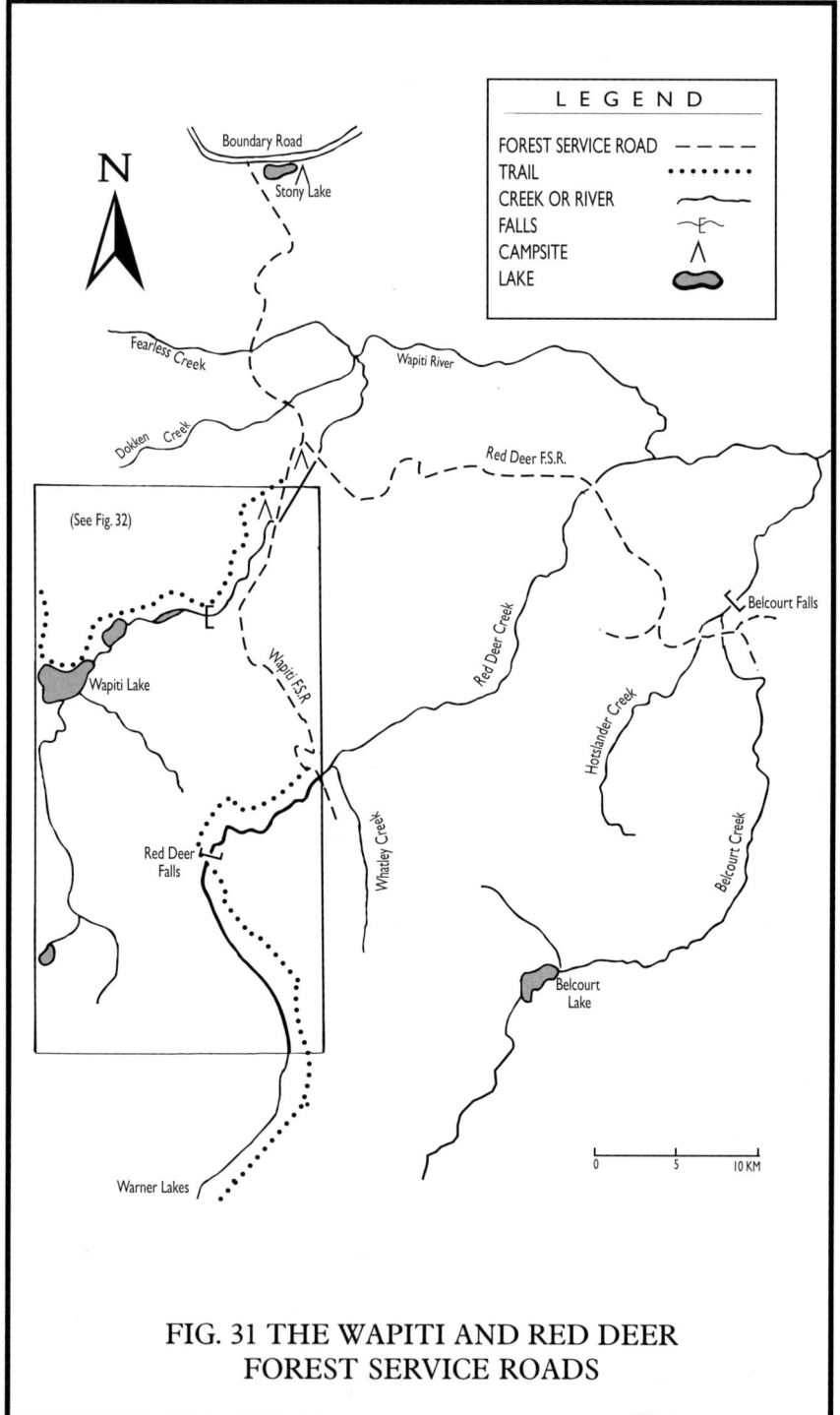

FIG. 31 THE WAPITI AND RED DEER FOREST SERVICE ROADS

crossing it splits into an east and west branch. Keep left here along the east branch. It first crosses Holtslander Creek, then enters some interesting rock scenery just before the bridge over the sizeable Belcourt Creek. On the right across the bridge is an attractive primitive campsite. This is 69 kilometres from the Boundary Road, 119 kilometres from Tumbler Ridge.

Below the bridge the creek cuts through interesting rock layers beneath towering cliffs to form Belcourt Canyon. The trail that starts opposite the campsite peters out quickly, and the best way to appreciate the canyon is to look for the quad track on the left just under a kilometre after the bridge. Follow this through the forest to its terminus and descend from there. You soon reach the rim of the canyon, where the swirling waters of the creek cut through vertical cliffs on either side. If you follow the game trail upstream along the canyon rim to the top end of this section, you can climb down to river level and there is a beach and pool.

Further down the canyon is the very impressive Belcourt Falls, a 30 metre drop augmented by falls from a side creek to form a unique sight (Plate 120). The rock in this area is notoriously untrustworthy, and landslides and fatalities have been recorded close to the falls. Be careful.

A few kilometres upstream from the bridge there is another remote waterfall. This can only be reached during times of low water. Start on the right before the bridge and head upstream, using game trails and the river bank, and be prepared to cross the creek whenever necessary. After a few mandatory crossings the falls are reached – not for novices and kids!

The road deteriorates soon after the bridge, but is being improved. Ultimately access to Belcourt Lake may be facilitated; currently a lengthy quad and horse trail leads in to this beautiful lake (Plate 121). For most visitors there is no option but to return the way you came and drive back to the junction on the Wapiti Forest Service road.

DESTINATION #93

NAME:
Belcourt Falls/Lake
FEATURE
Remote falls and lake
ACCESS:
2 KM on unmaintained quad trail and game trails to falls, long quad trail to lake

...

Destinations

Plate 119: The Back Meadows south of the Core Lodge offer some of the finest snowmobiling anywhere. Credit: Fred Banhan

Plate 120: Belcourt Falls. Credit: Leona Gibb.

Keeping right at the major junction on the Wapiti road leads to the start of the Wapiti Lake trailhead. This 30 KM (one way) trail ends at Onion Lake. A brochure has been put out by BC Forest Service, "Wapiti Onion Hiking Trail" and is available from the Travel Info Centre or from the Dawson Creek Forest District offices (phone 250 784 1200). Clear cutting near the trailhead may shorten access by a few kilometres. The 16 467 hectare Wapiti (or Wapiti Lake) Provincial Park was proclaimed in 1999.

The trail is generally level initially although a few rocky sections provide some relief, and there are a number of swampy sections worsened by the passage of pack trains. The trail leads past a number of beautiful lakes and ponds, and after seven kilometres there is a side trail down to the left that leads to Wapiti Falls (Plate 122). Although not high, these falls are pretty and wide, and lined by attractive overhanging rocks with pleasant pools.

DESTINATION #94

NAME:
Wapiti Falls

FEATURE
Falls on Wapiti River

ACCESS:
Short side trail 7 KM along Wapiti Lake Trail

At KM 15 there is an interesting shrine in a hollow in a cliff and a building that was dragged as a form of penance by Father Mariman, a Catholic priest, in the 1960s. He had met a helicopter pilot in Fort St. John who told him about the wild beauty of the Wapiti. Like sages through the ages, Father Mariman understood the value of solitude in seeking spiritual inspiration, and the power of Mother Nature to enhance faith. He sought out the Wapiti and returned to it time and again, and had a vision of a natural shrine that worshippers could walk into, something along the lines of the famous Our Lady of Lourdes in France. He passed away in the 1980s. The uncompleted shrine stands as testimony to his enlightenment.

At KM 17 Wapiti Lake is reached, and there is a forestry shelter at KM 19. This is one of the bigger and most beautiful mountain lakes in the region (Plate 123) and this was not lost on the early explorers. It is known that Gaetz was on its shores in 1898, and the Wapiti Pass was explored as a possible railway route in the early 1900s. Fay wrote the first description of the lake (which he called Sapphire Lake") in 1914:

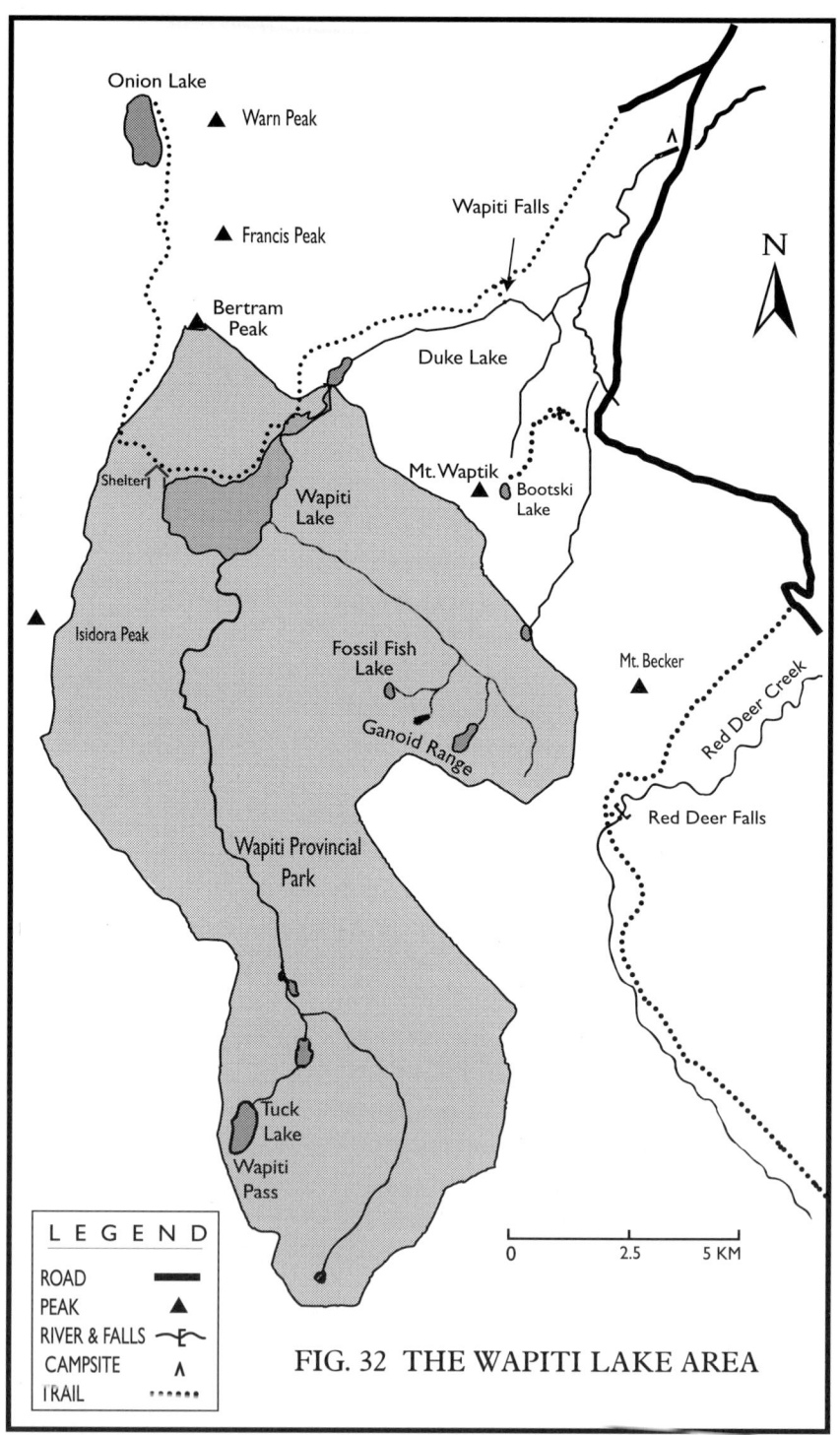

FIG. 32 THE WAPITI LAKE AREA

TUMBLER RIDGE *Enjoying its History, Trails & Wilderness*

"Finally we came to a beautiful lake about two miles by three miles of the most wonderful sapphire blue color, a very rare color for a lake in these mountains. On two sides it is surrounded by rocky cliffs which run into rocky peaks above and at the further end there is a gap where the river that drains it runs, one of the forks of the Wapiti."

DESTINATION #95

NAME:
Wapiti Lake

FEATURE
Beautiful lake in Wapiti Provincial Park

ACCESS:
At KM 17 of Wapiti–Onion Lake Trail

Prentiss Gray passed through in 1927:

"The lake…was one of the goals of our trip…the main lake is three miles long and one and three quarter miles wide. It nestles among high mountains that rise above timberline."

DESTINATION #96

NAME:
Onion Lake

FEATURE
Subalpine lake

ACCESS:
At KM 30 of Wapiti–Onion Lake Trail

At present the only formal continuation of the trail from Wapiti Lake is to head up over a pass to Onion Lake, a distance of another eleven kilometres. This lake is outside the park boundary. From the pass between Wapiti Lake and Onion Lake there is a huge area of alpine that may lure the adventurous, and most of the peaks can be climbed without technical gear. There are no trails in this beautiful wilderness. All the precautions that relate to alpine wilderness travel apply.

Onion Lake was first described by Prentiss Gray in 1927 and his words remain appropriate today (Plate 124):

"We found a delightful glacial lake (elevation 5100 feet) set in behind a typical terminal moraine and hemmed in by steep mountains that rose 2000 feet on all sides except at the head of the lake, where there appeared to be a pass."

…

Destinations

Plate 121: Prentiss Gray in the first photo of Belcourt Lake, 1928.
Reproduced with permission from
Sherman Gray and the Boone and Crockett Club

Plate 122: Wapiti Falls.

TUMBLER RIDGE *Enjoying its History, Trails & Wilderness*

The remainder of Wapiti Provincial Park holds much potential. The Fossil Fish Lake area and the Ganoid Range offer just one destination. But access remains exceedingly difficult and is recommended only for the committed and tough, who are prepared to bushwhack through miles of difficult vegetation, to earn the bliss of solitude in some of the finest mountain scenery. The least evil means of access is probably still from the Red Deer Valley.

DESTINATION #97

NAME:
Ganoid Range

FEATURE
Remote wilderness area

ACCESS:
Difficult wilderness access, best from Red Deer Valley

...

Back on the road the Wapiti West Recreation site is soon reached. Often full during the summer months, and another quadding favourite, the few forest service sites are situated just above the Wapiti River.

The road crosses the river and then continues southeast up a side valley that leads to the Red Deer Valley. The massif that looms to the right (southwest) is Mount Waptik. An old track leads up to a clearcut on its flanks. A four wheel drive vehicle with very high clearance may possibly be able to make it across the broken bridges, but most visitors who wish to enjoy the recommended Bootski Lake experience will have to park their vehicles next to the road, and walk the first few kilometres through uninspiring cleared areas.

At the very top of the highest clearcut the vague trail starts, and has been improved by members of the Wolverine Nordic and Mountain Society, although it is not yet an official trail, and is rough. Take stock of your situation at all times and consider how you will find the trail on your return if the weather worsens, especially when you get into the meadows. The treeline is reached surprisingly quickly, and you abruptly find yourself on an alpine ridge with great views ahead of Waptik Mountain. Dozens of goats can sometimes be seen here. Use your compass or GPS, turn left and follow the ridge in a southerly direction. You may find the remains of a large cross erected in the 1980s.

...

Plate 123: Wapiti Lake. Credit: Kevin Sharman.

Plate 124: Prentiss Gray took the first photo of Onion Lake in 1927. Reproduced with permission from Sherman Gray and the Boone and Crockett Club.

The best destination in the area for a campsite is Bootski Lake, a small body of water that is only unfrozen for about a month each year. It has no major inflow and its outlet is underground. It is set in a bowl below the sheer face and imposing strata of Waptik Mountain (Plate 125). Experts may wish to challenge this mountain with ropes in summer, and winter ascents have been made followed by ski descents. Ordinary humans don't try this sort of thing, and for them a hike up to the summits of the smaller ridge south of the lake offers quite enough scenery. The return trip is via the same trail.

 # 98
DESTINATION
NAME:
Bootski Lake/ Mt. Waptik

FEATURE
Alpine lake and peak

ACCESS:
Hike old forestry road, then up rough trail onto alpine ridge

...

The Wapiti Forest Service Road continues through a burned area past the ramparts of Mount Becker on the right, then descends into the Red Deer Valley. Immediately after a sharp switchback, look for a track that leads up the valley up its northern slopes (the right bank as you look upstream). This old road leads to Red Deer Falls and beyond through wonderful mountain country, but is no longer passable for motor vehicles, as the bridges have been intentionally broken. It also passes through a 1988 burn. The origin of the fire can be seen clearly – a fire pit near the falls. This serves as a good reminder to be careful with your fire. Hikers, mountain bikers, packhorses and quads now share the trail in summer, and it is a well–deserved favourite destination for each group, besides being a snowmobiling area (Plate 127).

Initially the track is flat, beneath the summit of Mount Becker on the right. The lighter bands of rock up on Mount Becker are composed largely of fossilised coral. Most of the mountain peaks have distinctive and rounded shapes, creating some unusual scenery. After five kilometres the track becomes much more interesting as it curves around and below spectacular cliffs. It ascends sharply to pass above some deep ravines that enter the awe–inspiring Red Deer Canyon below. Good views of the canyon scenery can be obtained from the trail, which begins to look less like an old road as it descends back down. (Believe it or not, the highest point of this part of the trail is the start of the

Plate 125: Camping at Bootski Lake.
Credit: Kevin Sharman

Plate 126: Prentiss Gray took the first photo of Red Deer Falls in 1927. Reproduced with permission from Sherman Gray and the Boone and Crockett Club.

dreaded and notorious bushwhack that leads enterprising/crazy diehards up through a pass. Experienced men and women are reduced to tears before they break out into the enchanting alpine scenery of the Ganoid Range in Wapiti Provincial Park.)

As the trail flattens out at the end of the descent, begin to look for a side trail to the left. This is sometimes well marked. If you reach the point where the trail reaches the river, you have gone about a kilometre too far. Do not give up, as you *have* to see Red Deer Falls, a lovely drop into a clear mountain pool backed by great mountain scenery. There is a smaller falls a short way upstream.

Prentiss Gray was the first to describe these falls, during his 1928 follow–up expedition (Plate 126):

> "We heard again the heavy zoom of falling water. Suddenly we came out on a rocky ledge directly above the river and there was seventy feet of sheer drop where the river plunged into a gorgeous pool, hemmed in by towering rocks. It paid for all the trip as we gazed at that silvery ribbon."

#99 DESTINATION

NAME:
Red Deer Falls

FEATURE
Spectacular waterfall

ACCESS:
10 KM hiking or mountain biking

#100 DESTINATION

NAME:
Warner Pass

FEATURE
Remote wilderness area

ACCESS:
Long route in from Red Deer Falls

As you can judge from the size of the creek, it drains a considerable area, and although the trail degenerates, it is feasible to get into the higher country at the head of the valley where the Warner Lakes lead to Warner Pass. This trail is suitable for mountain biking. Even this far into the mountains, hikers and cyclists will need to watch out for ATVs. It is 28 kilometres from the start of the trail to Warner Lakes, with a net elevation change of 156 metres. The road is no longer maintained so may deteriorate with time. ...

Destinations

Plate 127: Snowmobiling the Red Deer area.
Credit: Fred Banham.

Plate 128: Start of the Murray River canoe trip.

The summit of Mount Becker is another challenging destination for anyone looking for a remote rugged mountain that has only been climbed by a handful of people. A rope is advised as there are some gullies and bluffs that may prove problematic. Access is from the track to Red Deer Falls. The southwest ridge is probably the best route, but remember, few have been before you and there are no trails at all. This is not a trip for the inexperienced.

From the road bridge across the Red Deer, the summit of Mount Becker is seen to its full advantage. The subsidiary summit to the right has one of the most unusually symmetrical forms of any mountain, anywhere, and is the result of some particularly dramatic rock folding.

The Forest Service Road continues up Whatley Creek, and may be extended further in years to come, but has little else to offer at present. This is another of the typical mountain dead–end roads, leaving the traveler with no option but to return. The headwaters of Whatley Creek were the site of the incredible photograph by Prescott Fay of horses traversing a horrendously steep scree slope.

 # DESTINATION 101

NAME:
Mt. Becker

FEATURE
Remote alpine summit

ACCESS:
Wilderness travel, rope might be needed

■ THE MURRAY RIVER

A canoe trip down this river offers something to beginner and experienced canoeist alike. It is conveniently divided into two sections. The upper section is from Kinuseo Falls to Tumbler Ridge and is classified Grade 2. It takes one and a half days but has four conveniently placed bridges and can therefore be divided into shorter stages. The lower section is from Tumbler Ridge to the East Pine and is classified Grade 3. It takes three days and has no bridges or exits en route.

There haven't been any canoeing fatalities on the river, but it has certainly claimed lives, such as that of trapper Gesler who drowned trying to cross on a raft in 1935, and the family of eight that were swept away when an ice–jam broke in 1939. Many canoes have been lost on

Plate 129: Murray River Canoe Trip, Lower Section.
Credit: Kevin Sharman.

the lower section. Because the upper section is easier, it can lull people into complacency. Even this stretch can be difficult at very high water, and its inviting side channels may have sweepers or logjams that can upset the inexperienced canoeist. Neither section should be attempted unless you have the required skills for the relevant grade.

The bridges are numbered 1 – 4, assuming a start at Kinuseo Falls, and divide the trip into four stages.

The first stage takes three to four hours and involves a thrilling put-in at Kinuseo Falls, tempered only by the 1.5 KM portage to reach the river (Plate 128). There is a good campsite on the second island below the falls. After a few kilometres look for Diagonal Falls on the left. It has its origin in a cluster of springs just above. After a long flat section Club Creek enters on the left, then there is a long rapid. At the end of this Kinuseo Creek enters on the right, and here there is another good campsite. Further downstream look for a Bald Eagle nest and an Osprey nest. The take–out at the first bridge (KM 20 on the Murray Forest Service Road) is on the left, where there is another campsite.

DESTINATION #102

NAME:
Murray River upper section

FEATURE
Grade 2 canoeing river

ACCESS:
Put in at Kinuseo Falls or at bridges, take out at bridges

The second stage takes two to three hours. Tentfire Creek enters on the left, followed by a nice rapid which can be a bit scary for beginners. There is a good campsite at a big bend in the river towards the end of this stage. The take–out is just beyond the second bridge (side road at KM 12 on the Murray Forest Service Road) on the right.

The scenic third stage also takes two to three hours. A good stop is where Waterfall Creek enters on the right. At the end of a very long flat stretch there are rapids around a rocky island. Scout this first, but it is usually best to keep left, as there is a hidden rock in the right branch. The river then passes by some of the workings of the Quintette mine. The take–out is on the left just after the third bridge (KM 0 of the Murray Forest Service Road).

The fourth stage is the easiest and takes two to three hours. There are just a few sets of pleasant rapids. The Mighty Murray Raft Race has

Plate 130: Bergeron Falls.

been held on this section. You pass an old decrepit cabin on the left. Towards the end the railway line becomes visible on the right. The river then passes under the railway bridge and then the highway bridge, with the take–out following on the left. Note that the next take–out is two to three days downstream.

...

The lower section of the Murray River is a true wilderness trip of two to three days. Purists may complain about the occasional jet boat, but then again there have been a number of jet boat salvages of marooned canoeists. Otherwise there is scant evidence of human presence on this wild river. This contrasts with the Peace River that these waters enter downstream, its flow and cycle ravaged by a 1960s megaproject that has impacted traditional lifestyles downstream in the Peace-Athabasca delta.

 # DESTINATION 103

NAME:
Murray River lower section

FEATURE
Grade 3 canoeing river

ACCESS:
Three day wilderness trip, start at boat launch near Tumbler Ridge

 # DESTINATION 104

NAME:
Bergeron Falls

FEATURE
High waterfall

ACCESS:
Canoe/Jetboat down Murray River then 1 KM hike up creek

Putting in at the highway bridge, you pass the confluence with Flatbed Creek on the right, the Wolverine River on the left, then Quality Creek on the right. Then after the first steep banks on the left, look for a small creek on the left bank. Following this upstream leads to Bergeron Falls in less than a kilometre (Plate 130). This is a great sight in spring or after rain, tumbling 100 metres into an enormous amphitheatre. This is the highest waterfall in the area and has been ice–climbed.

The river passes through the beautiful Painted Canyon and past the towering formation known as the Anvil. Then there is a sharp bend to the left, and a small beach. High above on the open slopes you may see hikers on the Murray Canyon Overlook trail. Next look for Tepee Falls in the distance on the right. Salt Creek is more open and its waterfalls are distant. Gwillim River enters on the left, and from here on the river is Grade 3.

There are four specific hazardous sections and use of 1:50 000 topographic maps is suggested. These form river–wide ledges and chutes, and are very difficult to spot unless you are on your guard and prepared for them. Many canoeists have stumbled on them, been unable to avoid them, and lost all their gear here.

The second and third ledges are marked on the topographic map as rapids. The first ledge is not marked but is 12 KM before the second. The fourth is 9 KM before the end. These should all be read from the bank first and an educated decision taken whether to run these or portage around them. There is only one possible exit other than the East Pine: at Lone Prairie, which saves half a day, but this exit is not easy to identify.

Murray River Statistics

Mean flow:	56 cubic metres per second, dwindling to 10 in February, and rising to 193 in the June run-off.
Maximum recorded flow:	872 cubic metres per second in the 1990 flood.
Length from source to ocean:	3500 kilometres.

What happens if you just keep on going downstream? It's two days to the Peace River at Taylor. Then you could float for weeks down the Peace River, interrupted only by the Vermilion Chutes at old Fort Vermilion. You might get lost in the multiple channels of the Peace-Athabasca Delta before reaching the expanse of Lake Athabasca. From here the combined waters of these two great rivers form the Slave River, with a series of treacherous rapids with unfriendly names like "Rapids of the Drowned" near Fort Smith. Those rapids are the last real white water, as the river empties into massive Great Slave Lake. One of the world's great rivers, the Mackenzie, drains this lake and eventually spills into the Beaufort Sea of the Arctic Ocean, 3 500 kilometres from Tumbler Ridge.

TUMBLER RIDGE *Enjoying its History, Trails & Wilderness*

■ THE BC RAIL LINE

The final destination in this book is perhaps a destination no more. The 129 kilometres of electrified railway line was completed in 1983, after less than four years of intense effort, and is known as the Tumbler Branch Line. These formed the toughest kilometres of a 950 kilometre journey for Tumbler Ridge's coal to Ridley Island near Prince Rupert. But the last train from Quintette left on August 20 2000.

#105 DESTINATION

NAME:
Tumbler Branch Line

FEATURE
Dramatic railway route with two great tunnels

ACCESS:
Who knows?

The line was initially electrified because this was cheaper than installing ventilation for the two long tunnels that pierce the northern Rockies. This decision was based on a certain amount of projected traffic.

With coal only being shipped from the Bullmoose Mine, at the rate of a two or three trains per week, only diesel power was deemed necessary, and the last electrified train ran in October 2000.

Despite the obvious tourist potential of this line, recreational opportunities have been infrequent, although occasional trains have been specially organized for train enthusiasts. For the lucky ones, it has been a great trip. The route lies up the Wolverine Valley at a 1.21% grade, past a strange concretion and into the six kilometre Wolverine Tunnel with its sulphurous odour and water pouring out of a ditch at its north portal.

Perhaps the most attractive segment is the sudden emergence into light in the headwaters of the Sukunka Valley with its beckoning mountains. After just a few kilometres the nine kilometre Table Tunnel begins, with the highest point of the line just inside.

More waterfalls and peaks are evident on the far side, with Sentinel Peak dominating to the north. Throughout, the wildness and majesty of the Rockies is all around, and one's thoughts are concentrated on the immense amount of effort and planning that went into this line's construction.

It has all the potential to become a great train expedition, and the mind boggles at the possibilities The more adventurous may wish to be dropped off to hike to Upper and Lower Tunnel Falls. Some may wish to be dropped off and picked up at the entrance to the Table Tunnel, to facilitate their hike to the magnificent Bat Lake wilderness with its caves, peaks and lakes. (It is over three hours to this area by 4WD vehicle with high clearance, under an hour by train.)

A grand circular tour could be arranged from Prince George, hiking in on a reconstructed Monkman Pass trail, and returning by train through the mountains.

Politicians on special trains could hammer out deals at the summit in the murky darkness of the tunnel, and sign them in the glorious limelight of the Sukunka Valley.

But none of this may ever happen, if Bullmoose ceases production as is predicted for 2003, and the cost of maintaining the line becomes prohibitive.

Maybe the coal price will rise and the coal will continue to flow, maybe a new industry will recognize the value of this export route, maybe a wealthy entrepreneur will appreciate the tourist benefits. Maybe the line will simply cease to be and its evocative scenery will be reserved only for those who are prepared to make extra efforts to see it.

Will somebody please step in and save the Tumbler Branch Line?

14 HOW GOOD IS IT HERE?

I walk or cycle to work in summer and ski to work in winter. I see my kids at lunchtime most days. I seldom need to use our car. The wilderness begins at my back gate. These are obvious feel–good phenomena that are hard to quantify objectively. Along with many residents, I know that I live in a privileged environment. Is it possible to measure how good it is here? Here's an arbitrary attempt, divided into local, regional and global factors.

■ LOCAL

The people: Despite all the magnificence of its surroundings, Tumbler Ridge's major asset remains its people. There are no easily measurable "friendliness statistics", so one needs to rely on anecdotes such as this one from Al Galbraith:

> *"People in the street offer a friendly greeting – whether they know you or not. It's disarming at first. In Vancouver you put your hand on your wallet when you pass such friendly people."*

Those who have survived the tribulations of the last decade and are still here, are here because they want to be. Likewise those that have moved here recently with the opening up of the housing market have made a concrete positive choice. The old welcome the new with open arms, and the new appreciate their good fortune and respond in kind. It is a recipe for well–being.

How Good Is It Here?

Economic stability: Help from the B.C. Government in 2000 in paying off the municipal debt allowed Tumbler Ridge to move with the stroke of a pen from being the northern community with the highest per capita debt, to being debt free. Few communities share this advantage.

Crime: Year after year Tumbler Ridge posts one of the lowest per capita crime statistics in B.C. According to the publication put out by B.C.'s Ministry of the Attorney General, "Police and Crime Summary Statistics 1990-1999" the 1999 provincial average for reported criminal offences was 122 per thousand, whereas the figure in Tumbler Ridge was 88. (Parts of the Lower Mainland had the highest incidence, 196 per thousand.) The vast majority of these involved minor property offences or petty vandalism. And this figure has shown a consistent decrease over the years as Tumbler Ridge has evolved from a frontier town into a stable family community. It is gratifying to note that over 50% of cases were solved, a figure which is also well above the provincial average.

Education: In March 2000 the independent Fraser Institute published its assessment of British Columbia secondary schools in The Province newspaper. Tumbler Ridge was rated a creditable 120 out of 292. Another objective measurement assesses reading, writing and numeracy skills across the province at a Grade 10 level: Tumbler Ridge scored at the regional and provincial average level.

Health Care: I will be accused of being biased, but I believe that the level of health care that can be offered in small communities potentially exceeds in many respects what can be achieved in larger centres. There is a good reason why Tumbler Ridge has seen little of the turmoil in physician and nursing numbers that have characterised rural Canada recently: this is a fine place to live and to work. Waiting lists are seldom longer than a day or two, access to emergency treatment is rapid and efficient, and care by dedicated nurses has a personal touch that is virtually impossible to replicate in a larger facility.

Most services are provided under one roof, and a core of services are provided by visiting specialised practitioners.

That's all pretty good, but we desperately need hospital beds to prevent unnecessary transfers. Government has hinted that these would be looked at when the population climbed above 3 000 again, but there's nothing in writing… As the population climbs, we will need to regain the services we transiently lost, like full–time physiotherapy and ultrasound. And there is no valid reason why a mammography unit is not able to visit a few times a year.

I will never forget how in 1998, when physicians in centres like Tumbler Ridge were discriminated against by the provincial government, residents here rose up in our support, formed an action group, and attended protest meetings in huge numbers, with mine management and unions combining to form a potent voice. This embarrassed the provincial government into a position from which they had to back down. That support is something my colleagues and I try to reciprocate through the provision of quality and timely care that transcends the weakening health care system in Canada as a whole.

Isolation: We are all a part of the great mosaic of life. Some see isolation as something to fear. Such folks will not flourish here, almost a hundred kilometres from the next community. Others, fed up with the materialism that controls much of North America, irritated by contemporary life's triteness, find here a release from these vexations, a chance to reconnect with what is important in life, a chance to exert a degree of control over which aspects of the twenty–first century they bring into their lives. There are few places where a life of voluntary simplicity is so easy to achieve.

Recreation: For a community of its size, the recreation opportunities in Tumbler Ridge are hard to surpass anywhere. The Community Centre complex is something that in most of the rest of the world would be just a dream. We are privileged indeed. The opportunities that exist just beyond the periphery of town exhibit an alluring blend of being phenomenally good yet virtually unknown.

Recycling: One way to estimate how healthy a community is, is to gauge how much recycling is done per capita. In Tumbler Ridge 35 kilograms per person per year is being recycled, a figure which is increasing. One of the unusual features of the local program, which was started in 1997, is that it is run exclusively by volunteers. The wide spectrum of recyclable material is impressive, and there are facilities for community composting.

What should we eat?: North America trails the rest of the globe including the developing world in awareness of potential food hazards. At a local level, communities that eat what they grow and rely little on costly transport of foodstuffs can be considered healthy in many senses. Ellis Howard currently is alone in operating a commercial garden, and there is potential for other entrepreneurs to explore. Appropriate harvest of wild meat and fish offsets this deficiency, as does picking of the sumptuous and abundant berry crop each year.

■ REGIONAL

An edited version of Canada: If you drive Canada from coast to coast you may remark that it is a great country, but that it could do with some editing. In Tumbler Ridge three quarters of the country is squeezed into a small area. There is the Arctic tundra on the flat high summits, and below this is the beautiful mountain scenery. The forested upland of the Kiskatinaw Plateau resembles the boreal forests that cover much of northern Canada, and for those that miss the flatland sunsets, grain elevators, wind and snowdrifts, these can all be found just a few hours' drive east.

Parks: British Columbia is the first province in Canada to attain the goal of preserving 12% of its land base in parks, but this is not uniform across the province. Although the Peace area has the lowest percentage in the entire province, the amount of protected area increased significantly with the implementation of the Dawson Creek LRMP (Land Resource Management Plan) in 1999. This process sought input from multiple stakeholders and produced balanced recommendations.

TUMBLER RIDGE *Enjoying its History, Trails & Wilderness*

Air quality: This is an interesting question, for which there is no easy answer due to the unavailability of data. The air certainly feels clean, and the majority of people who relocate to Tumbler Ridge with respiratory ailments notice a major improvement in their health. Conversely, Tumbler Ridge residents who visit some of the other northern interior towns often immediately note the oppressive air pollution there. Our advantages here are space, the prevailing wind direction, and the absence of any major source of air pollution upwind.

A possible exception to this is the increasing amount of natural gas production, with sulfur dioxide and other emissions, which potentially can be harmful to human health. Concerns about this industry were raised in particular by Alberta farmers, who often had to deal with installations close to their dwellings. That magnitude of risk clearly does not occur in Tumbler Ridge, where the potential sources of emissions are many kilometres away. Some residents have considered establishing a monitoring station in town. On the positive side this industry appears to be moving towards a more environmentally responsible approach, endeavouring to return SO_2, H_2S and CO_2 back into underground sinks and thus decrease flaring.

Ownership of resources: I suspect that this is one of the areas where we fare the worst. When the coal mines were both in full production, there was a fair sense in the community of being associated with the resource, and Teck Corporation often showed itself to be a concerned corporate citizen. Nowadays we are faced with the depressing sight of dozens of logging trucks filled to the brim, roaring along the highway and bypassing Tumbler Ridge completely. Existing licences allow operators from out of the area to clear forested areas right on our doorstep. While impressive-sounding (although mandatory) presentations are made in the Community Centre about gas pipeline projects and the commitments of the companies to the worthy local population, those who have been to a few of these meetings take a cynical approach – they have heard this before and not seen the jobs materialize, while the resource flows out of the area and we still pay sky-high prices for it. A few levels up, the global economy reveals the impotence of governments in the face of the power of the giant multinational corporations.

Perhaps it seems idealistic to complain about this status quo and to envisage a system where communities take back ownership of their own resources, where citizens and town council have much more of a say in how the resources are utilized. Yet a growing body of opinion sees the substantial changes that would need to be made as imperative to the sustainability of rural communities.

Water quality: B.C. has 25% of the fresh flowing water in Canada. Contrary to popular belief, many parts of Canada including southern B.C. actually experience water shortages. This is simply not a problem in the north. The Tumbler Ridge water is currently of outstanding quality, in contrast to parts of the southern half of the province.

Measurements have been taken in the Murray River and downstream from both coal mines, with reassuring results. Yet one only has to look at the environmental oil spill disaster that befell the Pine River upstream from Chetwynd in 2000 to realise that clean water cannot be taken for granted.

As regards groundwater, Tumbler Ridge gets its drinking water supply from an aquifer near Flatbed Creek. 31% of such aquifers in B.C. are highly vulnerable to contamination; again that does not apply here. Analysis of the TR water for its mineral content reveals that it is wonderful water. Some of the limestone spring water has been sampled with a view to starting a bottled water business. Surprisingly, the local drinking water was actually found to be superior in quality! But it's better for drinking than showering - this is hard water that is tough on the skin, especially in winter.

As in most areas, there is a risk of contracting giardiasis (beaver fever) through drinking water in low–lying areas frequented by beavers and other animals. Obviously I cannot recommend drinking water in the alpine areas without boiling or otherwise purifying it, although I can comment that my alpine companions and I never do so, and have never become sick (yet). We theorise that our individual levels of toughness are inversely proportional to the altitude at which we begin to drink the water neat.

TUMBLER RIDGE *Enjoying its History, Trails & Wilderness*

Species at risk: British Columbia is Canada's most biologically diverse province, and biodiversity is crucial to long-term human and economic well-being. Across B.C., a total of 736 vertebrate and vascular plant species have been classified as threatened, endangered or vulnerable. Of these, only 48 occur in the Boreal Plains Ecoregion which includes Tumbler Ridge, and 41 in the Sub-Boreal Interior Ecoregion which begins just west of town. While these numbers are somewhat reassuring, they may just reflect less complex ecosystems in these ecoprovinces compared with coastal and southern parts of the province. In B.C. ten species have recently become extinct or been extirpated. None of these species have ever occurred in the Tumbler Ridge area.

While this too seems reassuring, an analysis of the broader picture suggests that a lot is missed by focusing just on the larger plants and animals, and that a truer understanding is obtained by examining the bacteria, fungi and other micro-organisms which ultimately sustain and control the more prominent life forms. Unfortunately, this vital knowledge remains largely unknown and unresearched, with minimal data available.

At the other end of the size scale, species such as Grizzly Bear and Caribou are conspicuous and easier to study. The research is in and what is needed to conserve them is the political will to make the changes to do so. Half of the world's Grizzlies live in Canada and of these half live in B.C. The North American distribution of these magnificent creatures has decreased by an alarming amount, and in the lower 48 states only pockets remain in the Yellowstone and Glacier parks. Mountainous areas such as Tumbler Ridge now serve as one of its remaining strongholds. The "Yellowstone to Yukon" initiative sought to address this by viewing the entire Rockies chain as one vast conservation area in which enough corridors had to be preserved to allow for the continued survival of species like the Grizzly and Wolf.

This concept scared many who viewed the mountains more in terms of their resource potential, and issues like this tend immediately to become emotionally clouded and polarised. In the case of the Tumbler Ridge area, this need not be the case. One only has to contrast what has happened in the Crowsnest Pass area in southern B.C., where the southeast coal development has taken place, with the northeastern

How Good Is It Here?

Tumbler Ridge development. In the former a highway bisects the mountain chain, accompanied by a string of towns on either side of it, and the coal mines extend this swath of disturbed land further into the mountains. The result is an almost impenetrable barrier to wildlife across the width of the Rockies. The Trans Canada Highway that crosses the mountains west of Banff, in a national park, is another example of an artificial barrier that has a profound effect on animal movements, not to mention road kills.

By contrast, the Tumbler Ridge experience is one of successful co-existence. The mines simply formed pockets of development in a huge wilderness, so that vital corridors were not affected. The backcountry of Monkman Park has intentionally been kept fairly inaccessible to preserve prime grizzly habitat. There does not seem to be any decline in populations in and around the mines. Strict legislation has prevented any interference with grizzlies at these mines, and they have thrived despite the close proximity of humankind and its machinery. The same applies to other big game animals. In the long term the aggressive reclamation work that is being done at the mines will actually provide for enhanced habitat for many species.

It appears that it is not necessarily contact with humans per se that is detrimental to these animal populations, but what humans choose to make of that contact. And such contact is now occurring on a greater scale than before, as a result of the increasing network of roads.

Roads: Probably the single most profound change that has occurred in the area over the past decade is the expansion of the road network, which now extends its tongues into many valleys and even in places reaches the alpine. Many of the destinations described in this book have only become relatively easily accessible because of this development. What previously demanded an arduous couple of days of bushwhacking now becomes accessible to a decent vehicle in a matter of hours.

The benefits to exploration and the enjoyment of the wilderness are immediately apparent, but the detrimental effects are often forgotten. Not only can it be argued that easy access cheapens the experience, but by bringing unprecedented numbers of people into an area, significant adverse environmental effects start happening. Poaching certainly becomes a lot easier, and represents one of the most significant threats to wildlife. Values have been calculated in kilometres of road per square kilometre, for a number of species. Above these values, populations are negatively affected:

Bull Trout 0.1 - 1.1; Grizzly Bear 0.4; Black Bear 1.25; Elk 0.6.

It is for this very reason that trail development in the Tumbler Ridge area is proceeding in an orderly and planned fashion, seeking to concentrate the majority of outdoors enthusiasts in a select number of highly interesting areas, while allowing for opportunities further into the less accessible wilderness for the minority that are prepared to rough it to some degree.

■ GLOBAL:

Climate change: Overwhelmingly, the scientific community has indicated that elevated levels of greenhouse gases are causing a change to the global climate, and Canadian politicians have displayed a combination of denial and irresponsibility in declining to tackle this issue appropriately. Precisely what this means for the Tumbler Ridge area is open to conjecture, and expert opinions differ widely. We can probably expect warmer winters with a shorter ski season (hence the planned high altitude ski trail), along with the possibility of increased fire hazards in summer, an obvious concern for a community so encircled by forest. Our glaciers are already tenuous and may disappear. However, we are far away from the coast, the zone which is likely to see the greatest change due to rising sea levels. Interestingly, the interior of British Columbia appears to have warmed at twice the rate of the global average over the past century.

Some may point a finger at Tumbler Ridge because of its early dependence on an obvious fossil fuel energy industry. However, such criticism is invalid, as none of this coal has been used for energy production, being metallurgical coal, and there is currently no large scale alternative to the use of coal in the production of steel.

Ultraviolet radiation: Yes, we live nearer to the North Pole than do most folks, and that means we are closer to the ozone hole and the sunlight we receive has less ultraviolet radiation filtered out of it. And there is certainly no shortage of sunlight: summer days include many hours of potential sunshine and in winter the absence of hours is more than made up for with the brightness of light reflected from snow. The potential good news is that our grandchildren may not be exposed to the same risk, and the phasing out of CFCs in the late twentieth century may be seen as one of the few success stories of global cooperation.

■ CONCLUSION

I won't forget a remark by a troubled patient a few years ago. He complained bitterly about living in Tumbler Ridge and the difficulties of surviving in such a remote area. "All you can do here is work, go out into Nature, and spend time with your family" he told me.

As family physicians we are trained to empathise with the problems of our patients, and not to resort to arguing a point. So I did not suggest that he go some place where he couldn't find a job, and would be stuck in a metropolitan jungle, where his family could find ways to avoid him. He has long since left, but the point remains that we are all part of the great web of life, and what drove this man to depression is precisely what inspires many people to visit Tumbler Ridge or to call it home.

This is how we like it and how many of us want it to stay. This is an area of the future. Watching that future unfold is exciting, with the challenge to "get it right".

I feel as if Wordsworth's lines

" *Bliss was it in that dawn to be alive*"

were written about Tumbler Ridge in the beginning of the 21st century. May the Golden Years be long and fulfilling.

APPENDIX A

■ ORIGIN OF PLACE–NAMES IN THE TUMBLER RIDGE AREA

The value of remembering the past is increasingly being realised. In 1996, after an extensive review of available literature, and interviews with old–timers, geographical features with historical names were identified. Submissions were made to the provincial Geographical Names Commission. These included a number of traditional Cree names, following an interview with the elders of Kelly Lake. Twenty-five of these were officially accepted and will be shown on future maps of the area.

Official naming of geographical features falls under the responsibility of the Geographical Names Office in Victoria. There are detailed guidelines and a specific process to follow. Once officially accepted, names appear on subsequent maps including topographical maps. This process has not prevented the unofficial naming of numerous other features. Ministry of Forests, for example, tends to name features and print these on forestry maps. The Geographical Names Office supports a Commemorative Names Project, in remembrance of British Columbians who died in war service overseas, and many names in the Tumbler Ridge area reflect the successful implementation of this project. Janet Mason of the Geographical Names Office has been most helpful in providing information on the origin of many of these names.

Appendix A – Origin of Place Names in the Tumbler Ridge Area

Albright (Ridge) – Named after Bruce Albright, pilot in RCAF, killed in action while flying over Germany. Albright was one of the pioneers at Kinuseo Falls in the construction of the cabins there in 1939, and in guiding in the area.

Babcock (Creek, Falls, Mount) – Mount Babcock is the prominent rounded mountain south of Tumbler Ridge, and was the site of some of the operations of the Quintette mine. It is named after Pte. Orville Babcock, of Rose Prairie killed in action, 1944.

The Bald Spot – Descriptive name for striking feature on hill immediately above Tumbler Ridge.

Barbour (Creek, Falls) – Named after Harry Barbour (1907-1988) who served the area as a forest ranger for 25 years.

Barton (Mount) – Named after Corporal Frank Barton of Prince George, killed in action in 1944.

Bearhole (Lake) – Officially adopted in 1961, this established name, of uncertain origin, was already in use in Gwillim's time. This large lake is the source of the Kiskatinaw River.

Becker (Mount) – Massif between Wapiti and Red Deer Valleys, named after Robert Becker, RCAF, of Pouce Coupe, killed in action, 1945.

Belcourt (Creek, Falls, Lake) – Originally known as Fish or Muinok, named after the Belcourt family of Kelly Lake by the Boundary Commission.

Bennett (Mount) – A hill north of Tumbler Ridge, named after P.O. Richard A.J. Bennett of Dawson Creek, killed in action, 1944.

Bergeron (Falls, Mount) – Mount Bergeron forms the prominent cliff–lined ridge north of Tumbler Ridge. The creek draining its northern flank drops 100 metres down Bergeron Falls, the highest waterfall in the area. P.O. John A. Bergeron, RCAF, of Pouce Coupe, was killed in action, 1944.

Bertram (Peak) – Near Onion Lake, this unofficial name is shown on Forestry maps to honour Bud Bertram, forester.

The Big Spring – Descriptive name for this powerful resurgence phenomenon east of Kinuseo Falls. In the late 1930s it was renowned as the place to cool off on the way to Kinuseo Falls.

Blackhawk (Lake) – Origin of name uncertain for this large, albeit shallow lake on the Kiskatinaw Plateau, officially accepted in 1961.

Bone (Mountain) – Origin of established name uncertain for this mountain massif north of Wapiti Lake, officially adopted in 1961.

Boone Taylor (Peak) – Prominent peak on southern horizon that forms a pair with The Shark's Fin, named after Boone Taylor (1887–1953) trapper, fur trader, pioneer farmer from Tupper. Accepted in 1982.

Boot (Lake) – Still marked on many maps as Foot Lake, the new name is now widely accepted, and confirmed by the presence of an old boot hanging from a prominent tree. "Foot Lake" may have been a descriptive name for the shape of the lake.

Bootski (Lake) – Descriptive name for the favourite activity of latterday adventurers that visit this pristine, usually frozen alpine tarn.

Brooks (Falls) – At the highest of The Cascades, the waters of Monkman Creek plummet over these impressive falls, discovered in 1937 by Carl Brooks, one of the pioneers and trailblazers of the Monkman Pass highway. In 1939 he was a guide for tourists from Kinuseo Falls to Monkman Lake. He was killed in a plane crash in Kakwa in 1945. The name was officially accepted in 1998.

Bulley (Creek, Glacier, Mount) – Outstanding pointed peak at the head of Bulley Creek, difficult to reach and seldom climbed, named after Pte. K.L. Bulley of Gundy, killed in action, 1945.

Bullmoose (Creek, Falls, Mine, Mountain) – Origin uncertain. Name already in use by Gwillim in 1919. First recorded ascent of Bullmoose Mountain was by Holzworth.

Calliou (Creek, Lake) – Named after William Calliou, one of the first to settle in Kelly Lake.

Cascades , The – The name given by the pioneers to the remarkable series of ten waterfalls on Monkman Creek (including Monkman, Brooks and Moore Falls). Known as Sagahiganiweitic in Cree, meaning "the place where the river widens out to become a series of lakes".

Castle (Mountain) – Descriptive name for the well–known and often–photographed backdrop to the usual photograph of Kinuseo Falls. This name was in common usage in the 1930s, and was officially accepted in 1998. Occasionally known as the "Three Brothers" because of its distinctive shape, although there is another mountain of this name in northeastern B.C.

Chain (Lakes) – A descriptive name for a series of lakes on Thunder Creek, submitted by Forestry Engineering Services in 1961. Known to the inhabitants of Kelly Lake as Kananawaustegwow – this alternative name has also been recorded by the Geographical Names Office.

Chamberlain (Mount) – A mountain northwest of the Bullmoose Mine, named after Spr. John H.J. Chamberlain, Army of Dawson Creek, killed in action, 1944.

Appendix A – Origin of Place Names in the Tumbler Ridge Area

Chambers (Ridge) – Situated southeast of Kinuseo Falls, this long ridge is named after Ted Chambers, one of the trailblazers of the Monkman Pass highway.

Collier (Mount) – This mountain forms the uppermost level of the Bullmoose Mine, and although many believe the name is related to coal, it is named after Pte. Wilfred E. Collier, Army of Gundy, killed in action, 1944.

The Core Lodge – Headquarters of the Ridge Riders Snowmobile Club, and named after the core drilling samples obtained there in the exploration days.

Club (Creek) – Origin uncertain, name in widespread use, officially accepted in 1998. This creek enters the Murray River north of Kinuseo Falls.

Courtipat (Falls, Mountain) – In the southeast section of Monkman Park, these features are named after Alfred Courtipat, trapper of Kelly Lake, who worked the area. Residents of Kelly Lake used to refer to the Upper and Lower Blue Lakes as the Courtipat Lakes. Courtipat Falls spouts out of a cliff–face below Lupin Lake.

Cowmoose (Mountain) – Mountain that towers to the northeast of Bullmoose Mine, so named because it forms a pair with Bullmoose Mountain.

Crum (Mount) – Near the headwaters of Windfall Creek, this mountain is named after P.O. Wallace Crum, RCAF of Dawson Creek, killed in action, 1944.

Devil's (Creek) – Creek northeast of Monkman Lake, exact origin uncertain. The pioneers called a neighbouring feature the Devil's Garden, and nearby Mt. Watts used to be known as Devil's Mountain.

Dickebush (Creek) – This creek is crossed on the highway between Tumbler Ridge and Chetwynd, named after the World War 1 site near Ypres.

Dokken (Creek) – Creek north of Wapiti River, named after Pte. S.A. Dokken of Rolla, killed in action in 1944.

Duke (Mountain) – Hill east of Stony Lake, named after Cliff Duke, guide and trapper in the area, and possibly the first to notice the fish fossils that the mountains are famous for.

Elephant (Ridge) – This descriptive name for the ridge north of Gwillim Lake was in use by Spieker in 1920 as Elephant Mountain.

Fearless (Creek) – Name submitted by Forest Engineering Services in 1961, origin uncertain.

Fellers (Lake) – On Wapiti–Onion hiking trail, this unofficial name is shown on Forestry maps to honour Bud Fellers, forester.
Five Cabin (Creek) – Five cabins stood at one of the favourite destinations of the trappers of Kelly Lake, near the confluence of this creek with Kinuseo Creek.
Flatbed (Creek, Falls) – This large creek joins the Murray River near Tumbler Ridge. It was originally named Rhubarb River by Prescott Fay in 1916, then recorded as Flat Creek by Gwillim in 1919 and Holzworth in 1923. However, it was recorded as Flatbed Creek by Spieker in 1920.
Footprint (Lake) – A descriptive name for the shape of this lake near Thunder Mountain, as seen from the air.
Fortress (Mountain) – A descriptive name for this massive foothill that rises above the Terry ranch, and forms part of the western skyline as seen from Tumbler Ridge.
Fossil Fish (Lake) – Internationally famous amongst palaeontologists, this small lake south of Wapiti Lake is incorrectly marked on some maps. Its name is descriptive for the sizeable fish fossils found near it.
Francis (Peak) – Near Onion Lake, this is a name put forward by Forestry to honour a dedicated forester.
Ganoid (Range) – Range of mountains south of Wapiti Lake named for the Ganoid fish fossils that occur in it.
Gauthier (Mount) – Named after St Pierre Gauthier, one of the founders of Kelly Lake, this alpine peak overlooks Monkman Lake. Gauthier is credited by many for the discovery of Monkman Pass. Accepted in 1981.
The Green Bowl – Named in the early 1930s by Isobel McNaught of Beaverlodge, this cliff–surrounded lakelet was one of the highlights for the pioneers who built the Monkman Pass. The road to Kinuseo Falls passes the Green Bowl about three kilometres before the falls. Submitted by Beaverlodge and District Historical Society and accepted in 1991.
Greg Duke (Memorial Recreation Area) – This area includes six lakes, all unofficially named by Ministry of Forests: Irene, Norden, Barber, Barton, Greg Duke and Pearl. They are sometimes known as the
Kinuseo Lakes – They are also known as the Chain Lakes, clearly in error as they are not connected, and this only creates confusion with the true Chain Lakes on Thunder Creek. Greg Duke was a prominent forester in the region.
Gwillim (Lake, River) – Named after Professor J.C. Gwillim of the B.C. Dept. of Lands, who explored the area in 1919. It was previously known as Rocky Mountain Lake.

Appendix A – Origin of Place Names in the Tumbler Ridge Area

Hambler (Creek) – The Hamelin family were amongst the first residents of Kelly Lake. The name was erroneously officially recorded as 'Hambler', but this new name persisted.

Hambrook (Creek, Lake) – A lake below Thunder Mountain, named after a forest service employee who died firefighting in the area

Happy Face (Hill) – A happy face was painted on the road at the start of the big climb on the Heritage Highway out of Tumbler Ridge onto the Kiskatinaw Plateau.

Heartbreak (Hill) – This hill on the Heritage Highway presented significant construction difficulties, and was referred to as a great heartbreak by the chief engineer.

Hell's Half Acre – Very descriptive name for one of the toughest stretches of the old Monkman Pass Highway, littered with enormous rocks from an old slide. Submitted by the Beaverlodge and District Historical Society and accepted in 1991.

Hermann (Mount) – Subalpine summit overlooking the Murray River near the Quintette Mine, named after an executive of Denison Mines.

Holmes (Lake) – Named in 1987 to commemorate Pte. Maxwell Holmes, of Pouce Coupe, killed during training in 1944.

Honeymoon (Creek) – One of the main tributaries of Kinuseo Creek, this creek was bridged by the volunteers constructing the Monkman Highway in 1937. Two newlywed couples were the first to cross the bridge.

Hook (Creek, Lake) – A descriptive name for this great lake which has an obvious hooked shape as seen from the air, submitted in 1961 by Forest Engineering Services. Previously known as Avalanche Lake and Avalanche Creek.

Horsetail (Creek, Falls) – A descriptive name for the falls, which can be seen from a considerable distance in Monkman Park.

Hourglass (Creek, Lake) – Another descriptive name for a lake with a perfect hourglass shape as seen from the air.

Imperial (Canyon, Creek) – Name was required for forestry access purposes, and submitted by forest service in the absence of any known name for this large creek that joins the Murray River above Kinuseo Falls.

Isidora (Mountain)– 7 100 foot summit immediately west of Wapiti Lake, known by this name to residents of Kelly Lake after Isidora Gladue, pioneer and trapper.

Jade (Falls, Lake) – Presumably descriptive name to describe colour of this lake east of Kinuseo Falls.

Jezebel (Creek) – Unknown origin of name for this creek that flows into the Gwillim River. It already appeared on Gwillim's 1919 geological reconnaissance map.

Jim Young (Mount) – Accepted in 1982. Jim Young (1883–1976) was the pioneer trader, store-owner and fur buyer at Kelly Lake in the 1920s, responsible for the establishment of its first school.

Joan (Lake) – Small lake east of Kinuseo Falls, named in 1937 by Ted Chambers after his infant daughter Joan (now Joan Jones of Beaverlodge). Officially accepted name in 1998.

Kinuseo (Falls, Creek)– The falls were recorded as such by Prescott Fay on his collecting expedition of 1914, with the explanation that it is the Cree word for fish, on account of the enormous numbers of trout above and below the falls. The name was officially accepted in 1920. Prentiss Gray recorded the Cree name for the falls: Kapaca Tignapy, meaning "falling water". Kinuseo Creek was recorded by the pioneer Guy Moore as being called "Kisitchewan" for "water running home". It was also known as "Contrary River" for the fact that it flows a considerable distance from east to west, to join the Murray River.

Kiskatinaw (Plateau, River) – Origin uncertain for this important tributary of the Peace River, which has its source in Bearhole Lake. Previously known locally as "Cutbank River" and "Mud River".

Kostuik (Mount) – Distinctive ridged summit above the Core Lodge, named after Paul Kostuik, of Denison Mines. Officially accepted in 1996, following widespread usage.

Kwoen (Hills) – These hills between Martin Creek and the Sukunka Valley, west of Gwillim Lake, were named by J. Templeton of the B.C. Land Survey, in 1930, for the Sekanias word meaning "burnt over".

Lower Blue (Lake) – A descriptive term for this subalpine lake.

Lupin (Lake) – Previously known as Gaines Lake, this beautiful alpine lake in Monkman Park is named for the profusion of Arctic Lupins in the area.

Martin (Canyon, Creek, Falls) – Exact origin uncertain, but likely named after a prominent local family, already found on Spieker's 1920 map, and recorded as such by Holzworth in 1923. Name was changed to 'Spieker Creek' in 1930 to avoid confusion with four other Martin Creeks, but was changed back to Martin Creek in 1954 to reflect widespread local usage.

Meikle (Creek, Mount) – A symmetrical subalpine summit south of Gwillim Lake, and adjacent creek, named after Bert Meikle, the cook on Spieker's expedition of 1920.

Merrick (Mount) – Named after Keith W. Merrick, Army of Pouce Coupe, killed in action, 1944.

Moe (Hill) – One of the hills frequented by snowmobilers above the Core Lodge, named after a local snowmobiler.

Monkman (Creek, Falls, Lake, Park, Pass) – Alex Monkman was the inspiration behind the Monkman Pass Highway, and is credited by many with the discovery of the pass. Born in Manitoba in 1870, he changed his plans to go to the Klondike, settling in the Lake Saskatoon area of Alberta. He died on his farm in 1941, soon after it became clear that the dream of building the highway through the pass which bears his name would not be realised.

Moore (Falls) – One of the Cascades, Moore Falls is named after Guy Moore, a pioneer of the Monkman Pass Highway in 1937 and 1938. He continued to take an active interest in the area throughout his life, and in a 1990 letter noted that these falls were his favourite. They were officially named after him in 1996.

Moose (Lake) – Established local name for popular fishing lake south of Gwillim Lake.

Murray (Canyon, River) – This great river bisects the Tumbler Ridge area from south to north. Its upper reaches were known as the Slate River until the 1940s. To add to the confusion, its lower reaches were known as the East Pine. It is named after N.F. Murray, who surveyed the river for the B.C. Forest Branch, and was killed in action in France in World War I.

Muskeg (Lake) – A descriptive name for this lake on the old and new routes to Pouce Coupe and Dawson Creek, name already in widespread usage by the 1920s.

Nesbitt's Knee (Falls) – A favourite ice climbing destination, this impressive falls is on Waterfall Creek, that drains the western flanks of Mt. Babcock and Mt. Kostuik. It is named after Don Nesbitt, a resident of Tumbler Ridge, who sustained a knee injury at the pool at their base.

Notogosogunwachi – A hill north of Stony Lake, Cree for "Old Woman's Back".

Onion (Creek, Lake) – Accepted in 1961, established local name, origin uncertain.

Paxton (Lake, Peak) – A high summit in Monkman Park with adjacent alpine lake, named after B. Paxton of Prince George, killed in action in 1944.

Perry (Creek) – Already mentioned in Holzworth's 1923 report, named after George Perry, a Californian trapper who died in a cabin in the area.

Puggins (Mount) – A large hill far to the north of Tumbler Ridge, with an old fire tower on its summit, named by J.F. Templeton after the pet name of his daughter Margaret.

Pyramid (Peak) – A descriptive name for this beautifully symmetrical peak as seen from the Quintette Mine.

Quality (Creek, Falls, Lake) – Origin unknown, submitted by Forest Engineering Division in 1961.

Quintette (Mountain, Mine) – This is a source of much confusion, as the Quintette Mine is not on Quintette Mountain! Quintette Mountain lies to the east of Mount Roman and is well seen from the Boundary Road. Its name reflects the "five heads" of its summit.

Red Deer (Creek, Falls) – Old established name for this large creek that drains into the Wapiti River.

Redwillow (River) – Originally known as Stony Creek, as one of its sources is Stony Lake. Submitted as an 'established name' by residents of Beaverlodge in 1947.

Reesor (Mount) – Part of the Tumbler Ridge western skyline, this alpine peak is named after P.O. Robert D. Reesor, RCAF of Pouce Coupe, killed in action, 1942.

Robert (Mount) – The flat–topped mountain northwest of Gwillim Lake, named by J.F. Templeton in 1930, after his father Robert.

Roman (Mountain) – The rounded double summit of Roman Mountain forms a distinctive part of the Tumbler Ridge southern horizon. It is named after Stephen Roman, business tycoon and head of Denison Mines. The annual Emperor's Challenge Mountain Race is run on its slopes and over its summit, and features on the route play on the Roman theme, e.g. The Roman Road, The Via Appia. Like Mount Everest, it also has a North Col and a South Col.

Serpent (Lake)– Descriptive name for the narrow, winding lake east of Kinuseo Falls.

The Shark's Fin – Excellent descriptive name for the most outstanding feature of the horizon from above Tumbler Ridge, this great peak is curved on the west and sheer on the east.

Smokehouse (Creek)– Named after the smokehouse of an early trapper, this is a long–established name for the creek that flows into Gwillim Lake from the west.

Appendix A – Origin of Place Names in the Tumbler Ridge Area

Spieker (Mount) – This enormous table–top mountain, previously known as Porcupine Mountain, forms the bulk of the mountainous western horizon as seen from Tumbler Ridge. It is named after Edmund Spieker, who conducted the 1920 oil survey in the region.

The Stone Corral – Descriptive name for recently discovered karst area near Kinuseo Falls.

Stony (Lake) – Old established name for this large lake near the Boundary Road, probably descriptive, also spelled Stoney Lake.

Sukunka (Falls, River) – Formerly known as the Middle Pine River, it slowly acquired the name Sukunka in the 1920s. Exact origin uncertain.

Suprenant (Mount) – Hill west of Gwillim Lake, named after Pte. Ambrose Suprenant, Army of Kelly Lake, killed in action, 1944.

Tepee (Creek, Falls) – Unknown origin of name of creek that flows off the Kiskatinaw plateau into the Murray River. A 1917 map already records this name. Gwillim spelled it 'Teepee Creek' in 1919.

Tentfire (Creek) – In the 1980s a serious fire spread through the catchment area of this creek, which drains into the Murray north of Kinuseo Falls. The fire was accidentally started by a party of campers. Officially accepted in 1998.

The Terminator – This name may inspire terror into the heart of a snowmobiler. It is a favourite snowmobiling mountain south of the Core Lodge.

Thunder (Mountain) – Probable descriptive name for this substantial hill with fire tower, southeast of Tumbler Ridge.

Trapper (Creek) – Unknown origin for creek that feeds Gwillim Lake from the north. This name already appears on Gwillim's 1919 map.

Tuck (Lake) – Named after Spencer Tuck, possibly the first Caucasian to explore the region, in 1907, this lake lies in the summit of Wapiti Pass.

Tumbler (Ridge) – Gwillim's 1919 map mentions "Tumbler Range", allegedly due to the frequency of rockfalls. Spieker changed the name to Tumbler Range. Gwillim's map shows it to be the lengthy ridge north of the town culminating in Mount Bergeron, but current maps denote it as the lower ridge east of the town.

Tunnel (Falls) – Series of two waterfalls on unnamed creek, adjacent to Wolverine Railway Tunnel.

Turning (Mountain) – Origin unknown for this foothill between the Murray River and Barbour Creek.

Two (Creek) – Tributary of the Wolverine River, named in 1919 by J.C. Gwillim.

Upper Blue (Lake) – Descriptive name for subalpine lake in Monkman Provincial Park.

Vreeland (Glacier, Mount) – Great mountain at the head of Monkman and Parsnip Glaciers, named after New Yorker F.K. Vreeland, who climbed it in 1915.

Wapiti (Falls, Lake, River) – Originally called Callahou after the family that first settled in the area, Wapiti is Cree for 'elk'.

Waptik (Mountain) – Bulky high peak southeast of Wapiti Lake, Cree for 'mountain–goat'.

Warn (Peak) – East of Onion Lake, this high summit was named by Ministry of Forests after Bill Warn, legendary trapper of the Murray River.

Watts (Mount) – Alec Watt was one of the pioneers of the Monkman Pass Highway, cutting the pack trail on the heels of the trailblazers. It is possible that this massive mountain in Monkman Park was named after him.

Weaver (Peak) – This great pointed summit southeast of Monkman Park was named after Pte. T.F. Weaver, of Hutten Mills, killed in action, 1944.

Windy (Ridge) – Descriptive name for the playground of the Ridge Riders Snowmobile Club, and site of the annual Hillclimb.

Windfall (Creek, Lake) – Origin uncertain for this tributary of the Sukunka River.

Wolverine (River) – Major tributary of the Murray River, already known as the Wolverine around 1915, and marked as such on Gwillim's map in 1919.

Yoho (Mountain) – Hill east of Stony Lake; one explanation of name is that in 1939 a hiking party got lost on its slopes and repeatedly shouted "Yoo-hoo" for help. When a survey party heard of this incident, they initially called it Yoo–hoo Mountain. Alternative explanation is that Yoho is a Cree exclamation of surprise.

APPENDIX B
BIRDS

BIRDS RECORDED IN THE TUMBLER RIDGE AREA

Pacific Loon
Common Loon
Red-necked Grebe
Horned Grebe
Eared Grebe
Western Grebe
Pied-billed Grebe
American White Pelican
Double-crested Cormorant
Great Blue Heron
Sandhill Crane
Whooping Crane
Tundra Swan
Trumpeter Swan
Canada Goose
American Wigeon
Gadwall
Green-winged Teal
Mallard
Northern Pintail
Blue-winged Teal
Northern Shoveler
Ruddy Duck
Redhead
Canvasback
Ring-necked Duck

Lesser Scaup
Greater Scaup
Harlequin Duck
Oldsquaw
Surf Scoter
White-winged Scoter
Black Scoter
Barrow's Goldeneye
Common Goldeneye
Bufflehead
Hooded Merganser
Common Merganser
Osprey
Bald Eagle
Northern Harrier
Sharp-shinned Hawk
Northern Goshawk
Red-tailed Hawk
Rough-legged Hawk
Golden Eagle
American Kestrel
Merlin
Peregrine Falcon
Spruce Grouse
Blue Grouse

Willow Ptarmigan
White–tailed Ptarmigan
Ruffed Grouse
Sora
American Coot
Common Snipe
Upland Sandpiper
Greater Yellowlegs
Lesser Yellowlegs
Solitary Sandpiper
Spotted Sandpiper
Long-billed Dowitcher
Semipalmated Sandpiper
Western Sandpiper
Least Sandpiper
Baird's Sandpiper
Pectoral Sandpiper
Stilt Sandpiper
Red-necked Phalarope
Wilson's Phalarope
Semipalmated Plover
Killdeer
Mew Gull
Ring-billed Gull
Herring Gull
Bonaparte's Gull
Black Tern

344

Caspian Tern
Common Tern
Rock Dove
Mourning Dove
Great Horned Owl
Barred Owl
Great Gray Owl
Northern Hawk Owl
Northern Pygmy Owl
Boreal Owl
Northern Saw-whet Owl
Short-eared Owl
Long-eared Owl
Snowy Owl
Common Nighthawk
Black Swift
Calliope Hummingbird
Rufous Hummingbird
Belted Kingfisher
Yellow-bellied Sapsucker
Downy Woodpecker
Hairy Woodpecker
Three-toed Woodpecker
Black-backed Woodpecker
Northern Flicker
Pileated Woodpecker
Eastern Kingbird
Olive-sided Flycatcher
Western Wood-pewee
Yellow-bellied Flycatcher
Alder Flycatcher
Least Flycatcher
Pacific-slope Flycatcher
Hammond's Flycatcher
Dusky Flycatcher
Eastern Phoebe
Say's Phoebe
Scissor-tailed Flycatcher
Blue Jay
Steller's Jay
Gray Jay
Clark's Nutcracker
Black-billed Magpie
American Crow
Common Raven
Blue-headed Vireo

Philadelphia Vireo
Red-eyed Vireo
Warbling Vireo
Northern Shrike
Bohemian Waxwing
Cedar Waxwing
American Dipper
Mountain Bluebird
Townsend's Solitaire
Swainson's Thrush
Hermit Thrush
American Robin
Varied Thrush
Ruby-crowned Kinglet
Golden-crowned Kinglet
European Starling
Red-breasted Nuthatch
White-breasted Nuthatch
Winter Wren
House Wren
Tree Swallow
Violet-green Swallow
Northern Rough-winged Swallow
Bank Swallow
Barn Swallow
Cliff Swallow
Black-capped Chickadee
Boreal Chickadee
Mountain Chickadee
Chestnut-backed Chickadee
Horned Lark
American Pipit
House Sparrow
Pine Siskin
American Goldfinch
Hoary Redpoll
Common Redpoll
Rosy Finch
Purple Finch
Pine Grosbeak
Red Crossbill

White-winged Crossbill
Evening Grosbeak
Orange-crowned Warbler
Tennessee Warbler
Yellow Warbler
Magnolia Warbler
Yellow-rumped Warbler
Townsend's Warbler
Black-throated Green Warbler
Blackpoll Warbler
Black-and-white Warbler
American Redstart
Ovenbird
Northern Waterthrush
Connecticut Warbler
Mourning Warbler
MacGillivray's Warbler
Common Yellowthroat
Wilson's Warbler
Lapland Longspur
Snow Bunting
Fox Sparrow
Song Sparrow
Lincoln's Sparrow
Swamp Sparrow
Harris' Sparrow
White-crowned Sparrow
White-throated Sparrow
Golden-crowned Sparrow
Dark-eyed Junco
Savannah Sparrow
Le Conte's Sparrow
American Tree Sparrow
Chipping Sparrow
Clay-coloured Sparrow
Vesper Sparrow
Western Tanager
Rose-breasted Grosbeak
Northern Oriole
Yellow-headed Blackbird
Red-winged Blackbird
Western Meadowlark
Common Grackle
Rusty Blackbird
Brewer's Blackbird
Brown-headed Cowbird

Appendix B – Birds

B.C. NORTHEASTERN SPECIALS
(OF INTEREST TO BIRDERS FROM SOUTHERN AND WESTERN BC AND WESTERN USA)

Yellow-bellied Sapsucker
common and easy to find around town

Yellow-bellied Flycatcher
surprisingly easy to find – try the Linking Trail along Flatbed Creek or the Mini-falls – arrives later than other migrants

Eastern Phoebe
only regularly found in the eastern areas near the Alberta border

Blue Jay
secretive and hard to find

Blue-headed Vireo
fairly common in forested areas

Philadelphia Vireo
a bird of deciduous forests – just reaches the flats below Tumbler Ridge – can be found more easily along the Heritage Highway towards Dawson Creek

Black-and-White Warbler
found near the Alberta border

Cape May Warbler
a rare find – almost always in spruce forest

Black-throated Green Warbler
just reaches Tumbler Ridge – listen for its distinctive song on the slopes above town or near Quality Falls

Ovenbird
found regularly near TR Point in deciduous forest

Mourning Warbler
just reaches the flats below town, commoner further east

Connecticut Warbler
occurs near the Alberta border – look along the old Monkman Pass Highway near Gunn Lake, otherwise off the Heritage Highway nearer Dawson Creek

Baltimore Oriole
occurs near the Alberta border, look in deciduous woodland around Gunn Lake

Rose-breasted Grosbeak
unpredictable but occurs regularly in the area including in Tumbler Ridge

Le Conte's Sparrow
just reaches some of the grassy sloughs of the Kiskatinaw Plateau

Canada Warbler
Bay-breasted Warbler
and
Nelson's Sharp-tailed Sparrow
are also Northeastern BC specials but have not yet been recorded in the Tumbler Ridge area.

WESTERN SPECIALS (OF INTEREST TO BIRDERS FROM EASTERN AND CENTRAL CANADA AND USA)

Western Grebe
look on larger lakes such as Bearhole in fall

Trumpeter Swan
breeding pairs on most lakes of the Kiskatinaw Plateau and Thunder Creek drainage

Harlequin Duck
easiest to find just above Kinuseo Falls

Blue Grouse
look just below treeline or in subalpine forest

White-tailed Ptarmigan
locally common on alpine summits

Black Swift
occurs over canyons and near waterfalls like Perry Canyon, Kinuseo Falls, Brooks Falls

Rufous Hummingbird
comes to many feeders in town

Calliope Hummingbird
harder to find but comes to feeders

Say's Phoebe
fairly common in spring in open areas

Dusky Flycatcher
and
Hammond's Flycatcher
both species occur regularly in forested areas and brushy slopes – Linking Trail and Murray Canyon Overlook are good sites

Steller's Jay
occasionally comes as far west as Tumbler Ridge, commonly found just twenty kilometres into the mountains from town

Clark's Nutcracker
uncommon in the area, best found much further south

American Dipper
common in the right habitat – try Quality Falls, Babcock Falls, Imperial Creek campsite, Flatbed Creek

Townsend's Solitaire
fairly common – usually easily found on the TR Point Trail

Varied Thrush
commonest in spring but readily found in subalpine forest

Townsend's Warbler
distinctive song in subalpine forest in summer, fairly common in fall migration

MacGillivray's Warbler
common once you recognise its song – occurs frequently in second growth aspen forest and brush around town

Gray-crowned Rosy Finch
fairly common in spring near town – found in alpine areas in summer

APPENDIX C

■ PLANTS

COMMON FLOWERING PLANTS OF THE TR POINT TRAIL AND SURROUNDING TRAILS

Prickly Rose
High Bush-cranberry
Labrador Tea
Saskatoon
Soopallillie
Kinnikinnick
Twinflower
Common Dandelion
Rosy Pussytoes
Pasture Sage
Yarrow
Canada Goldenrod
Heart-leaved Arnica
Aster species
Fairybells
Star-flowered False Solomon's-seal
Wild Lily-of-the-Valley

Fairyslipper (Calypso Orchid)
Frog Orchid
Three-toothed Saxifrage
Wild Strawberry
Creamy Peavine
Vetch species
Showy Locoweed
White Sweet-clover
Red Clover
Early Blue Violet
Pink Wintergreen
One-flowered Wintergreen
Chickweed
Fireweed
Bunchberry
Tall Bluebell
Northern Bedstraw

COMMON FLOWERING PLANTS OF THE ALPINE ZONE

Crowberry
Pink Mountain Heather
White Mountain Heather
Kinnikinnick
Smooth-leaved Mountain-aven
Northern Goldenrod
Alpine Arnica
Arctic Aster
Arctic Daisy
Indian Hellebore
White Bog-orchid
Three-toothed saxifrage
Narcissus Anemone

Alpine White Marsh-marigold
Subalpine Buttercup
Mountain Monkshood
Tall Larkspur
One-flowered Cinquefoil
Arctic Lupine
Alpine Sweetvetch
Stream Violet
Moss Campion
Lance-leaved Stonecrop
Tall Bluebell
Mountain Harebell

LARGE TREES OF THE TUMBLER RIDGE AREA

White Spruce
Engelmann Spruce
Black Spruce
Subalpine Fir
Lodgepole Pine

Tamarack
Trembling Aspen
Paper Birch
Black Cottonwood

To the south is the northern limit of Whitebark Pine.

APPENDIX D

■ ACKNOWLEDGEMENTS

This book was made possible through the invaluable help I received from many interested and helpful people.

My wife Linda and kids Daniel and Carina have assisted in more ways than I can count, and given up precious family time. (I am now searching for a replacement excuse for avoiding chores).

My parents Herbert and Erina Helm in South Africa, and in–laws Karl and Jeanette Zimmer in Saskatchewan have stood by in support and helped with proofreading. (My parents made their third visit to Tumbler Ridge in 2000, learned to cross–country ski and hiked the trails. My father did not let his 87 years interfere with learning to rappel. I am proud of them both.)

If there is one person I must single out that has helped me with historical data, it is Mike Murtha of Prince George. We share a passion for local history, only he is better than me at ferreting out information from dusty files and remote repositories of data. Fortunately he shares with me what he finds.

The stalwarts of the Wolverine Nordic and Mountain Society have enabled me to write the section on destinations – Lucinda Lindsay, Don Nesbitt, Kevin and Birgit Sharman, Al Tattersall, Fred and Ruth Walkley and others have shared their trove of knowledge with me as well as many hundreds of hours in the wilderness.

Others, hearing of this project, have readily come forth and helped me in areas where my own knowledge is dangerous, and some have written sections of the book: Fred Banham, Mark Bernadet, Mike

Paul de Greeff, Fern Duperreault, George and Janet Hartford, Daniel Helm, Mike Hunter, Dan McNeil, Don McPherson, Birgit and Kevin Sharman, Peter Sherrington, Linda Taylor and Mark Turner. Kevin Sharman also helped me understand the basics of local geology, and developed the astounding Wolverine Nordic and Mountain Society website which complements this book.

Regina Callahan and her able staff at the Tumbler Ridge Public Library have become used to my frequent requests for bizarre historical material, and are always prepared to go to great lengths to help, with a smile thrown in. Glenda Cornforth in the Jasper–Yellowhead Museum, appreciating the connections between Jasper and Tumbler Ridge, has also gone out of her way to be of assistance.

I have been privileged to make contact with scientists, experts in the field of palaeontology, like Andy Neuman and Phil Currie of the Royal Tyrrell Museum, Jim Basinger from the University of Saskatchewan, and Rich McCrea, the dinosaur trackway authority. Noted ornithologists Wayne Campbell, Joan Kerr and Peter Sherrington have been a constant source of encouragement to me in observing birds in the area and developing a database, and Clarence Hronek and Gerrit Van der Laan have done the same in their field of speleology.

I am indebted to Glen Gladu and the elders of the Kelly Lake First Nation for the insights into aboriginal history they have given me, as well as Art Napoleon of the Salteau First Nation and Murray Smith.

One of the greatest spin–offs from this kind of research is meeting the descendants of the worthy pioneers, like Prentiss Gray's son Sherman, Carl Brooks' son Richard, Ted Chambers' children Joan and Dale, and Alex Monkman's granddaughter Bev Whalen. The respect they show for the achievements of these pioneers is truly inspiring. Likewise, because this is a young area, many of the pioneer explorers are still alive, and tracking them down has been a fulfilling experience: Madelaine Suska and Cliff Rennie willingly shared details and photographs of their mid–twentieth century expeditions to this area, and John Terry was a source of personal inspiration to me.

Janet Mason of the Geographical Names Office in Victoria has always responded to requests for copies of maps and details on place–names with speed, courtesy and enthusiasm.

Appendix D – Acknowledgements

David Leonard is an historian from Edmonton with a special interest in the Peace Region who has kindly provided me with data and promoted an interest in local history. Grant and Paul Evaskevich were also gracious in sharing valuable historic information with me.

I have enjoyed developing excellent working relationships with Rob Bressette of BC Parks and Al Rodine of the Dawson Creek office of the Ministry of Forests. They have aided my understanding of the area significantly, and supported the creation of this book.

Photographers have willingly shared their work with me and allowed their photos to appear in this book: Peter Andrews, Fred Banham, Jim Basinger, Ivor Byren, Leona Gibb, Linda Helm, Ed Hillary, Darcy Jackson (who also permitted use of one of her watercolours), Paul Jurgens, Nigel Myers, Don Nesbitt, Birgit Sharman, Kevin Sharman, David Tolmie and Ruth Walkley.

Permission was obtained for the use of the historic photographs. Sherman Gray and the Boone and Crockett Club were particularly helpful, as were Glenda Cornforth and Megan Scammell of the Jasper-Yellowhead Museum and Archives, Dr W. Taylor, Donna Redpath of the Fort St. John North Peace Museum, Mrs. Beatrice Borden, Bob Vreeland, Gerry Clare, Bev Whalen, Dale Chambers and Joan Jones, Beaverlodge and District Historical Society, Richard Brooks and Cliff Rennie.

While I have no formal affiliation or relationship with the District of Tumbler Ridge in producing this book, their informal encouragement and readiness to answer queries has been much appreciated.

Adam Bonham-Carter, Lloyd Isaak, and Marek Szelag were happy to record distances and elevations and pass these on to me.

Ray Proulx and the members of the Mistahaya Wayatinaw Ecotourism Cooperative have understood the potential role of this book in promoting a healthy local tourism industry.

Most importantly, Loraine Funk is no ordinary publisher and Joan Zimmer is no ordinary artist – these are friends who share with me a glorious vision of the future Tumbler Ridge. Working together with people of this caliber has been a privilege I have thoroughly enjoyed.

My thanks go out to all these folks and all others who have contributed in any way to this book.

APPENDIX E

■ CHAPTER NOTES

CHAPTER 1:
OVERVIEW OF THE AREA
Dawson Creek Land & Resource Management Plan, 1977.
Master Plan for Monkman Provincial Park, July 1994.

CHAPTER 2:
CLIMATE
Gadd, Ben, Handbook of the Canadian Rockies, Corax Press, Jasper, 1999.

CHAPTER 5:
GEOLOGICAL HISTORY
Gadd, Ben, Handbook of the Canadian Rockies, Corax Press, Jasper, Alberta, 1999.

CHAPTER 6:
PALAEONTOLOGY
Rolf Ludvigsen, Life in Stone – A Natural History of British Columbia's Fossils: Chapter 9: Fishes of the Triassic – Trawling off Pangea, by Andrew Neuman; Chapter 12: On the Trail of the Cretaceous Dinosaurs, Scott Sampson & Phillip Currie; Chapter 15: Plant Life during the Great Cretaceous Transformation, James Basinger & Elisabeth McIver, UBC Press, Vancouver 1996

Andrew G. Neuman, Lower and Middle Triassic Sulphur Mountain Formation, Wapiti Lake, British Columbia, Summary of Geology and Fauna, <u>Contributions to Natural Science</u>, March 1992, Royal British Columbia Museum.

Zhihui Wan, The Lower Cretaceous Flora of the Gates Formation from Western Canada, thesis submitted to Dept. of Geological Sciences, University of Saskatchewan, Saskatoon, 1996.

Pers. comm. James Basinger, Phil Currie, Rich McCrea, Andrew Neuman

CHAPTER 7
PREHISTORY

Brian C. Apland & B.O.K. Reeves, "B.C. Rail Anzac to Quintette Branch Line, Heritage Resources Impact Assessment."

Margaret Kennedy and B.O.K. Reeves "Monkman Coal Project Stage II and Stage III Reports", Petro Canada.

Leakey, Richard, <u>The Sixth Extinction</u>.

Eric Poplin, "Final Report: Stage II Heritage Resource Impact Assessment, Quintette Coal".

B.O.K. Reeves, "Archaeological Overview and Selective Reconnaissance, Denison Coal Limited Quintette Development Area" Denison Coal Limited, Calgary 1977.

K. Walde et al, Heritage North Consulting Ltd., "Petrochemical Projects in N.E. British Columbia – Summary of Archaeological Assessments", 1994

CHAPTER 8
THE EXPLORERS

<u>The Journals and Letters of Sir Alexander Mackenzie</u>, Edited by W. Kaye Lamb, Published for the Hakluyt Society, University Press, Cambridge, page 294.

Report on Various Proposed Railway Routes for a Western Outlet to the Pacific from the Peace River District by a Joint Board of Engineers of the Canadian National and Canadian Pacific Railways, 1929. UNBC Library, Special Collections.

Bowes, Gordon E. <u>Peace River Chronicles: Eighty-one Eye Witness Accounts from the First Explorations in 1893 of the Peace River Region of British Columbia</u>, Prescott Publishing Co. Vancouver 1963

Spencer H. Tuck <u>Through the Wapiti Pass</u>, unpublished 1907.

S. Prescott Fay, "Journal of S. Prescott Fay of 1914 Expedition hunting sheep and other big game between the Yellowhead Pass and the Peace River along the Continental Divide of the Rocky Mountains in Alberta and British Columbia". Unpublished: Jasper Yellowhead Museum and Archives, Jasper, Alberta

L.C. Gunn collection, Fraser – Ft. George Regional Museum

Taylor, William C., <u>Tracks Across my Trail – Donald "Curly" Phillips, Guide and Outfitter,</u> Jasper-Yellowhead Historical Society 1984

Report of Wm Rindsfoos to Provincial Game Warden of B.C., Smithsonian Institution Archives

R.W. Cautley and A.O. Wheeler, <u>Report of the Commission Appointed to Delimit the Boundary between the Provinces of Alberta and British Columbia</u> Parts III-A and III-B 1918 to 1924 Office of the Surveyor General, Ottawa, 1925

Appendix E – Chapter Notes

John M. Holzworth, "Report on Trip taken in August, September and October 1923 in Northeastern British Columbia in the interests of the United States Biological Survey on the Subject of Mountain Sheep and Caribou Distribution."

Prentiss N. Gray, From the Peace to the Fraser, pp 209-332, Boone and Crockett Club 1994

Elmer Keith, Hell, I Was There! Petersen Publishing Company, Los Angeles, 1979.

Harry M. Snyder, Snyder's Book of Big Game Hunting, Greenberg Publisher, New York, 1950.

Sheldon, William G., Exploring for Wild Sheep in British Columbia in 1931 and 1931, Amwell Press, 1981.

Pers. comm. David Leonard, Mike Murtha

CHAPTER 9
THE SETTLERS
Andrews, G.S., Metis Outpost: Memoirs of the First Schoolmaster at the Metis Settlement of Kelly Lake, B.C., 1923-1925, Pencrest Publications, Victoria, 1985.

Robinson, Mike and Hocking, Dave, The Monkman Pass & Trail: a Brief History, Petro–Canada Coal Division, Calgary 1982. South Peace Historical Book Committee, The History of the South Peace – Tales of the Early pioneers to 1945.

Victoria Callihoo, The Iroquois in Alberta, Alberta Historical Review Volume 7, Number 2, 1959, Historical Society of Alberta.

Prentiss N. Gray, From the Peace to the Fraser, Boone and Crockett Club 1994.

John M. Holzworth, "Report on Trip taken in August, September and October 1923 in Northeastern British Columbia in the interests of the United States Biological Survey on the Subject of Mountain Sheep and Caribou Distribution."

Sheldon, William G., Exploring for Wild Sheep in British Columbia in 1931 and 1931, Amwell Press, 1981.

William Francis Warn, Trapping to Survive for Ninety Years. 1997

R. Waters, "Kate Edwards and John Terry – Settlers of the Wolverine Valley", Quintette Coal Limited 1981.

INDEX

Actinomyces 257
Aho, Aaro 126
Air quality 328
Alaska 44
Alaska Highway 41
Alberta 72, 91, 117, 328
Albertonia, 53, **54**
Albert's Point 40, 159, 185
Albright, Bruce 123, 195, 265
Albright Ridge 28, 29, 34, 51, 79, 121, 183, 189 – 196, **192, 193, 194, 196,** 248, 279
American Alpine Club 82,
American Museum of Natural History 103, 125
Ammonites 49
Anderson, Miss 134
Anderson Lake 283
Andrews, Gerry 106 – 107
Anvil, the 319
Aquatilavipes **60**, 61, 293
Arctic Ocean 321
Arctic Portage 84
Arras 38
Athabasca, Lake 321
Aurora Borealis 11
Avalanche Lake 219

Babcock Creek 23, 28, 33, 233, **234,** 285, 289, 291, 298
Babcock Falls 28, 41, 66, 67, 68, 285, 291, **292,** 294
Babcock Falls Trail 28, 294

Babcock, Mt. 33, 44, 81, 130, 231, 285, 287 – 289
Back Meadows 37, **304**
Bald Spot, the 89**, 154,** 155
Ball, Roger 248
Banff 45, 53, 73, 273, 331
Barbara Lakes 101
Barbour Creek 245, 247
Barbour Falls 28, 41, 243, **244,** 245
Barton, Mt. 1, 276
Basinger, Jim 63
Basset Road 24, 221
Bat Lake 29, 218, 323
Batoche 105
Bear, Black 13, 42, 285, 332
Bear, Grizzly 13, 42, 98, 127, 179, 181, 195, 253, 281, 285, 330, 331, 332
Bearhole Lake 3, 15, 18, 24, 25, 26, 36, 38, 97, **224,** 227 – 229
Bearhole Lake Provincial Park 15, 221, 227 – 229
Bearhole Lake Road 226 – 229
Beaver 42
Beaver Fever 329
Beaver Magazine, the 83
Beaver People 67 – 69
Beaverlodge 94, 117, 128, 231, 238
Becker, Mt. 34, 46, 51, 311, 315
Belcourt, Albert 107
Belcourt, Narcisse 106
Belcourt Canyon 303
Belcourt Creek 3, 41, 86, 94, 101, 237, 301, 303

Belcourt Falls 41, 303, **304**
Belcourt Lake 101, 109, 303, **308**
Belgian Congo 85
Belgium 94
Bennett, Bill 129
Bennett Dam 57, 129, 133
Bergeron Cliffs 34, 153, **164**, 165
Bergeron Falls 30, 41, 319, **320**
Bergeron, Mt. 8, 157, 165
Bering land – bridge 65
Berry picking 26, 27
Biathlon, Ridge Ramble 35, 153, 155
Big Flat, the 81, 145
Big Slough, the 239
Big Spring, the 117, **118**, 123, 138, 251
Biodiversity 330
Biogeoclimatic zones 5
Birding 14 – 16, 145, 147, 168, 225, 231, 235, 238, 251, 261, 275, 281, 293, 299
Bison 68, 105, 213
Blackhawk Lake 15, 18, 230
Blue Lakes 5, 98, 275
Boat launch 30, 163
Bobasatrania 53, **54**
Bobcat 42
Bone Mountain 98, 106, 301
Boone and Crockett Club 95
Boone Taylor Peak 283
Boot Lake 25, 230
Bootski Lake 17, 28, 29, 237, 309 – 311, **312**
Bootski Lake Trail 28, 29
Borden, Richard **102**, 103 – 104, 109
Botany 16 – 17, 218, 225, 241, 293
Boulder Gardens, the 28, 285, **286**, 287
Boulder Lake 17, 171
Boundaries, area 1
Boundary Commission 73, 89 – 93, **90**, **92**, 107, 138
Boundary Road 32, 33, 231 – 239, 285, 299, 300, 301
Brewster, Fred 77, **78**, 79, **80**, 82, 83
BC Department of Mines 128

BC Geographical Names Commission 121
BC Hydro 129
BC Parks 265, 273, 275, 277
BC Rail 21, 187, 322
Brooks, Carl 121, 273
Brooks, Richard 121, 123
Brooks Falls **120**, 121, 269, **271**, 272
Bull Trout 332
Bulley Creek 3, 5, 253, 275, 279
Bulley Creek Road 267, 275, 278 – 280
Bulley Glacier 3, 5, **6**, 34, 280
Bulley, Mt. 29, 34, 279 – 280
Bullmoose Creek 23, 74, 88, 89, 93, 167, 168, 181, 197, 203
Bullmoose Falls 29, 40, 199, 201, **202**
Bullmoose Flats 168
Bullmoose loadout 175
Bullmoose Marshes 168
Bullmoose Mine 32, 44, 56, 57, 61, 128, 129, 130, 136, 138, 181, 199
Bullmoose, Mt. 32, 36, 42, 181, 185, 197
Bullmoose – Windfall Creek Road 23, 24, 33, 168, 180, 197 – 207
Burnt River 93, 128, 213, 217
Burnt River Cave 217
Bus, the 38, 179

Cabin Pool 151 – 152
Cadomin 63
Calliou, Charlie 109
Calliou, Cliff 109
Calliou, Eddie 107
Calliou, Johnny 109
Calliou, Joseph 107, 109
Calliou, Pete 97, 98, 101, 104, 107, **108**, 109
Calliou, Sam 109
Calliou, William 107
Calliou Family 95, 106, 107
Calliou Creek 107
Calliou Lake 107
Calliou Outfitters 109
Calliou Trail 107

Index

Camel 47, 65
Campgrounds 17, 146, 169, 260, 267
Campsites, primitive 17, 18, 30, 168, 181, 191, 195, 215, 230, 235, 237, 238, 249, 269, 273, 281, 301, 303, 309, 317
Canadian Alpine Club 82
CMHC 136
Canadian Northern Railway (CNR) 73, 74, 99, 138
Canadian Pacific Railway (CPR) 72, 73, 74
Canary Creek 249
Canary Falls 249
Canoeing 17 – 19, 47, 175, 213, 227, 230, 235, 238, 315 – 321
Caribou 42, 66, 68, 86, 93, 94, 99, 180, 181, 199, 227, 290, 291, 330
Caribou Cave 20, 211
Caribou Highway **176**, 180
Cascades, the 30, 41, 46, 121, 253, 267, 269 – 273, **270, 271**
Castle Mountain 249, 261, 279, 281
Cautley, R.W. 73, 91, 107
Cave popcorn 260
Caving 19 – 21, 51, 191, 195, **196**, 209, 218, 257 – 260, **254**, 258
Chain Lakes 300
Chambers, Ted **118**, 119, 121, 249
Chambers Ridge 121
Charlie Lake Cave 66
Chetwynd 44, 97, 129, 175, 329
Chinooks 10 – 11
Chute, the 265, 267
Circular Run 153
Clams 49
Climate 7 – 11
Climate change 332
Close–to–the–edge Cave 19
Clovis Culture 65, 66
Club Creek 189, 317
Coal 44, 45, 91, 126, 128 – 131, 181, 322, 332
Coelacanth **52**, 53
Collier, Wilfred 201

Collier, Mt. 34, 128, 201
Community Directory 7
Coniopteris **60**
Consolation Cave 20, 218
Continental Ice Sheet 45
Contrary River 251
Copley 137
Coral **48**, 49, 51, 311
Corcoran, Marlene 291
Cordilleran Ice Sheet 45
Core Lodge, the 28, 33, 35, 36, 37, 40, 41, 42, 185, 285, 288, 289, 291, 294, 297, 298
Cornice Cave 19
Corral Cave 20, **250, 254**, 255, 257
Cougar 42
Courtipat Falls 275
Coutts, Katherine 113
Cowmoose Falls 29, 197, **200**
Cowmoose Mountain 42, 197
Coyote 42
Cree People 69, 71
Cretaceous Period 44, 61, 128
Crinoids 49, **50**, 51
Crooked River 97, 103
Cross, Charles Robert 77, **78, 80**, 82, 83
Cross – country skiing 21 – 23, 152, 153, 157, 159, 199, **202**, 203 – 205, **204, 206**, 227, **234, 236**, 237, 241 – 245, **244**, 247
Crowsnest Pass 331
Crum, Mt. 34, 46, 51, 205, **206**, 211
Culturally modified trees 69, 237
Cutbank River 97
Cycads **62**, 63
Cycling 31 – 32, 153

Dawson, George 72
Dawson Creek 8, 10, 15, 113, 115, 116, 119, 128, 226
Dawson Creek L.R.M.P. 171, 327
Dawson Creek Snowmobile Trail 38
Deer, Mule 42
Deer, White – tailed 42
Denison Mines 116, 128, 130

360

Department of Lands 88, 89
Devil's Club 257
Devil's Creek 273
Devonian Period 44
Dewing Lake 98
Diagonal Falls 317
Dimsdale, H.G. 74, 99, 101, 103
Dimsdale Lakes 101
Dinosaur trackways 49, 55 – 61, **58**, 70, 163, 293
Dipper, American 233, 281
Disabled access 27, 265
District of Tumbler Ridge 157
Divide, the 1, 89, 136, 218
Dixon, Jim 79, 263
Dog Sled Race 159
Dog sledding 23 – 25, 86, 159, 229
Dokken Creek 301
Dolly Varden 26, 79
Duck, Harlequin 261
Duke, Cliff 122, 126
Duke, Greg 249
Dunvegan formation 61

Eagle, Bald 317
Eagle, Golden 15, 177, 184 – 185, 197
Eagle's Nest, the 131
East Pine 18, 30, 31, 315, 321
Echo Ridge Trail 165
Ecoregions 5, 330
Edmonton 117, 124
Edson 82
Edwards, 'Aunt Kate' 113 – 116, **114**, 183
Edziza, Mt. 67
Elatides 62
Elephant Ridge 171
Elk 42, 66, 213, 332
Elmworth 238
Emperor's Challenge Mountain Half Marathon 7, 35, 40, 155, 285, 286, 289 – 293, 295, 297
Exploration 25

Fairy–slipper 265
Fang Cave 19

Faro Mine 126
Fay, Samuel Prescott 25, 34, 74, 76 – 83, **76**, **80**, 84, 94, 98, 137, 138, 145, 169, 261 – 265, 279, 305 – 306, 315
Fay Lake 83
Fearless Creek 301
Feller's Heights 116
Fern Fossils **60**, 63
Fire 71, 332
Fish Fossils 49, 52-56, 52, **54**, **56**, 124
Fishing 25 – 26, 68, 168, 173, 227, 230, 238
Five Cabin Creek 37, 106, 237, 297
Five Cabin Pass 295, 297
Five Peak Circuit 28, 295
Flatbed Creek 3, 18, 22, 24, 32, 46, 47, 55, 57, **58**, 81, 88, 89, 94, 97, 106, 126, 146, 147, 149, 151, 152, 163, 231, **234**, 235, 251, 319, 329
Flatbed East 235
Flatbed Falls 19, 41, 147, 149, **150**, 153
Flatbed Falls Regional Park 149
Flatbed Rock Pools 152
Flowers 16 – 17, 218, 225, 241, 293
Flowstone 257
Flycatcher, Yellow–bellied 147
Flyingshot Lake 105
Folded Falls 245
Fontoniko Creek 135
Footprint Lake 300
Forest Renewal BC 157, 162
Forestry 127
Forget Me Not Mountain 34, 121, 272
Fort Nelson 70
Fort Smith 321
Fort St. John 15, 66, 70, 103, 119
Fort Vermilion 321
Fortress Mountain 179
Fossil Fish Lake 52, 99, 125, 309
Fossils 48 – 64, **52**, **54**, **56**, **58**, **60**, **62**, **64**, 124, 257, 260, 293
Fraser, Simon 70
Fraser Institute 325
Fraser River 94
Fucoids 51

Index

Gaetz, Beau 74, 305
Galbraith, Al 136, 324
Ganoid Range 125, 309, 313
Gap Lake 237, 300
Gates Formation 61, 63
Gauthier, David 107
Gauthier, St. Pierre 106
Geographical Board of Canada 82, 84
Geological Survey of Canada 88, 125, 126, 138
Geology 43 – 47
Gesler, Frank 113, 315
Giardiasis 329
Gibson Lake 15, 237, 299
Ginkgo 63, **64**
Glacial Lake Peace 46, 47, 66
Glacial till 46
Glacier Park 330
Gladu, Isidora 107
Gladu family 106
Goat, Mountain 42, 66, 68, 99, 130, 197, 199, 290, 297, 309
Goatbone Grotto 19, 196
Golf and Country Club 158
Golfcourse 40, 157
Goodfare 231
Goodwin, Bill 112
Grand Trunk Pacific (GTP) 73, 74, 117
Grande Cache 44, 63, 107
Grande Prairie 8, 74, 75, 82, 86, 97, 105, 117, 124, 229, 231, 239
Gray, David 69, 106
Gray, Prentiss 25, 34, 74, 94 – 103, **96**, **100**, 109, 111 – 112, 138, 224, 229, 263 – 265, 300, 307, **308**, 312, 313
Gray, Sherman 95
Gray Pass 73, 74, 95, 99, 101, 103
Green Bowl, the 119, 253, 260
Greenland 53
Greg Duke Memorial Recreation Area 25, 28, 249
Grizzly Valley Days 35
Gulf of Mexico 44
Gunn, Luther 83

Gunn Lake 239
Gwillim, J.C. 88 – 89, 138
Gwillim Lake 3, 18, 25, 38, 67, 68, 81, 88, 168 – 169, **170**
Gwillim Lake Provincial Park 17, 40, 169, **170**
Gwillim River 3, 31, 88, 171, 319

Highway 29, 32, 166 – 175
Hadrosaurs 57, **58**, 59
Hambler, Albert 107
Hambler Creek 235
Hambrook Creek 69
Hamelin family 106
Hanington 72
Hansard 117
Happy Face Hill 221
Hart Highway 175, 223, 226
Hart Ranges 1, 299
Hartford, George 131
Hartford, Janet 79, 121, 131
Harvesting the wild 26 – 27
Hazards 12 – 13
Hell's Half Acre 119, 273
Helm, Daniel 57, 59
Heritage Highway 32, 97, 220 – 226, 229, 283
Hermann, Mt. 15, 241 – 242
Herrick River 117, 135
Heuer, Karsten 136
Hidden Valley 37, 296
Hiding Creek 238
Hillclimb – see Windy Ridge Challenge Annual Hillclimb
Hinman, Caroline 85
Hobi's Cabin 135
Hole in the Wall Provincial Park 21, 46, 215, **216**, 217
Holtslander Creek 303
Holzworth, John **92**, 93 – 94, 111, 138, 203
Holzworth Meadows 203
Honeymoon Cave 267
Honeymoon Creek 69, 237
Hoodoos 23, 168, 191, **193**

Hook Creek 3, 219
Hook Lake 3, 67, 104, 195, 219
Horseshoe Falls 23, 167
Horsetail Falls 269
Hourglass Lake 230
Hourglass Road 33, 221, 228 – 231, 239
Howard, Ellis 327
Hudson's Bay Company 107
Hudson's Hope 57, 70, **80**, 82, 89, 94, 97, 104, 107, 111, 112
Hummingbird, Rufous 267
Hunting 26, 68, 77, 86, 93, 94, 95, 98, 103
Hydrogen Sulphide 13, 243

Ice Caves 20
Ice Climbing 29 – 30, 197, 199, **200**, 246, **262**, 319
Ice – free corridor 47, 65
Ice Mountain 34, 84, **274**, 276
Ichthyosaurs 55
Ida, Mt. 300
Imperial Act 89
Imperial Canyon 281
Imperial Creek 37, 42, 280
Imperial Creek Road 267, 278 – 283
Irene Lake 249
Irenichnites **56**, 57
Iroquois People 69, 107
Isolation 326

Jackfish Lake 95
Jacobs, Rudi 123
Jade Creek 253, 260
Jade Falls 260
Jade Lake 253, 260
Japanese Steel Industry 129
Jarvis, E.W. 72
Jarvis Creek 99
Jarvis Pass 72
Jasper 45, 73, 75, 77, 82, 85, 88, 136
Jet Boating 30
Joan, Lake 119, 249
Jobe, Mary 85 – 86
Johnson Creek 296

Jones, Bob 77, **80**, 82, 83
Jones, Joan 119, 249
Jones, R.W. 74, 138
Jump BC Circuit 290

Kakwa 1, 79, 83, 121, 273
Kakwa lake 82
Kapaca Tignapy 98
Kayaking 17 – 19, 149, 163, **164**
Keith, Elmer 95
Kelly Lake 69, 71, 105 – 109, 231, 239
Kevin's Trail 28, 32, **150**, 151
Kicking Horse Pass 73
Kids' Triathlon 22, 143
Kinney, Reverend 85
Kinuseo Creek 3, 15, 46, 79, 106, 123, 126, 127, 237, 249, 251, 297, 317
Kinuseo Falls 15, 18, 25, 30, 37, 41, 46, 47, **78**, 79, 82, **96**, 97 – 98, 111, 119, **120**, 121, 123, 136, 138, 237, 253, 260, 261, **262**, 261 – 265, **264**, 297, 315, 317
Kinuseo Lakes 25, 249
Kiskatinaw Plateau 97, 226, 229, 300, 327
Kiskatinaw River 3, 97, 106, 231
Klin–Se–Za (Twin Sisters) 69
Klondike Gold Rush 111, 117
Kostuik, Mt. 37, 285, 295, 297
Kwarakante, Louis 'Karhiio' 107
Kwoen Hills 171

Lac St. Anne 105, 107
Lark, Horned 294
Late Oxbow Complex People 66
Lattice Creek 239
Laudon, Lowell 124
Laurentide Ice Sheet 45
Leake, R. 119, 120
Letendre, Clarence 107
Letendre, James 107
Lheidli T'enneh First Nation 69, 84, 276
Limestone Lakes 29, 74, 138, 253, 277
Linking Trail 27, 32, 35, 40, 147, 149
Lions 65

Index

Lions Flatbed Campground 17, 18, 32, 69, 126, 132, 146, 153
Lisa's Cave 20
Lithic Scatters 67
Little Prairie Lakes 238
Lone Mountain 126
Lone Prairie 88, 97, 175, 321
Loop Trail 31, 159
Lorette, Mt. 184
Lost Haven 9, 22, 31, **154**, 157
Louise, Lake 273
Lower Babcock Falls 23, 233
Lower Blue Lakes 5, 98, 275
Lower Tunnel Falls 41, 183, **188**, 323
Lupin Lake 275

M2O Canyon **236**, 241
M2O Creek 23, **236**, 239 – 242
M2O Creek Falls 241
Mackenzie 9
Mackenzie, Alexander 70, 71, 84, 128
Mackenzie River 321
Madagascar 53
Maidenhair Tree 63, **64**
Mammoth 47, 65
Maps 82, 89, 93, 128, 137 – 140
Mariman, Father 305
Marmots 181, 291
Martin Canyon 29, 172, 173
Martin Creek 93, 171, 215
Martin Falls 44, **172**, 173
Mast Creek 177, 242
Mast Creek Road 33, 177, 242
McBride 1, 94, 99
McCrea, Rick 59
McGinnis, Shorty 121
McNaught, Euphemia 119, 236, 238
Meikle Canyon 23, 168
Meikle Creek 23, 168 – 169
Metis 69, 71, 105 – 107
Microblade 66
Mighty Murray Raft Race 317
Mini Falls 147
Ministry of Forests 157
Missing Link, the 151

Mitchell, Charles 126
Moberly Lake 69, 81, 82, 95, 97, 104, 109
Moe Hill 285, 297
Monkeyflower Creek 253, 260
Monkman, Alex 73, 117 – 122, **118**
Monkman Cabin 69, 237
Monkman Coal Project 237
Monkman Creek 3, 5, 46, 74, 79, 84, 138, 269 – 273
Monkman Falls 269, **271**, 272
Monkman Glacier 3, **6**, 34, 84, 276
Monkman Lake 3, 5, 46, 74, 79, 84, 138, **266**, 269 – 273
Monkman Lake Trail 28, 266, 267
Monkman Pass 29, 34, 68, 73, 74, 103, 105, 117, 119, 121, 123, 135, 138, 272, 277, 323
Monkman Pass Highway 72, 117 – 123, 126, 237, 238, 249, 251, 253, 265, 269, 273, 277
Monkman Provincial Park 17, 20, 29, 34, 37, 41, 46, 49, 51, 123, 249, 252 – 277
Monkman Tarns 276 – 277
Monuments, Boundary 91, **92**, 93, 135
Moonmilk 257
Moore, Guy 121, 272
Moore Falls 269, **270**, **271**
Moose 42, 68, 86, 213
Moose Lake 17, 25, 88, 168
Mountain Biking 31 – 32, 179, 217, 242, 269, 296, 311
Mountain Death Camas 259
Muinok Creek 101
Mummy Cave People 66
Munroe, Henry 83
Mural, the **50**, 51, 257
Murray, N.F. 137
Murray Canyon 30, 111, 223
Murray Canyon Overlook Trail 15, 16, 28, 35, 46, 185, **222**, 223 – 225, 319
Murray Forest Service Road 231, 241, 243 – 251, 317

Murray River 3, 18, 47, 67, 74, 81, 88, 97, 109, 111 – 113, 136, 146, 157, 159, 161, 163, 219, 223, 225 – 226, 243, 265, 280, 315 – 321, **314**, **318**, 329
Murray River Canoe Trip 175, **314**, **318**, 315 – 321
Murray Station 61, 163
Murtha, Mike 75, 83
Mushrooms 27
Muskeg Lake 88, 94, 97, 116, 226
Muskrat 42
Muskwa–Kechika 45

Napoleon, Johnny **108**
Narraway River 57, 85, 86, 93, 99, 101, 135
National Museums of Canada 125
Natural Gas 44, 126 – 127, 328
Neck, the 183
Nelson 81, 169
Neoglaciation 66, 67
Nesbitt, Bert 126
Nesbitt's Knee Falls 28, 29, 41, 243, **244**, **246**
Nominister Abbey 151
North West Company 105
Northeast Coal Development 129, 288
Northern Lights College 35, 157

Obsidian 66, 67
Oil and gas Exploration 88-89, 126
Omineca Gold Rush 111
120th Meridian 89, **90**, 91, 138
One Hundred Mile Trail 38
One Island Lake Provincial Park 230, 239
Onion Creek 126
Onion Lake 25, 28, 97, 98, 106, 305, 307, **310**
Onion Lake Trail 28, 98, 305
Orchid, Calypso 265
Osprey 241, 265, 317
Ottawa 91
Our Lady of Lourdes 305

Overhanging Rock, the 152, 153
Ownership of Resources 328
Oysters (fossils) 49

Painted Canyon 30, 225, 319
Palaeontology 48 – 64
Pangaea 53
Parks 327
Parsnip Glacier 70
Parsnip River 70, 84, 97, 218
Pathfinder Car 119, 273
Paxton Lake 276
Paxton Peak 34, **274**, 276
Peace–Athabasca Delta 319, 321
Peace Canyon 93
Peace Pass 73
Peace River 3, 44, 57, 68, 70, 72, 77, 82, 97, 104, 111, 213, 218, 319, 321
Peak–bagging 34
Peck, Kathleen 94, 97, 104, **110**, 111 – 113
Peck, Victor 107, 111 – 113
Perry Creek 23, 32, 33, 177
Perry Falls 41, **176**, 177
Philips, Don 129
Phillips, Donald "Curly" 85 – 88
Photography 86, 98, 99, **100**, 109, 207
Phreatic Tube 257
Pine Pass 70, 72, 73, 103, 119
Pine River 82, 111, 113, 175, 213, 329
Pink Mountain 55, 66
Pinnacle Peak 28, 205, **206**, 207, **208**
Pioneer Range 48
Pipit, Water 294
Plant Fossils 49, 60 – 64
Plate Tectonics 43
Playground, the 276
Playpen, the 37, 181
Pleistocene Ice Sheet 44
Poaching 332
Poetry 116, 333
Poisonous Plants 16, 27, 259
Pond, the 185
Porcupine 259
Porcupine Cave 20, 255, **258**, 259

Index

Pouce Coupe 75, 91, 94, 111, 112, 113
Prehistory 65 – 69, 171, 219, 235, 263, 281, 295, 300
Prince George 10, 37, 277, 323
Prince Rupert 129, 322
Provincial Game Commission 109
Pseudocycas 63
Ptarmigan, white–tailed 181, 203, 291, 295
Ptarmigan, willow 203
Puggins Mountain 113, 127, 226
Pyramid Peak 34, 81, 195, 246

Quadra Camp 134
Quality Canyon 29, 40, **160**, 161, 162
Quality Creek 159, 227, 319
Quality Falls 41, 46, **160**, 161
Quality Lake 15, 17, 25, 38, 221, 227
Quality Mouth Trail 161
Quartzites 48, 67
Queen's University 88
Quintail Slough 15, 231
Quintette Lakes 235, 237, 294
Quintette Mine 32, 61, 129, 130 – 131, 136, 177, 239, 241, 288, 289, 322
Quintette Mountain 15, 28, 33, 37, 126, 231, 285, 288, **292**, 293

Radio–carbon dating 47, 67, 171
Railway Passes 72 – 74, 101 – 103
Rapids of the Drowned 321
Razorback, the 32, 151
RV Park 17
Recycling 327
Red Deer Canyon 101, 311
Red Deer Creek 3, 41, **76**, 77, 79, 101, 237, 301, 309, 311
Red Deer Falls 25, 28, 32, 41, 101, 109, 301, 311, **312**, 313, 315
Red Deer Forest Service Road 301
Red River 105
Redwillow Falls 239
Redwillow River 3, 73, 91, 106, 127
Redwood Fossils **62**, 63

Reesor, Mt. 23, 28, 33, 34, 38, 128, **176**, 177, 178, 179, 180, 201
Reesor Ridge 180, 201, **204**
Rennie, Cliff 126, 301
Reptile Fossils 49, 55
Ridge Ramble Biathlon 35
Ridge Ramble Ski Race 22
Ridge Riders Snowmobile Club 7, 36, 37, 136, 179, 195, 248, 285, 288, 296
Ridley Island 129, 322
Riel Rebellion 105
Rindsfoos, Bill 86 – 88
Rio Grande 117, 238
Road System 3, 4, 331
Road Touring 32 – 33
Robinson, Pearl 123
Rock Climbing 34, 195, 253, 255
Rocky Mountain Eagle Research Foundation 185
Rocky Mountain Fort 70
Rocky Mountain Lake 81, 88, 169
Rocky Tarn 181
Roger's Pass 38, 248
Rolla 97
Roman, Stephen 129, 290
Roman Road, the 290, 296, 297
Roman Mountain 28, 35, 37, 40, 44, 61, 231, 285, **286**, 288, 289 – 293, 296, 297, 298
Rose Prairie 106
Ross, Jim 103, 107
Royal Geographical Society 95
Royal Tyrrell Museum of Palaentology 55, 125
Running 35, 153, 225, 289 – 291

Saddle Club 31, 38, 40, 41
Sagenopteris **64**
Salt Creek 30, 97, 226, 319
Salteau First Nation 69, 109
Sanctuary Ranch 165
Sandstone 183
Sapphire Lake 305
Saskatoon, Lake 117
Saurichthys 53, **56**

Sausage Cave 20, 209
School District #59 Camp 168
Sea–lilies 51
Search and Rescue 13, 290
Sedimentary Rocks 43
Seed–ferns 63, **64**
Sekani People 67, 68, 69
Sentinel Peak 322
Serpent Creek 251
Serpent Lake 249
Sewage works 15, 47
Sharman, Kevin **150**, 151
Shark's Fin, the 29, 34, 37, 45, 227, 249, **282**, 283
Sheep 42, 66, 68, 77, 82, 93, 94, 96, 99, 103, 104
Sheep Creek 99
Shepherd, Kathleen 111
Sheldon, William 102 – 104, 109, 112
Sherman Lakes 101
Sherrington, Peter 15, 59
Showerbath Falls 219
Siberia 157
Sir Alexander, Mt. 77, 82, 85, 263
Ski Race 157
Skiing, see cross–country skiing
Skinner, Art 113
Skunk Creek 226
Slate River 269
Slave River 321
Smithonian Institute 86
Smokehouse Creek 169
Snowmobiling 23, 36 – 39, 179, 195, 203 – 204, 219, 229, 230, 237, 242, 275, 288, 296, 300, **304**, **314**
Snowshoeing 39 – 40, 161, 162, 167, 199, 241, 243, 245, 247, 248, 293
Snyder, Harry 95, 97
Sora Slough 237, 299
South Africa 53
Spieker, Edmund 89
Spieker, Mt. 15, 17, 23, 28, 32 – 36, 38, 41, 44, 177 – 181, **182**, 185, 197, 201
Spitsbergen 53

Springs 46, 215, 217, 253, 317
Stalactites 257
Stargazing 11
Stone Corral, the 9, 15, 16, 20, 21, 25, 27, 28, 46, 48, 50, 51, 138, 250, 253 – 260, **254**, **258**
Stony Lake 18, 117, 123, 125, 126, 236, 237 – 238
Stony Lake Advance 45, 46
Stromatoporoids 44
Sukunka Falls 41, 82, 104, 213 – 215, **216**
Sukunka Falls Provincial Park 213 – 215
Sukunka Lousewort Bag 215
Sukunka Ridge 219
Sukunka River 3, 5, 19, 29, 67, 81, 88, 93, 102 – 104, 109, 128, 173, 175, 213 – 218, 322, 323
Sukunka Road 33, 175, 213 – 218
Sulphur dioxide 328
Summit Lake 218
Summit Meadows 37, 296
Superbowl 37
Suska, Madelaine 34, 128, 138
Suski, Julian 128, 138
Swallow, Cliff 163
Swan Lake 239
Swan, Trumpeter 15, 226, 227, 230, 294, 299, 300
Swanson, Kris 290
Swift, Black 179
Swingbridge **266**, 269
Symes, Jack 77, **80**, 82, 83

Taylor, Bill **108**
Taylor, William C. 85 – 87
Taylor 321
Tattersall, Al 181, 199, **262**, 290
Teas 27
Teck Corporation 129, 130, 328
Telemarking 23
Temperature inversion 10
Tentfire Canyon 248
Tentfire Creek 247, 248, 317
Tepee Creek 225

Index

Tepee Falls 30, **224**, 225, 319
Terminator, the 37, 285, 296 – 298
Tern, Black 226
Terry, John 107, 113 – 116, **114**, 183
Thomas, Napoleon 69
1000 Man Camp 129, 133
350 Man Camp 242
Thunder Creek 239, 299
Thunder Mountain 36, 38, 97, 127, 237, 299
Thunder Mountain Road 299 – 300
Tiger, Sabre–toothed 65
Toronto Star 113, 115
Torrens Mountain 93
Tower Trail 40, 167
Townsend, Chris 135
Trace Fossils 49, **50**, 51, 257
Trackways 49, 55 – 61, **56, 58, 60**, 293
Trailriding 41
Trans Canada Highway 331
Trapper Creek 169
Trapping 111 – 113
Trees 16
Triassic Period 49, 53, 124
Triathlon, Kids 22
Trilobites 49
Tuck, Spencer 75
Tuck Lake 75
Tumbler Branch Line 322
Tumbler Range 89, 138
TR Point Bird Sanctuary 145
TR Point Trail 15, 27, 31, 35, 40, 145
Tumbler Ridge
- community centre 326
- crime 325
- economic stability 325
- education 325
- healthcare 325
- people 324
- recreation 326
- town 5, 131 – 134, **154**, 331

Tumbler Ridge Aquatic Centre 288
Tumbler Ridge Housing Corporation 136
Tumbler Ridge Museum & Archives 137
Tumbler Ridge Ornithology Group (TROG) 14, 231
Tumbler Ridge Tower 227
Tunnel Cave 20
Tunnel Falls 183, 187, 188
Tunnel Mountain 20, 25, 205, 211, **212**, 217
Tunnel, Table 29, 218, 219, 322, 323
Tunnel, Wolverine 177, 187, 218, 322
Turner, Mark 57, 59
Tuskoola Mountain 175
Two Creek 177

Ultraviolet Radiation 333
United States Biological Survey 77, 82, 93, 137
University of Alberta 61, 85, 125
University of Kansas 124
University of Saskatchewan 63
Upper Blue Lake 5, 98, 138, 275, 277
Upper Flatbed Canoe Trip 18, 235
Upper Flatbed Trail 28, 32, 151
Upper Quality Falls 41, 46, **160**, 161
Upper Tunnel Falls 41, 183, 187, 323

Vacco, Peter 135
Vancouver 130, 324
Vermilion Chutes 321
Via Appia 290, 291
Violet, Stream 267
Vireo, Philadelphia 146
Vreeland, Frederick 34, 73, **80**, 84 137
Vreeland, Mt. 34, 70, 84, 276

Wan, Zhihui 63
Wapiti East Forest Recreation Site 301
Wapiti Falls 41, 305, **308**
Wapiti Forest Service Road 33, 237, 301 – 315
Wapiti Lake 3, 24, 51, 55, 75, 79, 98, 106, 124, 237, 277, 305 – 307, **310**

368

Wapiti–Onion Trail 17, 28, 98, 305
Wapiti Pass 29, 68, 73, 277, 305
Wapiti Provincial Park 29, 125, 239, 301, 305 – 309, 313
Wapiti River 3, 24, 41, 57, 75, 85 – 88, 93, 94, 100, 106, 301
Wapiti West Forest Recreation Site 309
Wapitisaurus 55
Waptik Mountain 309
Warbler, Connecticut 239
Warn, Bill 113
Warn, Olga 107
Warner Lakes 32, 313
Warner Pass 313
Water Quality 329
Waterfall–bagging 41
Waterfall Creek 247, 319
Watt, Alec 123
Watts, Mt. 51, 121, 269, 273, 276
Websites 7, 107
Weigeltisaurus 55
West Kiskatinaw River 230
West Pine River 175
Westcoast Pipeline 37
Whale, the 269
Whatley Creek **76**, 315
Wheeler, A.O. 91
Whiteia 52
Wildlife watching 42
Wilson, Mark 59
Wind 8
Windfall Creek 20, 93, 104, 205, 207, 209, 215
Windfall Creek Road – See Bullmoose-Windfall Creek Road
Windfall Lake 17, 29, 205, 207, **208**, 209 – 211, 213
Windy Ridge 37, 285, 297
Windy Ridge Snowmobile Hillclimb 37, 288, 296
Wolverine 42
Wolverine Forest Service Road 33, 167, 174 – 189, 242

Wolverine Nordic and Mountain Society 21, 22, 35, 136, 152, 155, 157 – 159, 217, 289, 290, 309
Wolverine Pools 163
Wolverine River 3, 18, 24, 47, 81, 94, 113 – 116, 126, 163, 183, 189, 209, 242, 248, 319
Wolverine Trails 22, 31, 35, 41, 157
Wolverine Waterfalls 41, 183, 187 – 188
Wolves 42, 86, 330
Wong, Buck 132, 242
Wong Way, the 163, 242
World War I 81, 82, 86, 88, 94
World War II 104, 106, 115, 117, 119, 123, 124, 126, 195, 263
Wordsworth 333
Worm Burrows 48

Y
Yellowhead Pass 73, 74, 117
Yellowstone Park 330
Yellowstone to Yukon 136, 330
Young, Jim 106
Young, Louis 107

Charles Helm has been a keen outdoorsperson since his childhood near Cape Town in South Africa. He qualified as a medical doctor at the University of Cape Town in 1981, and practiced medicine in a variety of remote southern African locations before immigrating to Canada in 1986, where he met his wife Linda. In between working in Saskatchewan and northern Manitoba, the Helms travelled extensively, until they settled down in Tumbler Ridge in 1992 to raise their family.

Charles soon discovered that unearthing the history of this little–studied corner of British Columbia, and exploring its mountains and valleys, beat international travel hands down. He has discovered forgotten wilderness treasures and found many new ones. He has exhaustively studied maps, and obtained and researched the records of the pioneers. A founding member of the Wolverine Nordic and Mountain Society, he is an inspiration in the community of Tumbler Ridge, drawing people outside their limits into the backcountry. Occasionally against their will, occasionally providing only the most encouraging details when proposing an outing, Charles takes people on adventures they didn't know they needed, and leaves them asking for more.

This book is the product of eight years of research and exploration, and is a sample of his enthusiasm for the outdoors in Tumbler Ridge.

Al Tattersall